LONGMAN
KEYSTONE

C

Anna Uhl Chamot

John De Mado

Sharroky Hollie

PEARSON
Longman

LONGMAN KEYSTONE C

Pearson Education, 10 Bank Street, White Plains, NY 10606

Staff credits: The people who made up the Longman Keystone team, representing editorial, production, design, manufacturing, and marketing, are John Ade, Rhea Banker, Liz Barker, Danielle Belfiore, Don Bensey, Virginia Bernard, Kenna Bourke, Anne Boynton-Trigg, Johnnie Farmer, Maryann Finocchi, Patrice Fraccio, Geraldine Geniusas, Charles Green, Henry Hild, David L. Jones, Lucille M. Kennedy, Ed Lamprich, Emily Lippincott, Tara Maceyak, Maria Pia Marrella, Linda Moser, Laurie Neaman, Sherri Pemberton, Liza Pleva, Joan Poole, Edie Pullman, Monica Rodriguez, Tania Saiz-Sousa, Donna Schaffer, Chris Siley, Lynn Sobotta, Heather St. Clair, Jennifer Stem, Siobhan Sullivan, Jane Townsend, Heather Vomero, Marian Wassner, Lauren Weidenman, Matthew Williams, and Adina Zoltan.

Smithsonian American Art Museum contributors: Project director and writer: Elizabeth K. Eder, Ph.D.; Writer: Mary Collins; Image research assistants: Laurel Fehrenbach, Katherine G. Stilwill, and Sally Otis; Rights and reproductions: Richard H. Sorensen and Leslie G. Green; Building photograph by Tim Hursley.

Text design and composition: Kirchoff/Wohlberg, Inc.

Text font: 11.5/14 Minion
Acknowledgments: See page 480.
Illustration and Photo Credits: See page 482.

Library of Congress Cataloging-in-Publication Data
Chamot, Anna Uhl.
  Longman keystone / Anna Uhl Chamot, John De Mado, Sharroky Hollie.
    p. cm. -- (Longman keystone ; C)
  Includes index.
  ISBN 0-13-239445-6 (v. C)
  1. Language arts (Middle school)--United States. 2. Language arts (Middle school)--Activity programs. 3. Language arts (Secondary)--United States. 4. English language--Study and teaching. I. Demado, John II. Hollie, Sharroky III. Title.
  LB1631.C4466 2008
  428.0071'2--dc22

                        2007049279

ISBN-13: 978-0-13-239445-1
ISBN-10: 0-13-239445-6

PEARSON LONGMAN ON THE WEB

Pearsonlongman.com offers online resources for teachers and students. Access our Companion Websites, our online catalog, and our local offices around the world.

Visit us at **www.pearsonlongman.com**.

Printed in the United States of America
3 4 5 6 7 8 9 10 11 12—DWL—12 11 10 09 08

About the Authors

Anna Uhl Chamot is a professor of secondary education and a faculty advisor for ESL in George Washington University's Department of Teacher Preparation. She has been a researcher and teacher trainer in content-based second-language learning and language-learning strategies. She co-designed and has written extensively about the Cognitive Academic Language Learning Approach (CALLA) and spent seven years implementing the CALLA model in the Arlington Public Schools in Virginia.

John De Mado has been an energetic force in the field of Language Acquisition for several years. He is founder and president of John De Mado Language Seminars, Inc., an educational consulting firm devoted exclusively to language acquisition and literacy issues. John, who speaks a variety of languages, has authored several textbook programs and produced a series of music CD/DVDs designed to help students acquire other languages. John is recognized nationally, as well as internationally, for his insightful workshops, motivating keynote addresses, and humor-filled delivery style.

Sharroky Hollie is an assistant professor in teacher education at California State University, Dominguez Hills. His expertise is in the field of professional development, African-American education, and second-language methodology. He is an urban literacy visiting professor at Webster University, St. Louis. Sharroky is the Executive Director of the Center for Culturally Responsive Teaching and Learning (CCRTL) and the co-founding director of the nationally acclaimed Culture and Language Academy of Success (CLAS).

Reviewers

Sharena Adebiyi
Fulton County Schools
Stone City, GA

Jennifer Benavides
Garland ISD
Garland, TX

Tracy Bunker
Shearer Charter School
Napa, CA

Dan Fichtner
UCLA Ed. Ext. TESOL Program
Redondo Beach, CA

Trudy Freer-Alvarez
Houston ISD
Houston, TX

Helena K. Gandell
Duval County
Jacksonville, FL

Glenda Harrell
Johnston County School Dist.
Smithfield, NC

Michelle Land
Randolph Middle School
Randolph, NJ

Joseph E. Leaf
Norristown Area High School
Norristown, PA

Ilona Olancin
Collier County Schools
Naples, FL

Jeanne Perrin
Boston Unified School Dist.
Boston, MA

Cheryl Quadrelli-Jones
Anaheim Union High School Dist.
Fullerton, CA

Mary Schmidt
Riverwood High School
Atlanta, GA

Daniel Thatcher
Garland ISD
Garland, TX

Denise Tiffany
West High School
Iowa City, IA

Lisa Troute
Palm Beach County School Dist.
West Palm, FL

Dear Student,

Welcome to LONGMAN
KEYSTONE

Longman Keystone has been specially designed to help you succeed in all areas of your school studies. This program will help you develop the English language skills you need for language arts, social studies, math, and science. You will discover new ways to use and build upon your language skills through your interactions with classmates, friends, teachers, and family members.

Keystone includes a mix of many subjects. Each unit has four different reading selections that include literary excerpts, poems, and nonfiction articles about science, math, and social studies. These selections will help you understand the vocabulary and organization of different types of texts. They will also give you the tools you need to approach the content of the different subjects you take in school.

As you use this program, you will discover new words, use your background knowledge of the subjects presented, relate your knowledge to the new information, and take part in creative activities. You will learn strategies to help you understand readings better. You will work on activities that help you improve your English skills in grammar, word study, and spelling. Finally, you will be asked to demonstrate the listening, speaking, and writing skills you have learned through fun projects that are incorporated throughout the program.

Learning a language takes time, but just like learning to skateboard or learning to swim, it is fun! Whether you are learning English for the first time, or increasing your knowledge of English by adding academic or literary language to your vocabulary, you are giving yourself new choices for the future, and a better chance of succeeding in both your studies and in everyday life.

We hope you enjoy *Longman Keystone* as much as we enjoyed writing it for you!

Good luck!

Anna Uhl Chamot
John De Mado
Sharroky Hollie

Learn about Art with the
Smithsonian American Art Museum

Dear Student,

At the end of each unit in this book, you will learn about some artists and artworks that relate to the theme you have just read about. These artworks are all in the Smithsonian American Art Museum in Washington, D.C. That means they belong to you, because the Smithsonian is America's collection. The artworks were created over a period of 300 years by artists who responded to their experiences in personal ways. Their world lives on through their artworks and, as viewers, we can understand them and ourselves in new ways. We discover that many of the things that concerned these artists still engage us today.

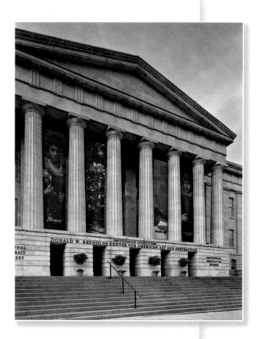

Looking at an artwork is different from reading a written history. Artists present few facts or dates. Instead, they offer emotional insights that come from their own lives and experiences. They make their own decisions about what matters, without worrying if others agree or disagree. This is a rare and useful kind of knowledge that we can all learn from. Artists inspire us to respond to our own lives with deeper insight.

There are two ways to approach art. One way is through the mind—studying the artist, learning about the subject, exploring the context in which the artwork was made, and forming a personal view. This way is deeply rewarding and expands your understanding of the world. The second way is through the senses—letting your imagination roam as you look at an artwork, losing yourself in colors and shapes, absorbing the meaning through your eyes. This way is called "aesthetic." The great thing about art is that an artwork may have many different meanings. You can decide what it means to you.

This brief introduction to American art will, I hope, lead to a lifetime of enjoyment and appreciation of art.

Elizabeth Broun
The Margaret and Terry Stent Director
Smithsonian American Art Museum

Glossary of Terms

You will find the following words useful when reading, writing, and talking about art.

abstract a style of art that does not represent things, animals, or people realistically

acrylic a type of paint that is made from ground pigments and certain chemicals

background part of the artwork that looks furthest away from the viewer

brushstroke the paint or ink left on the surface of an artwork by the paintbrush

canvas a type of heavy woven fabric used as a support for painting; another word for a painting

composition the way in which the different parts of an artwork are arranged

detail a small part of an artwork

evoke to produce a strong feeling or memory

figure the representation of a person or animal in an artwork

foreground part of the artwork that looks closest to the viewer

geometric a type of pattern that has straight lines or shapes such as squares, circles, etc.

mixed media different kinds of materials such as paint, fabric, objects, etc. that are used in a single artwork

oil a type of paint that is made from ground pigments and linseed oil

paintbrush a special brush used for painting

perception the way you understand something you see

pigment a finely powdered material (natural or man-made) that gives color to paint, ink, or dye

portrait an artwork that shows a specific person, group of people, or animal

print an artwork that has been made from a sheet of metal or a block of wood covered with a wet color and then pressed onto a flat surface like paper. Types of prints include lithographs, etchings, aquatints, etc.

symbol an image, shape, or object in an artwork that represents an idea

texture the way that a surface or material feels and how smooth or rough it looks

tone the shade of a particular color; the effect of light and shade with color

watercolor a type of paint that is made from ground pigments, gum, and glycerin and/or honey; another word for a painting done with this medium

Contents

Contents

 What are the benefits
of facing challenges? **68**

Contents

Contents

 What does home mean? 204

DEUTSCHE BUNDESPOST
60
ANNE FRANK · 12.6.1929 · 31.3.1945
1979

Contents

UNIT 5

What is the human spirit? 266

Contents

THE BIG Q QUESTION

How can change improve people's lives?

HOME WASHING MACHINE & WRINGER.

HOME WASHER

DEPOT 24 CORTLANDT ST., NEW YORK.
DEPOT 13 BARCLAY ST., NEW YORK.

This unit is about change. You will read informational texts that describe life in a new land and how new inventions change lives. You will also read literature about the first woman to vote and a girl who begins a community garden. Reading, writing, and talking about these topics will give you practice using academic language and help you become a better student.

READING 1: Social Studies Article

■ "The First Americans"

READING 2: Novel Excerpt

■ From *Riding Freedom* by Pam Muñoz Ryan

READING 3: Science Article

■ "Early Inventions"

READING 4: Novel Excerpt

■ From *Seedfolks* by Paul Fleischman

Listening and Speaking

At the end of this unit, you will choose a topic and give a **presentation** about it.

Writing

In this unit you will practice **descriptive writing**. This type of writing describes things, or tells what things look, sound, feel, smell, or taste like. After each reading you will learn a skill to help you write a descriptive paragraph. At the end of the unit, you will use these skills to help you write a descriptive essay.

QuickWrite

In your notebook, write the word *change*. List some words or phrases that you associate with this word. Then share your list with a partner.

What You Will Learn

Reading

- Vocabulary building: *Context, dictionary skills, word study*

- Reading strategy: *Preview*

- Text type: *Informational text (social studies)*

Grammar, Usage, and Mechanics
Order of adjectives

Writing
Describe a group of people

THE BIG QUESTION

How can change improve people's lives? A movement of large groups of people from one place to another is called *migration*. How do you think the migration of people can change a landscape? How can it change the lives of those who migrate? Discuss with a partner.

BUILD BACKGROUND

"The First Americans" is an informational text about the first people to inhabit the Americas. The purpose of an informational text is to inform the reader about real facts, people, or events.

The first Americans probably came from northern Asia many thousands of years ago. They may have crossed a land bridge that is now underwater. Look at the map. The arrows show possible migration routes of those early peoples.

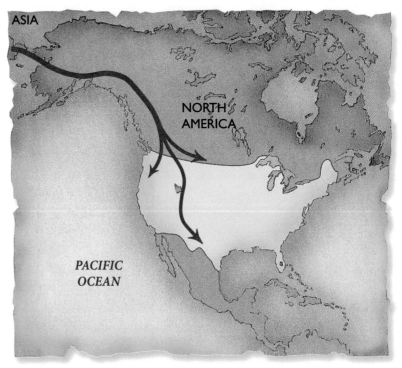

▲ Migration routes of early peoples

VOCABULARY

Learn Key Words

Read these sentences. Use the context to figure out the meaning of the red words. Use a dictionary to check your answers. Then write each word and its meaning in your notebook.

Key Words

climate
customs
irrigate
natural resources
nomads
tribe

1. In the summer, the **climate** in the Northeast is hot and humid.
2. Every culture has developed its own **customs**, such as ceremonies and festivals to celebrate special events.
3. Some tribes had to **irrigate** the land where they grew their crops because there was so little rain.
4. Tribes often used **natural resources** such as trees to build shelter.
5. Some Native Americans settled in one place, but others were **nomads** who traveled from one place to another.
6. The Penobscot **tribe** is a group of Native Americans from the Northeast.

Practice

Workbook
Page 1

Write the sentences in your notebook. Choose a red word from the box above to complete each sentence. Then take turns reading the sentences aloud with a partner.

1. Members of the same _____ lived together in the same place.
2. The area has many _____, like trees, water, and soil.
3. _____ moved from one place to another to hunt buffalo.
4. The tribes had different _____ and languages.
5. The warm _____ makes it possible to grow crops all year long.
6. They have to _____ the crops to help them grow.

◀ A painting of a tribe of Plains Indians

5

Learn Academic Words

Study the **red** words and their meanings. You will find these words useful when talking and writing about informational texts. Write each word and its meaning in your notebook. After you read "The First Americans," try to use these words to respond to the text.

affects = produces a change in someone or something	→	Climate **affects** crops either by helping them grow or by damaging them.
available = able to be used or seen	→	The tribes used the natural resources that were **available** to them.
environment = the land, water, and air in which people, animals, and plants live	→	Native Americans used plants from their **environment** for food and shelter.
region = large area	→	Many Native Americans settled in the Southwest **region** of North America.

Practice  Workbook Page 2

Work with a partner to answer these questions. Try to include the **red** word in your answer. Write the sentences in your notebook.

1. Can you think of one way in which the climate in your area **affects** the way you live? Explain.

2. What natural resources are **available** in your area? What are they used for?

3. How do your actions change the **environment**?

4. What **region** of the United States do you live in—the Northwest, Southwest, Plains, Northeast, or Southeast?

▲ A mountainous region in the western United States

Word Study: Spelling Long *a* and *e*

The text you are going to read contains words with long vowel sounds, such as *a* (*game*) and *e* (*creek*). There are different ways to spell each of these sounds. Look at the chart below.

Long *a*		Long *e*	
Spelling	**Examples**	**Spelling**	**Examples**
a	major	e	be, cedar
a_e	game, snake	ee	tree, between
ai	Plains, rain	ea	beans, northeast
ay	day, may	eo	people
ea	great	y	city, history

Practice  Workbook Page 3

Work with a partner. Copy the chart below into your notebook. Take turns reading the words in the box. Then write each word in the correct chart column. Circle the letters that stand for the long *a* and *e* sounds.

breed	pottery	state	theory
native	regions	steak	today

Long *a*	Long *e*

READING STRATEGY   PREVIEW

Previewing a text helps you understand the content more quickly. To preview, follow these steps:

- Look at the title and headings.
- Look at the visuals and read the captions or labels.
- Think about your purpose for reading the text.
- Read the first and last sentences of each paragraph.

Before you read "The First Americans," think about what you already know about this subject. What more would you like to know?

 Workbook Page 4

Set a purpose for reading As you read, identify the different regions in which the first Americans settled. How did they change these lands?

THE FIRST AMERICANS

Where Did the First Americans Come From?

According to one popular theory, the first Americans came from northern Asia. Some scientists believe that they crossed a land bridge between northern Asia and North America between 15,000 and 30,000 years ago. Some of those peoples stayed in North America, and others traveled into Central and South America. In the 1970s, a scientist found a campsite in southern Chile that is one of the oldest known human dwelling places in the Americas. It is at least 12,500 years old and contains remains of people's homes and tools.

Stone tools found at Monte Verde, a very old campsite in Chile, include items used for chopping, scraping, and pounding. ▼

---

theory, idea that tries to explain something
peoples, groups of people
campsite, place with shelter where people stay for a short time
dwelling, living

8

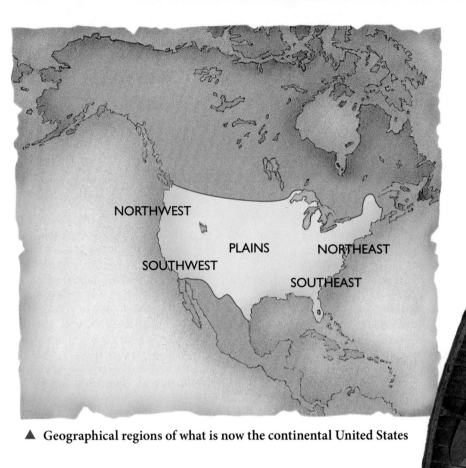

▲ Geographical regions of what is now the continental United States

▲ A Malecite canoe

Native Americans in the United States

By 1500 C.E., about 3–5 million people lived in the different regions of North America that are now the United States. Each tribe lived in a specific region and developed its own customs and language. The climate and geographical features of the different regions affected how the tribes lived. Several of the major regions are described below.

The Northeast

The Northeast had great forests and many rivers and lakes. It was rich in game and fish. Many native peoples, including the Iroquois, the Penobscot, and the Malecite, lived in the eastern forests. These tribes made tools and canoes. They hunted deer and birds and fished in the lakes, rivers, and ocean. They also grew corn, squash, and beans.

---

geographical features, parts of Earth, such as oceans and mountains
game, animals that people hunt for food
canoes, long, narrow boats that are moved by using paddles

BEFORE YOU GO ON

1 What did a scientist find in Chile?

2 What did people in the Northeast do to get their food?

On Your Own
Describe the climate in your region. Is it hot or cold? Wet or dry?

9

The Plains

▲ Sioux villages ▼

The Plains stretch north to south for approximately 3,200 kilometers (2,000 mi.) between the Rocky Mountains and the Mississippi River. They are huge, flat, grassy lands. The Native Americans of the Plains lived in villages. The women grew beans, corn, and squash, and the men hunted deer and some buffalo. After the Spanish brought horses to the area, the Native Americans of the Plains rode them during their buffalo hunts. Then these people became nomads, following the buffalo herds from place to place. They ate buffalo meat, and they made clothes, tepees, tools, and drums from buffalo skins, hair, and horns. The Native Americans of the Plains made medicines from plants. For example, they used skunk cabbage root as medicine for asthma.

By 1800, about 150,000 Native Americans, in thirty tribes, lived on the Plains. Among those tribes were the Pawnee and the Dakota (also called the Sioux).

---

villages, small towns
herds, large groups of animals
tepees, cone-shaped tents
asthma, illness that causes difficulty
    in breathing

10

▲ A painting of a buffalo hunter

The Southwest

The hot, arid Southwest was home to many Native American tribes. The Pueblo tribes learned to irrigate crops with the little water that was available. The Pueblo also performed rituals, or special ceremonies. For example, they performed a nine-day Snake Ceremony to bring rain and a good harvest. The history of the Pueblo goes back 2,000 years. Today, some Pueblo people live in stone and clay villages that are more than 1,000 years old.

The Southwest was also home to the Navajo and the Apache. The Navajo came to the Southwest in about the year 1400. They lived in the territory that is now northern Arizona and New Mexico and in part of southern Colorado and Utah. The Apache settled in modern-day Texas in the 1520s.

The Navajo and Apache were hunters. Later, they learned farming from the Pueblo. The Navajo also learned weaving, pottery making, and sand painting from the Pueblo.

When horses arrived in the Americas, the Navajo and Apache quickly learned to breed them.

---

arid, very dry with little rain
harvest, gathering of crops
weaving, cloth making
breed, help animals reproduce

BEFORE YOU GO ON

1 What animals were important to the Native Americans of the Plains? Why?

2 What was the purpose of the Pueblo's Snake Ceremony?

On Your Own
Why do you think some tribes farmed and others hunted?

11

◀ A community house supported by totem poles, Ketchikan, Alaska

The Northwest

The thirty tribes that lived in the forests of the Northwest were unique in several ways.

First, unlike Native Americans in other regions, they didn't become farmers. Instead, they caught fish and hunted game for their food.

Second, they had social classes. For example, some people were nobles, the highest social class. Others were commoners, and some were slaves.

Third, the Native Americans of this region were excellent builders and architects. Their huge houses were made of cedarwood.

Finally, members of many of these tribes made wooden totem poles to record their family tree. Every family chose a spirit in the form of an animal, such as a raven, wolf, bear, or eagle. They carved images of these spirits on their totem poles.

The Makah people lived in what is now northwestern Washington. The Makah were very skilled at fishing. Traditionally, they built big canoes from red cedar and hunted whales in the ocean.

---

unique, special and good
architects, people who design buildings
family tree, visual representation of family members, such as parents, grandparents, and great-grandparents

▲ A family's spirit images

12

Like many northwestern tribes, the Makah had potlatches—large feasts where people gave away blankets and other property. By giving away property, people earned a high position in society. Potlatches were a way to pass on important cultural information from one generation to the next.

The Southeast

Native Americans who settled in the Southeast enjoyed a mild climate and an environment rich in natural resources. The first settlers, sometimes known as the Temple Mound Builders, were skilled builders and farmers. They built large towns. The Mound Builders have vanished, but you can still see the flat-topped mounds of their cities in parts of Louisiana today.

By the late 1500s, the Choctaw, Cherokee, Chickasaw, Creek, and Seminole peoples had created a remarkable civilization in the Southeast. These tribes lived in planned villages and were good farmers and hunters. They started schools and had knowledge of diseases and medicines. European settlers called them the "Five Civilized Tribes."

Most of these southeastern peoples were forced to move west because European settlers wanted their land. Between 1830 and 1850, the government moved the Cherokee, the Choctaw, and other peoples to land west of the Mississippi River. Many died traveling there, and the journey of the Cherokee became known as the Trail of Tears.

---

generation, group of people who are about the same age
mild, not too cold, wet, or hot
vanished, disappeared
mounds, hills
civilization, developed society

◀ A Creek council house

BEFORE YOU GO ON

1 Why did the tribes of the Northwest make totem poles?

2 Why was the journey of the Cherokee known as the Trail of Tears?

On Your Own
If you could design your own totem pole, what animals would you carve into it? Why?

13

COMPREHENSION

Workbook
Page 5

Right There

1. Where did the first Americans come from?
2. What affected how the tribes lived within their regions?

Think and Search

3. In what regions of North America did the first Americans live?
4. How were tribes in the Northwest region different from tribes in other areas?

Author and You

5. Why do you think the author decribes the Native Americans by their regions?
6. Do you think it is important for people today to know about these tribes? Why or why not?

On Your Own

7. How would you describe your daily life?
8. How would you describe the region in which you live?

IN YOUR OWN WORDS

Use the words and phrases in the chart below to tell a partner about the first Americans and the regions in which they lived.

▲ A traditional coiled basket

Region	Vocabulary
The Northeast	tools, forests, lakes, game
The Plains	grassy lands, villages, buffalo, nomads
The Southwest	hunting, farming, weaving, pottery making
The Northwest	game, social classes, builders, totem poles
The Southeast	villages, schools, natural resources, Trail of Tears

DISCUSSION

Discuss in pairs or small groups.

1. Why do you think the first Americans migrated to North America?
2. How were the tribes in this article alike? How were they different?
3. Would you like to live the way the first Americans did? Why or why not?

Q How can change improve people's lives? Think of your environment. How would a migration affect it? Would it improve the environment? If so, how?

)) Listening TIP

Listen carefully to other people's ideas.

READ FOR FLUENCY

It is often easier to read a text if you understand the difficult words and phrases. Work with a partner. Choose a paragraph from the reading. Identify the words and phrases you do not know or have trouble pronouncing. Look up the difficult words in a dictionary.

Take turns pronouncing the words and phrases with your partner. If necessary, ask your teacher to model the correct pronunciation. Then take turns reading the paragraph aloud. Give each other feedback.

EXTENSION

Workbook Page 5

Learn about a Native American tribe that lives in your area today or that used to exist there. Work with a partner. Copy the chart below into your notebook. Use the Internet or do research at the library to complete the chart. Share your results with the class.

Tribe:
Location:
Number of members:
Customs:

A totem pole ▶

Grammar and Writing

Order of Adjectives

Writers use adjectives to describe people, places, or things. Sometimes more than one adjective is used to describe a noun. When this happens, adjectives must be listed in the order given in the following chart.

Order of Adjectives					
Opinion or Quality	Size	Age or Temperature	Shape	Color	Material
fast	tiny	new	round	brown	cedarwood
smart	medium	ancient	square	yellow	glass
pretty	huge	elderly	oval	pink	cloth
remarkable	big	cold	triangular	green	plastic

Read the examples below. Pay attention to the order in which the adjectives are listed.

> They built **huge cedarwood** houses.
> He owns a **fast brown** horse.
> We're studying a **remarkable ancient** civilization.

Practice

Work with a partner. Complete each sentence. Write each pair of adjectives in the correct order. Take turns reading the completed sentences aloud.

1. The family lived in the _____ hut. (grass, small)
2. They fished in the _____ lake. (blue, calm)
3. The tribe was the first to live in the _____ area. (large, wooded)
4. The women of the tribe planted the _____ seedlings yesterday. (young, green)
5. The boys found a _____ coin on the ground. (metal, round)

16

WRITING A DESCRIPTIVE PARAGRAPH

Describe a Group of People

At the end of this unit, you will write a descriptive essay. To do this, you will need to learn some of the skills writers use to describe people, places, and things.

Group	
Trait	Example

When writers describe a group of people, they often include details and adjectives to describe the group's traits, or characteristics, such as their values, relationships, customs, and/or activities. For example: *The Makah tribe had potlatches, or large feasts where people gave away their property. By giving away property, people earned a high position in society.*

Here is a model paragraph. The writer used a T-chart to list traits that describe the Cherokee people. She used this information to write her paragraph. Notice how she includes details and adjectives.

Katie Veneziano

The Remarkable Civilization of the Cherokee People

The Cherokee are a Native American tribe. For many centuries, the Cherokee made their home in the mountains and forests of what became the southeastern United States. Traditionally, Cherokees hunted, fished, and farmed crops such as corn and squash. They lived in villages with houses constructed of river cane and plaster. Their houses looked slightly similar to log cabins. For ceremonial purposes, Cherokees built larger seven-sided buildings. Besides being good builders, Cherokees created wonderful artwork. They made beautiful, useful baskets out of river cane, and they carved wooden masks for ceremonies and battles. Cherokees often traded their goods with neighboring Native American peoples. At times, the Cherokee went to war with other Native American tribes such as the Creek and Shawnee, but on other occasions they were allies.

Practice **Workbook** Page 7

Write a descriptive paragraph about another Native American tribe or about another group of people you know. Before you write, list details about the group in a graphic organizer. Be sure to use adjectives in the correct order.

Writing Checklist

IDEAS:
☑ I described a group's characteristics.

WORD CHOICE:
☑ I used details and adjectives to support and develop my description.

What You Will Learn

Reading
- Vocabulary building: *Literary terms, word study*
- Reading strategy: *Analyze historical context*
- Text type: *Literature (novel excerpt)*

Grammar, Usage, and Mechanics
Sequence words

Writing
Describe an event or experience

THE BIG QUESTION

How can change improve people's lives? In most places, people are supposed to follow rules and obey laws. But are these rules and laws always right? Are there any rules or laws that you think are not right? How would your life improve if these rules or laws changed? Discuss with a partner.

BUILD BACKGROUND

In this section, you will read an excerpt from the historical fiction novel ***Riding Freedom***. Historical fiction uses real events, places, or people in a fictional story.

The story is about Charlotte Parkhurst, a real person who lived during the 1800s. As a young girl, Charlotte loved horses, but girls weren't supposed to work in the stables. Taking care of horses was a boy's job. Girls were expected to cook and clean.

As an adult, Charlotte lost the use of one eye after a horse kicked her in the face. But she loved horses so much that she became an expert horse rider and a stagecoach driver. In her time, women weren't allowed to do these things. In fact, there were many things that women weren't permitted to do, such as voting and owning property. However, Charlotte found ways to do the things she wanted.

▲ A stagecoach in the Old West

VOCABULARY

Learn Literary Words

A **plot** is the sequence of related events in a story. Most plots include a problem, or **conflict**, the events that lead toward solving the conflict, and the solution to the conflict. Plots usually move forward in time. They have a beginning, a middle, and an end.

A conflict is a struggle that can occur between the following forces:

- Character versus self
- Character versus another character
- Character versus society
- Character versus nature

Conflict is important in stories because it sets the plot in motion and makes the story interesting and suspenseful.

Practice  Workbook Page 8

Work with a partner. Read the following paragraph. Identify the conflict, the events leading to the solution, and the solution itself.

> Frank looked up to see three women enter the building. A group of men began complaining loudly. Frank knew the men were behaving badly; he reminded the men that it was now legal for women to vote. The men looked at one another. They respected Frank and his opinions and slowly stopped calling out to the women. Instead, they stood by quietly and watched as the women cast their ballots and left the building.

◀ Women voting at the polls

Learn Academic Words

Study the **red** words and their meanings. You will find these words useful when talking and writing about literature. Write each word and its meaning in your notebook. After you read the excerpt from *Riding Freedom*, try to use these words to respond to the text.

achieved = succeeded in doing something, especially by working hard	→	Women **achieved** the right to vote in 1920.
attitudes = thoughts or feelings about something or someone	→	In the 1800s, some men had negative **attitudes** about women and their desire to vote.
discrimination = unfair treatment of some people because of their race, ethnic group, religion, or gender	→	In the 1800s, **discrimination** kept women from voting and purchasing land.
illegal = not allowed by law	→	A long time ago, it was **illegal** for women to vote in presidential elections.

Practice
Workbook
Page 9

Work with a partner to answer these questions. Try to include the **red** word in your answer. Write the sentences in your notebook.

1. What goals have you **achieved** in your lifetime?

2. Are people's **attitudes** toward women today different from the way they were years ago? If so, how?

3. Do you think **discrimination** affects people today? If so, who and why?

4. What do you think should happen to someone who does something **illegal**?

▲ A 1920s magazine cover

Word Study: Double Consonants

Adding an ending, such as *-ed* or *-ing*, to a word can change its meaning. When endings are added to a single-syllable word that ends in a vowel + a consonant, the final consonant is doubled. For words with more than one syllable, the consonant doubles only if the stress is on the final syllable of the word.

Base Word	+ Ending	= New Word
grin	-ed	grinned
run	-ing	running
occur	-ed	occurred
begin	-ing	beginning

Practice

Work with a partner. Copy the chart above into your notebook. Add four blank rows. Then add *-ed* and *-ing* to the words below and add them to the chart.

clap	rebel	regret	visit

READING STRATEGY | ANALYZE HISTORICAL CONTEXT

Analyzing the historical context of a story or text can make it more meaningful and easier to understand. Historical context includes the political and cultural changes that happened during a particular time period. To analyze historical context, follow these steps:

- As you read, pay attention to the events in the text.
- Think about how the location of the story affects the characters.
- Consider what you already know about the place or the time of the story.
- Notice how the characters are reacting to the events as they happen.

As you read *Riding Freedom*, think about the time and place of the story. What new historical information do you learn?

Set a purpose for reading Read the excerpt to find out how Charlotte Parkhurst made it possible for a woman to vote in the 1868 presidential election. How did her actions change people's perceptions of women?

from RIDING FREEDOM

Pam Muñoz Ryan

Dressed as a man, Charlotte "Charley" Parkhurst bought land in California. Her friend Hayward comes to her new home for a visit. In this scene, Charlotte prepares to say good-bye to him—and to reveal her secret plan.

Hayward stayed for a month of Sundays, and Charlotte couldn't bear thinking about him leaving again.

The morning he left she said, "Hay, you can stock tender for me as long as you like."

"Charlotte, I'm beginning to think you like having me around," he teased. "I never thought I'd see the day. But first, I got work to finish in Missouri. Then I got to help my folks move out here."

He hesitated, then said, "Charlotte, come with me."

"It'll take me over a year, Charlotte. You could get someone to watch the place. Won't you come?"

She turned and looked at him. "I can't, Hay. I don't want to leave. I worked my whole life for this. I belong *here*. I want to build up my horse stock, and I got apples to pick, and things I got to do. Besides, there's something I been thinking on for some time that I feel real strongly about."

She knew she could tell Hay anything but she wasn't sure how he'd react to this. "I registered to vote in Santa Cruz County. The election's in a few weeks, and I don't want to miss it."

Hayward stared at her and shook his head. "Charlotte, you'll be going against the law."

---

stock tender, take care of horses and cattle
folks, parents
registered, officially enrolled

✔ **LITERARY CHECK**

With whom does Charlotte have a conflict?

"Hay, I know more about who to vote for than most. Women are citizens of this country just like you. They work hard and make decisions sound as a man's."

"There's a lot of folks who don't agree."

"There's a lot of *men* who don't agree," said Charlotte.

Hayward grinned at her.

"I ain't one of them," he said. "I just don't understand what you'll be provin' if no one *knows* you're a woman."

"I guess I'm proving that here I am, a member of this county that most folks respect. Most of them ask *me* who *I'm* voting for! And the only reason I can walk in and vote is because they *think* I'm a man. Sooner or later, they'll all know I was a woman and my point will be made."

"So, someday you're gonna let people know you're a lady?" he asked.

"Maybe. But whether I let them know or not, I'll be wearin' these same clothes and tendin' my horses and runnin' this ranch, same as always."

He considered what she said and shook his head. "You know your mind, Charlotte, and that's fine by me. You know how I feel about you."

"I know."

He gave her a big hug and acted like he was never going to let go. Then he got on his horse and rode down the lane, past the corral. Charlotte stood on the porch and watched him ride away. He stopped halfway down the road and waved his hat.

Charlotte waved back.

---

sound, practical, based on good judgment
corral, pen for horses or cattle

BEFORE YOU GO ON

1. Why doesn't Charlotte want to leave with Hayward?

2. Why does Charlotte feel women should have the right to vote?

On Your Own
Do you think Charlotte's plan is a good one? Why or why not?

23

It was sprinkling when Charlotte rode into town that November afternoon, but a little rain couldn't stop her. She hoped it wouldn't stop other folks from getting out and doing what they had to do, either. Luckily, by the time she got to town, the sun had come out. She hitched the mustang and walked down the street and nodded to the people walking by. A big sign in the window of the hotel said POLLS. Some of the ladies in town went about their errands and didn't seem to give a second thought to the long line of men in front of the hotel. Others gathered out front, in twos and threes, waiting for their men-folk, and acted like there was nothing special going on inside. Charlotte wondered if they really didn't care. Or if they were going about playing their roles like she was playing hers.

One man came up and clapped her on the back.

"Glad to see ya, Charley," he said.

Another man said, "Pretty excitin' day, ain't it, Charley?"

Charlotte didn't say much. She shook hands all around and got in line with the men. She listened to them banter and joke around her.

"Heard Wyoming's gonna give women the right to vote. I thought I'd heard everything."

"What's this country comin' to?"

"What do you think, Charley?"

---

hitched, tied
mustang, small wild horse
polls, place for voting
errands, short trips to buy something

24

Charlotte said, "I don't think it hurts nothin'. Guess they know their minds as well as us."

"Don't hurt nothin'! Them women fightin' for this is just plain crazy, stirrin' up trouble all over. They'll be the ruination of this country. I told my wife that she wouldn't ever be votin' as long as she's married to me, no matter what the law says. What does she know about politics?"

Several other men added their opinions.

The line inched up the hotel steps.

A little boy ran up, found his father in line, and tugged on his hand.

"Papa, Papa! The Tayor boy said Sarah and I can't play ball 'cause I'm little and she's a girl. And she's fightin' him in the street and he's twice as big as her. Hurry, Papa!"

The father shook his head. "We told her and told her about fightin'. When's that girl gonna learn?"

The men chuckled, and the father and the little boy left.

The line moved closer to the desk.

Charlotte got to the front and signed the book.

The registrar handed her the ballot. She studied the names. Horatio Seymour or Ulysses S. Grant, the conservative Democrat or the much talked-about Republican. She had listened to the talk and heard people's debates. She had heard good things and bad things about both men but she knew her own mind and what she thought was right.

---

ruination, destruction, downfall
politics, the issues of running a country
registrar, official who records votes
ballot, piece of paper that you use to vote
Democrat, member of one of the two major political parties in the United States, the Democratic party
Republican, member of the other major political party, the Republican party

BEFORE YOU GO ON

1 Which state was the first to give women the right to vote?

2 What does the boy report about his sister, Sarah?

On Your Own
Why do you think the men had negative opinions about the idea of women voting?

25

"You know who you're votin' for, Charley?" asked the man next to her.

"Yes, I do," said Charlotte.

"Old Jake couldn't make it today because he's ailin'. Felt real bad about not comin', but I told him one vote won't make no difference."

Charlotte nodded to the man. Would her one vote make a difference? Why was she doing this? Someday when people found out, would they just think she had been crazy, too? Or would they wonder that she had a good reason?

Yes, she told herself. She had a good reason.

This was something she could do for those women out front who were pretending they didn't mind that they couldn't vote. And for that little girl outside who was already standing up for herself.

She smiled. And for me, she thought. Because I'm as qualified as the next man.

She marked her choice for president of the United States.

She turned in her ballot, then faced the crowd of men still waiting in line. She tipped her hat.

"Gentlemen," she said, "may the best man win."

Then she walked out of the hotel, got on her horse, and rode home.

✔ LITERARY CHECK

Which line best expresses the turning point, or climax, in the plot?

---

qualified, capable

26

From the Author

This fictional novel is based on the true story of Charlotte Darkey Parkhurst.

Posing as a male, by the 1860s, she was a noted "whip" or "jehu" (a Biblical term referring to a charioteer) of the time. Charlotte retired from driving at a ranch near Watsonville, California.

After Charley's death, it was discovered that she was a woman. Deeds and records confirm that Charlotte, disguised as Charles Parkhurst, owned property in Watsonville. Charlotte's cabin was near the Seven Mile House, a former stagecoach stop and hotel. This way station for travelers on the Santa Cruz to Watsonville stage line was located on a road that was later named Freedom Boulevard. Charlotte also registered to vote in Santa Cruz County, fifty-two years before any woman would be allowed to vote in federal elections in the United States.

▲ A stagecoach station

We will never really know Charlotte's motives for choosing to live her life the way she did. Possibly, she did what she had to do to survive during a time when there were very few opportunities for young women. I suspect that she stumbled upon the chance to become a stage driver, that she was good at it, and that it gave her personal freedoms that she would have never experienced as a girl. That freedom would have been very hard for anyone to give up once they had experienced it.

---

charioteer, driver of an ancient vehicle called a chariot
deeds, official papers that say who owns a piece of land
way station, rest stop
federal, governmental

ABOUT THE **AUTHOR**

Pam Muñoz Ryan has written numerous award-winning novels and picture books for young readers. She started her career as a teacher and later began writing on the advice of a friend. Today she lives in Southern California with her husband and four children.

BEFORE YOU GO ON

1 What motivated Charlotte to place her vote?

2 When did people discover that "Charley" was actually a woman?

On Your Own
Imagine yourself "in Charlotte's shoes." Would you have acted similarly in order to gain your personal freedoms?

27

Review and Practice

READER'S THEATER

Act out the following scene between Charlotte and a man at the polls.

Man: I was hoping to see you here, Charley.

Charlotte: I wouldn't miss voting today.

Man: Yeah, all the *men* should come and vote. But have you heard the news? Women in Wyoming are going to be allowed to vote soon, too. Can you imagine what would happen if we let women vote?

Charlotte: Why shouldn't women vote? They can make up their own minds.

Man: No, they can't. Women don't know what to think, and they don't know anything about politics.

Charlotte: You might be surprised. The women I know can think for themselves.

Man: If we let women vote, the country will be ruined.

Charlotte: I don't agree with you at all. I think you're mistaken.

Man: I don't think so. I hope I'm not alive to see the day a woman in this country is allowed to vote.

Charlotte: [*grinning*] Something tells me you'll be here to see it happen. Just wait.

COMPREHENSION

Workbook
Page 12

Right There

1. What were the other ladies in town doing while Charlotte stood in line to vote?

2. What did the men think would be the ruination of the country?

Think and Search

3. How are Sarah (the little girl who was fighting) and Charlotte similar?

4. Who was Charlotte referring to when she said, "May the best man win"?

Author and You

5. How do you think the men in town would have reacted if they knew Charlotte was a woman?

6. What is the author's attitude about personal freedom? Do you agree with her? Why or why not?

On Your Own

7. Have you ever voted? Who or what did you vote for and why?

8. Do you think discrimination against women still exists today? Why or why not?

DISCUSSION

》⑨ Listening TIP

Give the speaker your full attention. Don't talk to your classmates.

Discuss in pairs or small groups.

1. How do you think Charlotte felt after she turned in her ballot?

2. Do you think Charlotte was right to disguise herself as a man in order to vote? Why or why not?

⬤ **How can change improve people's lives?** How have women's rights changed over the past century? How have their lives improved?

RESPONSE TO LITERATURE

Workbook
Page 12

How do you think *Riding Freedom* would have ended if someone had discovered Charlotte's secret? Work with a partner to rewrite the story's ending. Write a paragraph that explains how Charlotte gets caught voting as a woman and who discovers her secret. Then share your version of events with the class.

Grammar and Writing

Sequence Words

Writers often use sequence words, such as *first*, *next*, *then*, and *finally*, to write about a series of events. Sequence words help the reader understand when events take place within a story. For example, look at how sequence words were used in this passage from *Riding Freedom*.

> The morning he left she said, "Hay, you can stock tender for me as long as you like."
>
> "Charlotte, I'm beginning to think you like having me around," he teased. "I never thought I'd see the day. But **first**, I got work to finish in Missouri. **Then** I got to help my folks move out here."

Sequence words help the reader understand the order in which Hayward has to complete his tasks.

> **First**, Hayward has work to finish in Missouri.
> **Then** he will help his parents move.
> **Finally**, he will care for Charlotte's horses.

Practice

Below are some events that happened in the excerpt from *Riding Freedom*. Work with a partner. Indicate the order in which the events happened by writing a number next to each sentence. Then use the sentences to write a paragraph. Include sequence words.

_____ Charlotte stood in line and talked to the men about women voting.

_____ Charlotte rode into town on a November afternoon.

_____ Charlotte moved to the front of the line, got her ballot, and voted.

_____ Charlotte hitched her mustang and walked down the street to the polls.

30

WRITING A DESCRIPTIVE PARAGRAPH

Describe an Event or Experience

You have learned how to describe a group of people using details and adjectives. Now you will learn how to describe an event or an experience.

Descriptive texts usually tell about events in chronological order, or the order in which they happened. Writers often use sequence words like *first*, *then*, *next* and *finally* to make the order of events clear.

Here is a model paragraph. The writer listed the details of her experience in a sequence-of-events organizer. Then she used sequence words within the paragraph to make the order of events clear.

First
Next
Then
Finally

Haley Coy

My First School Formal

Getting ready for my first school formal was busy and exciting. First, I had my hair done at a professional salon. Countless bobby pins and squirts of hairspray were used before the style was complete. The updo gave me an elegant look for the rest of the evening. Next, came the gentle brush-strokes of makeup, finished with small amounts of glitter on my cheeks. Then it was time to put on my black dress and high heels. The heels gave me enough height so that my dress just grazed the floor. Finally, my escort arrived to pick me up. He looked great in his elegant black tuxedo. As he placed a yellow rose corsage on my wrist, my parents started snapping pictures of us. Now I'll have plenty of photographs to remember just how incredible we looked on that memorable night.

Practice

Workbook Page 14

Write a descriptive paragraph about an exciting event you participated in or attended, for example, a sports event, a party, or a family celebration. Before you write, list the events in chronological order, using a graphic organizer. Be sure to use sequence words in your descriptions.

Writing Checklist

ORGANIZATION:
☑ I used chronological order.

WORD CHOICE:
☑ I used sequence words to make the order of events clear to the reader.

Prepare to Read

What You Will Learn

Reading

- Vocabulary building: *Context, dictionary skills, word study*

- Reading strategy: *Recognize sequence*

- Text type: *Informational text (science)*

Grammar, Usage, and Mechanics
Simple past: regular and irregular verbs

Writing
Describe an object

THE BIG QUESTION

How can change improve people's lives? What kinds of tools or machines do you use on a daily basis? A toothbrush? Television? Computer? Pen? Copy the chart below into your notebook. List objects you use every day. Include a brief description of how you use each item. Then, share your chart with a small group. Discuss how people's everyday lives have been changed by these items.

Tool or Machine	How I Use It

BUILD BACKGROUND

"Early Inventions" is a science article about inventions, or things that people design to improve their lives. Many of these inventions have made a big difference in how we live.

Inventions are created for various reasons. Some are created so people can do things they couldn't do before. For example, the music cylinder allowed people to record music and listen to it whenever they wanted. Some inventions, like the microwave oven, are designed to make the things we already do easier. Some inventions are made just for fun, like cotton candy. And some, as you will discover in "Early Inventions," are created purely by accident.

◀ An Edison gramophone

32

Learn Key Words

Read these sentences. Use the context to figure out the meaning of the **red** words. Use a dictionary to check your answers. Then write each word and its meaning in your notebook.

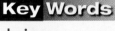

Key Words

designer
device
elements
invention
patent
periodic table

1. The **designer** sketched a picture of the tool he wanted to make.

2. The **device** opens metal cans.

3. Scientists are still discovering new **elements**, or simple chemical substances made of only one atom.

4. The **invention** of the vacuum cleaner made cleaning the house faster and easier.

5. The inventor applied for a **patent** from the government. He didn't want anyone else to make or sell his invention.

6. Students study the **periodic table** to learn more about chemical elements.

Practice  Workbook Page 15

Write the sentences in your notebook. Choose a **red** word from the box above to complete each sentence. Then take turns reading the sentences aloud with a partner.

1. All the chemical elements in the world are listed on the _____.

2. Max will sell the new video game he invented after he receives a _____ from the government.

3. The stapler is a _____ that fastens papers together.

4. The clothing _____ created all the costumes for the play.

5. Similar _____ are grouped together on the periodic table.

6. The _____ of the Internet allowed people to find information quickly.

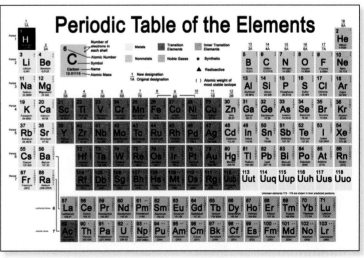

▲ The periodic table of chemical elements, invented in 1869

Learn Academic Words

Study the **red** words and their meanings. You will find these words useful when talking and writing about informational texts. Write each word and its meaning in your notebook. After you read "Early Inventions," try to use these words to respond to the text.

created = made or invented	➡	Alexander Graham Bell **created** a new way for people to communicate with each other—the telephone.
function = the purpose of something	➡	The **function** of a washing machine is to clean clothes.
significant = noticeable or important	➡	The invention of the computer had a **significant** impact on society. We will see the effects of this invention for many years to come.
technology = all the knowledge and equipment used in science	➡	As **technology** has improved, scientists have been able to develop many new products.

Practice  Workbook Page 16

Work with a partner to answer these questions. Try to include the **red** word in your answer. Write the sentences in your notebook.

1. Have you ever **created** something you were proud of? If so, what?
2. What is the **function** of an airplane?
3. In your opinion, what is one of the most **significant** inventions ever created?
4. What kinds of new **technology** might be invented in the future?

34

Word Study: Nouns That Modify Nouns

A noun is a person, place, or thing. Sometimes, a noun is used to decribe, or modify, another noun. For example, two nouns make up the phrase *bear cub*. However, the first noun acts as an adjective—*bear* gives you more information about the *cub*. Look at the sentences below for examples of other nouns that modify nouns.

She placed the tea bag in the mug.	➡	*tea* modifies *bag*
I cooked dinner in the microwave oven.	➡	*microwave* modifies *oven*
The first telegraph lines were built in the 1850s.	➡	*telegraph* modifies *lines*
I poured the juice into a paper cup.	➡	*paper* modifies *cup*

Practice
Workbook
Page 17

Work with a partner. Copy the sentences below into your notebook. Circle each noun modifier and underline the noun being modified.

1. The lie detector said that he wasn't telling the truth.
2. The telephone wire was sticking out of the wall.
3. Ben spilled juice on his computer keyboard.
4. She snapped her bubble gum loudly.
5. The ice pop melted in the sun.

READING STRATEGY   RECOGNIZE SEQUENCE

Recognizing sequence in a text is important because it helps you to understand the order in which things happen. To recognize sequence, follow these steps:

- As you read, look for words that the author uses to show sequence, for example, *first*, *then*, *next*, *finally*, *last*, *while*, *during*, and *after*.
- Look for dates and times, for example, *morning* and *Wednesday*.
- It may help you to draw a timeline of the events described.

As you read "Early Inventions," make a note of the sequence in which things were invented. What happened first, next, and last?

Workbook
Page 18

35

Set a purpose for reading As you read about inventions, consider how our ancestors' lives were different from ours today. What impact did these inventions have on us?

Early Inventions

The Nineteenth Century

In the nineteenth century, many new products and industries developed because of advances in science. Plastic, synthetic fabrics, electric light, telephones, photography, cars, and radio were just a few of the inventions that would change people's lives.

---

synthetic, manufactured, made in a factory

▲ A woman wearing bloomers

Bloomers
c. 1853
Amelia Bloomer

In the nineteenth century, people thought pants for women were outrageous. This may have been why American women's rights reformer Amelia Bloomer liked them. She believed that long, baggy pants gathered at the ankle would liberate women. When she appeared in her pants in about 1853, there was more laughter than liberation. But within thirty-five years, another invention made "bloomers" seem like a good idea—they were ideal for women who wanted to ride bikes.

Safety elevator
1853
Elisha Otis

Knowing that people were scared of elevators, Elisha Otis invented a safety hoist with arms that shot out and grabbed the sides of the elevator shaft if the supporting cable broke. In New York City, he demonstrated his invention's effectiveness by having the cable cut while he was in it. He installed his first passenger safety elevator in 1857 in a New York store.

---

reformer, person who tries to change society
gathered, tied or tightened
liberate, free
hoist, device that lifts and lowers
elevator shaft, chamber an elevator moves in

Transatlantic telegraph
1858
**Cyrus Field, Charles Bright,
William Thomson**

By the 1850s, there were several short underwater telegraph lines. American financier Cyrus Field wanted to go further. He wanted to link the United States and Britain with a cable across the Atlantic Ocean. Field hired many engineers and scientists, including Charles Bright and William Thomson. After heroic efforts, a transatlantic cable was laid in 1858. However, there were problems, which made the cable fail within weeks. But it proved that the idea worked. A permanent link between the two countries was finally established in 1866.

Periodic table
1869
Dmitry Mendeleyev

In 1866, Russian chemist Dmitry Mendeleyev listed the elements by atomic weight. He found that the list showed a pattern: similar elements appeared at regular intervals, or periods. Mendeleyev published his periodic table in 1869. In 1871, he created a version with gaps where there were breaks in the pattern. He said that the gaps represented undiscovered elements. Most chemists did not see the importance of this until at least twenty years later.

---

telegraph lines, electric wires used to carry messages
financier, person who lends large amounts of money
chemist, scientist who studies the interaction of atoms and molecules
atomic weight, the mass of a single atom of a certain element

▲ An advertisement

Jeans
1873
Jacob Davis, Levi Strauss

In the 1850s, the Gold Rush in California attracted people from everywhere. Levi Strauss had a business that supplied people with everything they needed, including pants. Tailor Jacob Davis started making denim pants with riveted pockets, to make them strong for hard work. He suggested to Strauss that they could make lots of money. So Strauss provided the cash to get started, and Davis supplied the know-how. In 1873, they got the first patent for jeans.

---

tailor, someone who makes clothes that are measured to fit exactly
riveted, fastened by small metal bolts

BEFORE YOU GO ON

1 Why did Amelia Bloomer believe wearing pants would help women?

2 How did both Jacob Davis and Levi Strauss contribute to the invention of jeans?

On Your Own
Which of these inventions have you heard of before?

The Twentieth Century

In the first fifty years of the twentieth century, new inventions and discoveries transformed both everyday life and the world of science. Ordinary people got radios, lifesaving drugs, and cars. Scientists created a new physics, which revealed the awesome energy hidden in matter. The modern world was nearly here.

Vacuum cleaner
1902
Hubert Booth

Early devices for removing dust just tried to blow it away. One day, British engineer Hubert Booth put a handkerchief over his mouth and sucked the upholstery of a chair. The dirt he collected convinced him that vacuum cleaning would be much better. He started a company to make vacuum cleaners in 1902. But the cleaners were so big they had to be parked outside the houses they cleaned.

---

physics, study of the basic laws of nature
matter, material that everything is made of
upholstery, material that covers furniture

Teddy bear
1902
Morris Mitchtom, Margarete Steiff

Popular American president Theodore "Teddy" Roosevelt became even more popular in 1902, when he went on a hunting trip but refused to shoot

▲ A Steiff bear

a defenseless bear cub. Cashing in on this, New York retailer Morris Mitchtom began selling cuddly toy bears. They had shoe-button eyes and jointed limbs. Mitchtom called them "Teddy's Bears." They were a huge success, and their name soon became "teddy bears." At about the same time, German designer Margarete Steiff started making similar bears. Although they weren't exactly like Mitchtom's bears, Steiff bears became the number one best-sellers.

---

retailer, person who sells goods from a store

▼ A 1902 vacuum cleaner

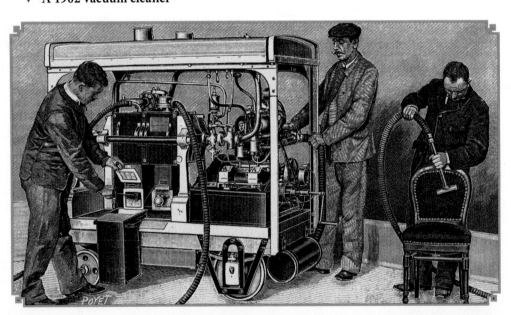

Electric washing machine
1907
Alva Fisher

For years, inventors tried to find a way of reducing the hours spent over a steaming washtub. Women spent many hours washing the family's clothes by hand. The first electric washing machine was designed in 1907 by American engineer Alva Fisher. It had a drum that turned back and forth to tumble clothes clean. Its motor was simply bolted on to the outside of the machine. It wasn't very safe, but it saved women many hours of work.

Ice pop
1923
Frank Epperson

Refreshing, flavored ice on a stick was patented by American salesman Frank Epperson in 1924. The legend is that Epperson invented the ice pop by accident in 1905, when he was a boy, by leaving a drink with a stirrer in it out on a cold night. His patent describes cylindrical ice pops made in ordinary test tubes.

---

legend, popular, probably untrue, story
cylindrical, round, but flat at top and bottom

◀ An early washing machine

Bubble gum
1928
Walter Diemer

Walter Diemer, a young accountant working for the Fleer Chewing Gum Company in Philadelphia, Pennsylvania, thought he could improve on the company's product. In 1928 he produced a gum that was so stretchy he could blow bubbles with it. He had created bubble gum. His company started selling it as Dubble Bubble. Diemer taught the sales force how to blow the perfect bubble, and the gum became a favorite worldwide.

Cat's eyes
1935
Percy Shaw

Cat's eyes are the little reflectors set in the road that make driving at night safer. Possibly inspired by real cats' eyes, British engineer Percy Shaw invented them in 1934, but they were not used until the following year. Their secret was in the rubber that housed the reflectors. Whenever a car ran over a cat's eye, a flexible "eyelid" wiped the reflectors clean, ready for the next driver. Shaw became a millionaire.

---

accountant, person who keeps track of money
reflectors, pieces of plastic that reflect light
rubber, stretchy, durable substance used in things like car tires

BEFORE YOU GO ON

1 Which invention was created by accident? How was it invented?

2 Who was Mitchtom's teddy bear named after?

On Your Own
If you could be the first to invent something, what would you invent?

COMPREHENSION

Workbook
Page 19

Right There

1. Who invented the electric washing machine?
2. What pattern did Mendeleyev find in his list of chemicals?

Think and Search

3. What is the same about the invention of the vacuum cleaner and the invention of the teddy bear?
4. Why did Cyrus Field want to build a transatlantic telegraph?

Author and You

5. Why do you think the author chose to write about these particular inventions?
6. Did the author use chronological order in the article? If so, how?

On Your Own

7. Which invention from the reading do you think is the most significant?
8. What characteristics do you think an invention must have in order for it to be significant? Why?

IN YOUR OWN WORDS

Review the reading. Choose four inventions that you think are the most significant. Look at the date of each invention. In your notebook, draw a timeline like the one below. Add the dates to the timeline in chronological order. Then write a sentence describing each of the four inventions. Present your timeline and summaries to the class.

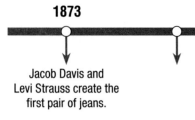

1873

Jacob Davis and
Levi Strauss create the
first pair of jeans.

A replica of the first lightbulb ▶

DISCUSSION

Discuss in pairs or small groups.

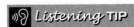

Listening TIP

Look at the speaker as he or she speaks.

1. The majority of the inventors that you read about were men. Why do you think that is?

2. What qualities do you think a person must have in order to be an inventor?

How can change improve people's lives? Name new technologies that have been invented during your lifetime. What was your life like before these inventions existed? How have they changed your life for the better?

READ FOR FLUENCY

When we read aloud to communicate meaning, we group words into phrases, pause or slow down to make important points, and emphasize important words. Pause for a short time when you reach a comma and for a longer time when you reach a period. Pay attention to rising and falling intonation at the end of sentences.

Work with a partner. Choose a paragraph from the reading. Discuss which words seem important for communicating meaning. Practice pronouncing difficult words. Give each other feedback.

EXTENSION

Workbook
Page 19

Choose an object that you use every day. Use the library or the Internet to research that object. Find out who invented it and when and how it was invented. Complete the chart below. Share the results with your class.

Object:
Inventor:
Year object was invented:
How object was invented:

Grammar and Writing

Simple Past: Regular and Irregular Verbs

In the article you just read, the author used the simple past to describe events or actions that began and ended in the past. Form the past tense of regular verbs by adding *-d* or *-ed* to the base form of the verb. If the verb ends in a *y*, change the *y* to an *i* and add *-ed*. Notice the regular verbs in the chart below.

Simple Present	Simple Past
It **proves** her theory is correct.	It proved her theory was correct.
Cyrus Field **wants** to go further.	Cyrus Field wanted to go further.
I **supply** him with the know-how.	I supplied him with the know-how.

Some verbs are irregular. The only way to learn the simple past forms of irregular verbs is to memorize them. Here are a few common irregular past tense verbs.

be → was, were	know → knew
do → did	make → made
find → found	put → put
get → got	take → took
have → had	think → thought

Practice  **Workbook Page 20**

Work with a partner. Rewrite each sentence below in the simple past. Take turns reading the sentences aloud with your partner.

1. We design clothes together.
2. They are in the workroom.
3. We work well together.
4. They modify the plans.
5. They make the job easier.
6. It is a new machine.

WRITING A DESCRIPTIVE PARAGRAPH

Describe an Object

You have learned how to describe a group of people and an event or an experience. Now you will describe an object.

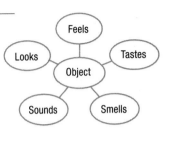

Writers often use sensory details to describe objects. Sensory details appeal to the reader's five senses. This helps the reader to imagine how an object sounds, smells, looks, feels, or tastes. For example, you might describe an ice pop as cold, cylindrical, and sweet. *Cold* describes how the ice pop feels, *cylindrical* describes how it looks, and *sweet* describes how it tastes.

Here is a model paragraph. First, the writer listed sensory details in a word web. Then he used those details to describe a faucet. Also notice his use of regular and irregular past tense verbs.

Pablo Espínola

The Faucet

It had to be 100 degrees in the kitchen. As I stood at the sink, the reflection of the sun on the faucet's metal hurt my eyes. I noticed the faucet's smooth curves, the knobs, and the gleaming spout. When I turned the cold-water knob, a river gushed out of the spout and hit the sink. Small droplets of water bounced out, leaving little wet marks along my arms. When I placed my hand on the metal spout, it felt icy from the cold water running through it. I got a glass from the cupboard and filled it. On a hot day, the water from the faucet tasted sweet and refreshing. After washing my hands and face, I felt cool and comfortable in my house on that hot, hot day.

Practice  **Workbook Page 21**

Write a descriptive paragraph about an object that you have used, eaten, or worn, such as a computer, an apple, or a sweater. List related sensory details in a graphic organizer. Include these details in your paragraph. Be sure to use regular and irregular past tense verbs correctly.

Writing Checklist

WORD CHOICE:
✔ I included sensory details to describe an object.

SENTENCE FLUENCY:
✔ I used regular and irregular past tense verbs correctly.

What You Will Learn

Reading

■ Vocabulary building: *Literary terms, word study*

■ Reading strategy: *Visualize*

■ Text type: *Literature* (*novel excerpt*)

Grammar, Usage, and Mechanics
Comparative and superlative forms of adjectives

Writing
Describe a place

THE BIG QUESTION

How can change improve people's lives? Do you know someone who has a garden? What kinds of plants grow there? What kind of changes take place in a garden? How could you benefit from having a garden? Discuss.

BUILD BACKGROUND

You will read an excerpt from the novel **Seedfolks**. It is a work of fiction about an empty lot that becomes a community garden. In some city neighborhoods, people plant gardens in vacant lots or empty areas of land. Each person plants flowers or vegetables in one part of the garden and then they take care of that area.

In *Seedfolks*, a different character narrates each chapter, telling about the garden from his or her point of view. Each chapter is like a short story. Short stories usually present a short sequence of events, and the main character usually experiences a problem or conflict. A girl named Kim narrates the first chapter you will read. She tells why she decided to plant beans in an empty city lot.

▲ A community garden

44

Learn Literary Words

Imagery is descriptive language used in literary works. Writers use sensory details to create imagery. This helps the reader see, feel, taste, touch, and smell what the writer is describing. Try to identify the use of imagery in the excerpt from *Seedfolks* below.

> **Literary Words**
>
> imagery
> setting

> The sidewalk was completely empty. It was Sunday, early in April. An icy wind teetered trash cans and turned my cheeks to marble. In Vietnam we had no weather like that. Here in Cleveland people call it spring. I walked half a block, then crossed the street and reached the vacant lot.

Notice how the words *icy* and *marble* appeal to your sense of touch, and the words *empty, teetered,* and *vacant* appeal to your sense of sight.

The **setting** of *Seedfolks* is an old, abandoned lot in Cleveland, Ohio. The setting of a literary work is the time and place of the action. *Time* can be a specific year, season, or time of day. *Place* can be a specific location on a map such as a town, state, or country. *Place* can also be a specific environment such as a garden or a junkyard.

Practice  **Workbook** Page 22

Work with a partner. Choose a setting from the box below. Create imagery by listing sensory details that describe the setting. Then rewrite your list, placing the most important details first. Read your list to the class.

beach	favorite restaurant
bedroom	house
classroom	local park

▲ Sensory details such as *empty* and *cold* could be used to describe this building.

Learn Academic Words

Study the **red** words and their meanings. You will find these words useful when talking and writing about literature. Write each word and its meaning in your notebook. After you read the excerpt from *Seedfolks*, try to use these words to respond to the text.

Academic Words

goal
involved
located
reacted

goal = something you want to do in the future	→	She's a new and inexperienced gardener. Her **goal** is to grow prize-winning flowers.
involved = included in a project or situation	→	She got **involved** in a garden club at school. She goes to their meetings every Friday.
located = in a particular place or position	→	The bean plants are **located** at the back of the garden.
reacted = behaved in a particular way because of what someone has said or done	→	Juan **reacted** with joy and excitement when the seeds began to grow.

Practice  **Workbook Page 23**

Work with a partner to answer these questions. Try to include the **red** word in your answer. Write the sentences in your notebook.

1. What is one **goal** you hope to accomplish before next summer?

2. What community service project would you like to become **involved** in?

3. Where is your house **located**?

4. How would you **react** if someone suggested a community garden for your neighborhood?

Prize-winning flowers ▶

Word Study: Apostrophes

As you read the excerpt from *Seedfolks*, you will see words that include an apostrophe ('). Use an apostrophe to make a noun show possession or to take the place of missing letters, as in a contraction.

To show possession:
- Add ' + s to the end of a singular noun.
- Add an apostrophe (') to the end of a plural noun.

> I found the **girl's plants**. [the plants that belong to the girl]
> The **plants' leaves** were wilting. [the leaves of the plants]

A contraction is two words combined into one with an apostrophe. Use the apostrophe to take the place of a missing letter or letters.

I'd never entered the lot before.	[I + had = I'd]
There's a garden in the lot.	[there + is = there's]

Practice  Workbook Page 24

Work with a partner. Read aloud the phrases in the box below. Combine the words in each phrase to make contractions or possessive nouns. Then, in your notebook, write a sentence using those words.

can not	seeds of the beans	had not	father of the girl	it is

READING STRATEGY   VISUALIZE

When you visualize, you make pictures in your mind of what you are reading. To visualize, follow these steps:
- As you read, think about what the author wants you to see.
- Pay attention to descriptive words and figurative language.
- Stop from time to time and visualize the story's characters, setting, and events.

As you read *Seedfolks*, ask yourself, "What language is the author using to create a picture of the characters, setting and events?"

 Workbook Page 25

Set a purpose for reading As you read, pay attention to Kim's actions. How do they affect other characters in the story?

from

Seedfolks

Paul Fleischman

Kim

I stood before our family altar. It was dawn. No one else in the apartment was awake. I stared at my father's photograph—his thin face stern, lips latched tight, his eyes peering permanently to the right. I was nine years old and still hoped that perhaps his eyes might move. Might notice me.

The candles and incense sticks, lit the day before to mark his death anniversary, had burned out. The rice and meat offered him were gone. After the evening feast, past midnight, I'd been wakened by my mother's crying. My oldest sister had joined in. My own tears had then come as well, but for a different reason.

I turned from the altar, tiptoed to the kitchen, and quietly drew a spoon from a drawer. I filled my lunch thermos with water and reached into our jar of dried lima beans. Then I walked outside to the street.

The sidewalk was completely empty. It was Sunday, early in April. An icy wind teetered trash cans and turned my cheeks to marble. In Vietnam we had no weather like that. Here in Cleveland people call it spring. I walked half a block, then crossed the street and reached the vacant lot.

I stood tall and scouted. No one was sleeping on the old couch in the middle. I'd never entered the lot before, or wanted to. I did so now, picking my way between tires and trash bags. I nearly stepped on two rats gnawing and froze. Then I told myself that I must show my bravery. I continued farther and chose a spot far from the sidewalk and hidden from view by a rusty refrigerator. I had to keep my project safe.

---

altar, table used for religious purposes
thermos, container that keeps liquids warm or cold
marble, hard, smooth stone
vacant, empty
scouted, looked around
gnawing, biting or chewing on something continuously

I took out my spoon and began to dig. The snow had melted, but the ground was hard. After much work, I finished one hole, then a second, then a third. I thought about how my mother and sisters remembered my father, how they knew his face from every angle and held in their fingers the feel of his hands. I had no such memories to cry over. I'd been born eight months after he'd died. Worse, he had no memories of me. When his spirit hovered over our altar, did it even know who I was?

I dug six holes. All his life in Vietnam my father had been a farmer. Here our apartment house had no yard. But in that vacant lot he would see me. He would watch my beans break ground and spread, and would notice with pleasure their pods growing plump. He would see my patience and my hard work. I would show him that I could raise plants, as he had. I would show him that I was his daughter.

My class had sprouted lima beans in paper cups the year before. I now placed a bean in each of the holes. I covered them up, pressing the soil down firmly with my fingertips. I opened my thermos and watered them all. And I vowed to myself that those beans would thrive.

---

hovered, floated in the air
patience, willingness to wait
vowed, made a promise
thrive, live well

BEFORE YOU GO ON

1. What kind of seeds did Kim plant?

2. Where did Kim plant her seeds? Describe the area.

💡 **On Your Own**
Have you ever planted seeds before? If so, what kind and why?

49

Wendell

My phone doesn't ring much, which suits me fine. That's how I got the news about our boy, shot dead like a dog in the street. And the word last year about my wife's car wreck. I can't hear a phone and not jerk inside. When Ana called I was still asleep. Phone calls that wake me up are the worst.

"Get up here quick!" she says. I live on the ground floor and watch out for her a little. We're the only white people left in the building. I ran up the stairs. I could tell it was serious. I prayed I wouldn't find her dead. When I got there, she looked perfectly fine. She dragged me over to the window. "Look down there!" she says. "They're dying!"

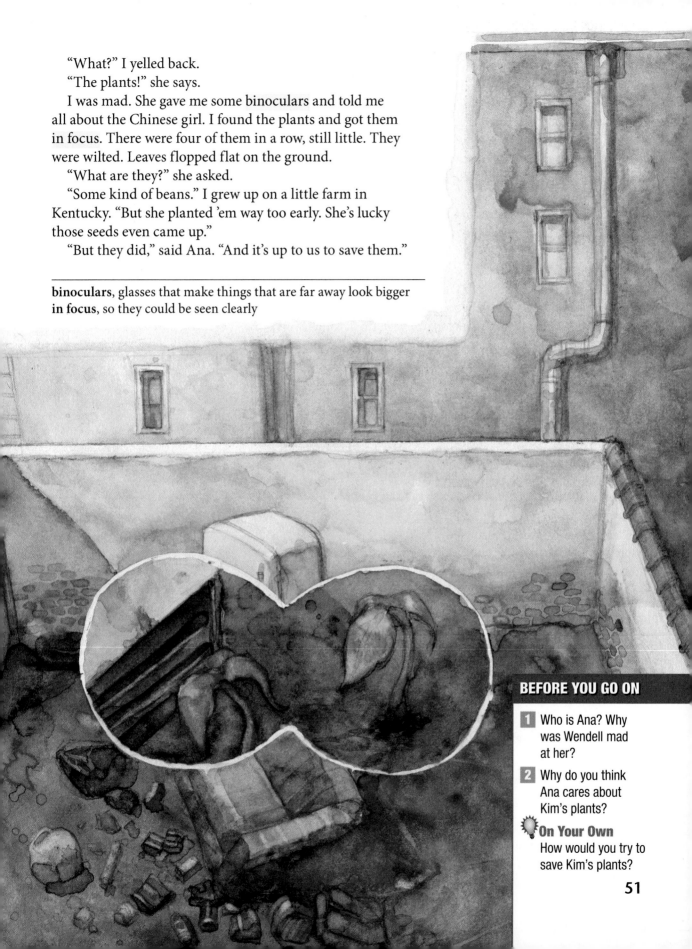

"What?" I yelled back.

"The plants!" she says.

I was mad. She gave me some binoculars and told me all about the Chinese girl. I found the plants and got them in focus. There were four of them in a row, still little. They were wilted. Leaves flopped flat on the ground.

"What are they?" she asked.

"Some kind of beans." I grew up on a little farm in Kentucky. "But she planted 'em way too early. She's lucky those seeds even came up."

"But they did," said Ana. "And it's up to us to save them."

---

binoculars, glasses that make things that are far away look bigger
in focus, so they could be seen clearly

BEFORE YOU GO ON

1 Who is Ana? Why was Wendell mad at her?

2 Why do you think Ana cares about Kim's plants?

On Your Own
How would you try to save Kim's plants?

It was a weekend in May and hot. You'd have thought that those beans were hers. They needed water, especially in that heat. She said the girl hadn't come in four days—sick, probably, or gone out of town. Ana had twisted her ankle and couldn't manage the stairs. She pointed to a pitcher. "Fill that up and soak them good. Quick now."

School janitors take too much bossing all week to listen to an extra helping on weekends. I stared at her one long moment, then took my time about filling the pitcher.

I walked down the stairs and into the lot and found the girl's plants. You don't plant beans till the weather's hot. Then I saw what had kept her seeds from freezing. The refrigerator in front of them had bounced the sunlight back on the soil, heating it up like an oven. I bent down and gave the dirt a feel. It was hard packed and light colored. I studied the plants. Leaves shaped like spades in a deck of cards. Definitely beans. I scraped up a ring of dirt around the first plant, to hold the water and any rain that fell. I picked up the pitcher and poured the water slowly. Then I heard something move and spun around. The girl was there, stone-still, ten feet away, holding her own water jar.

She hadn't seen me behind the refrigerator. She looked afraid for her life. Maybe she thought I'd jump up and grab her. I gave her a smile and showed her that I was just giving her plants some water. This made her eyes go even bigger. I stood up slowly and backed away. I smiled again. She watched me leave. We never spoke one word.

---

pitcher, container used to hold liquid
spades, symbols shaped like pointed leaves

I walked back there that evening and checked on the beans. They'd picked themselves up and were looking fine. I saw that she'd made a circle of dirt around the other three plants. Out of nowhere the words from the Bible came into my head: "And a little child shall lead them." I didn't know why at first. Then I did. There's plenty about my life I can't change. Can't bring the dead back to life on this earth. Can't make the world loving and kind. Can't change myself into a millionaire. But a patch of ground in this trashy lot—I *can* change that. Can change it big. Better to put my time into that than moaning about the other all day. That little girl showed me that.

The lot had buildings on three sides. I walked around and picked myself out a spot that wouldn't be shaded too much. I dragged the garbage off to the side and tossed out the biggest pieces of broken glass. I looked over my plot, squatted down, and fingered the soil awhile.

That Monday I brought a shovel home from work.

Bible, holy book of Christians

ABOUT THE **AUTHOR**

Paul Fleischman was born in Monterey, California, and grew up in Santa Monica. Today he lives in Aromas, California. Fleischman is the author of many books about music and natural history.

✔ **LITERARY CHECK**

Why is the setting especially important in this story?

BEFORE YOU GO ON

1 Why didn't Kim's seeds freeze in the cold weather?

2 What did Wendell realize after his encounter with Kim and her plants?

On Your Own
What changes did you read about in this story?

53

READER'S THEATER

🔊 *Speaking* TIP

Face the audience when speaking.

Act out the following scene between Ana and Wendell.

Ana: [*impatiently*] It's about time you got up here!

Wendell: What's the problem? I was afraid you were sick.

Ana: Quick, come over to the window. Look down there. They're dying.

Wendell: What are you talking about? What's dying?

Ana: The plants. The plants! Here, take my binoculars.

Wendell: [*looking through the binoculars*] Okay, I see them. So what?

Ana: Do you know what kind of plants they are?

Wendell: They look like beans. I used to grow beans on my farm.

Ana: They don't look good, do they? What's wrong with them?

Wendell: They were planted way too early. I can't even believe they came up.

Ana: Well, they did. And now it's our job to save them.

Wendell: Our job? What are we going to do?

Ana: *You* are going to water those plants. I can't because I twisted my ankle. Now, take this pitcher—fill it up with water. Quickly!

COMPREHENSION

 **Workbook Page 26**

Right There

1. In what city does this story take place?
2. Where did Kim live before she moved to Cleveland?

Think and Search

3. Why did Kim plant lima beans?
4. How did the location of Kim's plants help them grow?

Author and You

5. How does the author want the reader to feel about Kim?

6. Why did Kim plant her seeds in the early morning hours?

On Your Own

7. Is there a community garden in your neighborhood? If so, describe it.

8. Describe a time in your life when you experienced a change. What was it? How did it make you feel?

Listening TIP

If you can't hear the speaker, you may say, "Excuse me, could you speak louder, please?"

DISCUSSION

Discuss in pairs or small groups.

1. Why do you think Ana involved herself in helping Kim and her plants?

2. What was Wendell's life like before he became involved in helping Kim's plants grow?

How can change improve people's lives? Have you ever helped a stranger without being asked to do so? What did you do? How did you feel afterward? Do you think that small acts of kindness can change people's lives? If so, how?

RESPONSE TO LITERATURE

**Workbook
Page 26**

At the end of *Seedfolks*, Wendell decides to make a change in his life. How did Kim and her plants inspire this new beginning? What do you think this means for Wendell? What will he do? Write a paragraph that explains what you think Wendell will do and why. Trade papers with a partner and read each other's paragraphs aloud.

Grammar and Writing

Comparative and Superlative Forms of Adjectives

To compare two things, use the comparative form of the adjective and the word *than*. To compare three or more things, use *the* plus the superlative form of the adjective. Notice how spellings change with these forms:

Most one-syllable adjectives: add *-er* / *-est* Example: *young*	➡	She's **younger** than her brother. She's the **youngest** person in her family.
One-syllable adjectives (consonant-vowel-consonant): double the last consonant and add *-er* / *-est* Example: *big*	➡	The bean plants are **bigger** than the strawberry plants. The bean plants are the **biggest** plants in my garden.
Two-syllable adjectives that end in *y*: replace the *y* with *-ier* / *-iest* Example: *healthy*	➡	This garden is **healthier** than the garden I grew last summer. This is the **healthiest** garden I've ever had.
Most adjectives that have two syllables or more: use *more* / *most* in front of the adjective Example: *beautiful*	➡	Flowers are **more beautiful** than bean plants. These flowers are the **most beautiful** flowers I've ever seen.
Irregular adjectives: Some adjectives have irregular forms. They must be memorized. Example: *good*	➡	His new attitude is **better** than his old attitude. This is the **best** attitude he's had in a long time.

Practice  **Workbook** Page 27

Write the sentences below in your notebook. Complete each sentence by changing the adjective in parentheses to a comparative or a superlative.

1. The pumpkin seed is _____ than the apple seed. (big)
2. That lot is the _____ in the city. (dirty)
3. The weather in Cleveland is _____ in winter than in summer. (cold)
4. She is the _____ person in her family. (young)
5. Marco's report was the _____ report we heard. (interesting)
6. She is _____ than her neighbors. (curious)

WRITING A DESCRIPTIVE PARAGRAPH

Describe a Place

You have learned how to describe people, an event, and an object. Now you will learn how to describe a place.

Writers use details to describe places. Sometimes writers present details in a spatial order, or in order of location. For example, to describe your classroom, you might start at the back of the room and make your way toward the front, describing all the important features along the way. Words such as *inside, outside, on top of, underneath,* or *next to* can tell readers the position of people or things.

Here is a model paragraph. The writer used a three-column chart to organize her details. Within the paragraph, she presented the details in a spatial order. She also used comparative and superlative adjectives to describe objects.

The Garden		
Back	Middle	Front

Nicole Siley

The Garden

As I walked outside, I noticed my grandparents' garden. Looking at it, the first thing I noticed were the beautiful colors—red, yellow, purple, green, and orange. Then I noticed how the vegetables were arranged from back to front according to the size of the plants. In the far back, there were corn stalks, the tallest plants in the garden. Next, there were the biggest tomato plants I had ever seen. They sat in the middle of the garden with the eggplants. My favorite vegetables, the squash and the carrots, were in the front rows. Looking at these vegetables made me remember all the wonderful Sunday night dinners I've shared with my family. I never imagined that looking at vegetables could trigger such pleasant memories.

Practice  Workbook Page 28

Write a paragraph describing a place you are familiar with, such as a room in your home, a park, or your neighborhood. List your details in a graphic organizer. Present them in a spatial order. Be sure to include comparative and superlative adjectives.

Writing Checklist

ORGANIZATION:

✔ I used spatial organization.

WORD CHOICE:

✔ I used comparative and superlative adjectives correctly.

57

Link the Readings

Critical Thinking

Look back at the readings in this unit. Think about what they have in common. They all tell about changes. Yet they do not all have the same purpose. The purpose of one reading might be to inform, while the purpose of another might be to entertain or persuade. In addition, the content of each reading relates to changes differently. Now copy the chart below into your notebook and complete it.

Title of Reading	Purpose	Big Question Link
"The First Americans"	*to inform*	
From *Riding Freedom*		*It describes the first American woman to vote in a presidential election.*
"Early Inventions"		
From *Seedfolks*		

Discussion

Discuss in pairs or small groups.

● How is Charlotte in *Riding Freedom* similar to the inventors in "Early Inventions"?

Q **How can change improve people's lives?** Compare and contrast the ways in which each of the readings in this unit describes change. Think about the people in the readings. How were their lives improved by the changes they experienced? Does change always improve people's lives? Explain.

Fluency Check

Work with a partner. Choose a paragraph from one of the readings. Take turns reading it for one minute. Count the total number of words you read. Practice saying the words you had trouble reading. Take turns reading the paragraph three more times. Did you read more words each time? Copy the chart below into your notebook and record your speeds.

	1st Speed	2nd Speed	3rd Speed	4th Speed
Words Per Minute				

Projects

Work in pairs or small groups. Choose one of these projects.

1 Use modeling clay to create a family totem pole. Carve an animal that best represents each of your family members into the clay. Present the totem pole to a partner.

2 American women called suffragettes began to fight for the right to vote in the 1820s. They were rewarded for their work in 1920, when women won the right to vote. Research a suffragette and how her actions helped women. Share your results with the class.

3 Think of an invention you would like to create. What would it do? How would it help people? Illustrate your invention. Then write a descriptive paragraph about it. Share your work with a partner.

4 Create a community garden. Map out an area on a piece of posterboard. Draw and label the plants you want to include in your garden. Then take your classmates on a "tour."

Further Reading

To find out more about the theme of this unit, choose from these reading suggestions.

Inventions that Changed the World, David Maule
This Penguin Reader® looks at some of the most important inventions from ancient times to the present day. Topics include printing, mathematics, navigation, weapons, flight, communications, and computers.

Give Me Liberty: The Story of the Declaration of Independence, Russell Freedman
The author describes the events before, during, and after the American Revolution. We get to know the people whose views helped shape a new nation and to understand the significance of the Declaration of Independence, both then and now.

The Story of Thomas Alva Edison, Margaret Cousins
Here is the life story of the man who brought us the phonograph, motion pictures, and the electric light bulb—revolutionary inventions that forever changed the way we live.

Put It All Together

LISTENING & SPEAKING WORKSHOP

Small-Group Presentation

You will give a group presentation describing a person, place, object, or experience that has changed your school or community for the better.

1 **THINK ABOUT IT** Look back over the readings in this unit. Talk in small groups about change. Think of changes that have occurred in your school or community recently.

Work together to develop a list of beneficial changes that have taken place, for example:

- The new hire of an inspirational teacher
- A new community center
- The purchase of new school equipment
- The development of a new recycling plan

2 **GATHER AND ORGANIZE INFORMATION** As a group, choose a topic from your list. Then write down everything you know about that topic. Include any questions you have about it.

Research Use the library and/or the Internet to get more information. You may also wish to interview school or community leaders. Take notes on what you find.

Order Your Notes Share your notes with the group. Discuss which sensory details could be used within the presentation to create a picture in the minds of the audience members. Write them in a graphic organizer, such as a word web. Choose a logical order in which to present this information.

Use Visuals Make or use existing visual aids such as photos, maps, and illustrations to enhance your presentation. Make sure they are large enough for audience members to see easily.

3 PRACTICE AND PRESENT Keep your graphic organizer nearby as you practice your presentation as a group. Speak clearly and confidently, and use your visual aids to support key ideas. Make sure each group member has a part, and work on making smooth transitions from one speaker to the next. Keep practicing until you no longer need to look at your graphic organizer.

Deliver Your Group Presentation Look at your audience as you speak. Emphasize key ideas by pointing to your visual aids. Slow down when you come to the most important points, or restate them at the end of your presentation.

4 EVALUATE THE PRESENTATION
You will improve your skills as a speaker and a listener by evaluating each group presentation you give and hear. Use this checklist to help you judge your group's presentation and the group presentations of others.

☑ Was the group's topic clear?

☑ Did the speakers use sensory details to help listeners create a picture in their minds?

☑ Could you hear and understand each speaker easily?

☑ Were the transitions between speakers smooth and logical?

☑ What suggestions do you have for improving the group presentation?

Speaking TIPS

Have your first speaker introduce your topic in an interesting way.

You may want to use words like *first*, *then*, *next*, and *finally* to help identify a sequence of events for the audience.

Listening TIPS

Listen carefully to your fellow group members, and learn your *cues*—words or actions that signal when it is your turn to speak.

Write down key details as you listen. Use them to picture what the speakers are describing.

WRITING WORKSHOP
Descriptive Essay

You have learned how to write a variety of descriptive paragraphs. Now you will use these skills to write a descriptive essay. An essay is a group of paragraphs that focus on one topic. Most essays begin with a paragraph that introduces the topic. Two or more body paragraphs develop the topic by adding ideas and details. A concluding paragraph sums up what the essay is about. In a descriptive essay, the writer describes a person, group, place, thing, event, or experience. Descriptive essays often include adjectives and sensory details that appeal to a reader's senses.

Your assignment for this workshop is to write a five-paragraph descriptive essay about an experience or change in your life that had an important effect on you.

1 **PREWRITE** Brainstorm possible topics for your essay in your notebook. What experiences had an impact on your life, feelings, or ideas? You might write about meeting a new friend, moving to a new place, or trying a new activity. Choose an experience or change that you can describe clearly and vividly.

Organize Your Ideas After selecting a topic, use a graphic organizer such as a word web or a sequence of events chart to develop your essay. A student named Nicole wrote about going to middle school. She used a word web to gather ideas and details for her essay.

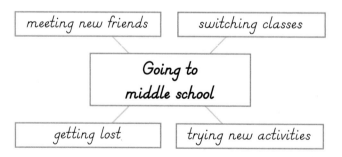

2 **DRAFT** Use the model on page 65 and your graphic organizer to help you write a first draft. Include an introductory paragraph, three body paragraphs, and a concluding paragraph. Use sensory details to help create a picture in readers' minds.

3 **REVISE** Read over your draft. As you do so, ask yourself the questions in the writing checklist. Use the questions to help you revise your essay.

SIX TRAITS OF WRITING CHECKLIST

☑ **IDEAS:** Does my essay describe an experience or change that had an important effect on me?

☑ **ORGANIZATION:** Are my ideas presented in an order that makes sense?

☑ **VOICE:** Does my writing express who I am?

☑ **WORD CHOICE:** Do I use words that describe events and feelings?

☑ **SENTENCE FLUENCY:** Do my sentences flow smoothly?

☑ **CONVENTIONS:** Does my writing follow the rules of grammar, usage, and mechanics?

Here are the changes Nicole plans to make when she revises her first draft:

A Big Step

In my town, three elementary schools ~~go~~ *combine* into one middle school. I used to think my elementary school was the larg*est* school in town, with the most students. *Now* I realize that the middle school is so much larger! Going there has been a *n*ew ⟨exciting⟩ experience that has changed me in many ways.

At first, I had feelings of concern about going to middle school. I *worried* ~~worried~~ about the responsibility of getting my own locker and remembering the combination. I also ~~worried~~ *felt nervous* about getting lost There were so many *busy* classrooms and *long* hallways! Getting lost is a scary thing to think about *when you're young.*

For a while, other things bothered me too. There were lots of

When I started,

strangers. ∧I didn't know many of the students or any of the teachers.

Also I had to switch classes for the first time, so I had to learn the

schedule. ∧Different classes began on different days at different times.

(It seemed very confusing!)

Finally,

∧I realized that everything was going to be fine. The teachers in

the school helped us find our way during the first week, so we didn't

private and safe

get too lost. I began to like having my own locker to keep my stuff. ∧

switching classes gave everybody a chance to meet up with old friends

Also there are tons of fun clubs to join.

and to make new friends from other schools. ∧

The step from elementary school to middle school changed me. I

adjusted very well to the challenges. I learned that students are given

to watch over them and help them

more freedom as they get older, but that they still have people there. ∧

Best of all, middle school expanded my horizons by allowing me to

experience new activities and to meet new friends.

---

4 **EDIT AND PROOFREAD**  **Workbook Page 29**

Copy your revised essay onto a clean sheet of paper. Read it again. Correct any errors in grammar, word usage, mechanics, and spelling. Here are the additional changes Nicole plans to make when she prepares her final draft.

Nicole Siley

A Big Step

In my town, three elementary schools combine into one middle school. I used to think my elementary school was the largest school in town, with the most students. Now I realize that the middle school is so much larger! Going there has been an exciting new experience that has changed me in many ways.

At first, I had feelings of concern about going to middle school. I worried about the responsibility of getting my own locker and remembering the combination. I also felt nervous about getting lost. There were so many busy classrooms and long hallways! Getting lost is a scary thing to think about when you're young.

For a while, other things bothered me too. There were lots of strangers. When I started, I didn't know many of the students or any of the teachers. Also I had to switch classes for the first time, so I had to learn the schedule. It seemed very confusing! Different classes began on different days at different times.

Finally, I realized that everything was going to be fine. The teachers in the school helped us find our way during the first week, so we didn't get too lost. I began to like having my own locker to keep my stuff private and safe. switching classes gave everybody a chance to meet up with old friends and to make new friends from other schools. Also there are tons of fun clubs to join.

The step from elementary school to middle school changed me. I adjusted very well to the challenges. I learned that students are given more freedom as they get older, but that they still have people there to watch over them and help them. Best of all, middle school expanded my horizons by allowing me to experience new activities and to meet new friends.

5 **PUBLISH** Prepare your final draft. Share your essay with your teacher and classmates.

Workbook
Page 30

Invention and Change

*T*he *United States has always been a country of invention and change. When the first European settlers arrived in the 1500s, they called their new homeland the New World. Since then, the country has grown and changed in ways the first settlers could never have imagined. The theme of change runs throughout the work of many American artists.*

Hans Hofmann, *Fermented Soil* (1965)

In *Fermented Soil*, Hans Hofmann did not paint faces or objects that you would recognize. Instead, he used thick and thin brushstrokes. He also used the flat edge of a knife to apply layers of color. Hofmann purposely used paints made from colors that come from the earth. Then he layered these colors one on top of another until he created a field of yellows, golds, and browns. Hofmann even tried to "turn" the paint with the flat knife as though he were turning dirt. The end result is a "garden" of paint on a huge canvas.

When something *ferments*, it breaks down and then changes into something new. Hofmann called this work *Fermented Soil* because he began with simple brown paint. Then he had the brown paint "ferment" with other layers of color until it became something new.

▲ Hans Hofmann, *Fermented Soil*, 1965, oil, 48 x 60 in., Smithsonian American Art Museum

66

▲ Samuel Colman, *Storm King on the Hudson*, 1866, oil,
32⅛ x 59⅞ in., Smithsonian American Art Museum

Samuel Colman, *Storm King on the Hudson* (1866)

In *Storm King on the Hudson*, Samuel Colman shows the
new world of steam-powered engines. These great ships arrived
on American rivers in the mid-1800s. On the left side of this
painting, steam-powered boats move down the mighty Hudson
River in New York State. The rowboats in their path look very
small and weak. In the distance, on the right side of the canvas,
the white sails of several sailboats stand out against the sides of
Storm King Mountain. Colman wanted to show the two worlds
that existed on the Hudson River at the time: the new and the
old, or the new steam-powered ships versus boats powered by
people, such as the sailboat and rowboat.

But this change came with a price, as Colman shows in his
painting. Dirty air from the smokestacks on the steamers fills
the sky. The artist shows this in contrast with the clean white
color of the clouds in the background. Sometimes change also
signals the end of good things.

Hofmann's work captures the exciting side of change,
while Colman's painting shows both the good and the bad.
Even though Colman's painting is more realistic, both artists
capture a tension that all of us connect with change.

Apply What You Learned

1 In what way are these
artworks about inventing
something new?

2 How do both Colman and
Hofmann show tension in
their paintings?

 Big Question
How could you capture
the idea of change in an
artwork? Explain.

 Workbook
Pages 31–32

THE BIG QUESTION

What are the benefits of facing challenges?

This unit is about challenges. You will read texts that describe how people have faced various challenges and the benefits they experienced as a result. Reading, writing, and talking about these topics will help you practice the language you need to use in school.

READING 1: Social Studies Article and Song
- "The Train to Freedom"
- "Follow the Drinking Gourd"

READING 2: Personal Narrative and Poetry
- "Five New Words at a Time" by Yu-Lan (Mary) Ying
- "Quilt" by Janet S. Wong

READING 3: Science Article
- "The Great Fever"

READING 4: Interview and Novel Excerpt
- "An Interview with Gary Paulsen" by Leonard S. Marcus
- From *Hatchet* by Gary Paulsen

Listening and Speaking

At the end of this unit, you will choose a topic and present a **personal narrative**.

Writing

In this unit you will practice **narrative writing**, or writing that tells a story. After each reading you will learn a skill that will help you write a narrative paragraph. At the end of the unit, you will use these skills to write a fictional narrative.

QuickWrite
What does *challenge* mean to you? Write your own definition. Share it with a partner.

Prepare to Read

What You Will Learn

Reading

- Vocabulary building: *Context, dictionary skills, word study*

- Reading strategy: *Skim*

- Text type: *Informational text (social studies) and song*

Grammar, Usage, and Mechanics
Prepositions of location: where and in what direction

Writing
Write a story with a starter

THE BIG QUESTION

What are the benefits of facing challenges? Do you know what it means to "face a challenge"? It means trying something even though you might fail. Some challenges are worth accepting; others can be dangerous. Have you ever accepted a difficult challenge? What was it? Was the outcome beneficial? Discuss with a partner.

BUILD BACKGROUND

"The Train to Freedom" is a nonfiction article about the secret routes that escaping slaves followed to freedom.

In the mid-1800s, slavery was illegal in the northern states, but it was still legal in the South. Many slaves in the South tried to escape. Their journeys were filled with challenges and dangers.

For example, discussing escape routes could be dangerous for the escaping slaves and others. Sometimes slaves hid this information in the songs they sang. You will read one of these songs called **"Follow the Drinking Gourd."**

Escape routes slaves used to travel north ▶

VOCABULARY

Learn Key Words

Read these sentences. Use the context to figure out the meaning of the **red** words. Use a dictionary to check your answers. Then write each word and its meaning in your notebook.

Key Words

fugitive
heritage
network
runaway
shelter
Underground Railroad

1. The **fugitive** slaves were caught and sent back to where they came from.

2. The discoveries, art, events, and accomplishments of our country's past make up our national **heritage**.

3. Many people created a **network** to help escaping slaves find food and a safe place to sleep.

4. Some people received rewards for catching and returning **runaway** slaves.

5. People who were against slavery offered their homes as **shelter** to slaves.

6. We learned that thousands of slaves escaped to freedom using the **Underground Railroad**.

Practice  **Workbook Page 33**

Write the sentences in your notebook. Choose a **red** word from the box above to complete each sentence. Then take turns reading the sentences aloud with a partner.

1. The police looked all over the city for the _____ woman.

2. The fugitives found _____ in an old barn during the storm.

3. The woman was only one of many in the _____ who provided fugitive slaves with supplies.

4. Fugitive, or _____, slaves often became ill from traveling on foot.

5. Freedom is a part of America's _____.

6. Many people supported the _____ , helping slaves escape to freedom.

A reward poster for the capture of a runaway slave ▶

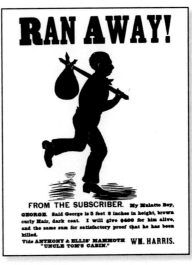

RAN AWAY!

FROM THE SUBSCRIBER. My Mulatto Boy, GEORGE. Said George is 5 feet 8 inches in height, brown curly Hair, dark coat. I will give $400 for him alive, and the same sum for satisfactory proof that he has been killed.
Vide ANTHONY & ELLIS' MAMMOTH "UNCLE TOM'S CABIN." WM. HARRIS.

Learn Academic Words

Study the **red** words and their meanings. You will find these words useful when talking and writing about informational texts. Write each word and its meaning in your notebook. After you read "The Train to Freedom" and "Follow the Drinking Gourd," try to use these words to respond to the texts.

Academic Words

accompanied
aid
challenge
code

accompanied = went somewhere with someone	⟹	She **accompanied** slaves on their journeys to freedom.
aid = help or support given to someone	⟹	The slaves received **aid**, such as food and shelter, from people who opposed slavery.
challenge = something difficult that you need skill or ability to do	⟹	The trip was a **challenge**. The weather was bad, and the slaves were in constant danger.
code = a way to use words, letters, or numbers to send secret messages	⟹	The song contained a **code**. It told the slaves where to go.

Practice

Workbook
Page 34

Work with a partner to answer these questions. Try to include the **red** word in your answer. Write the sentences in your notebook.

1. Who **accompanied** you to school this morning?
2. Have you ever received **aid** from a classmate? Explain.
3. What is your biggest **challenge** at school?
4. Have you ever sent a message that contained a secret **code**? If so, what kind of code did you use?

Word Study: Words with *ch* and *tch*

Ch and *tch* are consonant clusters. They sound the same but are spelled differently. Look at the words *which* and *scratch*. The final sound in each word is the same, but the words are spelled differently. English words may begin with the letters *ch*, but never with the letters *tch*. Read the examples in the chart below.

Spelling	Initial Position	Final Position
ch	**ch**allenge **ch**ance	mu**ch** ea**ch**
tch		ma**tch** fe**tch**

Practice

Copy the sentences below into your notebook. Fill in the missing letters of each word and check the spelling in a dictionary. Then read the sentences aloud with a partner.

1. We gave him a _____eese and tomato sandwi_____ for lun_____.

2. They took a _____ance offering shelter to fugitives.

3. Dogs were used to ca_____ the fugitive. They _____ased him for many miles.

4. He hid in a deep di_____.

READING STRATEGY | SKIM

Skimming a text helps you get a general understanding of what the text is about before you read it more carefully. It also helps you set a purpose for reading. To skim a text, follow these steps:

- Look at the title and visuals to get an idea of what the text is about.
- Read the first paragraph quickly. Then read the first sentence of the paragraphs that follow.
- Don't stop at any words you don't know—skip over them.
- After you skim the text, try to summarize what you learned before you go back and read it again.

Before you read "The Train to Freedom," skim the text quickly. Then stop and think about what you read. What do you already know about the subject? What more do you think you will learn?

Set a purpose for reading As you read, think about how slaves traveled on the Underground Railroad. What challenges did they face? Who helped them along the way?

The Train to Freedom

Risk Takers

People who tried to escape from slavery in the United States took a dangerous chance. Slave catchers and their dogs continually hunted runaway slaves. When they were caught, they might be beaten. Sometimes they were hanged. Even if runaways did not get caught, they often became ill from traveling on foot while tired, cold, wet, and hungry.

---

continually, constantly

◄ Slaves picking cotton

Many free African Americans and others also took risks to help slaves who were running away. People who helped runaways could be punished. Yet many people did not think slavery was right, and they found ways to help the slaves escape.

The Underground Railroad

The Underground Railroad wasn't really underground, and it was not a real railroad. It was called "underground" because it was secret. And it was called a "railroad" because it helped fugitive slaves travel to places where they could be free. A network of people supported the Underground Railroad, helping the slaves escape.

Many of the words connected to the Underground Railroad were railway terms. For example, slaves on the Underground Railroad were called "passengers." The homes, businesses, and churches where they could stop for food or shelter were known as "stations" and "depots." The people who lived in these homes or ran these businesses were called "stationmasters."

▲ Harriet Tubman

"Conductors" were courageous people who went with slaves on their journeys. Levi Coffin, a white Quaker from Cincinnati, was a well-known conductor. But the most famous conductor was Harriet Tubman, a woman who had been a slave herself.

Harriet Tubman

Harriet Tubman knew the evils of slavery. She was born a slave and worked as a maid, a children's nurse, and a field worker. When she was in her early teens, she tried to help a runaway slave. When she was caught trying to help, she was hit in the head with a heavy weight and almost died. As a result of this injury, she suffered from blackouts throughout her life.

Quaker, member of a Christian religious group that opposes all forms of violence
blackouts, periods of unconsciousness

BEFORE YOU GO ON

1 What was the Underground Railroad?

2 Why were stations important to slaves on the Underground Railroad?

💡 **On Your Own**
If you worked on the Underground Railroad, would you rather have worked as a stationmaster or a conductor? Why?

▲ **Harriet Tubman (left) helped many slaves escape to freedom.**

Harriet Tubman was twenty-nine years old when she made her own escape from slavery. Her journey was difficult, but she was successful and settled in Philadelphia. She worked as a dishwasher and began to make plans to rescue her family. Over the next few years, she brought her sister's family and her brothers to the North, where they were free.

However, Harriet Tubman was still not satisfied. Over a ten-year period, she traveled back to the South nineteen times to help more than 300 slaves escape. She was known along the Underground Railroad as Moses because, like Moses in the story of Exodus, she led her people to freedom.

Harriet Tubman became a hero among slaves and among abolitionists, but others hated her. Large rewards were offered for her capture. She wore clever disguises so no one would recognize her.

Harriet Tubman's accomplishments were not limited to her work on the Underground Railroad. During the Civil War, she became a spy for the Union army. She later worked in Washington, D.C., as a government nurse. She died at the age of ninety-three.

Exodus, Bible story in which people escape from slavery
abolitionists, people who wanted to end slavery
spy, person who watches other people secretly to discover information about them
Union, northern states during the Civil War

Travel on the Underground Railroad

What was it like traveling to the North on the Underground Railroad? Although it was different for each person, it was never easy. Slaves had to find out how to escape from the slaveholders' property. Sometimes they had to leave family members or friends and risk never seeing them again. Slaves who wanted to escape could not talk about their plans. Discussing escape plans could be dangerous for the escaping slave or for others.

It was often a challenge for fugitives to find their way from one stop to the next. Sometimes fugitive slaves had a conductor with them from the beginning of the journey, but sometimes they didn't. Runaway slaves had to trust strangers to help them. They often spoke in code, using one word to mean another. (Some of these code words can be found in the spirituals and other slave songs that have become part of our American heritage. The codes used by travelers and helpers on the Underground Railroad could be hidden in these songs.)

Runaway slaves often tried to cover between 10 and 20 miles a night. During daylight, they rested at depots or stations—homes, shops, and churches—when they could. Sometimes they slept in barns or in the woods.

The Underground Railroad operated in many states. Ohio, especially, had numerous Underground Railroad stations. Thousands of runaway slaves followed the Underground Railroad into Ohio. To do this they had to cross the Ohio River.

---

cover, travel

Free States	
California	New Hampshire
Connecticut	New Jersey
Illinois	New York
Indiana	Ohio
Iowa	Oregon
Maine	Pennsylvania
Massachusetts	Rhode Island
Michigan	Vermont
Minnesota	Wisconsin

Slave States	
Alabama	Mississippi
Arkansas	Missouri
Delaware	North Carolina
Florida	South Carolina
Georgia	Tennessee
Kentucky	Texas
Louisiana	Virginia
Maryland	

◄ The free states and the slave states in 1860

BEFORE YOU GO ON

1 Who was Harriet Tubman?

2 What is a code?

On Your Own
What would be the hardest thing for you to leave behind if you were a runaway slave? Why?

Other Supporters of the Underground Railroad

Slavery did not occur only in the South of the United States. Many of the slaves brought to North America arrived at northern cities and were sold to slave owners in the North. However, slavery was more widespread in the South, and it lasted much longer there.

More and more people in the North heard about the Underground Railroad. They formed groups to raise money and provide food and shelter for runaway slaves. These groups, known as "vigilance committees," helped settle fugitive slaves, who were faced with a very different climate and environment in the North. The vigilance committees helped the former slaves find jobs.

We do not have a complete history of the Underground Railroad. There are few written accounts of the Underground Railroad or the experiences of former slaves. Because of this, no one knows exactly how many slaves escaped on the Underground Railroad to free states, Canada, or Mexico. We also don't know how many people took the risk of helping the fugitive slaves on their way, or who these people were. But some historians estimate that as many as 100,000 slaves rode the Underground Railroad to freedom.

---

widespread, common
accounts, descriptions
historians, people who study history
estimate, guess, based on available information

Abolitionists printed pamphlets and newspapers against slavery. ▶

78

Follow the Drinking Gourd

This song contains a secret code. The "drinking gourd" is what the fugitive slaves called the Big Dipper. One of the stars in the Big Dipper points to the North Star, which the fugitive slaves used as a guide to the North.

When the sun comes back and the first quail calls,
Follow the Drinking Gourd.
For the old man is waiting for to carry you to freedom,
If you follow the Drinking Gourd.

Chorus:
Follow the Drinking Gourd. Follow the Drinking Gourd.
For the old man is awaiting to carry you to freedom if you
Follow the Drinking Gourd.

The river bank makes a very good road,
The dead trees show you the way,
Left foot, peg foot, traveling on
Follow the Drinking Gourd.

Chorus
The river ends between two hills,
Follow the Drinking Gourd.
There's another river on the other side,
Follow the Drinking Gourd.

Chorus
Where the great big river meets the little river,
Follow the Drinking Gourd.
For the old man is awaiting to carry you to freedom,
If you follow the Drinking Gourd.

▲ A dipper is a cup with a long handle. It is used to collect drinking water. The slaves thought of the Big Dipper as a dipper made from a gourd, like this one.

Big Dipper, group of stars in the shape of a bowl with a long handle
quail, wild, fat bird with a short tail
peg foot, refers to Peg Leg Joe, who went from farm to farm teaching the song to slaves

BEFORE YOU GO ON

1 How did the vigilance committees help fugitive slaves?

2 What information is hidden in "Follow the Drinking Gourd"?

On Your Own
What do you think it would have been like to travel at night, following the North Star?

79

Review and Practice

COMPREHENSION

Workbook
Page 37

Right There

1. Where did fugitive slaves rest during daylight?
2. What happened to fugitive slaves who were caught?

Think and Search

3. Why was the North Star important to escaping slaves?
4. In what ways did people offer aid to fugitive slaves?

Author and You

5. Why do you think Harriet Tubman became a spy for the Union army?
6. Some slaves did not escape when they had the chance. Why?

On Your Own

7. Would you risk your life in order to obtain freedom? Explain your answer.
8. Would you risk your life in order to help another person in need? Why or why not?

▲ Graue Mill in Oak Brook, Illinois, is believed to have been an Underground Railroad station.

IN YOUR OWN WORDS

The chart below lists the section headings from "The Train to Freedom." Write the main idea of each section in the chart. Then use this information to summarize the article for a classmate.

Heading	Main Idea
Risk Takers	Fugitive slaves, and the people who helped them escape, took a dangerous chance.
The Underground Railroad	
Harriet Tubman	
Travel on the Underground Railroad	
Other Supporters of the Underground Railroad	

DISCUSSION

Discuss in pairs or small groups.

1. Do you think it would have been more dangerous to be a stationmaster or a conductor on the Underground Railroad? Why?

2. Do you think the people who aided fugitive slaves gained anything from the experience? Explain.

Q **What are the benefits of facing challenges?** Do you know of other groups of people who faced challenges as they tried to achieve freedom? Who are they? What did they do? Do you think any benefits (other than freedom) are gained from facing such challenges?

Listening TIP

Do not interrupt the speaker. Save your comments until the speaker is finished.

READ FOR FLUENCY

It is often easier to read a text if you understand the difficult words and phrases. Work with a partner. Choose a paragraph from the reading. Identify the words and phrases you do not know or have trouble pronouncing. Look up the difficult words in a dictionary.

Take turns pronouncing the words and phrases with your partner. If necessary, ask your teacher to model the correct pronunciation. Then take turns reading the paragraph aloud. Give each other feedback on your reading.

EXTENSION  Workbook Page 37

Imagine that you are a conductor on the Underground Railroad. You are helping a group of fugitive slaves travel north to the Ohio River. You know how to find the Big Dipper, the North Star, and stations where people will help you. It is a cold winter night. The river is frozen, making it easier for you to cross. In your notebook, write a journal entry that describes your experience.

Grammar and Writing

Prepositions of Location: Where and in What Direction

Writers use prepositions to show where or in what direction an action occurs. Prepositions are always followed by a noun or noun phrase. This is called the object of a preposition. The prepositions in the chart below tell where and in what direction an action occurs.

Where	Sometimes fugitive slaves slept **in** the woods. During daylight, they rested **at** depots or stations. They crossed a river that ran **between** two hills.
In what direction	Fugitive slaves traveled **to** places where they could be free. It was difficult for fugitives to find their way **from** one stop **to** the next. Thousands of runaway slaves followed the Underground Railroad **into** Ohio.

Practice

Work with a partner. Copy the sentences below into your notebook. Choose the correct preposition(s) to complete each sentence.

1. Slavery did not only occur (in / between) the South.

2. Many people helped slaves escape (from / at) the South.

3. Some fugitive slaves traveled through the southern states and (into / at) Mexico.

4. Others escaped (to / at) Canada.

5. Fugitive slaves had to be especially careful as they traveled (in / from) one station (to / between) another.

6. The slaves took shelter (in / from) abandoned buildings.

7. They rested (between / at) the church.

8. Harriet Tubman traveled (at / between) the North and the South.

WRITING A NARRATIVE PARAGRAPH

Write a Story with a Starter

At the end of this unit, you will write a fictional narrative. To do so, you will need to learn some of the skills writers use to write narratives, or stories. An important aspect of a story is its setting. To describe a setting, you need to include details about the time (year, month, time of day) and place (country, state, neighborhood, home) of a story's action.

Here is a model of an opening paragraph in a story. The writer used the following story starter: *The moon was glowing brightly in the dark of night*. Then she used a word web to organize details that describe the story's setting. Notice how she uses prepositions to describe where and in what direction an action happens.

Madeline Shaw

A Journey on the Underground Railroad
   The moon was glowing brightly in the dark of night. A warm autumn breeze rustled the remaining leaves on the trees as we escaped and ran towards the river. The water was cold as we waded through it. It was the beginning of a journey that would take us to the North, where we would be free. Each night, we traveled anywhere from 10–20 miles a night, always reaching the next stop as daylight approached. Then caring, decent people would provide us with places to rest. We slept in old barns, in cold basements, or even in the woods that surrounded their properties. We continued to travel in this way for a long time. It was a long and difficult journey, but well worth it, as we were finally rewarded with freedom.

Practice

Workbook Page 39

Write a fictional narrative of your own. Begin your story with the following starter: *The view was unlike anything I had ever seen before.* Add details about your story's setting to a graphic organizer. Refer to it as you write your paragraph. Be sure to use prepositions that describe where and in what direction the action in the story takes place.

Writing Checklist

IDEAS:
☑ I used an interesting story starter.

WORD CHOICE:
☑ I used words that clearly establish the setting.

83

What You Will Learn

Reading

- Vocabulary building: *Literary terms, word study*

- Reading strategy: *Identify problems and solutions*

- Text type: *Literature (personal narrative and poetry)*

Grammar, Usage, and Mechanics
Gerunds as subjects and objects

Writing
Rewrite a familiar story

THE BIG QUESTION

What are the benefits of facing challenges? Moving to a new city, state, or country can be overwhelming. You have to say good-bye to your friends, you might have to go to a new school, and you might live among people who speak a different language or have different beliefs or customs than your own.

Have you ever moved to a new place? Where did you move? What challenges did your family face there? How was the move beneficial for your family? Discuss with a partner.

▲ A family moves into their new home.

BUILD BACKGROUND

In this section, you will read a personal narrative called **"Five New Words at a Time"** and a poem, **"Quilt."** In a personal narrative, the writer tells about something he or she experienced. In the narrative you are about to read, the writer tells about moving to a new country and having to learn a new language.

Learn Literary Words

As you have learned, a plot is a sequence of related events within a story. The people or animals involved in those events are called **characters**. You can learn about a character's traits, feelings, and actions by paying attention to their involvement in story events, what they say, and what other characters in the story say about them.

Point of view refers to the narrator, or person telling the story. When a person tells a story using the pronouns *I, me, my,* or *we*, the story is in the first-person point of view. Personal narratives use the first-person point of view.

> **First-person point of view:**
> Today is my first day at this school. I'm nervous. I don't know English that well, and I'm afraid this will keep me from making new friends.

In other stories, the narrator uses the pronouns *he, she,* or *they* to refer to the characters. These stories are told from the third-person point of view.

> **Third-person point of view:**
> Leila was nervous on her first day of school in the United States. She missed her friends and teachers in Ecuador.

Literary Words
characters
point of view

Practice

Write the sentences below in your notebook. Identify the point of view in each sentence. Then change those sentences in the first-person point of view to the third person, and those sentences in the third person to the first person. Take turns reading the sentences aloud with a partner.

1. I moved to America earlier this year.

2. His English tutor was very friendly.

3. We meet every day after school.

4. "How do you like your tutor?" my teacher asked.

5. I answered, "He is very helpful."

▲ A student works with his tutor.

Learn Academic Words

Study the red words and their meanings. You will find these words useful when talking and writing about literature. Write each word and its meaning in your notebook. After you read "Five New Words at a Time" and "Quilt," try to use these words to respond to the texts.

approach = a way of doing something or dealing with a problem	➡	Our teacher's **approach** was a lot of fun. She encouraged us to play word games every day.
communicate = express your thoughts or feelings so other people understand them	➡	When I came to America, it was difficult to **communicate** with my classmates because I did not speak English.
resources = a supply of materials used to complete a task	➡	I used **resources**, like a dictionary and a thesaurus, to complete my homework.
response = something that is said, written, or done as a reaction or reply to something else	➡	My **response** to the teacher's question was correct.

Practice  **Workbook** Page 41

Work with a partner to answer these questions. Try to include the red word in your answer. Write the sentences in your notebook.

1. What **approach** do you use when trying to make new friends?

2. How do you **communicate** with someone who does not speak your language?

3. What kinds of **resources** do you use in school?

4. What is your **response** to the idea of an extended school year?

▲ This student uses resources, such as a microscope and a slide, in his science class.

Word Study: Prefixes *im-, over-, un-, after-*

Prefixes are groups of letters added to the beginning of base words to change their meanings. Knowing the meanings of prefixes will help you understand unfamiliar words.

Prefix	Meaning	Base Word	New Word
im-	not	perfect	imperfect
over-	too much	do	overdo
un-	not	equal	unequal
after-	after	noon	afternoon

Practice

Work with a partner. Look through "Five New Words at a Time" and find words with the prefixes shown above. Write a definition for each word. Then use a dictionary to check your work.

READING STRATEGY | IDENTIFY PROBLEMS AND SOLUTIONS

Identifying problems and solutions helps you understand a text better. Many texts include a problem that a person or character has to solve. To identify these problems and solutions, follow these steps:

- What problem or problems does the person or character have?
- Think about your own experience and what you would do to solve the problem.
- Remember that there may be more than one solution to a problem.
- Read on and find out how the person solves or tries to solve the problem.

As you read "Five New Words at Time," ask yourself what problems the characters experience. How do they try to solve their problems? Are they able to find solutions, or not?

LITERATURE

PERSONAL NARRATIVE
AND POETRY

Set a purpose for reading As you read, pay attention to the families described in the texts. How do these families respond to challenging situations?

Five New Words at a Time

Yu-Lan (Mary) Ying

My family came to America in 1985. No one spoke a word of English. In school, I was in an English as a Second Language class with other foreign-born children. My class was so overcrowded that it was impossible for the teacher to teach English properly. I dreaded going to school each morning because of the fear of not understanding what people were saying and the fear of being laughed at.

At that time, my mother, Tai-Chih, worked part time in a Chinese restaurant from late afternoon till late in the night. It was her unfamiliarity with the English language that forced her to work in a Chinese-speaking environment. Although her job exhausted her, my mother still woke up early in the morning to cook breakfast for my brother and me. Like a hen guarding her chicks, she never neglected us because of her fatigue.

---

dreaded, worried about
exhausted, tired
neglected, failed to take care of
fatigue, tiredness

So it was not surprising that very soon my mother noticed something was troubling me. When I said nothing was wrong, my mother answered, "You are my daughter. When something is bothering you, I feel it too." The pain and care in her moon-shaped eyes made me burst into the tears I had held back for so long. I explained to her the fear I had of going to school. "Learning English is not impossible," my mother said. She cheerfully suggested that the two of us work together to learn the language at home with books. The confidence and determination my mother had were admirable because English was as new to her as it was to me.

That afternoon I saw my mother in a different light as she waited for me by the school fence. Although she was the shortest of all the mothers there, her face with her welcoming smile and big, black eyes was the most promising. The afternoon sun shone brightly on her long, black hair creating an aura that distinguished her from others.

My mother and I immediately began reading together and memorizing five new words a day. My mother with her encouraging attitude made the routine fun and interesting. The fact that she was sacrificing her resting time before going to work so that I could learn English made me see the strength she possessed. It made me admire my mother even more.

---

confidence, belief in oneself
determination, strong desire to succeed
admirable, worthy of respect
aura, quality or feeling

✔ **LITERARY CHECK**
Who are the ***characters*** *in this story?*

BEFORE YOU GO ON

1 Why was Yu-Lan afraid to go to school?

2 What did her mother suggest to help Yu-Lan learn English?

On Your Own
Have you ever felt like Yu-Lan? What was your experience?

89

Very soon, I began to comprehend what everyone was saying and people could understand me. The person solely responsible for my accomplishment and happiness was my mother. The reading also helped my mother learn English so that she was able to pass the postal entrance exam.

It has been seven years since that reading experience with my mother. She is now forty-three and in her second year at college. My brother and I have a strong sense of who we are because of the strong values my mother established for herself and her children. My admiration and **gratitude** for her are endless. That is why my mother is truly the guiding light of my life.

✔ **LITERARY CHECK**
*From which character's **point of view** is this story told? How do you know?*

---

gratitude, thankfulness, appreciation

ABOUT THE **AUTHOR**

Yu-Lan (Mary) Ying received her doctorate degree in medicine from the University of Pittsburgh Medical School. She is currently in training at the American Academy of Otolaryngology.

90

Quilt

Janet S. Wong

Our family
is a quilt

of odd remnants
patched together

in a strange
pattern,

threads fraying,
fabric wearing thin—

but made to keep
its warmth

even in bitter
cold.

---

remnants, parts of something that
    remain after the rest of it is gone
fraying, becoming loose

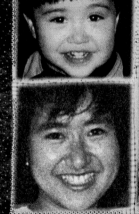

ABOUT THE **POET**

Janet S. Wong was educated at UCLA and
Yale Law School. After several years practicing
law, she began writing poetry and books for
young readers. She lives in New Jersey with
her husband and son.

BEFORE YOU GO ON

1 How did Yu-Lan's
mother benefit
from reading with
Yu-Lan?

2 What object does
the speaker of the
poem liken her
family to? Why?

On Your Own
What object would
you liken your
family to? Explain.

Review and Practice

READER'S THEATER

Speaking TIP

Speak naturally and with feeling.

Act out the following scene between Yu-Lan and her mother.

Yu-Lan: This is impossible! I'll never learn English.

Mother: What's the matter? You look so upset!

Yu-Lan: Nothing, I'm fine. How was work?

Mother: I can tell you're upset. What's wrong?

Yu-Lan: Oh, Mother, I'm so frustrated! I can't learn English. It's too difficult for me.

Mother: Don't they teach you English in school?

Yu-Lan: The class is so large. The teacher has no time to answer my questions.

Mother: I'm sorry to hear that, but learning English is not impossible. I need to learn English, too. Why don't we study together? Every day we will learn five new words.

Yu-Lan: Oh, Mother, do you really think we could?

COMPREHENSION

Workbook
Page 44

Right There

1. Why was it impossible for Yu-Lan's teacher to teach English properly?
2. Why was Yu-Lan's mother forced to work in a Chinese-speaking environment?

Think and Search

3. Why was it important for Yu-Lan and her mother to learn English?
4. What do the actions of Yu-Lan's mother tell you about her character?

Author and You

5. What did Yu-Lan's mother teach her daughter about facing challenges?
6. In the poem "Quilt," the speaker says the following about her family: *but made to keep/its warmth/even in bitter/cold.* What does this mean?

▲ Chinese restaurants

7. Have you ever had to learn another language? If so, what was your approach?

8. Do you think learning a new language is challenging? Why or why not?

DISCUSSION

Discuss in pairs or small groups.

1. Are the family relationships described in the personal narrative and in the poem similar in any way? If so, how?

2. Yu-Lan's mother encourages her daughter to learn English. Do you think it is easier to face challenges with the help and encouragement of other people? Explain.

Q **What are the benefits of facing challenges?** Have you ever helped someone overcome a challenge? What did you do? How did the experience make you feel?

Listening TIP

Respect each speaker. Listen politely even if you disagree with the speaker's ideas.

RESPONSE TO LITERATURE

Workbook Page 44

Can you think of a recent challenge you've had to face? Compare your experience to Yu-Lan's. Copy the chart below into your notebook. Complete the right column with information about your experience. Share your chart in a small group.

Experience	Yu-Lan	Me
Challenge	learned English	
Feelings about challenge	scared, frustrated	
Approach to challenge	read with her mother and learned five new words a day	
Outcome	both mother and daughter learned English	

Grammar and Writing

GRAMMAR, USAGE, AND MECHANICS

Gerunds as Subjects and Objects

A gerund is a verb that can be used like a noun in a sentence. Gerunds are formed by adding *-ing* to the base form of a verb. A gerund can be the subject of a sentence or the object of a verb in a sentence. The author of "Five New Words at a Time" included gerunds in her writing. Read the sample sentences below.

Subject of a Sentence	Object of a Verb
"**Learning** English is not impossible," my mother said.	I dreaded **going** to school each morning. [object of verb *dreaded*]
The **reading** also helped my mother learn English.	My mother and I began **reading** together. [object of verb *began*]

A gerund can also be the object of a preposition. Prepositions include such words as *of, before, from, in, on,* and *at.*

> I explained to her the fear I had <u>of</u> **going** to school.
> She was sacrificing her resting time <u>before</u> **going** to work.

Practice
Workbook
Page 45

Work with a partner. Copy the sentences below into your notebook. Change each verb in parentheses into a gerund. Use it to complete each sentence. Then decide if the gerund is the subject of the sentence, the object of the verb, or the object of a preposition.

1. _____ was very difficult for my family. (move)

2. I avoided _____ English at school. (speak)

3. My mother was good at _____ me. (help)

4. My mother believed _____ me was important. (encourage)

5. _____ English with my mother was fun. (study)

6. _____ hard was important to me and my mother. (work)

WRITING A NARRATIVE PARAGRAPH

Rewrite a Familiar Story

You have learned that setting is an important story element. The point of view from which a story is told is also significant.

    Stories may be written from different characters' points of view. For example, the personal narrative you just read is told from Yu-Lan's point of view. Yu-Lan describes the characters and events in the story and how she felt about them. But the same events could be narrated from another character's point of view, such as Yu-Lan's mother. How would her version of the story be different from her daughter's version?

    Here is a model paragraph. The writer used a T-chart to organize his ideas. Notice how a different point of view can change the way a reader thinks about the story's characters and events.

Yu-Lan's POV	Mother's POV

Austin Saiz

Five New Words at a Time

    Although we didn't speak English, my children and I moved to America in 1985. I quickly found a job at a Chinese restaurant. I like working there because I am able to understand what people are saying. But working long hours makes it difficult for me to spend time with my children. I am usually exhausted when I help them get ready for school in the morning. Even so, I noticed my daughter seemed unhappy. One day, I asked her what was wrong. She looked at me and burst into tears. She told me that learning English at school was impossible. I reassured her that learning a new language could be fun. In fact, I promised her that we would read books and learn the language together—five new words at a time.

Practice  Workbook Page 46

Think about a story you know well. Rewrite it from a different character's point of view. Use a graphic organizer to list your ideas. As you write, remember to use the pronouns *I*, *me*, or *we* if you write in the first-person point of view. Use *he, she,* or *they* if you write in the third-person point of view. Be sure to use gerunds as the subject of a sentence, the object of a verb, and/or the object of a preposition.

Writing Checklist

VOICE:

☑ I used a voice that captured the character's point of view.

WORD CHOICE:

☑ I used prepositions that correctly conveyed the character's point of view.

95

What You Will Learn

Reading

- Vocabulary building: *Context, dictionary skills, word study*

- Reading strategy: *Recognize cause and effect*

- Text type: *Informational text (science)*

Grammar, Usage, and Mechanics
Passive voice: simple past; regular and irregular past participles

Writing
Write a personal narrative

THE BIG QUESTION

What are the benefits of facing challenges? Think about a challenging problem you solved in the past. Why was it challenging? How did you benefit from the experience? Discuss with a partner.

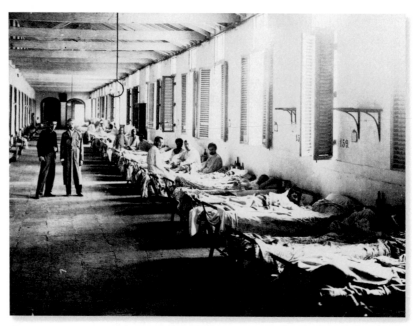

▲ Patients in a yellow fever hospital, Havana, Cuba

BUILD BACKGROUND

In this section, you will read a science article called **"The Great Fever."** It describes the struggle to find the cause of yellow fever. Discovering what caused this disease became a priority during the Spanish-American War in 1898. American troops were fighting in Cuba, and yellow fever was killing many U.S. soldiers.

Yellow fever was a mystery. It caused some people to become sick and even die. Others were not affected at all. Outbreaks occurred in some areas, but not in others. Finding the cause of this disease would be a slow, difficult, and life-threatening challenge.

VOCABULARY

Learn Key Words

Read these sentences. Use the context to figure out the meaning of the red words. Use a dictionary to check your answers. Then write each word and its meaning in your notebook.

1. Yellow fever is a **disease**. People who have it often experience headaches and backaches.

2. The scientist conducted an **experiment** to find the cause of the illness.

3. The girl is sick. She feels warm and has a **fever**.

4. The scientist formed a **hypothesis** about how the disease spread. He believed that insects were to blame.

5. Some **mosquitoes** can spread disease by biting animals and people.

6. The **virus** spread throughout the school and caused many students to become sick.

Practice  **Workbook Page 47**

Write the sentences in your notebook. Choose a red word from the box above to complete each sentence. Then take turns reading the sentences aloud with a partner.

1. An experiment proved that his _____ was incorrect.

2. Washing your hands can help stop a _____ from spreading.

3. I used bug spray to keep _____ from biting me.

4. The _____ was caused by a virus.

5. I used a thermometer to take my temperature. I have a _____.

6. We performed a chemistry _____ to test our hypothesis.

▲ Washing your hands can help keep you healthy.

Learn Academic Words

Study the **red** words and their meanings. You will find these words useful when talking and writing about informational texts. Write each word and its meaning in your notebook. After you read "The Great Fever," try to use these words to respond to the text.

objective = something that you are working hard to achieve	➡	The scientist's **objective** was to find the cause of the illness.
theory = an idea that explains how something works or why something happens	➡	He had to prove his **theory**—that a germ can cause disease.
transmit = send or pass something from one person to another	➡	Some sick patients may **transmit** their illnesses to others nearby.
volunteers = people who offer to do something without expecting to be paid	➡	The **volunteers** work at the hospital. They deliver flowers, clean rooms, and spend time with patients.

Practice

Work with a partner to answer these questions. Try to include the **red** word in your answer. Write the sentences in your notebook.

1. What is one **objective** you hope to achieve in school?

2. Have you ever had to prove a scientific **theory**? If so, what was the theory and how did you prove it?

3. What is one way a person can **transmit** an illness to someone else?

4. Do you know any **volunteers**? What do they do?

▲ A hospital volunteer reads to a child.

Word Study: Irregular Plurals

Most nouns in English are made plural by adding -s or -es to the end of the word. For some nouns, the spelling changes. Look at the examples below.

For a singular noun that ends in a consonant + y, change y to i and add -es.

Singular	Plural
enemy	enemies
laboratory	laboratories
priority	priorities

For a singular noun that ends in -is, change -is to -es.

Singular	Plural
crisis	crises
hypothesis	hypotheses
analysis	analyses

Practice  Workbook Page 49

Work with a partner. Take turns reading the words in the box below. Copy the words into your notebook. Change each singular noun to a plural noun. Use a dictionary if necessary.

army	colony	discovery	paralysis	theory
basis	diagnosis	emphasis	supply	thesis

READING STRATEGY | RECOGNIZE CAUSE AND EFFECT

Recognizing a cause-and-effect structure can help you better understand a text, especially informational texts. Most nonfiction and fiction texts tell about events that happen. Why an event happens is a cause. What happens as a result of a cause is an effect. To recognize causes and effects, follow these steps:

- As you read, look for events or actions in the text. These are the effects. Look for reasons for these events or actions. These are the causes.

- Look for words and phrases the author uses to talk about causes and effects, for example, *because, since, so that, therefore, as a result of, therefore.*

As you read "The Great Fever," look for causes and effects. Make sure you understand the relationship between each cause and its effect.

 Workbook Page 50

Set a purpose for reading As you read, think about the challenges scientists faced as they worked to find the cause of yellow fever.

The Great Fever

In 1801, a fierce rebellion broke out in Haiti. At the time, this small country belonged to France. Almost 30,000 soldiers were sent to battle the rebels. But the French forces lost. They were defeated by a deadly enemy—yellow fever. This terrible disease killed all but a few thousand French troops.

A Scientific Mystery

Yellow fever was among the most feared and mysterious of diseases. It first appeared in North America in the late 1600s. Yellow fever swept through both wealthy and poor areas. It appeared in some years, but not in others. No one understood what caused the disease, or how it spread.

Yellow fever was feared not only because of the thousands who died from it, but also because of the great suffering it caused. Victims would have symptoms such as headaches, backaches, and fever. When the symptoms briefly disappeared, patients would think they had gotten well. Then the disease would cause a condition

▲ Places in America that experienced major yellow fever outbreaks between 1793 and 1905

called jaundice. It would turn victims' skin and eyes a yellow hue. This is how yellow fever got its name.

In the last stages of the illness, patients' fevers would rise. Then, victims would begin to bleed internally. Some individuals would recover, but many others would not.

---

rebellion, act of fighting against a leader or
  government
rebels, people who fight against a leader or
  government

hue, color
internally, inside

A Doctor's Theory

Scientists began to discover clues about yellow fever after an epidemic that killed 20,000 people in 1878. However, scientists still did not know what caused and spread the disease. Did something in the water or the air create yellow fever epidemics? Did people spread the disease through human contact? How could epidemics be prevented?

Dr. Carlos Finlay had been interested in yellow fever for many years. He was from Cuba, a country with a warm, wet climate that experienced frequent epidemics. After reading scientists' theories and studying photographs of yellow fever victims, Finlay formed a hypothesis about how the disease spread. He believed that a biting insect—the mosquito—might transmit

---

epidemic, illness that spreads quickly to a lot of people

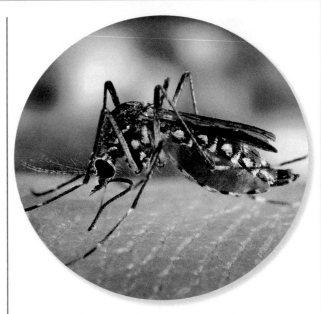

▲ An *Aedes aegypti* mosquito

yellow fever when it fed on animal and human blood. But since there are more than 2,000 types of mosquitoes, he wanted to find out which type might be responsible.

Finlay created a map that showed the locations of yellow fever epidemics and the habitats of different mosquitoes. He learned that the habitats of the *Aedes aegypti* mosquito and the locations of yellow fever epidemics were the same.

---

habitats, natural environments

▲ Dr. Carlos Finlay

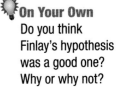

BEFORE YOU GO ON

1 How did yellow fever get its name?

2 What did Finlay's map show? Why was this significant?

On Your Own
Do you think Finlay's hypothesis was a good one? Why or why not?

▲ Major Walter Reed

▲ Dr. James Carroll

▲ Dr. Jesse Lazear

Jesse Lazear

Finding out more about yellow fever became an even higher priority two decades later. In 1898, the United States declared war on Spain. President Theodore Roosevelt sent 40,000 troops to seize Cuba, which was then a Spanish colony. While in Cuba, 2,000 American troops came down with yellow fever!

The problem was so serious that the army sent a surgeon, Major Walter Reed, to Cuba in 1900. He was placed in charge of a special commission to find the cause of yellow fever. Others on the commission included Dr. James Carroll and a young doctor and scientist named Jesse Lazear.

Reed, Carroll, and Lazear had heard about Finlay's experiments. They decided to visit the scientist at his home in Cuba. There had been many scientific advances since Finlay first proposed his mosquito theory. By 1900, scientists had linked certain germs with specific diseases. They also discovered a relationship between mosquitoes and a disease called malaria. Lazear thought that if mosquitoes could cause malaria, they might also transmit yellow fever.

Finlay had continued to study the *Aedes aegypti* mosquito. He gave Lazear the mosquitoes from his laboratory. Lazear took them back to commission headquarters and experimented on human volunteers.

Lazear even experimented on himself. He allowed mosquitoes that fed on yellow fever patients to bite him. To everyone's horror, Lazear contracted yellow fever and died from it. He was only thirty-five years old.

---

priority, thing that is most important and that needs attention before anything else
colony, country controlled by another country
came down with, got sick with
commission, group of people who have been given the official job of finding out about something

---

laboratory, room in which a scientist works

The Experiment at Camp Lazear

Lazear's sacrifice seemed to show that the *Aedes aegypti* mosquito transmitted yellow fever. However, more proof was needed.

Reed set up a new experiment with other men and women. He offered to pay them $100. The volunteers would receive an additional $100 if they became ill. The experiment's location was called *Camp Lazear*, in honor of that brave scientist.

The healthy volunteers at Camp Lazear were separated into two groups. One group lived in a tent among clothes, sheets, and other items that had been used by yellow fever patients. This tent was screened and kept completely free of mosquitoes. No one in this tent became ill.

In the second tent, mosquitoes that fed on yellow fever patients were set loose and allowed to bite healthy volunteers. Items used by yellow fever patients were not allowed in this tent. Even so, all the volunteers in this tent came down with the disease.

The scientific evidence was clear. Proof had been found that mosquitoes passed

---

proof, facts or information that proves something is true

in honor of, to show respect for

◀ Camp Lazear

---

yellow fever from sick people to healthy ones. These insects transmitted the disease when they fed on human blood.

More Discoveries

Once scientists proved that mosquitoes caused yellow fever, epidemics could be prevented. Places where mosquitoes bred, such as backyard containers that held water, could be covered. People were encouraged to screen their windows. Chemicals were used to kill the eggs of the *Aedes aegypti* mosquito. As a result, many countries experienced fewer cases of yellow fever.

▲ Howler monkeys, like this one, are one source of the yellow fever virus.

More discoveries about yellow fever followed. It was found that monkeys in the African rain forest were the original source of the yellow fever virus. In addition to the *Aedes aegypti*, scientists also identified other types of mosquitoes that carry and transmit the virus. Finally, in the 1930s, a vaccine was created to prevent yellow fever.

---

vaccine, substance that is put into a person's body to protect him or her from a disease

---

BEFORE YOU GO ON

1 What happened to Jesse Lazear after his meeting with Dr. Finlay? Why?

2 Describe Major Reed's experiment. What was the conclusion?

On Your Own
Would you have volunteered to participate in the experiments at Camp Lazear? Explain.

Review and Practice

COMPREHENSION

Workbook Page 51

Right There

1. What was discovered to be the source of yellow fever?
2. What was created to prevent yellow fever?

Think and Search

3. How did Dr. Finlay help find the cause of yellow fever?
4. How were Jesse Lazear's experiments similar to Major Walter Reed's experiments?

Author and You

5. Why do you think Dr. Finlay wanted to find the cause of yellow fever?
6. How does the author feel about Jesse Lazear? Explain.

On Your Own

7. Have you ever received a vaccine? What was it supposed to prevent?
8. What measures do you take to avoid mosquitoes?

▲ A flyswatter can be used to fight mosquitoes.

IN YOUR OWN WORDS

Work with a partner. Copy the chart below into your notebook. Fill in the blank boxes. Use the chart to summarize the article.

Cause		Effect
	➡	The army sent Major Walter Reed to Cuba.
Jesse Lazear allowed mosquitoes to bite him.	➡	
	➡	*Aedes aegypti* mosquitoes transmit yellow fever.
Governments worked to control yellow fever epidemics.	➡	

DISCUSSION

Discuss in pairs or small groups.

1. Do you think the United States government did enough to try and control the yellow fever epidemic in the late 1800s? Explain.

2. How were volunteers helpful in finding the cause of yellow fever?

Q **What are the benefits of facing challenges?** You read about doctors and scientists who worked to find the cause of yellow fever. What might motivate a person to accept such a challenge? In what ways could they benefit professionally?

))) Listening TIP

If you don't understand someone's answer, ask the speaker to repeat or explain it.

READ FOR FLUENCY

When we read aloud to communicate meaning, we group words into phrases, pause or slow down to make important points, and emphasize important words. Pause for a short time when you reach a comma and for a longer time when you reach a period. Pay attention to rising and falling intonation at the end of sentences.

Work with a partner. Choose a paragraph from the reading. Discuss which words seem important for communicating meaning. Practice pronouncing difficult words. Give each other feedback.

EXTENSION  Workbook Page 51

A yellow fever epidemic has not occurred in the United States for about 100 years. Still, yellow fever continues to be a problem in other countries.

Work with a partner. Go to the library or use the Internet to research areas around the world in which people continue to contract yellow fever. Then create a world map and flag these countries or regions. Share your map and findings with the class.

Grammar and Writing

Passive Voice: Simple Past; Regular and Irregular Past Participles

Form the passive voice with a form of the verb *be* + the past participle. Regular past participles are formed by adding *-d* or *-ed* to the base form of the verb. Irregular past participles, like the one below, must be memorized.

> **It was found** that monkeys in the African rain forest were the original source of the virus.

Here are a few more examples of irregular past participles.

Base Form of Verb	Simple Past	Past Participle
build	built	built
have	had	had
take	took	taken

Writers use the passive voice when the focus is on the receiver, not the performer, of an action. A *by*-phrase can be used to identify the performer. When the performer is unknown or not important, the *by*-phrase is left out.

> The experiment **was conducted by Jesse Lazear**.

> The healthy volunteers at Camp Lazear **were separated** into two groups.

Practice
Workbook
Page 52

Work with a partner. Rewrite the sentences below in your notebook, changing them into passive voice. Use the correct verb tense. Use the *by*-phrase if necessary.

1. The pharmacist delivered the medicine to the doctor's office.
2. They sprayed chemicals on the plants.
3. The U.S. government took action to eliminate the disease.
4. They built a yellow fever hospital in Cuba.
5. Hospital workers retrieved the supplies.
6. Dr. Finlay completed the research.

106

WRITING A NARRATIVE PARAGRAPH

Write a Personal Narrative

In the previous writing assignment, you wrote a short narrative from another character's point of view. Now you will write a personal narrative from your own point of view.

When you write a personal narrative, you tell the reader about an event in your life that was memorable and meaningful to you. Most often, the event you choose to write about will involve other people, or characters. It is important to describe and develop these characters for the reader. One way to do so is through the use of dialogue, or what the characters say to each other.

Here is a model of a personal narrative that includes dialogue. Before writing, the writer organized his ideas in a three-column chart. Notice how he included the use of the passive voice in his writing.

Who was there	What happened	What was said

Ari Janoff

As Pale as a Ghost

When I woke up last Tuesday, I wasn't lying in my room, but on the living room couch. My mother did not make me sleep in my room because I had a heavy cough the night before. I felt "under the weather" and nauseous. I looked like a sloth, lying motionless. I called to my mom for help. She came running down the stairs and exclaimed, "Oh my gosh! You're as pale as a ghost! What's wrong?!" She brought me cough drops and juice. But I didn't feel any better. In fact, as the day wore on, I felt worse. Finally, I was taken by my mother to the doctor. He ran some tests and concluded that I had the flu. He told me I wasn't allowed to return to school until I was better—I might transmit the virus to my classmates. In all, I missed six days of school!

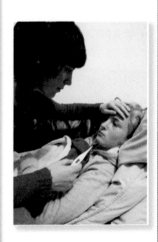

Practice Workbook Page 53

Write a personal narrative. You might write a paragraph about a memorable experience you had with a friend or a classmate. Before writing, list your ideas in a graphic organizer. Be sure to use the passive voice correctly.

Writing Checklist

IDEAS:
- [x] I described a memorable event.

VOICE:
- [x] I tried to sound like myself.

107

Prepare to Read

What You Will Learn

Reading
- Vocabulary building: *Literary terms, word study*
- Reading strategy: *Predict*
- Text type: *Literature (novel excerpt) and interview*

Grammar, Usage, and Mechanics
Simple and compound sentences

Writing
Write a personal letter

THE BIG QUESTION

What are the benefits of facing challenges? Imagine that you are on a camping trip. You become separated from your friends and now you are alone in the woods. What would you need in order to survive? List these items in your notebook. Then think about the challenges you would face while trying to obtain those items. Discuss with a partner.

BUILD BACKGROUND

In this section, you will read **"An Interview with Gary Paulsen."** In it, Paulsen, now an author, describes his challenging childhood experiences.

Remembering these times helped Paulsen write the fictional novel ***Hatchet.*** It is about a thirteen-year-old boy named Brian Robeson. Before Brian flies to Canada to visit his father, Brian's mother gives him a hatchet, or a small ax. Brian takes the hatchet with him as he boards a single-engine plane. During the flight, the pilot suffers a heart attack and dies. The plane crashes into the Canadian wilderness, leaving Brian alone with nothing more than his hatchet and the clothes on his back. Will this be enough to help Brian survive?

▲ A single-engine plane flying over a heavily wooded area

VOCABULARY

Learn Literary Words

Author's influences are factors that may affect an author's writing. These factors include the author's date and place of birth and cultural background, personal experiences, and world events that took place during the author's lifetime. Such influences can contribute to the kinds of conflict an author writes about.

Conflict, or a struggle between opposing forces, is an important story element because it causes the action. One kind of conflict takes place within the character's mind. The character struggles with his or her own thoughts and feelings.

Another kind of conflict is between a character and an outside force. The outside force might be another person or a force of nature, such as a wild animal or a hurricane. This kind of conflict is called an **external conflict**.

Literary Words

author's influences
external conflict

Practice

Workbook Page 54

Work with a partner. Read the paragraph below. Then answer the following questions: What kind of conflict is described? What is causing the conflict? Who is affected?

The sun was shining as Theo left the farm. Soon after, a large, dark cloud passed over the sun's bright rays. A chilly wind whipped across the sky. Theo pulled the collar of his jacket up around his neck and continued to trudge towards town. He was used to cold weather, but he wasn't prepared for the driving snow that showered from the sky minutes later. The road quickly became covered in white, the path to town no longer visible. Theo lost his sense of direction. Worse yet, the damp cold began to seep through his clothing.

Learn Academic Words

Study the red words and their meanings. You will find these words useful when talking and writing about literature. Write each word and its meaning in your notebook. After you read "An Interview with Gary Paulsen" and the excerpt from *Hatchet*, try to use these words to respond to the texts.

available = able to be used or seen	→	The boy looked for the closest **available** food source he could find.
injured = hurt	→	The fall from the ledge hurt his leg and left him badly **injured**.
structure = a building or something that has been built	→	He built a **structure** to live in. It is made of wood.
survive = continue to live after an accident or illness	→	The boy had one goal—to **survive** until someone came to rescue him.

Practice

Workbook Page 55

Work with a partner to answer these questions. Try to include the red word in your answer. Write the sentences in your notebook.

1. If you were lost in the wilderness, what kinds of food do you think would be available to you?
2. Have you ever been injured?
3. What kind of structure do you live in?
4. Would you be able to survive in unfamiliar surroundings? Why or why not?

▲ Wild berries can be a source of food in the wilderness.

Word Study: Closed Compound Nouns

Compound nouns are formed by combining two or more nouns together. Some compound nouns are written as one word. They are called closed compound nouns. The word *basketball* is a closed compound noun. It is made up of two nouns: *basket + ball*. Look at the chart below for more examples.

Noun	+ Noun	= Compound Noun
note	book	notebook
fire	fly	firefly
day	light	daylight

Practice  Workbook Page 56

Work with a partner. Copy the sentences below into your notebook. Use the words in the box to form a closed compound noun to complete each sentence. Then take turns reading the sentences aloud.

door	fire	stone	week
end	sand	way	wood

1. He bumped his head as he walked through the _____.
2. _____ is a kind of rock.
3. We are going on a trip to the mountains this _____.
4. He lit the _____ to keep himself warm.

READING STRATEGY | PREDICT

Predicting helps you better understand a text and focus on a story. Before you read, predict (or guess) what the story will be about. You can also make new predictions as you're reading. To predict, follow these steps:

- Stop reading from time to time and ask yourself, "What will happen next?"
- Look for clues in the story and in the illustrations. Think about what you already know. Make a prediction.

As you read the excerpt from *Hatchet*, stop and check to see if your prediction was correct. Make a new prediction if necessary.

 Workbook Page 57

Set a purpose for reading As you read, think about the kinds of challenges Gary Paulsen faced during his childhood. Then look for evidence of these experiences when you read the excerpt from *Hatchet*.

An Interview with Gary Paulsen

Leonard S. Marcus

Gary Paulsen first learned survival skills as a child growing up in a deeply troubled home. By the age of twelve, the future author of *Hatchet* (1987) had taught himself to keep house, make his own fun, and live for weeks at a time in the wilderness.

Leonard Marcus (LM): *What kind of child were you?*

Gary Paulsen (GP): I had a really rough childhood. So to me, childhood was mainly something to get through alive. Now, though, I'm actually grateful for some of those early experiences.

LM: *Grateful in what way?*

GP: Because I was pretty much on my own by the age of seven or eight, I learned about tenacity and independence and the willingness to fight. And I can go back now to some of the things that happened to me and write about them. They're like a mine that I can harvest.

---

tenacity, determination
independence, the freedom to take care of yourself without needing other people
mine, a deep hole in the ground from which gold, coal, etc., is dug
harvest, gather from

▼ Gary Paulsen plays with his dog on a hillside.

112

LM: *How did you survive?*

GP: At one time, when we were living in an apartment in a small Minnesota town, I moved down into the basement of our building by myself. I had found a place in back of the furnace, a sort of alcove, with a half-sized couch and a light hanging from the ceiling. That became my home. Half the time my parents wouldn't know I was gone.

LM: *Did you enjoy spending time alone in the woods, as so many of your characters do?*

GP: I fostered myself to the woods. Whenever I went into the woods, all the hassles of life were very quickly forgotten. It's still that way for me.

LM: *What kind of student were you?*

GP: A miserable one! I flunked ninth grade and barely got through high school.

LM: *When did you decide to become a writer?*

GP: Not until years later. I don't know why, but one night when I was about twenty-seven, it just came to me that I wanted to write. I had never thought of writing before then. I didn't even know what a manuscript was.

LM: *What do you tell kids who want to write?*

GP: Read. Read like a wolf eats! You can't learn anything watching television. It's very important to turn the box off—and carry a book with you all the time.

▲ Gary Paulsen often spent time in the woods as a child.

---

alcove, small space
hassles, troubles
manuscript, book before it is published

ABOUT THE **INTERVIEWER**

Leonard S. Marcus works in the field of children's literature as an author, critic, magazine editor, and professional lecturer. In fact, Marcus travels around the world speaking to teenagers in different countries. When he's not traveling, Marcus lives in Brooklyn, New York.

BEFORE YOU GO ON

1 How does Paulsen describe his childhood?

2 Does Paulsen enjoy spending time alone in the woods today? Why or why not?

On Your Own
What do you do to survive difficult times in your life?

113

from

Hatchet

Gary Paulsen

Brian Robeson was traveling to Canada to visit his father when the pilot of the single-engine plane in which he was flying had a heart attack. The plane crashed into a lake, leaving Brian alone in the Canadian wilderness. That was two days ago. Bruised and battered, Brian must find a way to survive in the wilderness alone, with nothing more than a thin jacket and a hatchet.

Using the sun and the fact that it rose in the east and set in the west, he decided that the far side was the northern side of the ridge. At one time in the far past it had been scooped by something, probably a glacier, and this scooping had left a kind of sideways bowl, back in under a ledge. It wasn't very deep, not a cave, but it was smooth and made a perfect roof and he could almost stand in under the ledge. He had to hold his head slightly tipped forward at the front to keep it from hitting the top. Some of the rock that had been scooped out had also been pulverized by the glacial action, turned into sand, and now made a small sand beach that went down to the edge of the water in front and to the right of the overhang.

It was his first good luck.

No, he thought. He had good luck in the landing. But this was good luck as well, luck he needed.

---

glacier, large, slow-moving mountain of ice
ledge, surface of rock
cave, deep hollow area in rock
pulverized, crushed

All he had to do was wall off part of the bowl and leave an opening as a doorway and he would have a perfect shelter—much stronger than a lean-to and dry because the overhang made a watertight roof.

He crawled back in, under the ledge, and sat. The sand was cool here in the shade, and the coolness felt wonderful to his face, which was already starting to blister and get especially painful on his forehead, with the blisters on top of the swelling.

He was also still weak. Just the walk around the back of the ridge and the slight climb over the top had left his legs rubbery. It felt good to sit for a bit under the shade of the overhang in the cool sand.

And now, he thought, if I just had something to eat.

Anything.

When he had rested a bit he went back down to the lake and drank a couple of swallows of water. He wasn't all that thirsty but he thought the water might help to take the edge off his hunger. It didn't. Somehow the cold lake water actually made it worse, sharpened it.

---

lean-to, shelter with a sloped roof, made by leaning fallen branches against a tree, a rock, or other branches
blister, swell with a clear liquid
rubbery, weak and unsteady

BEFORE YOU GO ON

1 Describe Brian's surroundings.

2 Why does Brian consider himself lucky?

On Your Own
What do you think Brian should do next?

115

He thought of dragging in wood to make a wall or part of an overhang, and picked up one piece to pull up, but his arms were too weak and he knew then that it wasn't just the crash and injury to his body and head, it was also that he was weak from hunger.

He would have to find something to eat. Before he did anything else he would have to have something to eat.

But what?

* * *

At first he was too far away to see what they were doing, but their color drew him and he moved toward them, keeping the lake in sight on his right, and when he got closer he saw they were eating berries.

He could not believe it was that easy. It was as if the birds had taken him right to the berries. The slender branches went up about twenty feet and were heavy, drooping with clusters of bright red berries. They were half as big as grapes but hung in bunches much like grapes and when Brian saw them, glistening red in the sunlight, he almost yelled.

His pace quickened and he was in them in moments, scattering the birds, grabbing branches, stripping them to fill his mouth with berries.

---

clusters, groups or bunches

✔ **LITERARY CHECK**

Describe some ***external conflicts*** *Brian struggles against.*

He almost spit them out. It wasn't that they were bitter so much as that they lacked any sweetness, had a tart flavor that left his mouth dry feeling. And they were like cherries in that they had large pits, which made them hard to chew. But there was such a hunger on him, such an emptiness, that he could not stop and kept stripping branches and eating berries by the handful, grabbing and jamming them into his mouth and swallowing them, pits and all.

He could not stop and when, at last, his stomach was full he was still hungry. Two days without food must have shrunken his stomach, but the drive of hunger was still there. Thinking of the birds, and how they would come back into the berries when he left, he made a carrying pouch of his torn windbreaker and kept picking. Finally, when he judged he had close to four pounds in the jacket he stopped and went back to his camp by the ridge.

Now, he thought. Now I have some food and I can do something about fixing this place up. He glanced at the sun and saw he had some time before dark.

---

bitter, bad tasting
tart, sharp, sour
pits, hard fruit centers, which hold the seeds
pouch, small bag
windbreaker, thin jacket that protects from wind and rain

BEFORE YOU GO ON

1 Why is Brian unable to collect wood for his shelter?

2 What food does Brian find in the woods?

On Your Own
Do you know how to find food in the woods? If so, what kind(s)?

117

If only I had matches, he thought, looking ruefully at the beach and the lakeside. There was driftwood everywhere, not to mention dead and dry wood all over the hill and dead-dry branches hanging from every tree. All firewood. And no matches. How did they used to do it? he thought. Rub two sticks together?

He tucked the berries in the pouch back in under the overhang in the cool shade and found a couple of sticks. After ten minutes of rubbing he felt the sticks and they were almost cool to the touch. Not that, he thought. They didn't do fire that way. He threw the sticks down in disgust. So no fire. But he could still fix the shelter and make it—here the word "safer" came into his mind and he didn't know why—more livable.

Kind of close it in, he thought. I'll just close it in a bit.

He started dragging sticks up from the lake and pulling long dead branches down from the hill, never getting out of sight of the water and the ridge. With these he interlaced and wove a wall across the opening of the front of the rock. It took over two hours, and he had to stop several times because he still felt a bit weak and once because he felt a strange new twinge in his stomach. A tightening, rolling. Too many berries, he thought. I ate too many of them.

But it was gone soon and he kept working until the entire front of the overhang was covered save for a small opening at the right end, nearest

---

ruefully, with regret
in disgust, with a strong feeling of dislike or disapproval
interlaced, joined together by crossing over each other
twinge, sudden pain

the lake. The doorway was about three feet, and when he went in he found himself in a room almost fifteen feet long and eight to ten feet deep, with the rock wall sloping down at the rear.

"Good," he said, nodding. "Good. . . ."

Outside the sun was going down, finally, and in the initial coolness the mosquitos came out again and clouded in on him. They were thick, terrible, if not quite as bad as in the morning, and he kept brushing them off his arms until he couldn't stand it and then dumped the berries and put the torn windbreaker on. At least the sleeves covered his arms.

Wrapped in the jacket, with darkness coming down fast now, he crawled back in under the rock and huddled and tried to sleep. He was deeply tired, and still aching some, but sleep was slow coming and did not finally settle in until the evening cool turned to night cool and the mosquitos slowed.

Then, at last, with his stomach turning on the berries, Brian went to sleep.

---

huddled, brought his knees to his chest

✔ **LITERARY CHECK**

*What may have **influenced** the **author**, Gary Paulsen, to write Hatchet?*

BEFORE YOU GO ON

1. Is fire important to Brian's survival? Why?

2. How does Brian make his shelter "safer"?

💡**On Your Own** What do you think Brian's efforts say about his personality?

119

Review and Practice

DRAMATIC READING

Speaking TIP

Face your fellow students during a discussion.

A good way to understand the flow of spoken conversation is to act out or recite an interview. Read "An Interview with Gary Paulsen" again with a partner. Work together to interpret any difficult or unknown words or phrases. Take turns reading the parts of the interviewer, Leonard S. Marcus, and Gary Paulsen. After you have practiced, recite the second page of the interview for the class.

COMPREHENSION  Workbook Page 58

Right There

1. What led Brian to the berries?

2. What does Brian use to protect himself from mosquitoes?

Think and Search

3. What does Brian's shelter look like?

4. What does Brian try to achieve by rubbing two sticks together?

Author and You

5. What caused Brian's bodily injuries?

6. How do you think the hatchet will be helpful to Brian in the wilderness?

On Your Own

7. Do you like spending time in the wilderness? Why or why not?

8. Have you ever been lost in the wilderness? If so, what did you do?

▲ A hatchet

DISCUSSION

Discuss in pairs or small groups.

1. In your opinion, what is the greatest challenge Brian must overcome in the wilderness?

2. What does Gary Paulsen mean when he says that he "fostered" himself to the woods?

 **What are the benefits of facing challenges?** How did Gary Paulsen benefit from his childhood challenges later in life? Could Brian benefit in the same way? Explain.

Workbook
Page 58

RESPONSE TO LITERATURE

Work with a partner. Describe what you think will happen to Brian next. Can he make a fire? Does he survive in the wilderness? Is he ever rescued? Share your predictions with the class.

▲ A campfire on the shore of a lake

»)⌒ *Listening* TIP

Think about the points others are making. Try to relate their ideas to what you already know.

Grammar and Writing

Simple and Compound Sentences

A simple sentence contains a subject and a predicate. The predicate tells what the subject does. A predicate always has a verb. Look at the examples below from *Hatchet*.

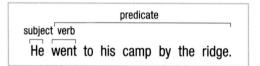

A compound sentence joins two simple sentences with a coordinating conjunction (*and, but, or,* and *so*). A comma usually comes before the conjunction.

> They were thick, **and** he kept brushing them off his arms.
> The sand was cool in the shade, **so** he sat for a while.

When the simple sentences both have the same subject, a comma is not always necessary.

> It wasn't very deep **but** it was smooth and made a perfect roof.
> He can rest **or** he can try to find his way home.

Practice

Rewrite the sentences below in your notebook. Create compound sentences by combining each set of simple sentences with a coordinating conjunction. Use a comma when necessary. Have a partner check your answers.

1. I went to the library. I checked out the book *Hatchet*.

2. The book was very interesting. It was very entertaining.

3. I didn't read the beginning of the story. I don't know why Brian was in the woods alone.

4. I think he was stranded. I'm not sure.

5. I could write about this book. I could write about a different book.

WRITING a NARRATIVE PARAGRAPH

Write a Personal Letter

You have learned how to write three different kinds of narrative paragraphs. On this page, you will write a narrative in the form of a personal letter. In a personal letter, you tell the reader a story about a memorable event or experience in your life. A personal letter has five parts: the date, the greeting, the body, the closing, and the signature. It is in the body of the letter that you include memories, ideas, and sensory details to make your story interesting to the reader.

Here is a model of a personal letter written by a student named George Delgrosso. The writer used a graphic organizer like the one here to put his narrative paragraph into a letter format. Notice how he included simple and compound sentences in the body of his letter.

Salutation (or greeting)	Date
Body	
	Closing, Signature

October 1, 2009

Dear Joe,

Hi, how are you? I've had many tests to study for recently and I have been really stressed out. So last weekend, I tried to relax. I went on a camping trip in the mountains with my cousins. It took us almost six hours to get to the campsite! We were exhausted by the time we got there and we still had to pitch the tent. We were almost finished when it started to rain. Luckily, we stayed dry and we got a good night's rest. The next day, we hiked to the other side of the mountain. We found a big, clear lake and jumped into it to cool off. Then we ate lunch. Before long, it was time to go home. I enjoyed spending time with my cousins. Maybe next time, you can come with us.

Write back soon!

Best,
George

Practice

Workbook
Page 60

Write a personal letter to a friend about a memorable event you've experienced. Use a graphic organizer to put your story into the correct format. Include simple and compound sentences in the body of your letter.

Writing Checklist

WORD CHOICE:
☑ I included vivid sensory details and memories in my narrative.

SENTENCE FLUENCY:
☑ I used simple and compound sentences in my letter.

123

Link the Readings

Critical Thinking

Look back at the readings in this unit. Think about what they have in common. They all tell about challenges. Yet they do not all have the same purpose. The purpose of one reading might be to inform, while the purpose of another might be to entertain or persuade. In addition, the content of each reading relates to challenges differently. Now copy the chart below into your notebook and complete it.

Title of Reading	Purpose	Big Question Link
"The Train to Freedom"		*It describes challenges slaves experienced as they traveled on the Underground Railroad.*
"Five New Words at a Time"		
"The Great Fever"		
From *Hatchet*	*to entertain*	

Discussion

Discuss in pairs or small groups.

- Compare and contrast the challenges faced by Harriet Tubman and Jesse Lazear. How were they the same? How were they different?

- **What are the benefits of facing challenges?** Think about the people in the readings. Does change always improve people's lives? Explain.

Fluency Check

Work with a partner. Choose a paragraph from one of the readings. Take turns reading it for one minute. Count the total number of words you read. Practice saying the words you had trouble reading. Take turns reading the paragraph three more times. Did you read more words each time? Copy the chart below into your notebook and record your speeds.

	1st Speed	2nd Speed	3rd Speed	4th Speed
Words Per Minute				

Projects

Work in pairs or small groups. Choose one of these projects.

1 Research songs that are part of our African-American heritage, such as slave songs or spirituals. Learn to sing the songs, and play or perform them for your classmates.

2 You read about Jesse Lazear and how his job as a scientist had dangerous consequences. Find out more about a job that involves risks and challenges, such as being a firefighter, police officer, paramedic, journalist, documentary filmmaker, or construction worker. Once you find facts about the job and what it requires, write a "help wanted ad" for it. Be sure to include the job requirements and explain some of the challenges involved.

3 Have you ever heard of survival skills courses? They are designed to teach people how to survive in the wilderness with little or no equipment. Use the Internet to research an organization that offers these courses. Use the information you find to make a brochure. Include the organization's address, contact information, course descriptions, and photographs. Then share your brochure with the class.

Further Reading

To find out more about the theme of this unit, choose from these reading suggestions.

Extreme Sports, Michael Dean
This Penguin Reader® describes the challenging world of extreme sports for those with a sense of adventure.

Women in Business, David Evans
Here are the stories of five successful businesswomen: Paloma Picasso, Anita Roddick, Madonna, Oprah Winfrey, and Hanae Mori.

The World I Live In, Helen Keller
This is Helen Keller's most personal work—one that highlights her extraordinary achievements. In it, she describes what it is like to experience the world as a deaf and blind woman.

Put It All Together

LISTENING & SPEAKING WORKSHOP

Personal Narrative

As you have learned, a personal narrative is a story about events in your life. You will present a personal narrative about a challenge you have faced.

1 **THINK ABOUT IT** Look back at the readings in this unit. Talk in small groups about challenges. Describe some challenges you have faced in the past.

Work together to develop a list of challenges you could tell about in a personal narrative, for example:

- A difficult class or homework assignment
- Trying to defeat a fierce sports opponent
- Relationships you've had with friends
- Issues within your neighborhood

2 **GATHER AND ORGANIZE INFORMATION** Choose a challenging experience from your group's list. Think about the setting and plot of your personal narrative. List the characters involved in your story.

Reflect Think about what made the challenge difficult. How did you meet the challenge? Why was the experience memorable? How was facing this challenge beneficial? Write down the most important points you would like to communicate to your classmates. Include specific details.

Order Your Notes List the events you want to share in chronological order.

Use Visuals Make a poster that illustrates the events in your story. Point to the poster as you tell your story. Be ready to answer questions.

3 **PRACTICE AND PRESENT** Use your list of events as the written outline for your presentation. Keep your outline nearby, but practice talking to your audience without reading from it word-for-word. If possible, use a tape recorder to record your storytelling. Then play back the recording and listen to yourself. Keep practicing until you are relaxed and confident, and know your presentation well.

Deliver Your Personal Narrative Look at your audience as you speak. Emphasize key events with your voice and actions. For example, slow down when you come to the most important events in your narrative, and point to pictures of them on your poster. Give your classmates a chance to ask questions at the end.

4 **EVALUATE THE PRESENTATION**
You will improve your skills as a speaker and a listener by evaluating each presentation you give and hear. Use this checklist to help you judge your presentation and the presentations of your classmates.

- ☑ Did the speaker clearly identify the challenge he or she faced?
- ☑ Was the setting clearly described?
- ☑ Did the speaker explain why the event was memorable?
- ☑ Did the speaker answer your questions?
- ☑ What suggestions do you have for improving the presentation?

Speaking TIPS

Be sure you emphasize key events. Ask your listeners for feedback. Did they understand which events were the most important?

Use facial expressions and gestures to show how you felt during this challenging experience.

Listening TIPS

Think about what you are hearing. Have you faced a similar challenge?

What else would you like to know about this challenging experience? Write down questions and ask them at the end of the presentation.

WRITING WORKSHOP

Fictional Narrative

In this workshop, you will write a fictional narrative. A fictional narrative is a story created from the writer's imagination. A good fictional narrative has a clear setting and interesting characters. Dialogue helps bring the characters to life. The events in a fictional narrative are called the *plot*. Most plots take place in sequence and focus on a conflict that is resolved by the story's end. Another important element of a fictional narrative is the point of view, or who tells the story. Sometimes the writer tells what happens. Sometimes a character in the story tells what happens.

Your assignment for this workshop is to write a fictional narrative about someone who faces a problem and successfully meets the challenge.

1 **PREWRITE** Brainstorm a list of possible challenges to write about. Invent a situation that interests you. You might write about someone who wins a contest, overcomes an illness, or stands up against injustice. After choosing a situation for your story, think about your main character. What are his or her traits? Will you tell your story from the main character's point of view or from a different point of view?

List and Organize Ideas and Details Use a story chart to organize ideas for your fictional narrative. A student named Austin decided to write about someone who has the leading role in a play. Here is Austin's story chart:

Characters	Setting	Problem	Solution
Julia Melissa	School auditorium Julia's house	Julia wins the part Has trouble learning the role	Melissa helps Julia practice Julia's performance is great

2 **DRAFT** Use the model on page 131 and your story chart to help you write a first draft. Remember to tell events in sequence. Include dialogue to help reveal what your characters are thinking and feeling.

3 **REVISE** Read over your draft. As you do so, ask yourself the questions in the writing checklist. Use the questions to help you revise your fictional narrative.

SIX TRAITS OF WRITING CHECKLIST

☑ **IDEAS:** Are my plot and characters interesting?

☑ **ORGANIZATION:** Are events presented in sequence?

☑ **VOICE:** Does my story have a clear point of view?

☑ **WORD CHOICE:** Does the dialogue suit my characters?

☑ **SENTENCE FLUENCY:** Do my sentences vary in length and type?

☑ **CONVENTIONS:** Does my writing follow the rules of grammar, usage, and mechanics?

Here are the changes Austin plans to make when he revises his first draft:

A Challenge and Success!

The New York streets were bustling with people as ~~I made my~~ [Julia] [her] way

to the audition. Lucky charm in hand, ~~I~~ [she] entered the auditorium of the

performing arts academy where ~~I~~ [she] attended school. The room was filled

with other students rehearsing lines, dancing, and singing.

Julia tried her best[,] [but] ~~.~~ She didn't think the director looked too

impressed with her performance. [In fact,] She was shocked and thrilled a week

later, when she learned that she had [been awarded] the leading role!

[The part was long and difficult.] One day, after rehearsing alone in her room, Julia began to doubt

she would ever learn her lines. "I don't even know one whole page, she

exclaimed. She repeated her lines over and over.

"I think I've got it!" she shouted Then, a minute later, she cried,

"Darn, I forgot them again." She threw her script ~~in~~ [on] the floor and

129

wondered, "Should I just drop out? NO! It would upset Mom and Dad so much."

The phone rang.
"Hello?" Julia said tiredly.

"JULIA, JULIA, OH, MY GOSH! How are you?" said her friend melissa.

"Stressed!" Julia answered.

"Why?" Melissa demanded.

Julia confessed all her fears.

"Don't worry," Melissa said. "Why don't I come over everyday to help you."

Julia thought about it for a second. Then, she admitted, "That would be great!"

"DEAL!" Melissa said.

Had rehearsing with Melissa really helped? On opening night, Julia was so nervous she almost couldn't breathe. After two hours, the last line of the show was said. Julia had done it! As she stood up to a standing ovation, she made eye contact with Melissa in the crowd and smiled a big thank-you.

Melissa silently mouthed the words, "You're welcome." Julia felt a rush of happiness and gratitude as she took her bow.

4 EDIT AND PROOFREAD

Workbook
Page 61

Copy your revised draft onto a clean sheet of paper. Read it again. Correct any errors in grammar, word usage, mechanics, and spelling. Here are the additional changes Austin plans to make when he prepares his final draft.

Austin Saiz

A Challenge and Success!

The New York streets were bustling with people as Julia made her way to the audition. Lucky charm in hand, she entered the auditorium of the performing arts academy where she attended school. The room was filled with other students rehearsing lines, dancing, and singing.

Julia tried her best, but she didn't think the director looked too impressed with her performance. In fact, she was shocked and thrilled a week later, when she learned that she had been awarded the leading role!

The part was long and difficult. One day, after rehearsing alone in her room, Julia began to doubt she would ever learn her lines. "I don't even know one whole page," she exclaimed. She repeated her lines over and over.

"I think I've got it!" she shouted. Then, a minute later, she cried, "Darn, I forgot them again." She threw her script on the floor and wondered, "Should I just drop out? NO! It would upset Mom and Dad so much."

The phone rang. "Hello?" Julia said tiredly.

"JULIA, JULIA, OH, MY GOSH! How are you?" said her friend melissa.

"Stressed!" Julia answered.

"Why?" Melissa demanded.

Julia confessed all her fears.

"Don't worry," Melissa said. "Why don't I come over everyday to help you."

Julia thought about it for a second. Then, she admitted, "That would be great!"

"DEAL!" Melissa said.

On opening night, Julia was so nervous she almost couldn't breathe. Had rehearsing with Melissa really helped? After two hours, the last line of the show was said. Julia had done it! As she stood up to a standing ovation, she made eye contact with Melissa in the crowd and smiled a big thank-you.

Melissa silently mouthed the words, "You're welcome." Julia felt a rush of happiness and gratitude as she took her bow.

5 **PUBLISH** Prepare your final draft. Share your essay with your teacher and classmates.

Workbook
Page 62

131

The Challenge of Illness

*M*ost people face illness at some point in their lives. Sometimes medicine alone cannot heal them. People need help from family and friends as well as their own personal strength to get well. American artists often celebrate the spirit that moves people to recover from disease or injury.

Alice Eugenia Ligon, *Embroidered Garment* (about 1949)

Alice Eugenia Ligon had to go to the hospital for a medical problem in 1949. Later, she turned the symbol of her illness—her hospital gown—into a holiday present and work of art for her children. She gives the viewer this information by sewing the story in green thread in the bottom left corner of the gown, under the second rainbow. Using every blank area, she also embroidered dozens of religious, patriotic, and personal phrases and images on the gown that held great meaning to her. This piece of folk art celebrates Ligon's ability to face the challenge of her illness and turn it into something positive. If she had to sit and heal, then she could also sit and create!

Alice Eugenia Ligon, *Embroidered Garment*,
about 1949, muslin, cotton, 43¾ x 38½ in.,
Smithsonian American Art Museum ▶

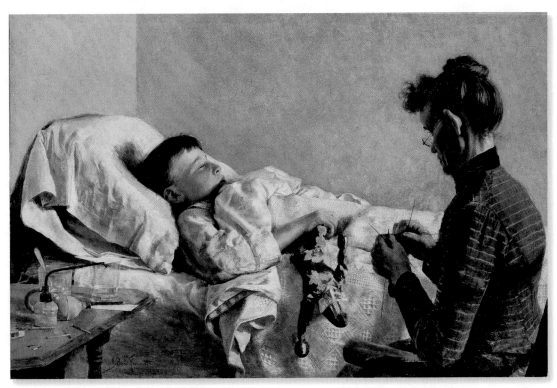

▲ J. Bond Francisco, *The Sick Child*, 1893, oil, 32 x 48 in., Smithsonian American Art Museum

J. Bond Francisco, *The Sick Child* (1893)

In J. Bond Francisco's *The Sick Child*, a mother sits nervously in her chair. She knits and stares through her glasses at a boy resting in bed. The boy holds a toy clown, which stands out in the center of the painting. It's uncertain if the boy will have enough strength to continue to hold on to the clown. It looks as if it might fall to the floor. Francisco leaves it unclear whether the boy will survive his illness. The mother faces the challenge the best way that she knows how: sitting by her son's side and keeping busy to pass the long hours.

Francisco painted *The Sick Child* at a time when medicine was still very limited. Unfortunately, many parents in the 1800s experienced the horror of watching a child die. This made it easy for them to understand the subject matter of Francisco's painting. Thousands of doctors' offices across the United States hung a copy of *The Sick Child* in their waiting rooms, which made Francisco's painting very well known.

Both artworks celebrate the human need to face challenges and to reach out to family during troubled times.

Apply What You Learned

1 What creates an air of uncertainty in Francisco's painting?

2 How does each of these artworks celebrate the spirit that helps people to recover from illness? In what ways are they similar and different?

 Big Question
What other kinds of challenges do people face besides illness, and how could they be shown in an artwork?

Workbook
Pages 63–64

How are relationships with others important?

This unit is about relationships. You will read informational texts and literature that describe different kinds of relationships and how they change the lives of the people or animals involved. Reading about these topics will give you practice using academic language and help you become a better student.

READING 1: Novel Excerpt
- From *Salsa Stories,* "Aguinaldo" by Lulu Delacre

READING 2: Social Studies Articles
- "Sowing the Seeds of Peace" by Mandy Terc
- "Seeds of Peace: Cultivating Friendships"

READING 3: Legend Excerpt
- From *Blue Willow* by Pam Conrad

READING 4: Science Article
- "Partnerships in Nature"

Listening and Speaking

At the end of this unit, you will choose a topic and deliver a **how-to demonstration** about it.

Writing

In this unit you will practice **expository writing**, which presents factual information about a topic. After each reading you will learn a skill to help you write an expository paragraph. At the end of the unit, you will use these skills to help you write an expository essay.

QuickWrite
List the different kinds of relationships that you have with other people. Circle the three relationships that are the most important to you.

Prepare to Read

What You Will Learn

Reading

- Vocabulary building: *Literary terms, word study*

- Reading strategy: *Analyze cultural context*

- Text type: *Literature (novel excerpt)*

Grammar, Usage, and Mechanics
Imperatives

Writing
Write instructions

THE BIG QUESTION

How are relationships with others important? There is an old saying that when you help someone, you are really helping yourself. What do you think that means? Do you think it is important to reach out to others? Discuss with a partner.

BUILD BACKGROUND

In this section, you will read **"Aguinaldo,"** an excerpt from the novel *Salsa Stories*. It is about a young Puerto Rican girl named Marilia. Her class is going on a field trip to a nursing home where her classmates plan to deliver surprise Christmas gifts, or *aguinaldos*, to the elderly people who live there. However, Marilia is afraid to participate; her only grandmother died in a nursing home the year before, and the thought of returning to one makes her sad.

Currently, more than 1.5 million elderly Americans live in nursing homes, or places where elderly people live. Some of them cannot care for themselves. They receive medical care, healthy meals, opportunities to participate in organized activities, and companionship.

◄ A caregiver hugs an elderly nursing-home resident.

Learn Literary Words

Foreshadowing is an author's use of clues to hint at what might happen later in a story. Writers use foreshadowing to build readers' expectations and to create suspense.

Irony is the difference between what the reader expects to happen and what actually happens in a story. Writers include ironic situations in stories to create surprise and amusement. Read the example of irony below.

Literary Words

foreshadowing
irony

> Jonathan didn't want to study in France, but his parents thought it would be beneficial for him to experience another culture. After saying good-bye to his parents at the airport, Jonathan made a mental list of all the reasons why he *should not* be flying to France: He didn't speak the language, none of his friends lived there, he didn't even like French food.
>
> ★ ★ ★
>
> Three months later, Jonathan decided to call his parents—it wouldn't hurt to ask. He was nervous as he listened to the phone ring. His mother answered. "Hi, Mom. Do you think I could stay here for the rest of the school year?"

What is ironic about Jonathan's situation?

Practice
Workbook
Page 65

In a small group, discuss a movie you have seen that contains an ironic situation. Describe the difference between what you thought would happen and what actually happened. Also, describe any foreshadowing that may have occurred.

Learn Academic Words

Study the red words and their meanings. You will find these words useful when talking and writing about literature. Write each word and its meaning in your notebook. After you read "Aguinaldo," the excerpt from *Salsa Stories*, try to use these words to respond to the text.

distributes = gives something to different people or places	➡	Our class **distributes** gifts to needy people each year.
positive = good or useful	➡	Simonese enjoyed her visit to the nursing home. It was a **positive** experience.
rejected = decided not to do something	➡	Aaliyah **rejected** the opportunity to visit the nursing home.
residents = people who live in a place	➡	The **residents** of the nursing home were happy to have visitors.

Practice

Workbook
Page 66

Work with a partner to answer these questions. Try to include the red word in your answer. Write the sentences in your notebook.

1. Is there a shelter in your area that distributes food or clothing to the needy? Have you ever volunteered to work there?

2. Do you think volunteering is a positive use of your time? Why or why not?

3. Have you ever rejected the opportunity to volunteer somewhere? Explain.

4. Are there residents that volunteer to pick up trash in and around your neighborhood? How would the area be different if these people did not volunteer their time and energy?

These volunteers work to keep school grounds clean. ▶

138

Word Study: Spelling *s-* Blends

A consonant blend is the sound that two or three consonants make when they come together in a word. You can hear the sound of each consonant in the blend. Identifying *s-* blends can help you spell new and unfamiliar words. Read the *s-* blends and examples in the chart below.

sw- (/sw/)	sp- (/sp/)	st- (/st/)	str- (/str/)
swept	**sp**ecial	**st**ay	**str**anger
swim	**sp**ace	**st**omach	**str**ong

Practice

Work with a partner. Copy the sentences below into your notebook. Read the sentences aloud. Complete each sentence with the correct *s-* blend.

1. We are ＿＿＿＿ending the day at the nursing home.
2. The building is across the ＿＿＿＿eet.
3. The woman told me ＿＿＿＿ories about her childhood.
4. She ＿＿＿＿oke softly.
5. I ＿＿＿＿allowed the ＿＿＿＿eets.
6. She ＿＿＿＿ared at the card.
7. The ＿＿＿＿udents decorated the room with ＿＿＿＿eamers.

READING STRATEGY | **ANALYZE CULTURAL CONTEXT**

Analyzing the cultural context of a story or text helps you visualize and understand what's happening. Cultural context includes the beliefs, art, ideas, and values of a particular community. To analyze cultural context, follow these steps as you read:

- Think about the characters' native language and country.
- Think about what you already know about the place and the people.
- Notice how the author describes the houses, food, music, and clothing.
- Pay attention to the characters' ideas and beliefs.

As you read "Aguinaldo," think about the place where the story happens. Compare and contrast it with your own experience.

Set a purpose for reading As you read, notice how Marilia's views about the nursing home change. What are the reasons for this change?

from
Salsa Stories

Águinaldo

Lulu Delacre

On New Year's Day, a neighbor gives Carmen Teresa a blank notebook. Although she is grateful for the gift, Carmen Teresa has no idea how to fill it. Her guests suggest she use it to record family stories. When she agrees, her family members eagerly share their childhood experiences. This excerpt is Tía Marilia's tale.

When I was growing up in Puerto Rico, I went to a small, Catholic girls' school. Every December, Sister Antonia, our religion teacher, insisted that students visit the nursing home in Santurce. Bringing Christmas cheer to the old and infirm was an experience she felt all students should have.

"I'm not going," I whispered to my friend Margarita.

"You have to, Marilia," she said. "Everyone has to go."

All of my classmates looked forward to the trip. But ever since my only grandma died in a nursing home, the thought of going back to one made me feel sad. I didn't want to go.

As I sat at my desk making the Christmas card that I would give to a resident, I tried to figure out how I could skip this field trip. Maybe they

---

Tía, aunt
infirm, weak or sick
field trip, trip students take with their classmates and teacher

would let me help at the library. Maybe I could write a special book report at school while they were out. Or better yet, I could wake up ill and stay home from school. As soon as the recess bell rang, I ran over to the library to try out my first plan.

"Hola, Marilia," Señora Collazo greeted me.

"Hola, Señora Collazo," I said, smiling sweetly. "I came to ask you if I could stay here tomorrow to help you paint posters for the book fair. I really don't mind spending the whole day at the library."

"Aren't you going on a field trip tomorrow?" Señora Collazo asked.

"My class is going. But I could be excused if you need my help." The librarian thanked me and said that if I wanted to help I could join the other students who had already volunteered to stay after school to do the posters. Biting my lip, I left the library in a hurry. It was time to try my second plan.

I marched right back to my classroom. Sister Antonia was grading papers at her desk as I went in.

"Sister Antonia," I said softly.

"Yes, Marilia," Sister Antonia answered.

I stared for a moment at the buckles of my shoes. Then without looking up, I took a deep breath, swept back my black curls, and asked, "May I stay in school tomorrow to do an extra book report?"

"I'm afraid not, Marilia," Sister Antonia said firmly. "Tomorrow is our trip to the nursing home. But if you want to do an extra book report, you can do it over the weekend."

---

hola, *hello*
Señora, *Mrs.*

BEFORE YOU GO ON

1 What does Sister Antonia insist her students do every year? Why?

2 How does Marilia feel about going to the nursing home? Explain.

On Your Own
Would you want to go on this field trip? Why or why not?

141

I glanced across the room to the trays of *besitos de coco*, the coconut sweets that my class had prepared to bring to the nursing-home residents as an *aguinaldo*. *Aguinaldos*, surprise Christmas gifts, were fun to receive. But still, I wasn't going, so it wasn't my concern. I whispered thank you to the sister, and left.

That evening at dinnertime, I put my third plan into action. To my parent's surprise, I had two big helpings of rice and kidney beans, two helpings of dessert, and three glasses of mango juice. I *never* ate so much. I figured that with all this food, I was sure to get indigestion. I went to bed and waited. I tossed and turned. I waited for several hours expecting a stomachache any second, but instead, the heavy meal made me tired and I fell sound asleep.

"Marilia, get dressed!" Mami called early the next morning. "We have to leave soon for school!"

How unlucky. I woke up feeling quite well. There was only one thing left to do, I ran to the bathroom, let the hot water run, and drank a full glass of it. Then I went back to bed.

"Marilia." Mami came in. "Get up! What is going on with you?"

"I feel warm, Mami," I mumbled.

Mami looked with concern. She touched my forehead and my neck. She left the room and in a few minutes came back with the thermometer in her hand. I opened my mouth and she slipped it under my tongue.

---

mango, sweet tropical fruit
indigestion, stomach pains from eating too much food
mumbled, spoke quietly and unclearly
concern, worry
thermometer, instrument that measures the temperature of your body

When the time was up, Mami pulled the thermometer out and read it.

"One hundred and six degrees?" she exclaimed. "That's impossible. You look perfectly fine to me."

After a little questioning, I confessed what I had done. I told Mami how much I didn't want to go on the field trip.

"You know, Marilia," she advised, "you might enjoy yourself after all. Besides, I've already promised Sister Antonia two trays of *tembleque* to bring as an *aguinaldo* to the residents of the home."

There was no way out. I had to go.

In the big lobby of the nursing home, paper streamers hung from the tall windows. The residents were scattered everywhere. Sister Antonia took out her guitar and at the sound of the first bar we began to sing a medley of carols. Meanwhile, the residents clapped and sang along while a student passed around our cards for us to give to them later. As I watched how happy our music made the residents, memories of my grandma rushed to me, making me dizzy with sadness. Suddenly, I saw that everybody was visiting with their residents. I was alone. I didn't feel like joining one of the groups. Maybe I could quietly slip away until the visit was over. I hoped it would be soon. Then I noticed a chair against the yellow wall. I sat there still holding the card I had made.

---

tembleque, dessert made from coconut milk
scattered, spread out
dizzy, unsteady

BEFORE YOU GO ON

1 What are *aguinaldos*? What *aguinaldos* do Marilia's class take to the nursing home?

2 How does Marilia feel when she goes to the nursing home? Why?

On Your Own
Have you ever known someone who lived in a nursing home?

143

Across the room there was a frail old lady in a wheelchair. She was alone, too. I looked at my card again. It was rather pretty. I had painted it with shades of blue and gold. Maybe I could just hand it to her and leave. It might brighten her day. So gingerly, I crossed the lobby and stood next to her.

"Who is there?" the old lady asked as she coquettishly fixed her silver bun with the light touch of her manicured hand.

"My name is Marilia," I said. "I brought you a card."

"*Dios te bendiga,*" the old woman said. "God bless you."

She reached for the card but her hand was nowhere near it. Her gaze was lost in the distance, and I knelt down to place the card in her hand. It was then that I saw the big clouds in her eyes. She was blind. *What was the use of a card if you couldn't see it?* I felt cheated. I stood up to go back to my chair.

"My name is Elenita," she said as I tried to slip away. "Tell me, Marilia, what does your card look like?"

I knelt down beside her and, in as vivid detail as I could, described the three wise men I had drawn. Then, Elenita's curious fingers caressed every inch of the card. She couldn't have enjoyed it more if she had seen it.

---

gingerly, cautiously
coquettishly, in a feminine way
manicured, professionally cared for
vivid, clear, specific
wise men, kings who came to see the baby Jesus
caressed, felt in a gentle way

144

When the coconut sweets were passed around, she mischievously asked for two.

"I bet you are not supposed to eat one of these," she giggled.

"No," I replied. "Sister Antonia told us that the sweets were just for residents."

"Well," she whispered. "Nobody said I couldn't give you one of *mine*."

I liked Elenita. I placed the *besito de coco* in my mouth and relished it even more. Especially since I wasn't supposed to have it. I enjoyed being her partner in mischief. After all, she asked me if I liked music and if I knew how to dance.

"Ay," I said, "I love to listen to music and dance."

Then she told me how, when she was young, she had been a great dancer.

"I used to dance so well that men would line up for a chance to dance with me. I had many, many suitors at one time," she said. "I had suitors that serenaded me in the evening and others that brought me flowers. But I didn't go out with all of them. You have to be selective, you know."

Too soon we were interrupted by Sister Antonia. It was time to get on the bus and return to school. I didn't want to leave.

---

mischievously, playfully
relished, enjoyed
suitors, men who want to marry a woman
serenaded, sang a romantic song to

✔ **LITERARY CHECK**
*What is the **irony** of Marilia's trip to the nursing home?*

BEFORE YOU GO ON

1 Why does Elenita ask Marilia to describe the card?

2 How does Marilia feel when she leaves the nursing home?

On Your Own
Did you like Elenita? Why or why not?

145

"Thank you for the card, Marilia," Elenita said. She opened her hand and gestured for me to give her mine. "I'll keep this card to remember you by."

"I'm sorry you can't see it," I said as I squeezed her hand. For a moment it felt as warm and giving as my own grandma's. "I wish I had brought you a better *aguinaldo*."

"The best *aguinaldo*," Elenita said, "was your visit, Marilia."

As I left, I felt light and warm and peaceful. On the bus ride back, I told my friend Margarita all about our visit. I couldn't wait to come back next year. I already knew what I would bring Elenita. I would make her a collage. That way she would be able to feel the many textures of my picture, even if she couldn't see it. And maybe I could make a picture of her dancing. I knew she had been very pretty when she was young.

"Are you going to wait until next Christmas to give her your collage?" Margarita asked.

I thought for a moment. "Maybe Mami could bring me back sooner," I said.

As I looked out the window, I remembered how good Elenita's hand felt to touch. It's funny how sometimes things change unexpectedly. Just that morning I didn't want to go at all. But then, I couldn't wait to visit my new friend again. We had gone to the nursing home to give *aguinaldos*. And what a very special *aguinaldo* I had been given—Elenita's friendship.

✔ **LITERARY CHECK**
Look back at the story. Identify one instance of **foreshadowing**.

---

gestured, made a motion
collage, work of art made by sticking pictures, photographs, cloth, etc.
  onto a surface

146

Marilia's Besitos de Coco

(Coconut Kisses)

3¼ cups fresh frozen grated
   coconut, firmly packed
1 cup brown sugar, firmly packed
8 tbs. all-purpose flour
¼ tsp. salt
4 tbs. butter, at room temperature
3 lg. egg yolks
½ tsp. vanilla

Preheat oven to 350°F. Place grated coconut in a bowl. Add brown sugar, flour, salt, butter, yolks, and vanilla. Mix well. Grease a 9- by 13-inch glass baking dish. Take mixture by the tablespoon, shape into balls, and arrange in baking dish. Bake for about 35 minutes or until golden. Let cool in baking dish for 10 minutes. With a small spatula, remove *besitos* carefully and place upside down onto platter. Let cool completely and turn over.

Makes about 35.

---

tbs., short for tablespoon, which is a large spoon used for measuring food
tsp., short for teaspoon, which is a small spoon used for measuring food
lg., large

ABOUT THE **AUTHOR**

Lulu Delacre was born in Puerto Rico to Argentine parents. She showed an early interest in drawing and attended painting classes in Argentina when she was ten. Later she studied fine arts in Puerto Rico and France. The stories in her books, which she both writes and illustrates, come from her cultural heritage.

BEFORE YOU GO ON

1. What *aguinaldo* does Marilia receive during her trip to the nursing home?

2. What are *besitos de coco*? What are they made of?

On Your Own
Do you think it is important for young people to develop and maintain relationships with elderly individuals? Explain.

READER'S THEATER

Act out the following scene between Marilia and her mother.

Mami: [*reading a thermometer*] One hundred and six degrees! You don't look that sick. Marilia, what's going on?

Marilia: Mami, I don't want to go on the field trip to the nursing home.

Mami: Why not?

Marilia: [*sounding sad*] It reminds me of Grandma. I miss her.

Mami: I know, I miss her, too. But Marilia, you might enjoy your trip to the nursing home more than you think.

Marilia: [*shaking her head no*] I don't think so, Mami.

Mami: Besides, we have to bring *aguinaldos* for the residents. Now, get ready. We have to leave soon.

Marilia: [*sounding defeated*] Okay, Mami, I'm coming.

COMPREHENSION

Workbook
Page 69

Right There

1. In what country does the story take place?
2. What will Marilia bring on her next visit to the nursing home? Why?

Think and Search

3. In what ways does Marilia try to skip the field trip?
4. What activities do the students participate in at the nursing home?

Author and You

5. Why does Sister Antonia think it is important for the students to bring Christmas cheer to the old and infirm?
6. How does the students' visit affect the nursing home residents?

On Your Own

7. Do you have elderly friends? Why are they important to you?
8. Describe a special recipe that you like to share with friends.

DISCUSSION

Discuss in pairs or small groups.

1. How are Marilia and Elenita similar?

2. How do you think Marilia's experience at the nursing home might affect her the next time she has to do something she's afraid to do?

Q **How are relationships with others important?** In what ways did Marilia help herself by reaching out to Elenita? Has someone ever reached out to you in this way when you needed a friend? Explain.

RESPONSE TO LITERATURE

Workbook
Page 69

Marilia dreads having to go on the school field trip to the nursing home. Prior to leaving, she discusses her fears with her mother.

Work with a partner. Write a dialogue that occurs between Marilia and her mother after the field trip. In it, include Marilia's description of events—what she saw at the nursing home, what she did there, and who she met. Include her plans to return to the nursing home. Perform your dialogue for the class.

>))♀ **Listening TIP**

Respect each speaker. Listen politely, even if you disagree with the speaker's ideas.

149

Imperatives

Imperatives are often used to give instructions. Imperatives are formed using the base form of the verb. The subject of the sentence is *you*. However, we do not say or write *you*. To make the negative form of an imperative, use *don't* before the imperative.

Imperatives can be used in many situations. For example, teachers often use them to tell you to do something in class or to explain the rules of a game. Imperatives are also used in recipes like the one below.

Marilia's Besitos de Coco

Preheat oven to 350° F. **Place** grated coconut in a bowl. **Add** brown sugar, flour, salt, butter, yolks, and vanilla. **Mix** well. **Grease** a 9- by 13-inch glass baking dish. **Take** mixture by the tablespoon, **shape** into balls, and **arrange** in baking dish. **Bake** for about 35 minutes or until golden. **Let** cool in baking dish for 10 minutes. With a small spatula, **remove** *besitos* carefully and **place** upside down onto platter. **Don't turn over** until completely cool.

Practice

Work with a partner. Read the paragraph below. Rewrite the verbs in the imperative form, changing the paragraph into a recipe. Then name it.

First, you slice some strawberries, peaches, and bananas. Then you take a cup of yogurt, and you put it into a bowl. Next, you add the sliced fruit to the yogurt. You should not forget to mix it well. Finally you measure 3 tablespoons of granola or your favorite cereal, and you add it to the fruit and yogurt. Now you enjoy!

WRITING AN EXPOSITORY PARAGRAPH

Write Instructions

Expository writing explains or informs. Instructions are one kind of expository writing. They explain how to do or make something. For example, the recipe on page 147 teaches the reader how to make *besitos de coco*. First, the recipe lists the ingredients, such as coconut and brown sugar. Then a clear sequence of steps tells the reader how to mix the ingredients together. Finally, the recipe instructs the reader how to cook the treats.

There are also instructions in the expository paragraph below. In it, the writer tells the reader how to find volunteer opportunities. She used a sequence chart to determine the order of the steps involved. In the paragraph itself, she included transition words, such as *first*, *then*, *next*, and *finally*, to keep the order clear.

First
↓
| Then |
↓
| Next |
↓
| Finally |

Haley Coy

How to Find Volunteer Opportunities in Your Area

Volunteering is a great way to help your community. One way to find a volunteer opportunity is to look on the Internet. To do this you will need a computer with Internet access, a pen or a pencil, and a phone. First, do a search. Use the key word volunteer and your zip code to find nearby places in which to volunteer, such as nursing homes, hospitals, food banks, and homeless shelters. Next, collect information about each place that interests you. Be sure to find out what skills or experience you need in order to volunteer at these places. Then call your friends and ask them if they are interested in volunteering, too. It'll be fun to volunteer together. After you decide on a place to volunteer, write down the address, telephone number, and the name of a person to contact. Finally, call or visit the organization to find out more about it.

Practice **Workbook Page 71**

Write a set of instructions. Be sure to write about something you know how to do well, such as baking cookies or using an MP3 player. Use a graphic organizer to sequence the necessary steps. Be sure to use imperatives correctly.

Writing Checklist

ORGANIZATION:
☑ I explained the steps in the correct order.

SENTENCE FLUENCY:
☑ My instructions are clear and easy to follow.

What You Will Learn

Reading
- Vocabulary building: *Context, dictionary skills, word study*
- Reading strategy: *Compare and contrast*
- Text type: *Informational text (social studies)*

Grammar, Usage, and Mechanics
Independent and dependent clauses

Writing
Write a critique

THE BIG QUESTION

How are relationships with others important? Think about one of your friends. What beliefs do you share with him or her? What beliefs don't you share? Sometimes a difference in beliefs can cause conflict between people. Was this ever true for you and your friend? How did you resolve the conflict? Discuss with a partner.

BUILD BACKGROUND

In this section, you will read two informational articles: **"Sowing the Seeds of Peace"** and **"Seeds of Peace: Cultivating Friendships."** The Seeds of Peace International Camp brings teenagers from the Middle East together to confront the conflict that has defined the region for more than fifty years. In doing so, the camp hopes to teach these future leaders the communication and leadership skills they will need to interact with each other, to work toward peace, and to develop lasting relationships with one another.

▲ Campers at the Seeds of Peace International Camp in Maine

Learn Key Words

Read these sentences. Use the context to figure out the meaning of the **red** words. Use a dictionary to check your answers. Then write each word and its meaning in your notebook.

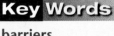

Key Words

barriers
confrontation
cultivate
enemies
political
violence

1. There were personal **barriers** that kept the girls from becoming friends.

2. Maria and Nimesh had a **confrontation** about their personal differences. They argued for a long time.

3. Hassan and Anastasia **cultivate** their friendship by calling each other every day.

4. Rashad and Hassan do not speak to one another. They are **enemies**.

5. The students debate about **political** issues that relate to government and the rights of people.

6. The fighting between the countries has continued for more than fifty years. The **violence** in that region is frightening.

Practice  **Workbook Page 72**

Write the sentences in your notebook. Choose a **red** word from the box above to complete each sentence. Then take turns reading the sentences aloud with a partner.

1. The president works hard to _____ relationships with other world leaders.

2. The country's government has made great _____ progress in improving relations with its neighbors.

3. There are _____ that make it difficult to achieve world peace.

4. The leaders wanted to avoid a _____ about their differing beliefs.

5. _____ erupted when the citizens of one country attacked those of another.

6. Members of the warring nations are _____.

▲ Two students conduct a political debate.

Learn Academic Words

Study the red words and their meanings. You will find these words useful when talking and writing about informational texts. Write each word and its meaning in your notebook. After you read "Sowing the Seeds of Peace" and "Seeds of Peace: Cultivating Friendships," try to use these words to respond to the texts.

Academic Words

assumed
focus
individuals
similarities

assumed = thought that something was true without having proof	→	I **assumed** the test would be easy to pass because I studied hard.
focus = pay special attention to a particular person or thing instead of others	→	It was noisy in the library. I had to **focus** very hard to study for the test.
individuals = people; not a whole group	→	A few **individuals** passed the test easily, but for most students it was difficult.
similarities = the qualities of being similar, or the same	→	There are **similarities** in all people. We are all alike in some ways.

Practice  Workbook Page 73

Work with a partner to answer these questions. Try to include the red word in your answer. Write the sentences in your notebook.

1. Have you ever **assumed** that a class would be easier than it actually was? Explain.

2. What is your main **focus** at school?

3. Which **individuals** in your classroom do you work well with? Why?

4. What are three **similarities** that all people share?

▲ Only a few individuals passed the test.

154

Word Study: Suffixes *-er, -or*

A suffix is a letter or group of letters placed at the end of a base word. Adding a suffix changes the meaning of the base word.

The most common meaning of the suffixes *-er* and *-or* is "one who." For example, a learner is one who learns; a visitor is one who visits. The only way to know which of these two suffixes to use is to check the dictionary. Remember, if a base word ends with an *e*, drop the *e* before adding the suffix. Study the examples in the chart below.

Base Word	+ Suffix	= New Word
travel	-er	travel**er**
bake	-er	bak**er**
act	-or	act**or**
educate	-or	educat**or**

Practice

Copy the sentences below into your notebook. Complete each sentence by adding *-er* or *-or* to the word in parentheses. Use a dictionary if necessary. Have a partner check your work.

1. The camp _____ led the students in a variety of activities. (counsel)
2. Each student was allowed to invite one _____ to the camp. (visit)
3. A _____ encouraged students to discuss political issues. (facilitate)
4. Each _____ presented a persuasive argument. (debate)
5. Andrea, a _____, performed during cultural night. She is a good _____. (camp, sing)

READING STRATEGY | COMPARE AND CONTRAST

Comparing and contrasting helps you to understand what you read more clearly. When you compare, you see how things are similar. When you contrast, you see how things are different. To compare and contrast, follow these steps as you read:

- How are the people, events, experiences, and settings in the stories similar? How are they different?
- Think about your own experiences. Do they help you better understand the text?

As you read "Sowing the Seeds of Peace," compare and contrast the teenagers and their beliefs.

Set a purpose for reading As you read, look for examples of the conflicts between the two groups of teenagers. How has the politics of their countries affected their relationships with each other?

Sowing the
Seeds of Peace

Mandy Terc

One rainy rest hour at a summer camp in Maine, fifteen-year-old Noor from the Palestinian West Bank was learning to write her name. She glanced back quickly at the example that sixteen-year-old Shirlee, a Jewish Israeli from a seaside town, had provided. After a few more seconds of intense writing, Noor triumphantly handed the piece of paper to me, her bunk counselor. Parading across the top of the paper in large, careful print were the Hebrew letters that spelled her Arabic name.

A spontaneous lesson on the Hebrew and Arabic alphabets probably does not happen at most summer camp bunks, but the Seeds of Peace International Camp challenges the traditional definition of what teenagers can learn and accomplish at a summer camp. Seeds of Peace brings Middle Eastern teenagers from Israel, Palestine, Jordan, Egypt, and other countries to Maine to help them confront

▲ Seeds of Peace campers

the conflict and violence that has defined their region for more than fifty years.

At this camp, things like table and bunk assignments, sports teams, and seating are never accidental. They are all part of encouraging interaction. Here, Israelis and Arabs not only meet for the first time but also sleep side by side, share a sink and participate in group games. In the

---

bunk, cabin

interaction, action or communication between or among people

close quarters of tiny cabins and bunk beds, bunk counselors encourage the campers to ignore national and ethnic boundaries as they make friends with their immediate neighbors.

The three weeks spent in Maine combine ordinary camp activities with a daily two-hour coexistence session, during which trained facilitators encourage discussion of political and personal issues. The remainder of the day is spent in traditional summer camp activities.

Teenagers are asked to analyze questions that have perplexed world leaders, and even bedtime can become a political forum. In my bunk, I asked the girls to summarize one positive and one negative aspect of their day before going to sleep.

---

boundaries, borders or barriers
traditional summer camp activities, typical, well-known games and sports
perplexed, confused
forum, meeting in which people have a chance to publicly discuss important subjects

Sometimes, the discussions were about quite ordinary and uncontroversial things.

At other times, our bedtime discussions reflected the complexity and difficulties of living with perceived enemies. On one occasion, Adar, a strongly nationalistic Israeli, began by expressing frustration with a Palestinian girl's comment that Israel unjustly occupied Jerusalem, which the Palestinian felt truly belonged to the Palestinian people.

Instantly, eight bodies snapped from snug sleeping positions to tense, upright postures. Jerusalem is the most contentious issue between the Arab and Israeli campers, and each girl in the bunk was poised to take this opportunity to talk about her opinion on the disputed city. Adar asked if all Palestinians refused to recognize Israelis as legitimate residents of the city.

---

contentious, likely to cause an argument
legitimate, lawful

▲ Campers participate in a traditional summer camp activity.

BEFORE YOU GO ON

1 What is the goal of the Seeds of Peace International Camp?

2 What issue caused a serious discussion at bedtime?

On Your Own
Would you like to go to a summer camp? If so, what kind?

Almost before Adar could finish her question, Aman was ready to answer. Aman is a strong, athletic Palestinian who does not waste her words. When she begins to speak, she is both intimidating and impressive as she defends her opinions.

Calm and composed, she explained to Adar that the presence of Muslim holy sites in Jerusalem meant that the Palestinians were the rightful proprietors of the city. With an equally rapid response, Adar reminded her that Jerusalem also contained Jewish holy sites.

Aman seemed prepared for this answer. "We would be very nice to you [the Jewish people]. We would always let you come visit your sites, just like all the other tourists," she replied.

Adar had no intention of allowing her people to become theoretical tourists in this debate: "Well, we have the city now," Adar said. "You can't just make us leave, because it's ours. We might decide to give some of it to the Palestinians, but it belongs to us now."

---

intimidating, aggressive
composed, thoughtful
proprietors, owners

I spent such times in the bunk listening. I only sporadically interjected my voice, reminding them not to hold each other, as individuals, responsible for the actions of their governments.

The conversation eventually wound down. As the girls drifted off to sleep, I felt relieved. As much as I want the girls in my bunk to express all their concerns and thoughts, any conversation about such a sensitive issue keeps me tense. The bunk must feel safe but issues of conflict can't be ignored or downplayed. As a bunk counselor, I must provide campers with the safety and security they need to continue the process of breaking down barriers.

---

sporadically, from time to time
tense, nervous and worried

▲ **Cultural Night activities**

ABOUT THE **AUTHOR**

Mandy Terc has worked at the Seeds of Peace International Camp in Maine and also in Seeds of Peace's New York development office. She is currently a doctoral candidate at the University of Michigan.

Seeds of Peace: Cultivating Friendships

Author John Wallach founded Seeds of Peace in an effort to bring understanding to the Middle East. In the summer of 1993, Wallach invited forty-six Israeli, Palestinian, and Egyptian teenagers to his camp in Maine. There, the teens lived alongside those they were previously taught to hate. They participated in activities designed to confront the fears, mistrust, and prejudices that continue to fuel the conflicts in their home countries. Through such interactions, Wallach and his staff worked to ensure that the leaders of tomorrow are friends, rather than enemies.

Since that first camp, Seeds of Peace has expanded its programming to include participants from twenty-five different nations. To date, over 3,000 teens have graduated from Seeds of Peace.

Following graduation, many teenagers continue to participate in follow-up conferences and workshops. Below, two campers speak of their experiences, the lessons they learned, and the friendships they continue to cultivate.

Eitan Paul (New Jersey)

We arrived as separate delegations, debaters of our country's positions; we would leave as friends, aware that coexistence is possible.

Every day teenagers wearing the green Seeds of Peace T-shirts accomplish something that world leaders struggle to achieve. They listen to each other, suspending personal agendas, cultivating meaningful friendships.

John Wallach always used to say, "Make one friend." I made many.

Marisa Gorovitz (Maitland, Florida)

Camp was more amazing than I ever imagined. I learned an incredible amount about Arabic culture, Israel, the Palestinians, Islam, and the history of the Middle East.

Leaving camp and my new friends was the hardest thing I've ever done. We shared unforgettable moments, from debating, to climbing, to dancing. I keep in touch with my friends through e-mail, the phone, and the mail. I hope to visit them in their various countries!

fuel, make worse
suspending, stopping for a short time

BEFORE YOU GO ON

1 What was the author's advice to the campers during the discussion?

2 How did the campers change during Eitan Paul's stay at camp?

On Your Own
Do you have political discussions with others? What do you discuss?

159

COMPREHENSION  Workbook Page 76

Right There

1. Who founded the Seeds of Peace International Camp? Why?
2. What two groups of people meet for the first time at the camp?

Think and Search

3. In what ways does the camp encourage interaction among campers?
4. In what kinds of daily activities do campers participate?

Author and You

5. Why do you think the camp is called Seeds of Peace?
6. Why does the author feel tense about some of the political discussions that occur in the bunk?

On Your Own

7. Do you think a camp is a good place to bring people with opposing views together? Explain.
8. Have you ever been to a summer camp? If so, what kind of camp was it? What did you do there?

▲ Seeds of Peace campers learn how to sail.

IN YOUR OWN WORDS

Work with a partner. Copy the chart below into your notebook. Write the missing information in the chart. Use this information to summarize the article for your partner.

Seeds of Peace International Camp	
Location	Maine
Campers	
Activities	
Goals	

DISCUSSION

Discuss in pairs or small groups.

1. Compare and contrast Adar's and Aman's views of Jerusalem.

2. Do you think Seeds of Peace can make a difference in the world? Why or why not?

Q **How are relationships with others important?** Describe a time when you met someone whose views were different from your own. Did you try to understand that person's way of thinking? Were you able to get along?

»)) Listening TIP

Listen to the verbs and adjectives the speaker uses. Try to visualize, or picture in your mind, the event that the speaker is describing.

READ FOR FLUENCY

It is often easier to read a text if you understand the difficult words and phrases. Work with a partner. Choose a paragraph from the reading. Identify the words and phrases you do not know or have trouble pronouncing. Look up the difficult words in a dictionary.

Take turns pronouncing the words and phrases with your partner. If necessary, ask your teacher to model the correct pronunciation. Then take turns reading the paragraph aloud. Give each other feedback on your reading.

EXTENSION  Workbook Page 76

The relationship between Arabs and Israelis is constantly in the news. Work with a partner. Find two articles about current events happening in this region. Use newspapers, news magazines, or the Internet. Then summarize each article and present the information to your classmates.

Grammar and Writing

Independent and Dependent Clauses

An independent clause has a subject and a verb. It is a complete sentence. Coordinating conjunctions, such as *but, and, yet, or,* and *so,* can join two independent clauses. A comma is often used before the conjunction. Read the example below from "Sowing the Seeds of Peace."

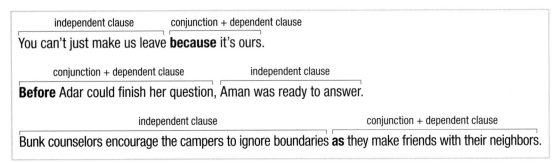

independent clause	conjunction + independent clause

"We might decide to give some of it to the Palestinians, **but** it belongs to us now."

A dependent clause has a subject and verb, but it is not a complete sentence. It must be connected to an independent clause. Subordinating conjunctions, such as *before, because,* and *as* introduce a dependent clause.

independent clause	conjunction + dependent clause

You can't just make us leave **because** it's ours.

conjunction + dependent clause	independent clause

Before Adar could finish her question, Aman was ready to answer.

independent clause	conjunction + dependent clause

Bunk counselors encourage the campers to ignore boundaries **as** they make friends with their neighbors.

Practice

Workbook Page 77

Copy the sentences below into your notebook. Label the independent clauses and the dependent clauses. Circle the conjunction.

1. Few people signed up for the camp, but it was still a success.
2. Before the camp started, there wasn't any place where Middle Eastern teenagers could meet.
3. The counselors worked hard as they encouraged the teenagers to talk with each other.
4. The campers sometimes got angry because they had to analyze difficult political questions.
5. The teens learned to interact with each other, and they had a good time, too.

162

WRITING AN EXPOSITORY PARAGRAPH

Write a Critique

You have learned that an expository paragraph explains or gives information. Another type of expository writing is a critique. When you write a critique, you judge a work or an experience based on standards, or a level of quality that is acceptable to you. You tell what the standards are and then explain why the work or experience did or did not meet them. For example, imagine that you and your friends like video games that include a lot of action. If a friend asked you about the two games you played yesterday, you could judge the games based on this standard.

The model below is a critique of an after-school program. The writer began by listing her ideas in a graphic organizer. Then she critiqued the program based on her standards.

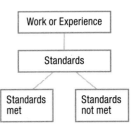

Work or Experience

Standards

| Standards met | Standards not met |

Nicole Siley

The Community Arts Center After-School Program

Last year, I attended an after-school program at the Community Arts Center in my town. It had many of the qualities I was hoping it would have: kids my age, good instructors, and fun activities. Many of my classmates attended. Even so, I was able to meet new students from other schools, and we still keep in touch with one another. Unfortunately, a lot of kids—more than 100—signed up for the program. Our instructors, however, kept things moving and made the program fun. There were many activities to choose from, such as painting, drawing, dancing, and acting. I took a painting class. I learned how to paint and took a trip to the art museum. Even though it was crowded, I'm going to sign up for the after-school program again this year.

Practice  Workbook Page 78

Write a critique of a story, movie, video game, or place you have visited, such as a restaurant. List your ideas in a graphic organizer. Be sure to use dependent and independent clauses correctly.

Writing Checklist

IDEAS:
☑ I clearly identified the standards I used to judge a work or an experience.

CONVENTIONS:
☑ I used dependent and independent clauses correctly.

What You Will Learn

Reading

- Vocabulary building: *Literary terms, word study*

- Reading strategy: *Identify with a character*

- Text type: *Literature (legend)*

Grammar, Usage, and Mechanics
Expressions to compare and contrast

Writing
Write to compare and contrast

 THE BIG QUESTION

How are relationships with others important? As you know, people can be involved in different kinds of relationships. Work with a partner. Discuss the relationships you have with others. Then answer the following questions: How and when did each relationship begin? What makes you value each relationship? How would you feel if you could not experience these relationships?

BUILD BACKGROUND

In this section, you will read an excerpt from a legend called **Blue Willow**. A legend is a story that is often based on fact. However, over time, details in legends move further away from factual events to describe people and actions that are more fictional than real.

The *Blue Willow* legend explains the Blue Willow china pattern, which always includes a willow tree, a bridge, and a moon pavilion, or a decorative building. Plates with this pattern were produced in England during the eighteenth century—a time when the English were inspired by Chinese culture.

Set in ancient China, the legend describes the relationship between Kung Shi Fair, the daughter of a wealthy merchant, and a village fisherman named Chang the Good. The couple wants to marry, but the merchant will not grant his permission. This causes a series of events that no one could have anticipated.

◀ A plate with a Blue Willow pattern

VOCABULARY

Learn Literary Words

Long before there were books, there were stories. Storytelling was a form of entertainment in ancient cultures. Stories were passed along by word of mouth from one generation to the next. This is called the **oral tradition**.

A **legend** is one kind of story that was originally shared by oral tradition. Because legends were told orally and were not written down, they moved away from factual events to describe more fictional events and characters.

Character motive is the reason for a character's thoughts, feelings, actions, or speech. Characters are often motivated by needs, such as food and shelter. They are also motivated by feelings, such as fear, love, and pride. Knowing characters' motives helps the reader understand the characters and the story better. Read the passage below. What is Lisa's motivation?

> Lisa longingly looked out the window. This was the fourth day in a row that she had stayed after school to work on her science project. "I'd rather be with my friends," Lisa thought to herself as she sighed loudly. She turned her head from the window. Out of the corner of her eye, she caught a glimpse of the science fair poster. She focused on the words printed in bright red letters: *Grand Prize Winner—$200.* All thoughts of her friends faded as Lisa got back to work.

Practice

Workbook
Page 79

Work with a partner. Share a story that has been passed down in your family from generation to generation in the oral tradition. Is the story a legend? Try to identify the main characters' motivations.

Learn Academic Words

Study the red words and their meanings. You will find these words useful when talking and writing about literature. Write each word and its meaning in your notebook. After you read the excerpt from *Blue Willow*, try to use these words to respond to the text.

Academic Words

authoritative
consent
encounter
reaction

authoritative = respected and trusted as being true, or making people respect or obey you	➡	My mother makes the rules in our home. She is the most **authoritative** member of our family.
consent = permission to do something	➡	We have to get her **consent** before we can leave the house with friends.
encounter = an occasion when you meet someone without planning to	➡	I had an unexpected **encounter** with my friend at the mall.
reaction = the way you behave in response to someone or something	➡	My friend and I had the same **reaction**. We were both surprised and happy to see each other.

Practice

Workbook
Page 80

Work with a partner to answer the questions. Try to include the red word in your answer. Write the sentences in your notebook.

1. In your opinion, who is the most authoritative person in your school?

2. Do you have to receive your teacher's consent before leaving the classroom?

3. Who did you have an encounter with at school today?

4. What was your reaction to this encounter?

▲ This teacher is the authoritative figure in her classroom.

166

Word Study: Synonyms

Synonyms are words that have the same or nearly the same meaning. The words *clever* and *intelligent, glisten* and *shine,* and *toss* and *throw* are synonyms. Writers often choose one synonym over another to express a specific idea or emotion. Look at the chart below for examples.

Synonym	Meaning	Sentence
claim (verb)	to say something without proof or evidence	They **claimed** to have heard the leopard cries.
state (verb)	to say something in a strong and formal way	Her father **stated** that she could not marry him.

Practice  Workbook Page 81

Work with a partner. Copy the chart above into your notebook, leaving the columns blank. Fill in the first column with the pairs of synonyms in the box below. Use a dictionary or thesaurus to find the meaning of each synonym. Then write the meaning and a sentence for each one.

drift/float	look/gaze	shriek/yell
special/unusual	startle/surprise	love/adore

READING STRATEGY   IDENTIFY WITH A CHARACTER

Identifying with a character helps you better understand and enjoy a story. When you identify with a character, you understand his or her actions and feelings. To identify with a character, follow these steps as you read:

- Think about the character's actions. What does he or she do?
- How do you think the character feels?
- Think about your own experiences. How would you feel? Would you act in the same way as the character?

As you read the excerpt from the legend *Blue Willow,* imagine how you would feel if you were the main character. Think about the things you would do differently.

 Workbook Page 82

Set a purpose for reading As you read, notice
how Kung Shi Fair's relationship with Chang the Good
affects her father. How does his reaction affect the
young couple's relationship?

from

Blue Willow
Pam Conrad

Many years ago, there was a river called Wen that flowed past a small and
peaceful village.

On one side of the Wen River, in a large mansion, lived a wealthy merchant.

Everyone knew that he had one daughter, Kung Shi Fair. She was a beautiful
girl with hands as small as starfish, feet as swift as sandpipers, and hair as
black as the ink on her father's scrolls. As she grew, the people of the village
wondered who she would marry, because they all knew that the merchant
always gave her whatever she asked for.

One day Kung Shi Fair was sitting in her moon pavilion when she saw
something glistening on the bank of the river. She made her way to the water.
When she got there, she saw it was only a broken shell. She picked it up, then
looked up and saw for the first time a boat and a young man pulling his
d ipping nets out of the water.

This was Chang the Good who lived across the river. He was a
young fisherman.

---

merchant, person who makes money by selling things
sandpipers, wading birds
scrolls, books written on long sheets of papers that roll up
moon pavilion, decorative building
glistening, shining

Now Kung Shi Fair and Chang the Good were both startled to see each other. The fish spilled out of his nets. The shell dropped from Kung Shi Fair's hand. Tossing the nets on the floor of his boat, Chang the Good picked up his oars, and he rowed across the river to her.

When he reached the shore, Kung Shi Fair watched as he pulled the boat onto the land. She came close and touched his nets. "How beautiful," she said.

"I made them myself," he told her, thinking he, as well, had never seen something so beautiful this close.

"And what a wonderful bird!" she exclaimed as the cormorant held out its wings to dry in the breeze.

"I fish with her. She dives for fish and—because I have trained her so well—she brings the fish to me."

"You are very clever," she said, turning her gaze full on him.

"Can I tell you something?" he asked her softly.

She nodded, silent.

"One morning I came down to the river, thinking my boat would be anchored where I had left it, but the currents had taken it away. All day long I searched along the river for my boat. Then, when I had given up hope, I came upon a cove, and there it was, drifting toward me. My heart swelled with love."

Kung Shi Fair tilted her head. "And so?"

"And so, this is how I felt just now, seeing you here on the bank of the river."

---

anchored, kept in place by a heavy weight that is connected to the boat and dropped into the water.
currents, moving waters
cove, small area of water that is surrounded by land

BEFORE YOU GO ON

1 Who is Kung Shi Fair? Who is Chang the Good?

2 How do Kung Shi Fair and Chang the Good meet?

On Your Own
Chang the Good talks about loving Kung Shi Fair within moments of their first meeting. Do you think love at first sight is possible? Explain.

169

Kung Shi Fair frowned. "My boat has never been in the river," she said. "So I have never lost a boat, or found one." Then she smiled at him. "But I came to the river just now thinking I saw something glistening on its bank, and now I know I came for you."

But it so happened that Kung Shi Fair's father was watching from the window of his mansion. He watched as his daughter led the fisherman across the stone footbridge, and he watched her lead Chang the Good to her moon pavilion.

That night he said nothing to his daughter about what he had seen. They were drinking their tea, sitting quietly, when one of the servants came panting onto the veranda.

"There is terrible news, Master. It seems there is a wild leopard on a rampage."

"This is frightening," the merchant said. "You must tell me if you hear news of the leopard coming in this direction."

The merchant looked at his daughter. "Perhaps, until the leopard is caught, you should not go down into your moon pavilion."

Kung Shi Fair laughed, "Don't be silly, silly father. My pavilion is perfectly safe."

* * *

The next day and every day after that, when the work of the fishing was through, Kung Shi Fair and Chang the Good would meet on the shore. First they would go to the pavilion. Then they would trail peony petals down the path to the bridge, where they would sit and talk, and eat mulberries beneath the cool willow tree.

Finally, after many days of this, Chang the Good came with a bundle.

"I have something to show you," he said.

Very carefully, he unfastened the knot and opened his bundle on the floor before her. There were brooches and necklaces, bracelets, and pendants hung not on gold chains as she was used to, but on rough silk cords dull with wear.

He told her, "These belonged to my mother, who died when I was very young."

---

servants, people who are paid to clean someone's house, cook food, etc.
panting, breathing quickly with short noisy breaths
veranda, porch with a roof
leopard, large cat with black spots
on a rampage, behaving wildly or violently
brooches, jewels that can be attached to clothing

BEFORE YOU GO ON

1 What news does the servant have for the merchant?

2 What is in the bundle Chang the Good brings to Kung Shi Fair? Why are its contents special?

On Your Own
Do you own a special piece of jewelry? If so, describe it and explain why it is important to you.

171

"And this was her own ring," Chang the Good was saying, and he slipped a small jade ring onto her thumb.

"Beautiful," Kung Shi Fair told him.

"I want you to have them," he told her. "I want you to be my wife."

Kung Shi Fair held very still.

"Yes, I would like this, too," she said. "But I must tell my father."

* * *

That night Kung Shi Fair went to her father. She said to him, "I would marry now, Father."

And he answered, "Not yet, my daughter, not yet."

"But, Father, you have always been so good to me. And this is what I want more than anything. If not now, then when?"

"When I find a copper coin in my path," he said.

Kung Shi Fair ran from the room to hide her tears, past the servant who was coming to tell the merchant that the leopard was terribly close.

Chang the Good could not be discouraged. Sitting in Kung Shi Fair's moon pavilion, he thought of a plan. He did not stay that day for he had special work to do, and he told Kung Shi Fair to sit by her window at dawn.

The next morning, Kung Shi Fair leaned on the window. Her father was preparing to go to a meeting concerning the rampaging leopard.

She saw the servants bring the carriage around to him, and just as her father was about to climb on, he looked down and saw coins strewn at his feet—hundreds of little copper coins. He looked up at his daughter in the window.

She saw no anger in his face, just sadness. She smiled kindly at him. "Now, Father? Can I now?"

He shook his head. "Not yet, my daughter, not yet."

Her smile turned to tears. "Then when, Father? Oh, then when?"

"When there's a rainbow over the stone bridge that leads to your moon pavilion," he told her, and he drove away.

Later the servants claimed to have heard Kung Shi Fair's sad crying that morning, even above winds that whistled over the river's surface. They decided she had gone to find Chang the Good, to tell him his plan had failed.

The village women later whispered about how she went down to the bank of the tumbling Wen River, to her boat. She had watched many times as Chang the Good had sailed away, and now—hoping she could remember how—she awkwardly pushed her boat into the surging river.

✔ LITERARY CHECK
*What is the merchant's **motive** in refusing to let the couple marry?*

---

jade, green stone
discouraged, persuaded to lose the confidence needed to do something
strewn, lying
surging, quickly moving

Turning her face into the wind, she steered bravely through the river's foam and rapids. When she was halfway across the river, the wind ripped the fig leaf sails from their mast, and the cassia bark hull snapped apart, tipping the merchant's beautiful daughter into the torrential river. For a few moments her silken robe could be seen floating near the surface, and then it was gone.

In the village, Chang the Good had gone to the meeting to hear the news about the rampaging leopard. Everyone was frightened that the leopard would come and kill their families. Then the merchant spoke to them.

"While the storm is raging," he said, "we must go out, seek the leopard, and slay him before he comes to our village again."

"Yes!" "Yes!" the villagers cried. "Kill the leopard now!"

Chang the Good had thoughts only for Kung Shi Fair. He had no heart for a hunt. Without being seen, he stepped out into the rain. He thought to himself how once the winds calmed, he would sail over and see her and ask her how things had gone with her father and the coins.

Meanwhile the swords were brought out and the bows and arrows, the spears and the clubs, and everyone received a weapon. The villagers poured out of the hall, and they took to the rain-slick road, in search of the leopard.

---

rapids, fast-moving waters
hull, body of the boat
torrential, quickly flowing
slay, kill

BEFORE YOU GO ON

1 How does Kung Shi Fair react to her father's denial? What is the result of her actions?

2 What do the villagers determine they have to do? Why?

On Your Own
Are you able to relate to Kung Shi Fair's feelings? Explain.

173

It was dark when the winds finally calmed and the river slowed its fury. The cormorant perched on the back of Chang the Good's boat, as he eased it into the river. Chang the Good gave it a final push and jumped in. Slowly and carefully, he made his way across, peering into the darkness of the pavilion to see if Kung Shi Fair waited for him. But there was no sign of her.

He pulled his boat ashore and called, "Kung Shi!" There was silence.

He ran to the pavilion and threw back the rain-soaked silks, "Kung Shi!"

Frightened, he turned towards her father's house that was dark and lifeless. His feet barely touched the ground. He ran from room to room, calling her name and hearing the silence answer. He knew something terrible had happened.

Slowly he left the house. The song of small green frogs carried him to the stone bridge and he decided to sit there and wait for her.

Suddenly the cormorant flapped her wings, shrieked, and dived into the water and disappeared. Then she flew straight up and landed beside Chang the Good. She dropped what she was carrying into her master's hand.

It was a small, jade thumb ring.

---

shrieked, yelled in a high-pitched voice

Chang the Good saw it and at that moment, he knew. He jumped up, and his eyes searched the shore for the cassia boat and he knew. He saw the whole story before him and threw back his head. He knew it was too late.

Just as the moon began to slip into sight, the weary villagers were returning home empty-handed. As they came back toward the village, they heard a sound coming from across the water near the merchant's house. "The leopard!" they whispered. At that, three of them jumped into a boat and sailed silently across the river to the place where the sound came from.

Now for many years after, the villagers tried to describe to each other what the sound was like. Most thought it sounded like the ragings of a leopard before it strikes. Later they all knew it was the sound of Chang the Good, crying his heart into the night.

Silently the boat slipped onto the riverbank, and the three men crept up the shore. In the moonlight they saw their enemy. In one thrust they all shot arrows, threw spears, and sent clubs sailing through the wailing air. Their mark was made, and Chang the Good toppled into the river beneath the bridge.

If this was the end of the story, it would probably have been forgotten by now, it was so long ago. But because the merchant was so heartbroken, he cried his sorrows to whomever would listen to him, and the entire village soon knew he had kept his daughter away from the man she loved.

It was some time later, while the last leaves were still on the willow, that there was a cloudburst in the late afternoon. The merchant heard the villagers cry out, and he went to the window.

His heart leapt at the sight, for just above the footbridge that led to his daughter's pavilion, there appeared a most wondrous rainbow of every color. While the villagers and the merchant watched, two swallows fluttered above the willow tree and kissed.

---

weary, very tired
strikes, attacks
toppled, fell
sorrows, feelings of grief and sadness
swallows, small birds

ABOUT THE **AUTHOR**

Pam Conrad (1948–1996) wrote stories for both children and adults. Before her death, she authored twenty-nine books. Often she used her own experiences as inspiration for many of her award-winning tales.

✔ **LITERARY CHECK**
*This **legend** was originally shared with others as part of the **oral tradition**. Retell the story to a partner. How does your oral version differ from the written story?*

BEFORE YOU GO ON

1. How does Chang the Good find out what happened to Kung Shi Fair?

2. What happens to Chang the Good at the end of the story?

💡 **On Your Own**
Did the story end as you thought it would? Why or why not?

READER'S THEATER

Act out the following scene between Kung Shi Fair and Chang the Good.

Kung Shi Fair: These nets are beautiful.

Chang the Good: I made them myself. I use them to catch fish.

Kung Shi Fair: And this lovely bird! What kind of bird is it?

Chang the Good: It's a cormorant. She's very smart! I have taught her how to catch fish and bring them to me.

Kung Shi Fair: Then it is you who is smart!

Chang the Good: Can I tell you something? One morning the currents took away my boat during the night. I searched for my boat all day long. Finally, I found it in a small cove. My heart was filled with joy.

Kung Shi Fair: Why are you telling me this?

Chang the Good: Because that is how I felt when I saw you.

🔊 **Speaking** TIP

Read the lines in a way that reflects your character's personality. This will help to make your character seem real.

COMPREHENSION

Workbook
Page 83

Right There

1. Why do the people of the village wonder who Kung Shi Fair will marry?

2. What do the villagers mistake Chang the Good's crying for?

Think and Search

3. What is the significance of the willow tree, the bridge, and the moon pavilion in the story?

4. What does the merchant say has to happen before Kung Shi Fair and Chang the Good can marry?

Author and You

5. Who places the copper coins in the merchant's path?

6. Why do you think the author chooses to share the *Blue Willow* legend with others in the form of a written story?

▲ A copper coin

On Your Own

7. Do you think it is important to be able to choose your own friends? Explain.

8. What kinds of relationships would your parents object to you having?

DISCUSSION

»)🦻 *Listening* TIP

Think about what you are hearing. Try to relate what you hear to what you already know.

Discuss in pairs or small groups.

1. Could the merchant have prevented his daughter's death? If so, how?

2. In your opinion, was the merchant right to deny his daughter marriage? Why or why not?

Q **How are relationships with others important?** Do you think parents have the right to put an end to certain relationships between their children and other people? Explain.

RESPONSE TO LITERATURE

Workbook
Page 83

Because legends were often shared orally, many versions of the *Blue Willow* legend exist. Work with a partner. Find an account that is different from the one you read in class. Use library resources or the Internet. Then compare both stories. Copy the chart below into your notebook. Add information about the characters, settings, story events, and conclusions. Share this information with your classmates. How many different versions were presented?

Blue Willow				
Version	**Setting**	**Characters**	**Story Events**	**Conclusion**
Pam Conrad's				
Internet				

GRAMMAR, USAGE, AND MECHANICS

Expressions to Compare and Contrast

To compare ideas, writers use expressions such as *and so . . . and and . . . too.* If the verb *be* is used in the first half of the sentence, it should also be used in the second half of the sentence.

> Chang the Good was young, **and so was** Kung Shi Fair.
> Chang the Good was young, **and** Kung Shi Fair **was**, **too**.

When other verbs are used in the first half of the sentence, use a form of *do* in the second half of the sentence.

> Chang the Good loved Kung Shi Fair, **and so did** her father.
> Chang the Good loved Kung Shi Fair, **and** her father **did**, **too**.

To contrast ideas, writers use *but . . . not* and *and yet.*

> Kung Shi Fair wanted to marry, **but** her father did **not** want her to.
> The merchant loved his daughter, **and yet** he wouldn't let her marry.

Practice  Workbook Page 84

Work with a partner. Combine the sentences with expressions used to compare and contrast. Write the sentences in your notebook. More than one answer may be possible.

1. Chang the Good thought the cormorant was wonderful.
   Kung Shi Fair thought the cormorant was wonderful.

2. The servant was frightened by the leopard.
   The master was frightened by the leopard.

3. Chang the Good wanted to marry Kung Shi Fair.
   Her father would not let them marry.

4. Kung Shi Fair's father was sorry for his actions.
   He could not bring his daughter back.

WRITING AN EXPOSITORY PARAGRAPH

Write to Compare and Contrast

You have learned that expository writing involves presenting facts about a topic. Instructions, critiques, and compare-and-contrast paragraphs are all examples of expository writing.

A compare-and-contrast paragraph looks at the similarities and differences between two people, places, or things. For example, you can compare and contrast two friends. First, write down the ways your friends are similar and different. Then write your paragraph. In your introduction, tell your reader about the friends you are comparing and contrasting. Next, tell how your friends are the same. Then write about how they are different. Include specific examples that emphasize their similarities and differences.

Here is a model paragraph. After choosing his topic, the writer used a Venn diagram to organize his ideas. Also notice how he used comparison and contrast structures in his paragraph.

Kung Shi Fair   Chang the Good

Both

Austin Saiz

Blue Willow

Kung Shi Fair and Chang the Good are the two main characters in <u>Blue Willow</u>. They are similar in some ways, but they are also very different. First, both characters are similar in age. Also, at the time they meet, both Kung Shi Fair and Chang the Good have lost their mothers. Kung Shi Fair lives with her wealthy father in a mansion near the Wen River. Chang the Good also lives near the Wen River. However, Chang the Good lives in the village. His family isn't wealthy at all. In fact, he's a poor fisherman. Despite the differences in their backgrounds and lifestyles, Kung Shi Fair and Chang the Good see something good in each other and fall in love.

Practice

Workbook Page 85

Write a paragraph that compares and contrasts two people, places, or things you know well. List your ideas in a graphic organizer. Be sure to use comparison and contrast structures correctly in your writing.

Writing Checklist

ORGANIZATION:
☑ I used a compare-and-contrast organization.

WORD CHOICE:
☑ I used comparison and contrast structures correctly.

179

What You Will Learn

Reading

■ Vocabulary building: *Context, dictionary skills, word study*

■ Reading strategy: *Classify*

■ Text type: *Informational text (science)*

Grammar, Usage, and Mechanics
Compound and complex sentences

Writing
Write a classifying paragraph

THE BIG QUESTION

How are relationships with others important? Think of a time when you had to work with a partner in order to complete an assignment. How did you divide the tasks? Were they equally difficult and time-consuming? What would have happened if your partner hadn't done his or her share of the work? Discuss with a partner.

BUILD BACKGROUND

Humans are not the only organisms that enter into partnerships with others. Some organisms, such as animals, plants, bacteria, and viruses, also work together in order to obtain protection, food, and/or shelter. You will learn more about these relationships as you read the science article **"Partnerships in Nature."**

▲ Partners working together to complete an assignment

VOCABULARY

Learn Key Words

Read these sentences. Use the context to figure out the meaning of the **red** words. Use a dictionary to check your answers. Then write each word and its meaning in your notebook.

Key Words

commensal
mutualistic
nature
parasites
protection
symbiosis

1. Some animals participate in **commensal** partnerships. One animal is helped, while the other animal is neither helped nor hurt.

2. Unlike a commensal partnership, a **mutualistic** partnership benefits both partners.

3. Orchids are plants that are found in **nature**.

4. I think **parasites** are disgusting—they live in plants, animals, or people and get food from them.

5. In some relationships, one animal provides another animal with **protection** from its enemies and other dangers.

6. Mutualism, commensalism, and parasitism are examples of **symbiosis**.

Practice  Workbook Page 86

Write the sentences in your notebook. Choose a **red** word from the box above to complete each sentence. Then take turns reading the sentences aloud with a partner.

1. Animals, plants, and weather are all part of _____.

2. Clownfish hide among sea anemonies for _____. The sea anemonies conceal the clownfish from its predators.

3. Mosquitoes are _____. They feed on human blood.

4. Hibiscus flowers and honeybees have a _____ partnership with one another. Both organisms are helped by this relationship.

5. _____ is important to many organisms in nature. Without these partnerships, many organisms could not survive.

6. Frogs and certain tropical plants have a _____ partnership. The frog benefits, and the plant is neither helped nor harmed.

▲ A mosquito

Learn Academic Words

Study the **red** words and their meanings. You will find these words useful when talking and writing about informational texts. Write each word and its meaning in your notebook. After you read "Partnerships in Nature," try to use these words to respond to the text.

beneficial = good or useful		Having a partner can be **beneficial** to organisms. They can help each other survive.
interact = talk to other people and work together with them		The partners **interact** with one another as they work together.
partnership = a relationship in which two or more people, organizations, etc., work together to achieve something		The green sea anemone and the crab work together. They have a **partnership**.
role = the position or job that something or someone has in a particular situation or activity		The sea anemone's **role** is to protect the crab from predators.

Practice

Workbook Page 87

Work with a partner to answer these questions. Try to include the **red** word in your answer. Write the sentences in your notebook.

1. How can working with a partner in the classroom be **beneficial**?
2. Can you think of a time when you worked with a classmate to complete a project? How did you **interact** with one another?
3. What did or did not make this **partnership** successful?
4. What was your **role** within the partnership?

The partnership between the green sea anemone and the crab benefits both organisms. ▶

182

Word Study: Greek and Latin Roots *para*, *sitos*, *virus*, *nutrire*

Many English words have their origins in the Greek and Latin languages. Knowing word roots can help you understand the meanings of unfamiliar words. Read the words and roots in the chart below.

Word	Greek or Latin	Root(s)	Meaning
parasite	Greek	para sitos	beside food
virus	Latin	virus	poison, sap of plants
nutrition	Latin	nutrire	nourish

Practice

Workbook Page 88

Work with a partner. Copy the chart below into your notebook. Complete the chart with an English word that originates from each Greek and Latin root. Use a dictionary if necessary.

Root	Greek or Latin	Meaning	Word
auto	Greek	self	
dent	Greek	teeth	
script	Latin	write	
terra	Latin	earth	

READING STRATEGY   CLASSIFY

Classifying information helps you organize new ideas and facts. It also makes it easier to understand the text. To classify, follow these steps:

- As you read, make a list of new information that you learn.
- When you finish, review your list. Decide which facts are most important. Think about how the ideas or facts are similar and different. Think about how they are related.
- Group the facts and ideas together under different headings, according to their subject.

As you read "Partnerships in Nature," list all of the new information that you learn. When you finish reading, group similar information together. Use a graphic organizer to help you.

Workbook Page 89

Set a purpose for reading As you read, identify the different function(s) of each partnership. Which partner has the most to gain from the relationship?

Partnerships in Nature

Many kinds of relationships exist in nature. One of these relationships is called symbiosis. It is a partnership between different organisms. The word *symbiosis* means "life together."

Organisms enter symbiotic relationships for many reasons: to find food, shelter, or protection, or to keep themselves clean.

Many symbiotic relationships are mutualistic. Mutualistic organisms help each other survive. Both partners gain something from the relationship. The photograph below shows two organisms in a mutualistic relationship.

---

organisms, living things

The bird, a red-billed oxpecker, often rides on the buffalo's body. It is difficult to imagine that a small bird like an oxpecker could help a large animal like the buffalo. However, the oxpecker provides the buffalo with protection. It calls out a warning if it sees the buffalo is in danger. If the buffalo does not respond quickly, the oxpecker will peck at the buffalo's head.

The oxpecker also pecks ticks off of the buffalo's body. Then the oxpecker feeds on the ticks and the blood they took from the buffalo.

---

peck, strike or eat by making quick stabbing motions with its head

ticks, tiny insects that live on other animals and drink their blood

Red-billed oxpeckers ride on a buffalo. ▶

▲ An acacia bush and stinging ants

Did you know that a bush can be part of a mutualistic relationship? For example, the acacia bush and stinging ants work together to survive.

The acacia bush is covered with thorns that keep small animals away. But larger animals are still able to eat the thorns; the acacia bush needs additional protection to survive. So it produces a nectar, or sweet liquid, at the base of its leaves. This nectar attracts stinging ants. To stay near this new food source, the ants hollow out the bush's thorns, and they create colonies within them.

In return, the ants sting insects, animals, or humans that come into contact with the bush. They provide the bush with additional protection.

How important are the ants to the bush? In an experiment, scientists killed the ants on an acacia bush with insecticide. Without its partners, the bush was unable to survive.

thorns, sharp needles that grow on some plants
hollow out, remove everything from inside
colonies, communities

insecticide, a chemical that kills insects

BEFORE YOU GO ON

1 What does *symbiosis* mean?

2 Describe the relationship between the acacia bush and stinging ants.

On Your Own
Do you know of any other mutualistic relationships in nature? What are they?

185

▲ An orchid grows within the fork of a tree.

In a commensal relationship, one partner benefits from the relationship, while the other partner is neither helped nor harmed.

Orchids and trees are commensal partners. Orchids are plants. Some orchids live on trees in the tropical rainforest. By living high above the ground, the orchids get the light, air, and water they need for photosynthesis. If the orchids lived on the forest floor, the dense tree cover above would keep them from getting the nutrients they need to survive. In addition, living high above the forest floor protects the orchids from land-based animals or predators. The trees are neither helped nor harmed by this relationship.

Many birds gather grasses and twigs to make nests in trees. The birds and the trees are commensal partners. The birds receive protection and shelter. The trees are neither helped nor harmed by this relationship.

---

tropical rainforest, forest near the equator that gets a lot of rain
photosynthesis, process by which plants turn sunlight into food
dense, thick

---

nutrients, chemicals in food
predators, organisms that live by eating other organisms

186

Remora fish participate in commensal relationships. The remora fish has a special suction cup on its head. The remora uses this disk to attach itself to larger creatures like manta rays, sea turtles, whales, or sharks. For example, look at the remora on the right. It has attached itself to a napolean fish.

By attaching itself to the napolean fish, the remora fish gains protection from predators. It also gets a free ride from place to place. Most importantly, the napolean fish provides the remora with food—it leaves food scraps floating in the water. The remora quickly swims free and helps itself to these leftover scraps.

Barnacles and whales engage in a similar relationship. Barnacles attach themselves to a whale. They feed on the whale's leftover scraps. Like the napolean fish, the whale does not gain from this partnership, but it is not harmed by it either.

▲ A remora fish attached to a napolean fish

---

suction cup, device that sticks to something by creating a vacuum

▲ Barnacles attached to a whale

BEFORE YOU GO ON

1 Who benefits in a commensal relationship?

2 Which organism, the orchids or the tree, benefits from their commensal relationship? In what way(s)?

On Your Own
Have you ever witnessed one of these commensal relationships in nature? If so, which one? Where did you see it?

187

In a parasitic relationship, one partner, called a parasite, often benefits from a larger organism, called a host. A parasite is like a predator. It hurts the host animal. Some parasites can also spread infectious, sometimes deadly, diseases. However, the parasite never directly kills the host. After all, if the host dies, the parasite can also die.

Animals such as horses, dogs, and cats often play unwilling hosts to parasites. For example, horses often host worms called leeches. A leech can burrow beneath a horse's flesh and suck its blood.

A flea is another kind of parasite that feeds on blood. A flea often attaches itself to a dog or a cat. However, a flea does not stay with its host for long. After the flea bites the host, it jumps away. Like the flea, some parasites find new hosts often. Other parasites stay with the same host their entire lives.

---

burrow, dig
flesh, soft part of a body

▲ A flea

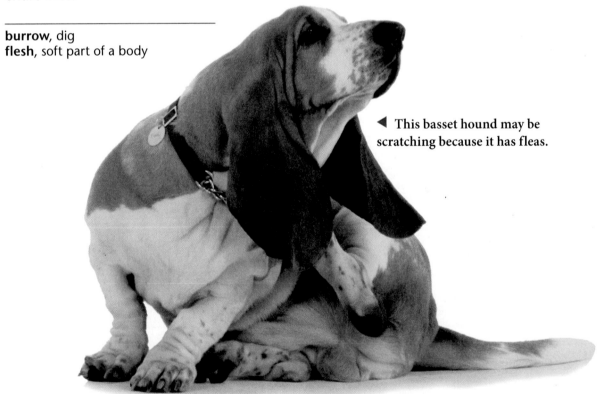

◀ This basset hound may be scratching because it has fleas.

188

Humans can also be hosts in parasitic relationships. Have you ever been bitten by mosquitoes? They are parasites that feed on your blood.

A tick is a parasite that lives in a wooded or grassy area. After attaching itself to a person or an animal, a tick burrows beneath the host's skin and feeds on its blood. Ticks can also be hosts to other parasites, some of which carry and transmit Lyme disease.

Unlike mosquitoes and ticks, most parasites live within their hosts. Have you ever had a cold or the flu? These illnesses are caused by microscopic parasites, called viruses. A virus lives inside your body. The virus receives shelter from your body and nutrition from your body's cells, which help the virus reproduce. In the process, the parasite makes you sick.

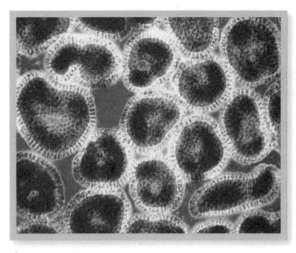

▲ The influenza virus

◀ The influenza virus is a parasite that often causes people to become ill.

BEFORE YOU GO ON

1 What is a parasitic relationship?

2 How do the relationships between some parasites and their hosts differ from others?

On Your Own
In what different kinds of parasitic relationships can humans be involved?

189

COMPREHENSION

Workbook
Page 90

Right There

1. What kind of partnership do the red-billed oxpecker and buffalo have? How does each partner benefit from the relationship?

2. What special bodily feature allows a remora fish to attach itself to its partner?

Think and Search

3. Name three different symbiotic relationships.

4. Name the organisms involved in two different parasitic partnerships.

Author and You

5. What characteristics does the author use to categorize symbiotic relationships?

6. Why do you think the author chose to write about partnerships in nature?

On Your Own

7. Have you ever been a host to a virus? How did it make you feel?

8. Which partnership did you like reading about the most and why?

IN YOUR OWN WORDS

Copy the chart below into your notebook. In the second column, write examples of symbiotic relationships that were discussed in the reading. Then use the information in the chart to summarize the reading for a partner.

Type of Relationship	Example
Mutualistic	
Commensal	
Parasitic	

DISCUSSION

Discuss in pairs or small groups.

1. Discuss the benefits of each symbiotic relationship mentioned in the reading.

2. How can some symbiotic relationships be harmful to organisms?

Q **How are relationships with others important?** You read about the partnerships that some organisms in nature have with one another. What would life be like for these organisms without these relationships?

Listening TIP

Listen for key words and important details. Take notes to help you remember this information.

READ FOR FLUENCY

When we read aloud to communicate meaning, we group words into phrases, pause or slow down to make important points, and emphasize important words. Pause for a short time when you reach a comma and for a longer time when you reach a period. Pay attention to rising and falling intonation at the end of sentences.

Work with a partner. Choose a paragraph from the reading. Discuss which words seem important for communicating meaning. Practice pronouncing difficult words. Give each other feedback.

EXTENSION  **Workbook** Page 90

Work with a partner. Think about the three types of symbiotic partnerships described in the article. Which type did you think was the most interesting? Go to the library or use the Internet to learn about other organisms that participate in this kind of partnership. Pair this information with pictures to create your own science article. Share it with your classmates.

A student conducting research at the library ▶

Compound and Complex Sentences

A compound sentence is two or more simple sentences joined together. Each simple sentence is an independent clause. Remember, an independent clause has a subject and a verb and is a complete sentence. The conjunctions *and, but, or, so,* and *yet* are used to join two independent clauses. Read the examples below from "Partnerships in Nature."

> The ants hollow out the bush's thorns, **and** they create colonies within them.
>
> The whale does not gain from this partnership, **but** it is not harmed by it either.

A complex sentence has one independent clause and one or more dependent clauses. Remember, a dependent clause has a subject and a verb, but it is not a complete sentence. A dependent clause often begins with an adverb, such as *after, when, since, as,* or *before.* The first clause in a complex sentence may be dependent or independent. Use a comma when the first clause is a dependent clause.

> The flea flies away **after** it bites the host.
>
> **When** the napolean fish swims by, the remora fish attaches itself to its body.

Practice

Work with a partner. Take turns reading the following sentences to each other. Identify whether the sentence is compound or complex.

1. After it attaches itself to a person or an animal, a tick burrows beneath the skin.
2. As the shark eats, it leaves food scraps floating in the water.
3. The shark swam away as the whale approached the reef.
4. When a shark swims by, the remora fish attaches itself to the shark's body.
5. Thorns on the acacia bush keep small animals away, but larger animals are still able to eat them.

WRITING AN EXPOSITORY PARAGRAPH

Write a Classifying Paragraph

You have already learned about three types of expository writing: instructions, critiques, and compare-and-contrast paragraphs. Classifying objects and writing about them is another kind of expository writing.

Bald eagles	Bottlenose dolphins	Meerkats

Classification is the process of putting people or things into groups, called categories, according to the qualities they share. In the reading "Partnerships in Nature," the author classifies symbiotic relationships into three categories: mutualistic, commensal, and parasitic. Each relationship is defined by its positive or negative effects on other living creatures.

Here is a model paragraph. The writer used a three-column chart to organize her ideas before writing. Notice how she clearly explains and presents each category.

Katie Veneziano

Parenting Styles in Nature

Many animals care for their young until their offspring can survive on their own. The bald eagle, the bottlenose dolphin, and the meerkat all care for their young in different ways. Male and female bald eagles share the duty of sitting on their eggs. One parent watches the eggs while the other looks for food. After the eaglets hatch, they live with their parents for eight to fourteen weeks. Bottlenose dolphins mostly live in tropical waters, and the female dolphins usually have a baby about every three years. The baby, or calf, will live with its mother for up to six years. Unlike bald eagles, male dolphins are not involved in raising their young. Young meerkats are not cared for by their parents, but by surrounding female meerkats. When the young meerkats leave the burrow, these females protect them from predators.

Practice
Workbook
Page 92

Write a paragraph in which you classify something. For example, you could write about movies and classify them into three categories: comedy, drama, and action. List your ideas in a graphic organizer. Be sure to use compound and complex sentences correctly.

Writing Checklist

ORGANIZATION:
☑ I organized my writing in a way that makes my categories clear.

WORD CHOICE:
☑ I chose words that clearly explained the characteristics of each group.

193

Link the Readings

Critical Thinking

Look back at the readings in this unit. Think about what they have in common. They all tell about relationships. Yet they do not all have the same purpose. The purpose of one reading might be to inform, while the purpose of another might be to entertain or persuade. In addition, the content of each reading relates to relationships differently. Now copy the chart below into your notebook and complete it.

Title of Reading	Purpose	Big Question Link
"Aguinaldo," from *Salsa Stories*		*A young girl makes a new friend.*
"Sowing the Seeds of Peace"		
From *Blue Willow*		
"Partnerships in Nature"	*to inform*	

Discussion

Discuss in pairs or small groups.

● How are the relationships between the campers in "Sowing the Seeds of Peace" similar to the relationship between Marilia and Elenita in "Aguinaldo"?

Q **How are relationships with others important?** What do you think is important about each relationship within the readings? What are the most important relationships in your life? What makes them important to you?

Fluency Check

Work with a partner. Choose a paragraph from one of the readings. Take turns reading it for one minute. Count the total number of words you read. Practice saying the words you had trouble reading. Take turns reading the paragraph three more times. Did you read more words each time? Copy the chart below into your notebook and record your speeds.

	1st Speed	2nd Speed	3rd Speed	4th Speed
Words Per Minute				

Projects

Work in pairs or small groups. Choose one of these projects.

1 Think about foods that are part of your family's tradition. Write two or three of your favorite family recipes on note cards. Include a list of the necessary materials and instructions for what to do with those materials. Share the recipes with your classmates. Describe why your recipes are special. Then combine your recipes to make a class cookbook.

2 You read about the Seeds of Peace International Camp. Write an informational brochure that describes the camp's mission, location, and programs. The brochure should make people understand what makes this camp special. Then share it with the class.

3 In the legend *Blue Willow*, both Kung Shi Fair and Chang the Good die tragically. Rewrite the final scenes of the legend to include a description of their lives together had they lived. Illustrate your new ending. Then share it with the class.

Further Reading

To find out more about the theme of this unit, choose from these reading suggestions.

The Scarlet Letter, Nathaniel Hawthorne
In this Penguin Reader® adaptation of the classic story, a young woman in seventeenth-century New England is scorned by her community. She and her baby face a harsh punishment.

Under the Royal Palms: A Childhood in Cuba, Alma Flor Ada
The author recollects growing up in a small Cuban town and the many people who touched her life, including her grandmother, a mysterious uncle, and a dance teacher who helped her through a difficult year at school.

Shabanu: Daughter of the Wind, Suzanne Fisher Staples
Life is both sweet and cruel to strong-willed Shabanu, whose home is a windswept desert of Pakistan. When a tragic encounter with a wealthy landowner ruins the marriage plans of her older sister, Shabanu is asked to sacrifice everything she's dreamed of.

LISTENING & SPEAKING WORKSHOP

How-To Demonstration

You will tell and show the class how to do something.

1 THINK ABOUT IT Have you ever shown a friend or family member how to do something? Think about everyday tasks you know how to do well, such as washing dishes or making a bed. How would you tell someone else to do these tasks? Review the use of imperative verbs to give commands and instructions.

Work together to develop a list of ideas for a how-to demonstration. Think of interesting activities that you could demonstrate in class. For example:

- How to make a sandwich
- How to organize your CDs and DVDs
- How to use a digital camera
- How to ride a skateboard

2 GATHER AND ORGANIZE INFORMATION Choose a topic from your group's list. Begin by thinking about how you learned to do this activity. Then make a list of the steps involved. Remember to include small steps that are obvious to you but that someone else might not think about. Write down any remaining questions you may have about how to do the activity.

Research Go to the library, talk to an adult, or search the Internet for more information. Look for answers to your questions. Take notes on what you find.

Order Your Notes Revise your list of steps based on your research. Then write each step on a separate note card. Think about the best order in which to present the steps. Arrange your note cards in this order, and then number them.

Use Visuals Find or make props you can use to show key steps in your demonstration. You can also create posters, models, or other visuals to help you.

3 **PRACTICE AND PRESENT** Practice your demonstration until you know it well. Begin by telling your audience what you will demonstrate for them. Glance at your note cards while you speak, but don't read from them. Use your visuals and props to help you explain or act out each step. If possible, ask friends or family members to listen and give you feedback. Can they hear and understand what you are saying? Keep practicing until you feel relaxed and confident.

Deliver Your How-To Demonstration Make sure your note cards are in order and your visuals are ready before you begin. Look at your audience as you speak. Think about each step as you explain it. Emphasize imperative verbs by changing the tone of your voice. Slow down when you come to the most important points. At the end of the demonstration, give your audience a chance to ask questions.

4 **EVALUATE THE PRESENTATION**
You will improve your skills as a speaker and a listener by evaluating each presentation you give and hear. Use this checklist to help you judge your oral report and the reports of your classmates.

- ☑ Did the speaker present the steps in a clear sequence?
- ☑ Do you feel that you were given enough information to complete the activity on your own?
- ☑ Did the speaker use props and other visuals effectively?
- ☑ Did the speaker answer your questions?
- ☑ What suggestions do you have for improving the demonstration?

Speaking TIPS

Highlight the most important words on your note cards so that you can see them easily.

Use ordinal numbers (*first, second, third . . .*) and sequence words (*before, next, then, finally*) to clearly explain the order of your steps.

Listening TIPS

Watch and listen carefully. Give the speaker your full attention.

Think about what you are hearing. Does it make sense? Would you be able to explain the steps to someone else? Write down questions and ask them at the end of the demonstration.

WRITING WORKSHOP
Expository Essay

You have been learning how to write a variety of expository paragraphs. Now, you will use your skills to write an expository essay. An expository essay is a group of paragraphs that gives information about a topic. A good expository essay begins with a paragraph that introduces the writer's topic and purpose. The writer develops the topic in two or more body paragraphs. Each body paragraph presents a main idea supported by facts and details. A concluding paragraph sums up the important information in the essay.

Your writing assignment for this workshop is to expand one of the paragraphs you wrote for this unit into a five-paragraph essay.

1 **PREWRITE** Brainstorm a list of topics in your notebook. Are you fascinated by crocodiles? Do you like to read about pandas? Have you always wanted to know more about ostriches? Do reptiles, mammals, or birds most interest you? You will probably need to do some research to write your essay. Use sources such as books and magazines about animals, websites, or encyclopedias.

List and Organize Ideas and Details Use a graphic organizer such as a Venn diagram, T-chart, or three-column chart to organize information for your essay. A student named Katie decided to write about how three different animal species relate to their offspring. Here is her three-column chart:

Bald Eagle	Bottlenose Dolphin	Meerkat
bird species	mammal species	mammal species
both father and mother sit on and guard eggs	mother raises offspring	young raised communally by females in colony
eggs hatch after about 35 days	young stay with mother for up to 6 years	young leave burrow at 21 days old
young stay with parents until able to care for selves—about 14 weeks		group continues to protect young

2 **DRAFT** Use the model on page 201 and your graphic organizer to help you write a first draft. Remember to introduce your topic in your first paragraph and to support your main ideas with facts and details.

3 **REVISE** Read over your draft. As you do so, ask yourself the questions in the writing checklist. Use the questions to help you revise your essay.

SIX TRAITS OF WRITING CHECKLIST

☑ **IDEAS:** Is my topic about animal parents and their offspring in the wild?

☑ **ORGANIZATION:** Do I present information in an order that makes sense?

☑ **VOICE:** Does my writing show my knowledge of my topic?

☑ **WORD CHOICE:** Do I use linking words to connect ideas?

☑ **SENTENCE FLUENCY:** Do I include compound and complex sentences?

☑ **CONVENTIONS:** Does my writing follow the rules of grammar, usage, and mechanics?

Here are the changes Katie plans to make when she revises her first draft:

Animal Parents and Their Young

Many animals in the wild care for their young. ~~Then~~ *until* their offspring can survive on their own. *However* Animals have different ways of raising their young. The bald eagle, the bottlenose dolphin, and the meerkat are examples of animals that care for their young in different ways.

The bald eagle is the national bird of the united States. The male and female of this species share the duty of incubating the eggs. While one parent watches the eggs the other looks for nesting material or food. Incubation lasts about thirty-five days. *Once* The eaglets are hatched. They continue to live with their parents for eight to fourteen weeks. By then, the eaglets can fend for themselves.

The bottlenose dolphin is a marine mammal that lives mostly in
tropical waters. Usually, a female dolphin will have a baby, called a
calf, about every three years. A calf lives with its mother for up to
six years. Male ^bottlenose dolphins are not involved in raising their offspring.
~~During this time, a calf is taught how to find food and survive.~~

A meerkat is a small African mongoose that lives in communal
burrows. The male meerkat ^like the male bottlenose dolphin does not get involved in raising its young.
Instead, the young are communally raised with the assistance of other
females. After about twenty-one days, the young leave the burrow.
but
^They are still cared for by the group In fact, female "babysitter"
meerkats act as lookouts near the burrow to protect the young
from predators.

All three of these animal species brood their young. However,
different animals live with their parents for different periods of time.
In addition
^The young of some species are raised by both parents. ^and The young of
other species are raised by one parent or by the group. The examples
of the bald eagle the bottlenose dolphin, and the meerkat show
                              in how animal species care for their offspring
similarities and differences ^.

4 **EDIT AND PROOFREAD**
Workbook
Page 93

Copy your revised essay onto a clean sheet of paper. Read it again. Correct
any errors in grammar, word usage, mechanics, and spelling. Here are the
additional changes Katie plans to make when she prepares her final draft.

Katie Veneziano

Animal Parents and Their Young

Many animals in the wild care for their young until their offspring can survive on their own. However, animals have different ways of raising their young. The bald eagle, the bottlenose dolphin, and the meerkat are examples of animals that care for their young in different ways.

The bald eagle is the national bird of the united States. The male and female of this species share the duty of incubating the eggs. While one parent watches the eggs, the other looks for nesting material or food. Incubation lasts about thirty-five days. Once the eaglets are hatched, they continue to live with their parents for eight to fourteen weeks. By then, the eaglets can fend for themselves.

The bottlenose dolphin is a marine mammal that lives mostly in temperate and tropical waters. Usually, a female dolphin will have a baby, called a calf, about every three years. A calf lives with its mother for up to six years. During this time, a calf is taught how to find food and survive. Male bottlenose dolphins are not involved in raising their offspring.

A meerkat is a small African mongoose that lives in communal burrows. The male meerkat, like the male bottlenose dolphin, does not get involved in raising its young. Instead, the young are communally raised with the assistance of other females. After about twenty-one days, the young leave the burrow, but they are still cared for by the group. In fact, female "babysitter" meerkats act as lookouts near the burrow to protect the young from predators.

All three of these animal species brood their young. However, different animals live with their parents for different periods of time. In addition, the young of some species are raised by both parents, and the young of other species are raised by one parent or by the group. The examples of the bald eagle, the bottlenose dolphin, and the meerkat show similarities and differences in how animal species care for their offspring.

5 **PUBLISH** Prepare your final draft. Share your essay with your teacher and classmates.

Workbook
Page 94

Embracing Family, Friends, and Neighbors

All people have relationships in their lives. The way you act with a parent may be different from the way you act with a friend. But both relationships may offer something important to your life. American artists have used all sorts of media to capture this idea.

Franz Kline, *Merce C* (1961)

In this large oil painting, Franz Kline painted bold black brushstrokes against a white background. Kline wanted the painting to celebrate the talent of his friend Merce Cunningham, a dancer and choreographer. Kline uses only two colors, black and white, in *Merce C*, but the viewer feels motion and excitement anyway. Kline probably used his whole body to create the wide brushstrokes, which push against the border of the canvas. He even lets spatters and drops of black paint show on the canvas. Kline did this to celebrate the unexpected movements Cunningham made in his dances. Although this may not look like a traditional portrait of his friend, Kline's painting captures a very physical grace. Some people think it looks like dancers moving.

Franz Kline, *Merce C*, ▶
1961, oil, 93 x 74⅝ in.,
Smithsonian American Art Museum

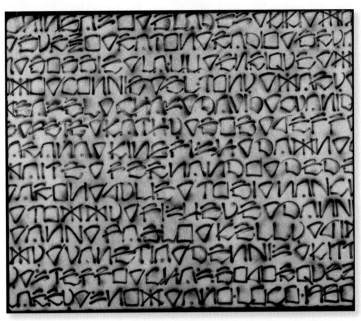

▲ Charles "Chaz" Bojórquez, *Placa/Rollcall*, 1980, acrylic, 68¼ x 83⅛ in., Smithsonian American Art Museum

Charles "Chaz" Bojórquez, *Placa/Rollcall* (1980)

In *Placa/Rollcall*, artist Charles "Chaz" Bojórquez uses stylized letters to create a painting. His painting is a wall of words that celebrates the names of his family, friends, and mentors, or teachers.

Bojórquez grew up in East Los Angeles, California. Gangs there often wrote graffiti on public places to list their members' names. Bojórquez turns this practice around. He celebrates people who have made a positive contribution to his life. He created his own secret alphabet to do it. For example, Bojórquez's *Y* is a triangle with a dot underneath it. He starts in the upper-left corner with his girlfriend's name and ends in the lower-right corner with the date. Once you adjust to the patterns in the lettering, you can find many names you'll recognize, including Tony, Tommy, Fernando, and Connie. Bojórquez sprayed the names against a huge 7-foot-wide gray-colored canvas so the painting would look like a wall or *placa* (Spanish for "plaque") of honor.

These two artists show how important caring relationships are, either in their own lives or in the lives of the people around them.

Apply What You Learned

1 In what way does a wall of words honor people's lives? Do you know about other walls of words that do this?

2 In what way are these artworks different from those you might expect to see about friends and family relationships? Explain.

Big Question
What kind of artwork would you create to celebrate the relationships in your life?

Workbook
Pages 95–96

UNIT 4

What does home mean?

This unit is about home. You will read texts about homes immigrants lived in long ago, how some whooping cranes learn to find their way home, and the feelings people experience when they are far from home. Reading, writing, and talking about these topics will give you practice using academic language and help you become a better student.

READING 1: Social Studies Articles

- "97 Orchard Street"
- "The Pros and Cons of Tenement Life"

READING 2: Short Story

- "Somebody's Son" by Richard Pindell

READING 3: Science Article

- "Operation Migration" by Joyce Styron Madsen

READING 4: Poetry

- *The Lotus Seed* by Sherry Garland

Listening and Speaking

At the end of this unit, you will choose a topic and deliver a **TV news show** about it.

Writing

In this unit you will practice **expository writing**, which tells factual information about a topic. After each reading, you will learn a skill to help you write an expository paragraph. At the end of the unit, you will use these skills to help you write an expository essay.

QuickWrite

In your notebook, write a few sentences that describe your home. Share them with a partner.

Visit *LongmanKeystone.com*

Prepare to Read

What You Will Learn

Reading
- Vocabulary building: *Context, dictionary skills, word study*
- Reading strategy: *Identify author's purpose*
- Text type: *Informational texts (social studies)*

Grammar, Usage, and Mechanics
Adjective clauses with *who* and *which*

Writing
Write a magazine article

 THE BIG QUESTION

What does home mean? Why might someone leave their home country? What do you know about immigrants that came to the United States in the mid-1800s to early 1900s? Take the quiz below to find out. Then share your answers with a partner.

1. All immigrants came from Europe.   True / False
2. Immigrants came to America for different reasons.   True / False
3. Most immigrants found high-paying jobs.   True / False
4. Immigrants in large cities often lived in large houses with lots of space.   True / False

BUILD BACKGROUND

"97 Orchard Street" is an informational article. It provides factual information about a tenement museum located in New York City. The article is followed by **"The Pros and Cons of Tenement Life."** It lists both the advantages and disadvantages of living in tenements.

A tenement is a large building that is divided into many apartments. At the turn of the twentieth century, many immigrants from around the world left their homelands to come to the United States. They came to find jobs, to escape violence and discrimination, to get an education, or to own property.

After they arrived, many poor immigrants lived in tenements. Often as many as eight to ten people lived in one small apartment, many of which did not have running water or indoor plumbing. This led to unsanitary conditions. In addition, the tenements themselves were often in disrepair and unsafe.

◀ Immigrants on Ellis Island, near New York City, in 1907

VOCABULARY

Learn Key Words

Read these sentences. Use the context to figure out the meaning of the red words. Use a dictionary to check your answers. Then write each word and its meaning in your notebook.

Key Words

exhibit
inspectors
mission
neighborhood
preserved
tenement

1. The museum **exhibit** displays children's toys from the 1800s.

2. The fire **inspectors** decided it was safe for people to live in the building.

3. The museum's **mission** is to provide its visitors with historical information about immigrants and how they lived.

4. There are many people who live in that area, or **neighborhood**.

5. The museum **preserved** the old buildings, or kept them from being destroyed.

6. Eight people lived together in one small apartment within the **tenement**.

Practice

Workbook Page 97

Write the sentences in your notebook. Choose a red word from the box above to complete each sentence. Then take turns reading the sentences aloud with a partner.

1. That family just moved into the apartment building across the street. They are new to the _____.

2. Early tools and inventions are displayed in the science _____.

3. The old wedding dress looks new. It has been carefully _____.

4. The _____ forced the building's owner to install lights in the stairways.

5. The crowded _____ was home to many families.

6. The school's _____ was to help immigrants learn English quickly.

▲ An immigrant family of seven in their one-room tenement apartment

Learn Academic Words

Study the **red** words and their meanings. You will find these words useful when talking and writing about informational texts. Write each word and its meaning in your notebook. After you read "97 Orchard Street" and "The Pros and Cons of Tenement Life," try to use these words to respond to the texts.

Academic Words

benefit
community
cultural
immigrants
items

benefit = something that helps you or gives you an advantage	➡	One **benefit** of living in a small town is that you know your neighbors.
community = all the people living in one place	➡	New York City's SoHo district is known as a **community** of artists.
cultural = relating to a particular society and its way of life	➡	The Jewish Museum offers many **cultural** programs. They teach art, music, and crafts.
immigrants = people who enter another country in order to live there	➡	In the early 1900s, many **immigrants** left their homelands and came to America.
items = things in a set, group, or list	➡	The museum displays **items** that immigrants brought from their home countries.

Practice  **Workbook Page 98**

Work with a partner to answer these questions. Try to include the **red** word in your answer. Write the sentences in your notebook.

1. What is one **benefit** of living in your town?
2. How would you describe your **community**?
3. What kinds of **cultural** events take place at your school or in your neighborhood?
4. Do you know any **immigrants**? Where are they from?
5. If you had to move to a new country, what **items** would you bring with you?

Immigrant artifacts ▶

208

Word Study: Silent Letters

In English there are certain letter combinations in which one letter is "silent." It is important to know these combinations when spelling many words. Here are some common combinations: *gn*, *bt*, *mb*, and *kn*.

Words with Silent Letters	Letter Combination	Sound	Silent Letter
campai**gn**	gn	/n/	g
de**bt**	bt	/t/	b
cli**mb**	mb	/m/	b
knock	kn	/n/	k

Practice  Workbook Page 99

Work with a partner. Take turns reading and spelling the words in the box. Copy the words into your notebook. Underline the letter combinations *gn*, *bt*, *mb*, and *kn* and circle the silent letters.

align	doubtful	knife	lamb
comb	foreign	know	subtle

READING STRATEGY | IDENTIFY AUTHOR'S PURPOSE

Identifying an author's purpose (or reason for writing) can help you analyze information better. Three of the most common reasons authors write are to inform, to entertain, and to persuade. To identify an author's purpose, ask yourself the following questions as you read:

- Is this entertaining? Am I enjoying this text?
- Am I learning new information from the text?
- Is the author trying to persuade me about something or change my opinion?

An author can have many reasons for writing. As you read "97 Orchard Street" and "The Pros and Cons of Tenement Life," try to identify what the purpose is, and also whether the author has more than one purpose for writing.

 Workbook Page 100

Set a purpose for reading As you read, think about what it was like for immigrants to live in tenements. How do you think immigrants made the tenements feel like home?

97 Orchard Street

Have you ever visited New York City and seen the Statue of Liberty? Have you ever walked through Ellis Island and strolled around Castle Clinton? These landmarks symbolize the welcoming of immigrants to a new life. But did you ever wonder what happened *after* immigrants arrived in the United States? We suggest you make one more stop on the Immigrant Heritage Trail—97 Orchard Street.

At this address, you will find a tenement building. It is located in the most famous immigrant neighborhood in America. Built in 1863, this structure is the first home of urban poor and immigrant people to be preserved in the United States. Restored and run by the Lower East Side Tenement Museum, the building allows us to travel back in time. Visitors can see firsthand the immigrant experience at the turn of the twentieth century.

---

landmarks, buildings or important, historical places
symbolize, represent
restored, made to look like it used to

The Lower East Side Tenement Museum ▶

▲ An unrestored tenement apartment

▲ The same tenement apartment after its restoration

The only way to explore the museum is through a guided tour. Carefully restored apartments reflect the lives of residents from different historical periods and cultures. You will hear the stories of immigrant families who struggled to make a life in America.

Learn about the impact of economic depressions on the Gumpertz family in the 1870s. Discover the imaginative ways this family made their way through hard times. A visit to the Levines' 1890 apartment illustrates the Lower East Side's connection to the nation's garment industry. It also shows the impact this type of work had on immigrant families.

In one museum exhibit, a costumed woman portrays immigrant Victoria Confino. This is a hands-on experience. You can touch any items in the apartment, try on period clothing, and dance to music played on a wind-up Victrola. Victoria will answer any questions about life in 1916.

An unrestored apartment in the building drives home the nineteenth-century reform movement's campaign for improved housing. Here you can participate in a program that lets you role-play. You can pretend to be a housing inspector: Determine what is acceptable housing at different times, and learn how people fought for better housing. Visitors also learn about housing rights today and how to report housing problems.

economic depressions, times when many people are out of work
garment industry, businesses that make clothes
period clothing, clothes that were worn long ago

Victrola, music player that sits inside a cabinet
reform movement, movement intended to bring about change
campaign, series of actions intended to achieve a particular result

BEFORE YOU GO ON

1 What is located at 97 Orchard Street?

2 What kinds of exhibits can visitors see there?

On Your Own
Would you want to visit the tenement museum? Why or why not?

▲ A Lower East Side street scene in early 1900s

The museum offers public tours and school tours. More than 25,000 schoolchildren each year participate in the site's original programs, which use history to teach tolerance. You can also take part in discussions of current issues such as immigration, labor, and social welfare. And walking tours of the Lower East Side describe the neighborhood's role as the nation's most famous gateway for immigrants.

An important part of the museum's mission is addressing current social issues by looking back at history. For example, immigrant students who visit the museum today use the diaries and letters of past immigrants to learn English.

To help unite the diverse community surrounding it, the museum has organized the Lower East Side Community Preservation Project. The project helps community leaders identify and restore local historic places. It is working currently to create historical markers at sites around the neighborhood. The sites represent the different groups who have lived in the neighborhood since the 1800s.

tolerance, the acceptance of other people and cultures as they are
social welfare, a government program that gives assistance to the poor

The Pros and Cons of Tenement Life

Pros (+):

Closeness to work: Tenement residents had a difficult time finding transportation to bring them to work. Living and working close together made life easier.

Fraternity: Immigrants sharing the same backgrounds often lived in the same neighborhoods. In this way, they found support in fraternal organizations. These groups offered help in finding jobs and places to live.

Assimilation: Living among people of the same background helped immigrants cope with the American way of life.

Amusements: Coney Island, nickelodeons, and dance halls offered nearby, inexpensive ways to have fun and relax. Taking strolls to see store windows and riding the trolley provided entertainment, too.

Cons (–):

Disease and poor sanitation: There was a high death rate among immigrants who lived in tenements. Health officials blamed this on overflowing garbage and lack of proper sanitary facilities.

Lack of outside air and ventilation: Prior to 1879, rooms in tenements were not required by law to have access to outside air. That meant that residents had to endure sweltering heat during the summer.

Darkness: One social worker nearly tripped over children sleeping in a tenement's dark hallway. Eventually, building owners were forced to install lights near the stairs.

Fire hazards: Wooden staircases, few windows, and overcrowding turned many tenements into death traps when a fire started.

---

fraternal organizations, groups of people, usually men, who consider each other brothers and support and help one another
nickelodeons, early movie theaters where a ticket cost five cents
sanitary facilities, services and equipment that keep buildings and streets clean
sweltering, extremely hot

BEFORE YOU GO ON

1 What is the Lower East Side Community Preservation Project? What is its goal?

2 In what ways were some tenements dangerous to live in?

On Your Own
Would you want to live in a tenement? Why or why not?

COMPREHENSION

Workbook
Page 101

Right There

1. When was the tenement at 97 Orchard Street originally built?

2. What can visitors to the museum's unrestored apartment learn about it?

Think and Search

3. In what ways could living in a tenement be beneficial to an immigrant?

4. What were some of the struggles immigrants faced in the United States?

Author and You

5. Why did so many immigrants choose to live in tenements?

6. What do you think was the author's purpose for writing this text?

On Your Own

7. Do you think the immigration experience is easier or harder today than it was 100 years ago? Explain.

8. People from all over the world continue to immigrate to the United States. Why?

▲ Nearby places like Coney Island in New York offered tenement residents inexpensive ways to have fun.

IN YOUR OWN WORDS

Copy the chart below into your notebook. Complete the chart with information from the article "97 Orchard Street." Then use the chart to summarize the reading for a partner.

"97 Orchard Street"	
Subject	**Details**
Museum location	97 Orchard Street, New York City
Museum exhibits	
Museum programs	

DISCUSSION

Discuss in pairs or small groups.

1. What are the missions of the tenement museum?
2. Which mission do you think is the most important and why?
Q **What does home mean?** Do you think it is difficult to create a new home in a new country? Why or why not?

Listening TIP

Listen for important details.

READ FOR FLUENCY

It is often easier to read a text if you understand the difficult words and phrases. Work with a partner. Choose a paragraph from the reading. Identify the words and phrases you do not know or have trouble pronouncing. Look up the difficult words in a dictionary.

Take turns pronouncing the words and phrases with your partner. If necessary, ask your teacher to model the correct pronunciation. Then take turns reading the paragraph aloud. Give each other feedback on your reading.

EXTENSION

Workbook Page 101

You have learned about immigrants that came to this country at the turn of the twentieth century. In particular, you learned about their reasons for coming, where they lived, their way of life, and how they worked.

What about immigrants today? How are they the same? How are they different? Work with a partner to find the answers to these questions on the Internet or in the library. Then organize your information in a Venn diagram like the one below. Write facts about each individual group in the corresponding circles. Write facts that are true about both groups in the middle of the diagram. Then share this information with the class.

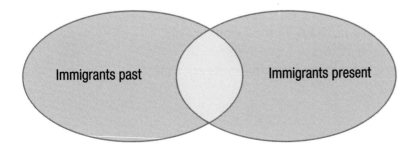

GRAMMAR, USAGE, AND MECHANICS

Adjective Clauses with *who* and *which*

Writers use adjective clauses to describe a noun in an independent clause. An adjective clause beginning with the relative pronoun *who* describes a person or people. In the following example the adjective clause *who lived in tenements* describes *immigrants*.

> There was a high death rate among immigrants. Immigrants lived in tenements.
>
>   independent clause   adjective clause
>
> There was a high death rate among immigrants **who** lived in tenements.

An adjective clause beginning with the relative pronoun *which* describes a thing or things. In the following example, the adjective clause *which teaches tolerance* describes *a program*.

> Students participate in a program. It teaches tolerance.
>
>   independent clause   adjective clause
>
> Students participate in a program **which** teaches tolerance.

Practice

Workbook Page 102

Copy the following sentences into your notebook. Choose *who* or *which* to complete each sentence. Then underline the noun that the adjective clause describes.

1. Many visitors (who / which) come to New York visit the Statue of Liberty.
2. There were charity workers (who / which) helped immigrants as they entered the country.
3. The museum ticket (who / which) is on the table is mine.
4. A costumed woman (who / which) portrays Victoria Confino discusses what it was like to live in 1916.
5. The diaries (who / which) were left behind by immigrants are used to teach students English.

WRITING AN EXPOSITORY PARAGRAPH

Who?	
What?	
Where?	
When?	
Why?	

Write a Magazine Article

At the end of this unit, you will write an expository essay. Expository writing tells factual information about a topic. A magazine article is one type of expository writing.

When you write a magazine article, you try to grab the reader's attention quickly with interesting information. Your article should answer as many of the 5Ws as possible. The 5Ws are *Who? What? Where? When?* and *Why?* The article "97 Orchard Street" answered the following questions: *Who created the tenement museum? What is displayed there? Where is it located? When was it built? Why was it created?*

Here is a model of a magazine article. Before writing, the writer listed her ideas in a graphic organizer.

Blaise Yafcak

A Museum Worth Visiting

Anyone who is curious about the way things work in nature should visit the lightning exhibit at the Museum of Science in Boston, Massachusetts. The Museum of Science is one of the most exciting science museums in the country, and the lightning exhibit, which is on permanent display, is a highlight of any tour. Visitors to Boston, residents of the city, kids, teenagers, and adults will all find the exhibit fascinating. It is located in a large amphitheater, which is where museum staff members describe how lightning is made. They explain how positive charges in the ground can be attracted to and collide with negative charges in a rain cloud. These collisions are what you see during a lightning storm. After the lesson, the museum staff actually replicates the process of colliding charges right in front of you! This thrilling exhibit can be seen whenever the museum is open to visitors. Check the museum's website for hours of admission.

Practice  **Workbook** Page 103

Write a magazine article about an event in your town such as the opening of a museum exhibit, a sporting event, or a concert. Use a graphic organizer. Be sure to include adjective clauses with *who* and *which* in your writing.

Writing Checklist

IDEAS:
☑ I answered the 5Ws in my article.

SENTENCE FLUENCY:
☑ I combined sentences using adjective clauses.

217

Prepare to Read

What You Will Learn

Reading
- Vocabulary building: *Literary terms, word study*
- Reading strategy: *Summarize*
- Text type: *Literature (short story)*

Grammar, Usage, and Mechanics
Adjectives and adverbs

Writing
Write a plot summary

 THE BIG QUESTION

What does home mean? We have all had arguments, or disagreements, with members of our family. Can you imagine ever being so angry that you would leave your family and home? Do you think it would be difficult to return home afterwards? Discuss with a partner.

BUILD BACKGROUND

In this section, you will read a fictional short story called **"Somebody's Son."** Like a novel, a short story consists of characters and a fully developed theme, or main idea. However, it is much shorter than a novel.

"Somebody's Son" is the story of a young man, named David, who ran away from home after arguing with his father. During his time away from home, David traveled by train and car to the West Coast, Mexico, and Canada. You will read about how David wanted to return home, how he wanted to repair the relationship with his father, and the journey that he took to get there.

Learn Literary Words

Literary Words

suspense
climax

Authors create **suspense** to keep readers interested. Suspense is a feeling of uncertainty about the outcome of a story. Suspense makes readers ask, "What will happen next?" Read the passage below to see how one author has created suspense.

> Jillian walked into the room. She had to find the missing letter. Surely, the letter would reveal who had stolen the diamond necklace. She could smell a faint, flowery perfume. Someone had just been there before her. But who? All of a sudden, she heard a rustling sound coming from the closet in the corner.

What questions does the passage leave you with? Are you curious to find out what happens next?

Most stories have a buildup of suspense that usually leads to a **climax**, or the moment of highest intensity. It is usually the most exciting part of the story. The passage below is an example.

> She whirled around and saw the closet door opening slowly. Jillian stepped back. Old Mrs. Wentworth came out of the closet. She was holding a piece of paper in her hand.
>
> "Mrs. Wentworth! What is that piece of paper?" Jillian asked.
>
> "It's the letter you're looking for, my dear. It tells who stole the diamond necklace," said Mrs. Wentworth.
>
> "Who stole it?" Jillian asked excitedly.
>
> Mrs. Wentworth walked toward the fireplace. She threw the paper into the burning flames and turned back to face Jillian.
>
> "I did, of course," she said. "And now, you have no way to prove it."

Practice  Workbook Page 104

In a small group, reread the passages above. Talk about how each passage made you feel. How was your response to the first passage different from your response to the second passage?

Learn Academic Words

Study the **red** words and their meanings. You will find these words useful when talking and writing about literature. Write each word and its meaning in your notebook. After you read "Somebody's Son," try to use these words to respond to the text.

correspond = write to someone and receive letters from him or her	⇒	Even though my cousin lives far away, we **correspond** by e-mail every day.
indicate = say or do something that shows what you want or intend to do	⇒	Students are supposed to **indicate** that they finished a test by laying their pencils on top of their papers.
occurs = happens	⇒	The reunion **occurs** every ten years.
transportation = the process or business of moving people or goods from one place to another	⇒	The only **transportation** available is a bus that leaves at 6:30 in the morning.

Practice

Workbook Page 105

Work with a partner to answer these questions. Try to include the **red** word in your answer. Write the sentences in your notebook.

1. How do you **correspond** with friends who live far away?

2. In what ways do you **indicate** to others how you feel about them?

3. Can you name an event that **occurs** in your town year after year?

4. What kinds of **transportation** do you use to get from place to place?

Using the computer is one way for friends to correspond with each other. ▶

Word Study: Homophones

Homophones are words that sound the same but are spelled differently and have different functions and meanings. For example, the words *see* and *sea* are homophones. *Sea* is a noun. *See* is a verb. Both words sound the same, but have different spellings and meanings.

| **sea** = a large area of salty water | The stormy *sea* has huge waves. |
| **see** = to perceive something with your eyes | The boy was sad to *see* the sun go down. |

Practice

Work with a partner. Read the sentences aloud. Copy them into your notebook. Then use one of the homophones in parentheses to complete each sentence. You can use a dictionary to help you.

1. (mail / male)
   a. The dog is not a female, it's a _____.
   b. They get their _____ at the post office.

2. (sun / son)
   a. Robert is Maria's _____.
   b. The _____ is shining brightly today.

3. (plane / plain)
   a. I like _____ yogurt, not the kind with fruit.
   b. The _____ is flying to California.

Now write sentences using these homophones: *cent / sent / scent*.

READING STRATEGY   SUMMARIZE

Summarizing helps you to understand and remember the most important points in the text. When you summarize, you find the main ideas and state them in a few short sentences. To summarize, follow these steps:

- Read the text. Then reread each paragraph or section.
- Decide what the main idea is in each paragraph or section. Make notes. Leave out details. Just focus on the most important points.
- Write a few sentences that summarize the main ideas. Use your own words.

As you read "Somebody's Son," stop from time to time to note the main ideas. Summarize the text in two or three sentences.

Set a purpose for reading As you read, think about why David wants to return home. What about his home is important to him?

Somebody's Son

Richard Pindell

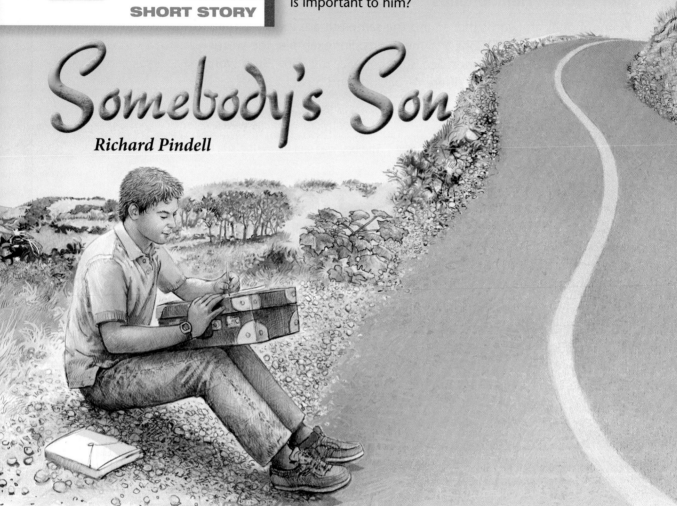

He sat, washed up on the side of the highway, a slim, sun-beaten driftwood of a youth. He was hunched on his strapped-together suitcase, chin on hands, elbows on knees, staring down the road. Not a car was in sight.

Now he was eager to write that letter he had kept putting off. Somehow, writing it would be almost like having company.

He unstrapped his suitcase and fished out of the pocket on the underside of the lid a small, unopened package of stationery. Sitting down in the gravel of the roadside, he closed the suitcase and used it as a desk.

---

stationery, special paper used for writing letters
gravel, small stones used to pave roads

222

Dear Mom,

If Dad will permit it, I would like to come home. I know there's little chance he will. I'm not going to kid myself. I remember he said once, if I ever ran off, I might as well keep on going.

All I can say is that I felt leaving home was something I had to do. Before even considering college, I wanted to find out more about life and about me. Please tell Dad—and I guess this'll make him sore all over again—I'm still not certain that college is the answer for me. I think I'd like to work for a time and think it over.

You won't be able to reach me by mail, because I'm not sure where I'll be next. But in a few days I hope to be passing by our place. If there's any chance Dad will have me back, please ask him to tie a white cloth to the apple tree in the south pasture—you know the one, beside the tracks. I'll be going by on the train. If there's no cloth on the tree I'll just quietly, and without any hard feelings toward Dad—I mean that—keep on going.

Love,
David

A series of headlights made a domino of the highway. High beams flickered over him curiously. He put out his thumb almost hesitantly, wishing he didn't have to emerge so suddenly, so menacingly. One by one, the cars passed him, their back draft slapping him softly, insultingly, on the cheek.

---

kid, fool
sore, angry
high beams, bright headlights from cars
menacingly, threateningly or in an angry way
back draft, wind that comes from passing by very fast
insultingly, offensively or in an impolite way

BEFORE YOU GO ON

1 Why did David leave home?

2 In his letter, what does David ask his mother to do?

On Your Own
Describe what you hope to do after high school.

223

Much later, turning woodenly to gaze after a car, he saw the glow of taillights intensify. Brakes squealed. The car careened wildly to a stop, and he was running down the road to capture it, his breath rushing against his upturned collar and the taillights glowing nearer as in a dream.

A door was flung open like a friendly arm reaching out to a tired swimmer. "Hop in, boy."

It was a gruff, outdoors voice. "I pret' near missed you. You ain't easy to see out there."

"Thanks, mister."

"Forget it. Used the thumb a lot myself when I was a kid."

"How far are you going?" asked David.

The man named a small place in Iowa about two hundred miles away.

"Where you headin'?" the man asked him.

David glanced at him. His nose was big; his mouth, wide and gentle.

The boy looked out on the highway with affection. It would be a good ride with a good companion. "Home," he said with a grin. "I'm heading home."

The man heard the smile in the boy's voice and chuckled. "That's a good feelin', ain't it? Where 'bouts?"

"Maryland. We have a farm about thirty miles outside of Baltimore."

"Where you been?"

"West Coast, Canada, a little of Mexico."

"And now you're hightailin' for home, huh?" There was a note in the man's voice as if this were a pattern he understood intimately.

---

intensify, get stronger
careened, moved from side to side
chuckled, laughed quietly
hightailin', traveling quickly
intimately, very well

"Yes, sir."

"Yeah," the driver was saying now, "I know how it is." The corners of his eyes crinkled as if he were going to smile, but he didn't. "I was out on that same old road when I was a kid. **Bummin' around.** Lettin' no grass grow under me. Sometimes wishin' it would."

"And then, afterward," David asked, "did you go back home?"

"Nope. I didn't have no home to go back to, like you do. The road was my only home. Lost my ma and pa when I was a little **shaver.** Killed in a car wreck."

"That's rough," David said with such feeling the man glanced at him sharply.

The boy was staring into the night. The man shifted his grip on the wheel. He spoke softly to the boy as if he were aware he was interrupting important thoughts. "Bet you could do with some sleep."

"You sure you won't be needing me later to help you keep awake?" David asked.

"Don't worry 'bout me none. I like drivin' at night. You just lean back there and help yourself."

"Well, okay," David said. "Thanks."

Sometime later, he was awakened by a sharp decrease in speed. They were entering a town. He sat up and jerked the letter out of his jacket pocket. He had almost forgotten.

---

bummin' around, wandering around without any particular place to go
shaver, young male child

BEFORE YOU GO ON

1 How does David get a ride?

2 What do David and the driver have in common?

On Your Own
Would you like to travel to new places? If so, where do you want to go and why?

225

"Excuse me, sir, but would you mind stopping at a mailbox so I can mail this? I want to make sure that it gets home before I do."

"Course not," the man said. "Here's one comin' up now." He pulled over to the curb and stopped.

When the boy got back in, the man smiled kindly. "Bet your folks'll be tickled to hear from you."

"I hope so, sir." David tilted his head back and closed his eyes.

The next day, rides were slow. They were what David called "farmer rides," a few miles here, a couple of miles there, with long waits in between.

Toward nightfall, he swung onto a panting, slow-moving freight aimed stolidly east. The train was hammering along beside a highway. He stared at the houses on the other side. How would it be at home? Would his house be like that one, the one with the porch light burning? Or would it be like that one, where the porch was dark and where over each of the lighted windows a yellow shade was pulled down firmly to the sill?

A couple of days later, in the middle of Maryland, maddeningly close to home, the flow of rides narrowed to a trickle and then ceased altogether. When cars weren't in sight, he walked. After a while, he didn't even bother to stop and hold out his thumb. Furiously, he walked.

Later, seated on the passenger train he wished with slow, frightened heartbeats that he were back on the road, headed the other way.

---

tickled, pleased
narrowed to a trickle, got fewer and fewer
ceased, stopped

Three inches from his nose was the dust-stained window through which in a few minutes he would look out across his father's fields. Two different pictures tortured him—the tree with the white cloth and the tree without it. His throat closed and he could hardly breathe.

He tried to fortify himself with the idea that whether or not he still was welcome, at least he would see the place again.

The field was sliding closer, one familiar landmark at a time. He couldn't stop the train. Nothing could postpone the denouement now. The tree was around the next bend.

He couldn't look. He was too afraid the cloth would not be there—too afraid he would find, staring back at him, just another tree, just another field, just another somebody else's strange place, the way it always is on the long, long road, the nameless staring back at the nameless. He jerked away from the window.

Desperately, he nudged the passenger beside him. "Mister, will you do me a favor? Around this bend on the right, you'll see an apple tree. I wonder if you'll tell me if you see a white cloth tied to one of its branches?"

As they passed the field, the boy stared straight ahead. "Is it there?" he asked with an uncontrollable quaver.

"Son," the man said in a voice slow with wonder, "I see a white cloth tied on almost every twig.

---

postpone, delay
denouement, conclusion or ending
nudged, gently poked
quaver, trembling voice
wonder, amazement or surprise

ABOUT THE **AUTHOR**

Richard Pindell received his doctorate from Yale University in 1971. He is now a popular and award-winning professor of English at the University of Binghamton in New York, where he specializes in teaching Southern and Civil War literature.

BEFORE YOU GO ON

1. What kept David from looking at the apple tree?

2. What did the stranger see when he looked out the window?

On Your Own
Were you surprised by the story's ending? Explain.

227

READER'S THEATER

Speaking TIP

Make eye contact with your partner.

Driver: Hi, get in. I almost missed you—it's so dark out there.

David: Thanks for stopping.

Driver: No problem. Where you headed?

David: Home. [*reaches into his pocket and feels the letter*] Oh! I almost forgot! Sir, would you mind stopping at a mailbox? I have a letter—I'd like it to get home before I do.

Driver: Not at all. In fact, here's a mailbox now.

[*pause while David mails the letter and gets back in the car*]

Driver: It'll be good to be back home, huh? I bet your parents will be happy to hear from you.

David: [*uncertainly*] I hope so. We'll see.

COMPREHENSION

Workbook
Page 108

Right There

1. Where is David's home?

2. Why couldn't the driver return to his childhood home?

Think and Search

3. What forms of transportation does David use on his journey?

4. Where has David been?

Author and You

5. Why do you think David wrote the letter to his mother instead of his father?

6. Why did David's father tie more than one white cloth to the apple tree?

On Your Own

7. Have you ever felt angry towards a parent or another relative? Explain.

8. What do you think is the best way to resolve a conflict?

DISCUSSION

Discuss in pairs or small groups.

1. How does David feel about college after his travels?

2. Is this a present-day story? Explain.

Q **What does home mean?** Some people say that young adults need to leave home and explore the world around them in order to discover more about themselves and what they want to do with their lives. Do you agree? Why or why not?

Summarize what the speaker says in your own mind. Do you agree or disagree?

RESPONSE TO LITERATURE

Workbook Page 108

Work in groups of three. Use your imagination as you discuss the following: What do you think happens when David returns home? How do his parents react? What does David say to his parents? Write a dialogue that answers these questions. Be sure to include parts for David, his mother, and his father. Then act out your dialogue in front of the class.

Grammar and Writing

Adjectives and Adverbs

Writers often use adjectives and adverbs to describe other words. An adjective describes a noun. An adjective appears before the noun it describes or after a verb, such as *be*.

> He wished with **slow, frightened** heartbeats that he was back on the road. The next day, the rides were **slow**.

An adverb usually describes a verb or shows how something is done. Many adverbs are formed by adding *-ly* to the adjective. For example, *slow/slowly, quiet/quietly, soft/softly, careless/carelessly*.

Adverbs ending in *-ly* appear before the verb or verb phrase when they are not the main focus of the sentence. Adverbs that are the main focus of the sentence usually appear after the verb or at the end of the sentence.

> I'll just **quietly** keep on going. (focus is the action itself)
> He spoke **softly** to the boy. (focus is on how the action was done)

Practice

Copy the sentences below into your notebook. Complete each sentence by using an adjective or adverb in parentheses.

1. The boy _____ stepped out of the darkness. (sudden / suddenly)
2. As they came around the bend, he _____ closed his eyes. (firm / firmly)
3. David was _____ about the driver's past. (curious / curiously)
4. He was _____ to know if his father had forgiven him. (desperate / desperately)
5. The _____ young man answered the questions. (nervous / nervously)
6. The train _____ chugged down the track. (loud / loudly)

230

WRITING AN EXPOSITORY PARAGRAPH

Write a Plot Summary

You have learned that a magazine article is one kind of expository writing. A plot summary is another kind of expository writing. A plot is what happens in a story. The events in most plots focus on a conflict or problem. Usually, it is resolved by the story's end. When you summarize a plot, describe, in a shortened form and in your own words, what happens. Introduce the main characters and the setting. Then describe the conflict or problem the character(s) face. Include the most important story events, and explain how the conflict is resolved.

Characters
Setting
Conflict
Main events
Resolution

Here is a model of a plot summary. The writer used a plot summary chart to organize his ideas. Notice how he describes the main character, the setting, and the most important events. He presents the conflict and tells how it is resolved.

Andrew Denkus

"Somebody's Son": A Summary

"Somebody's Son" is a short story about a teenager named David, who ran away from home after arguing with his father. Now, David wants to return home to Maryland, but he is not sure his parents will welcome him. Sitting in the hot sun by the side of a road, he writes a letter to his mother. In it, he asks his father to signal permission for David to return by tying a white cloth to an apple tree in the family's pastures. After mailing the letter, David still has a long journey ahead of him. He hitches rides from various strangers and eventually boards a train headed for Maryland. As it nears his parents' land, David nervously asks the passenger beside him to look out the window for the white cloth. The surprised passenger tells him that pieces of white cloth are tied to almost every one of the tree's branches!

ORGANIZATION:
☑ I included only the most important events in my summary.

WORD CHOICE:
☑ I included adjectives and adverbs in my summary.

Practice

Workbook
Page 110

Think about a story you know well. It may be a story presented in a book, film, or television show. Use a graphic organizer to list information about the plot. Then write a summary. Be sure to use adjectives and adverbs.

231

What You Will Learn

Reading

- Vocabulary building: *Context, dictionary skills, word study*

- Reading strategy: *Monitor comprehension*

- Text type: *Informational text (science)*

Grammar, Usage, and Mechanics
Subject-verb agreement

Writing
Write a problem-and-solution paragraph

 THE BIG QUESTION

What does home mean? Do you know what an endangered species is? Animals that are endangered are at risk of extinction, or of dying out. Work with your classmates to make a list of endangered animals that you know of. Then discuss the following with a partner: Did any of these animals become endangered as the result of losing their homes? Why would the loss of a home cause animals to become endangered?

BUILD BACKGROUND

In this section, you will read an informational science article called **"Operation Migration."** Migration occurs when a group of animals or birds move from one place to another year after year.

Whooping cranes are birds that migrate. Because humans took over much of their habitat, the whooping crane population decreased. By 1941, there were only fifteen whooping cranes left, and they were declared an endangered species. In an effort to raise the population, scientists conducted an experiment called Operation Migration.

▲ A whooping crane

Learn Key Words

Read these sentences. Use the context to figure out the meaning of the **red** words. Use a dictionary to check your answers. Then write each word and its meaning in your notebook.

Key Words
endangered species
migration
monitor
population
rare
refuge

1. Polar bears are an **endangered species**. There are only a few of these animals left on Earth.

2. The **migration** of monarch butterflies occurs both in the fall and spring. In the fall, the butterflies fly from north to south. In the spring, they return to their habitats in the north.

3. Scientists **monitor** the progress of the injured birds each day.

4. There are more bald eagles now than there were ten years ago. Their **population** has risen.

5. The giant panda is a **rare** animal. It is found only in China.

6. The birds live in a safe place—they live in a wildlife **refuge**.

Practice  **Workbook Page 111**

Write the sentences in your notebook. Choose a **red** word from the box above to complete each sentence. Then take turns reading the sentences aloud with a partner.

1. Because they were hunted by whalers, the _____ of blue whales dropped.

2. Salmon can travel hundreds of miles during their _____.

3. The whooping crane only exists in North America. It is a _____ bird.

4. You cannot hunt animals that live in a wildlife _____.

5. There are very few gray wolves left in the United States. They are an _____.

6. Bird-watchers _____ the migration of birds each year.

Polar bears ▶

233

Learn Academic Words

Study the red words and their meanings. You will find these words useful when talking and writing about informational texts. Write each word and its meaning in your notebook. After you read "Operation Migration," try to use these words to respond to the text.

Academic Words

interaction
outcome
route
substitute

interaction = the activity of talking with other people and working together with them	➡	There was constant **interaction** between the scientists as they performed the experiment.
outcome = the final result of a meeting, process, etc.	➡	The experiment's **outcome** was successful—the birds completed their migration.
route = the way from one place to another	➡	Migrating animals follow the same **route** home year after year.
substitute = someone who does someone else's job	➡	The scientist fed the chicks. He acted as a **substitute** for the chicks' mother.

Practice  Workbook Page 112

Work with a partner to answer these questions. Try to include the red word in your answer. Write the sentences in your notebook.

1. What kinds of daily interaction do you have with your classmates?

2. What was the outcome of the last test you took in this class?

3. What route do you take to school each morning?

4. Have you ever had a substitute teacher? What does a substitute teacher do?

▼ Migrating reindeer

Word Study: Suffix *-ion*

Learning about suffixes, or word parts, is a good way to build your vocabulary. The suffix *-ion* means "an act or a process". Adding *-ion* to the end of a base word changes its meaning. It also changes a verb into a noun.

Word	Definition	Example
subtract	**v.** to take one number from another	To find the answer, **subtract** 3 from 5.
subtraction	**n.** the process of taking one number from another	We learned **subtraction** in math class.

For words that end in a silent *-e*, drop the *-e* before adding *-ion*.

Word	Definition	Example
migrate	**v.** to travel at the same time each year from one part of the world to another	The birds **migrate** in the fall.
migration	**n.** the act of moving from one place to another	We studied the **migration** of birds.

Practice

Workbook Page 113

Work with a partner. Change these verbs to nouns: *populate*, *select*, *extinct*, *separate*. Write the words in sentences using nouns and then verbs. Use a dictionary to check your work.

READING STRATEGY | MONITOR COMPREHENSION

Monitoring comprehension helps you to understand difficult texts. To monitor comprehension, follow these steps:

- Reread the text.
- Make a list of words that are difficult. Try to figure out their meanings from the context. If you can't, look them up in a dictionary.
- Try to put the information you read into your own words.

As you read "Operation Migration," stop from time to time. Ask yourself whether you understood each section.

Workbook Page 114

235

Set a purpose for reading As you read, think about how human behavior impacts wildlife. In particular, what effect did human behavior have on the whooping cranes' habitat?

Operation Migration

Joyce Styron Madsen

Have you ever seen a pilot fly an "ultralight" plane? How about a bright yellow ultralight with the pilot dressed in a bird costume—and leading a formation of thirteen young sandhill cranes?

While this may sound like a wild publicity stunt, it's actually part of a long-term, well-researched plan to save the endangered whooping crane from extinction. The graceful whooping crane has always been a rare bird, found only in North America. In the late 1800s and early 1900s, American cities expanded rapidly. New buildings and roads took over much of the cranes' wetland habitat. The whooping crane population shrank year by year. By 1941, there were only fifteen left.

Fortunately, naturalists, biologists, and the government took action before it was too late. The whooping crane was declared an endangered species. It became protected by international law. The crane's wintering and breeding grounds became protected refuges. As a result of this careful study and care, the number of whooping cranes began to increase.

---

ultralight, airplane with a single seat that weighs less than
115 kilograms (254 lbs.)
publicity stunt, action performed to get attention
naturalists, people who study nature, or who work to preserve nature
biologists, scientists who study living things

A new community built where cranes' habitat once existed ▼

◀ A human caretaker dressed as a sandhill crane

By the 1990s, the whooping crane population had grown to more than 180. All of the cranes were part of one single, migratory flock. What would happen if a dangerous disease were to spread through the flock? To prevent such a disaster, government agencies joined together with such groups as the International Crane Foundation in Baraboo, Wisconsin. Together, they created a ten-year plan to encourage a second migratory flock. It would nest in Wisconsin and winter in Florida. They called the plan Operation Migration.

The plan was to be tested, using plentiful sandhill cranes instead of the rare whooping cranes. In the spring of 2000, sandhill crane eggs were removed shortly before hatching from their nests. The eggs were kept at the Necedah National Wildlife Refuge in Wisconsin and Patuxent Wildlife Center in Maryland. When the eggs hatched, both refuges were careful to let the chicks "stay wild."

For their own protection, the hatchlings needed to stay shy of humans. They also needed to become used to the sounds of the ultralight. Their human caretakers wore gray overalls and covered their hands with sandhill crane puppets. Loudspeakers played recorded sounds of ultralight engines and the calls of adult sandhills.

Soon the chicks were ready to be let out into the exercise yard. There they were met by the ultralight pilot. He was dressed in his crane costume and seated in the plane. Caretakers trained the chicks to run behind the very slow-moving ultralight. They followed it as they would follow a mama crane.

---

flock, group of birds
disaster, sudden, terrible event
hatching, breaking through an egg in order to be born
stay shy of, avoid

BEFORE YOU GO ON

1 What took over much of the cranes' wetland habitat?

2 What was the goal of Operation Migration?

💡 **On Your Own**
Would you be interested in participating in an experiment like Operation Migration? Why or why not?

Ordinarily when cranes migrate, they take off on a clear morning with a steady wind. A soaring breeze helps the cranes to glide a long distance with little effort. But when following the ultralight, a very calm day was needed. The cranes had to continually flap their wings to stay aloft. Without the winds to help them, the ultralight flight was much longer and more tiring for the cranes. A flight that usually would take about five days of gliding might take six or seven weeks of flapping.

After years of planning and months of training, Operation Migration took to the air on October 3, 2000, from the Necedah refuge. The route from Wisconsin to Florida was 1,250 miles. It was the longest bird migration ever led by a human. Following along by road was a team of support vehicles: a mobile veterinary van, a night pen for the cranes, and four mobile homes for the support crew. The team also included a larger, faster scouting plane to follow the ultralight and the cranes. The pilot of this plane would keep an eye on the entire formation.

The flight was carefully watched and tracked at every stage. The cranes were able to fly no more than a total of two hours and twenty minutes a day, depending on the weather. When it was time for a rest stop, the scouting plane would speed ahead and clear the landing site of any people or other animals.

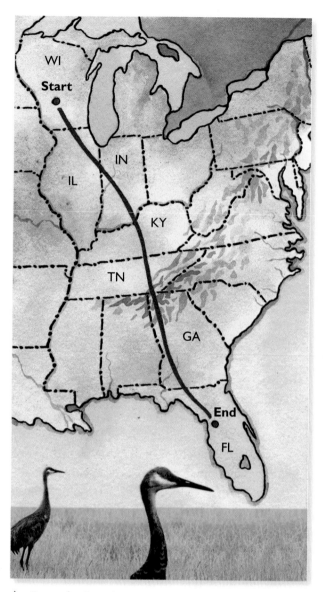

▲ Cranes' migration route

---

breeze, gentle wind
glide, easily move through the air
aloft, high up in the air
veterinary, relating to health care for animals

More about the whooping cranes . . .

- Whooping cranes stand about five feet tall.
- They're named for their loud, bugle-like call.
- Adults are white and have black-tipped wings and a patch of bare, red skin on their heads.
- The female usually lays two eggs, but often only one chick survives.

▲ An ultralight pilot leads a flock of six cranes as they fly south.

On Saturday, November 11, the sandhill cranes circled the St. Martin's Marsh Aquatic Preserve in Florida. After flying 1,250 miles in forty days, the cranes and their human companions touched down in their winter home. Of the thirteen sandhills that began the journey, eleven actually landed in the Florida refuge. Along the way, one crane left the flock and joined a different wild group. Unfortunately, another crane died in the overnight holding pen.

After the sandhill cranes' trailblazing migration and successful landing, Operation Migration moved into the next phase of its plan. The crew will continue to monitor the cranes because several questions remain: Will the cranes be able to find food and survive through the winter? Will they stay wild? In spring, will they migrate back to Wisconsin on their own? Once these questions are answered, Operation Migration will be one step closer to its goal—a second migratory flock of whooping cranes.

---

trailblazing, first ever

BEFORE YOU GO ON

1 Where did the cranes begin their migration? Where was their final destination?

2 Why did the experiment take place on a calm day? How did this affect the cranes?

On Your Own
Do you think the cranes were able to return to Wisconsin on their own? Why or why not?

239

COMPREHENSION  Workbook Page 115

Right There

1. What was the whooping crane population in 1941?
2. What are whooping cranes named for?

Think and Search

3. Why did the ultralight pilot dress in a crane costume?
4. How was Operation Migration monitored by scientists?

Author and You

5. The cranes' habitat was overrun by America's expanding cities. In what other ways does expansion threaten birds and animals?
6. Do you think the author believes in saving whooping cranes? Why or why not?

On Your Own

7. Do you think it's important to protect endangered species? Explain.
8. In what other ways can humans help prevent animals from becoming endangered?

▲ Litter can cause animal endangerment.

IN YOUR OWN WORDS

Work with a partner. Read the topics in the chart below. Then recall as many facts about those topics as you can from "Operation Migration." List these facts in the chart. Use this information to summarize the article for your partner.

Topics	Facts
Actions taken by scientists and government to save whooping cranes	
How Operation Migration worked	
Outcome	

DISCUSSION

Discuss in pairs or small groups.

Listening TIP

Be a careful listener so that you don't repeat what someone else has already contributed to the discussion.

1. What actions did the government take to increase the whooping crane population?

2. Have you ever been to a wildlife refuge? Where was it? What did you see?

Q What does home mean? The whooping crane population became endangered because humans disturbed their habitat. Do you think humans have a responsibility to preserve animal habitats? Why or why not?

READ FOR FLUENCY

When we read aloud to communicate meaning, we group words into phrases, pause or slow down to make important points, and emphasize important words. Pause for a short time when you reach a comma and for a longer time when you reach a period.

▲ Bird-watchers observe birds at a wildlife refuge.

Pay attention to rising and falling intonation at the end of sentences.

Work with a partner. Choose a paragraph from the reading. Discuss which words seem important for communicating meaning. Practice pronouncing difficult words. Take turns reading the paragraph aloud and give each other feedback.

EXTENSION
Workbook
Page 115

Scientists were successful in teaching sandhill cranes to migrate. However, were they successful in boosting the whooping crane population? Were they able to create a second migratory flock of whooping cranes as they had planned? Are whooping cranes still on the endangered species list? What is their population like today? Work with a partner. Use the Internet to find the answers to these questions. Then present your findings to the class. You may want to include visuals, such as a population graph, as you do so.

GRAMMAR, USAGE, AND MECHANICS

Subject-Verb Agreement

In order to convey a clear message when you write, it's important that subjects and verbs agree in your sentences.

A singular subject takes a singular verb.

> **The whooping crane is** a rare bird.
> **It was** part of a long-term, well-researched plan.

When the subject is singular or when the pronoun *he*, *she*, or *it* is the subject, add *-s* or *-es* to a verb in the simple present.

> **The bird lays** two eggs at a time.
> **He watches** the cranes closely.

A plural subject takes a plural verb.

> By 1941, only fifteen **whooping cranes were** left.

When the subject is plural or when the pronoun *I*, *we*, *you*, or *they* is the subject, do not add *-s* or *-es* to a verb in the simple present.

> **The cranes glide** on breezy days.
> **They call** the plan Operation Migration.

Practice
Workbook Page 116

Copy these sentences into your notebook. Complete each sentence with the correct form of the verb in parentheses.

1. Whooping cranes _____ (stand) about five feet tall.
2. The bird _____ (screech) when it is hungry.
3. International law _____ (protect) the cranes' breeding grounds.
4. He _____ (teach) the cranes how to fly.
5. Loudspeakers _____ (play) the recorded sounds.
6. The recorded call _____ (match) the call of a sandhill crane.
7. The egg _____ (hatch) in the spring.
8. The program _____ (work).

242

WRITING AN EXPOSITORY PARAGRAPH

Write a Problem-and-Solution Paragraph

You have learned that expository writing presents factual information about a topic. One way to organize your facts is by problem and solution. To write a problem-and-solution paragraph, begin by clearly stating the problem. Then tell the process that was used, or the steps that were taken, to solve the problem. If you write about this information in chronological order, include words such as *first*, *then*, *next*, and *after* to make the sequence of events clear. Also include supporting facts and details to help your readers understand how your solution worked.

Problem

↓

Solution

Here is a model paragraph. The writer used a problem-and-solution chart to organize his thoughts. In his paragraph, he clearly stated the problem and included facts that described the solutions.

> *Pablo Espínola*
>
> ### Future Looks Bright for Whooping Cranes
>
> When the whooping crane was threatened with extinction, government officials quickly declared it an endangered species. Its breeding grounds became protected refuges. However, scientists still faced a serious challenge. All of the cranes belonged to the same migratory flock. If a disease spread through this flock, the whooping cranes would again be in danger of extinction. So scientists launched an experiment, called Operation Migration, to create a second migratory flock. First, scientists removed whooping cranes' eggs from their nests. After the chicks hatched, scientists trained the chicks to fly behind an ultralight plane. Eventually, the cranes followed the ultralight plane along their migration route to their winter home. As a result of all of these these efforts, the whooping crane population has once again increased.

Practice

Workbook Page 117

Write a paragraph in which you describe a problem in your school. List your ideas in a graphic organizer. As you write your sentences, be sure that the subjects and verbs agree in number.

Writing Checklist

ORGANIZATION:
- ☑ I used a problem-and-solution organization to guide my writing.

CONVENTIONS:
- ☑ Subjects and verbs agree in number.

What You Will Learn

Reading
■ Vocabulary building:
*Literary terms,
word study*

■ Reading strategy:
*Analyze text
structure*

■ Text type: *Literature
(poetry)*

**Grammar, Usage,
and Mechanics**
Adverb clauses of time

Writing
Write a response to
literature

 THE BIG QUESTION

What does home mean? Imagine that you have to leave your home in a hurry. If you could take one possession with you, what would it be? Why is this item important to you? Discuss with a partner.

BUILD BACKGROUND

In this section, you will read a narrative poem called **The Lotus Seed**. A narrative poem, like a short story, has a plot and characters. However, the structure of a narrative poem looks different. It tells a story in verse.

The Lotus Seed is about a woman who was forced to leave her home country, Vietnam. For hundreds of years, emperors ruled Vietnam. The Vietnamese believed the emperor was wise about all things. The emperors lived in a magnificent palace that had beautiful gardens filled with lotus plants.

The last emperor was Nguyen Vinh Thuy, who became emperor at the age of twelve in 1926. He took the name Bao Dai, meaning "Keeper of Greatness." Because the French had conquered Vietnam in the late 1800s, he had little power, but was a symbol of Vietnam's heritage.

By 1945, many Vietnamese wanted to be independent from France. Bao Dai resigned as emperor in support of Ho Chi Minh, the leader of the independence movement. After a long war, the Vietnamese defeated the French in 1954.

Soon after, a civil war began between the northern and southern parts of the country. The United States helped the southerners. The war ended in 1975, when the south was defeated. As the northern armies began to move south, many Vietnamese left the country by boat. Most of them came to live in the United States.

◄ Refugees flee Vietnam in 1975.

244

VOCABULARY

Learn Literary Words

The **speaker** of a poem is the imaginary character, or voice, a poet uses when writing a poem. This voice is the one you "hear" when you read the poem. This speaker is often not identified by name. Read the excerpt from the poem below for an example.

I years had been from home,	Stare vacant into mine
And now, before the door,	And ask my business there.
I dared not open, lest a face	My business,—just a life I left,
I never saw before	Was such still dwelling there?
	—*Emily Dickinson*

A **symbol** is anything that stands for or represents something else. In addition to having its own meaning, a symbol stands for something other than itself, often an idea or a feeling. For example, a flag is a piece of cloth with a design on it that represents both a country and people's feelings of patriotism toward that country.

Practice  Workbook Page 118

Work with a partner. Copy the chart below into your notebook. Create a symbol for each idea. Then explain to your partner why you chose each symbol.

Idea	Symbol
happiness	
sadness	
Earth-friendly	
freedom	
victory	

◀ The American flag

245

Learn Academic Words

Study the **red** words and their meanings. You will find these words useful when talking and writing about literature. Write each word and its meaning in your notebook. After you read *The Lotus Seed,* try to use these words to respond to the text.

Academic Words

attached
removed
source
symbolize

attached = emotionally connected to	➡	I am very **attached** to that vase. It belonged to my grandmother.
removed = took something away from where it was	➡	When it was time to eat, I **removed** the vase from the table.
source = where something comes from	➡	Rose hips, or the fruit of roses, are a good **source** of vitamin C.
symbolize = represent a quality or a feeling	➡	To many people, yellow roses **symbolize** friendship.

Practice  **Workbook Page 119**

Work with a partner to answer these questions. Try to include the **red** word in your answer. Write the sentences in your notebook.

1. What is one family item that you are **attached** to?

2. How would you feel if someone **removed** this item from its current location without your permission?

3. Who or what is the **source** of this item?

4. What does the item **symbolize** to you?

A Chinese vase ▶

Word Study: Spelling Long *o*

Learning to identify sound-spelling relationships will help you read more fluently. The story you are going to read contains words with the long *o* sound. Here are a few different spellings: *o*, *oa*, *o_e*, and *ow*.

o	oa	o_e	ow
so	**boat**	**home**	**own**
lotus	**soak**	**throne**	**show**

Practice  Workbook Page 120

Work with a partner. Copy the headings from the chart above into your notebook. Take turns spelling the words in the box. Write each word in the correct column. Then write a sentence using each word.

alone	below	close	coast	golden	old	road	window

READING STRATEGY | ANALYZE TEXT STRUCTURE

Analyzing text structure can help you understand what kind of text you're reading. It can also help you set a purpose for reading. There are many different types of text structure, including poems, plays, and stories. To analyze the text structure of a poem, follow these steps:

- Poems are usually written in lines and groups of lines, called stanzas, and narrative poems are written in verse. Look at the way the lines are grouped in the poems you read.

- The punctuation doesn't always follow the same rules in poetry as it does in other types of text.

- Notice how the poet uses commas, dashes, periods, or line breaks to show you where to pause.

Review the text structure of *The Lotus Seed*. Discuss it with a partner.

 Workbook Page 121

Set a purpose for reading As you read, think about why Bà chose the lotus seed as a memory of home. What aspect(s) of home does the seed represent?

The Lotus Seed

Sherry Garland

My grandmother saw
the emperor cry
the day he lost
his golden dragon throne.

She wanted something
to remember him by,
so she snuck down
to the silent palace,
near the River of Perfumes,
and plucked a seed
from a lotus pod
that rattled
in the Imperial garden.

She hid the seed
in a special place
under the family altar,
wrapped in a piece of silk
from the ao dai
she wore that day.
Whenever she felt sad
or lonely,
she took out the seed
and thought of the
brave young emperor.

And when she married
a young man
chosen by her parents,
she carried the seed
inside her pocket
for good luck, long life,
and many children.
When her husband
marched off to war,
she raised her
children alone.

---

lotus pod, hard, natural pouch that
holds the seeds of the lotus plant
silk, soft, delicate material
ao dai, long dress

One day bombs fell
all around,
and soldiers
clamored door to door.
She took the time
to grab the seed,
but left her mother-of-pearl
hair combs lying
on the floor.

✔ **LITERARY CHECK**
*What is the symbol
in this poem?*

One terrible day
her family scrambled
into a crowded boat
and set out
on a stormy sea.
Bà watched the mountains
and the waving palms
slowly fade away.
She held the seed
in her shaking fingers
and silently said good-bye.
She arrived in a
strange new land
with blinking lights
and speeding cars
and towering buildings
that scraped the sky
and a language
she didn't understand.

---

clamored, shouted loudly
mother-of-pearl, shiny substance
found inside some seashells
palms, trees with broad, flat leaves
that grow only at the top

BEFORE YOU GO ON

1. What caused the
emperor to cry?

2. How does Bà feel
about the young
emperor? Why?

On Your Own
Name a person that
has had a strong
impact on your
life. Explain.

249

She worked many years,
day and night,
and so did her children
and her sisters
and her cousins, too,
living together
in one big house.

Last summer
my little brother
found the special seed
and asked questions
again and again.
He'd never seen a lotus **bloom**
or an emperor
on a golden dragon throne.

So one night
he stole the seed
from beneath the family altar
and planted it
in a pool of mud
somewhere near Bà's
onion patch.

Bà cried and cried
when she found out
the seed was gone.
She didn't eat,
she didn't sleep,
and my silly brother
forgot what spot of earth
held the seed.

bloom, open up its flowers

Then one day in spring
my grandmother shouted,
and we all ran
to the garden
and saw
a beautiful pink lotus
unfurling its petals,
so creamy and soft.

"It is the flower
of life and hope,"
my grandmother said.
"No matter how ugly the mud
or how long the seed lies **dormant**,
the bloom will be beautiful.
It is the flower
of my country."

When the lotus blossom
faded and turned
into a pod,
Bà gave each of
her grandchildren
a seed
to remember her by,
and she kept one
for herself
to remember the emperor by.

I wrapped my seed
in a piece of silk
and hid it
in a secret place.
Someday I will plant it
and give the seeds
to my own children
and tell them about the day
my grandmother saw
the emperor cry.

unfurling, unrolling and opening
dormant, inactive

✔ **LITERARY CHECK**
*What can you tell
about the **speaker**
by reading the
poem?*

ABOUT THE **POET**

Sherry Garland is the award-winning author of over twenty-five books for children and teenagers. Seven of her books focus on Vietnam and came about because of her close association with Vietnamese families in the Houston, Texas, area. She also traveled to Vietnam for research purposes. As a fifth-generation Texan, she sets many of her books in the Lone Star State. Ms. Garland currently lives in Central Texas.

BEFORE YOU GO ON

1 Why did Bà get so upset when she "lost" her lotus seed?

2 What does the speaker plan to do with the seed Bà gave her?

On Your Own
Why do you think Bà thought it was important to give a lotus seed to each of her grandchildren? Explain.

251

Review and Practice

DRAMATIC READING

🔊 *Speaking* TIP

Use facial expressions, gestures, and other movements to show the characters' feelings and actions.

One of the best ways to understand the pace and flow of a poem is to recite it aloud. Work with a partner. Take turns reading *The Lotus Seed* aloud. Work together to interpret any difficult words or phrases. After you have examined the poem carefully, memorize your favorite section and act it out for the class. Comment on one another's oral reading and make helpful suggestions for improvement.

COMPREHENSION

Workbook
Page 122

Right There

1. Where did the lotus seed come from?
2. Why did the speaker's grandmother pluck a seed from the Imperial garden?

Think and Search

3. Why did looking at the lotus seed help Bà when she felt sad or lonely?
4. The lotus seed represented many things to Bà. What were they?

Author and You

5. How did Bà feel when she left her homeland of Vietnam?
6. What country do you think Bà moved to?

On Your Own

7. How would you feel if you had to flee your homeland?
8. Name some items that symbolize your homeland.

▲ Mekong Delta, Vietnam

DISCUSSION

Discuss in pairs or small groups.

1. Do you think the lotus flower was more important to Bà before she left her country or after she left her country? Explain.

2. Do you think the lotus seed will ever mean as much to the speaker as it did to Bà?

Q **What does home mean?** The speaker says she plans to tell her children about the day her grandmother saw the emperor cry. Is there a story that is told over and over again in your family? How does passing stories along to family members keep a sense of home alive?

Listening TIP

Respect each speaker. Listen politely, even if you disagree with the speaker's ideas.

RESPONSE TO LITERATURE

Workbook
Page 122

Think about an item that is important to your family. Write a poem that describes this item and why it has so much meaning to you. Your poem can be short, or you can write a longer narrative poem like *The Lotus Seed*. Share the poem with your classmates.

Grammar and Writing

Adverb Clauses of Time

Adverb clauses of time express *when*. The adverbs *when* and *whenever* both express *when*, but they have different meanings. *When* refers to an event that happened once. *Whenever* refers to an event that happened many times.

An adverb clause is a dependent clause. It can come before or after a main clause. When an adverb clause comes before the main clause, use a comma to separate the two. Look at the examples from *The Lotus Seed* below.

---

adverb clause

When her husband marched off to war, she raised her children alone.

adverb clause

Whenever she felt sad or lonely, she took out the seed and thought of the brave young emperor.

Practice

Workbook Page 123

Work with a partner. Copy the sentences below into your notebook. Decide whether the event happened once or many times. Then complete each sentence with *when* or *whenever*.

1. My grandmother saw the emperor cry _____ he lost his throne.

2. She didn't eat or sleep _____ she found out the seed was gone.

3. _____ my grandmother shouted, we all ran to the garden.

4. Bà told her grandchildren the story of the emperor _____ they wanted to hear it.

5. _____ I see a lotus flower, I think of my grandmother.

WRITING AN EXPOSITORY PARAGRAPH

Write a Response to Literature

You have learned that expository works provide the reader with factual information.

A response to literature is a type of expository writing in which you explain, interpret, or respond to some aspect of a piece of literature. You should organize your response around a clear idea and support the idea with details and examples from the text.

Here is a model paragraph. Before writing, the writer organized her thoughts in a word web. Notice how she uses adverb clauses of time as she explains the significance of the lotus seed within the story.

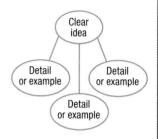

Madeline Shaw

The Lotus Seed

"The Lotus Seed" tells the story of Bà, a woman who flees her home in Vietnam to go to the United States. Bà takes only one thing with her: a lotus seed. She had taken the lotus seed from the emperor's garden on the day he lost his throne. It reminded her of his bravery and gave her courage. She carried the seed for luck when she got married. And she clutched it in her hand as she sailed away from home. One night her grandson steals the seed and plants it, breaking her heart. But in the spring Bà discovers that her seed has grown into a beautiful lotus blossom. She calls it "the flower of life and hope." Throughout Bà's life, the seed stands for many things. First it reminds her of the emperor's courage. When she weds, it represents good luck and long life. When she first comes to the United States, it represents Vietnam. When the lotus flower blooms, it represents life and hope. Finally, when the lotus flower produces its own seeds, it represents the continuing cycles of life.

Practice
Workbook Page 124

Write a response to a story or another piece of literature. Use a graphic organizer to list your ideas. Be sure to use adverb clauses of time in your writing.

Writing Checklist

ORGANIZATION:
☑ I organized my response around a clear idea.

WORD CHOICE:
☑ I supported my ideas with evidence from the text.

Link the Readings

Critical Thinking

Look back at the readings in this unit. Think about what they have in common. They all tell about home. Yet they do not all have the same purpose. The purpose of one reading might be to inform, while the purpose of another might be to entertain or persuade. In addition, the content of each reading relates to home differently. Now copy the chart below into your notebook and complete it.

Title of Reading	Purpose	Big Question Link
"97 Orchard Street" "The Pros and Cons of Tenement Life"		
"Somebody's Son"	*to entertain*	
"Operation Migration"		
The Lotus Seed		*A young woman must leave her home country.*

Discussion

Discuss in pairs or small groups.

- "97 Orchard Street" and *The Lotus Seed* are both about immigrants who left their home countries. What other similar experiences did the people in each reading share?

- **Q** **What does home mean?** What ideas do the readings in this unit share? Which reading do you relate to the most? Why?

Fluency Check

Work with a partner. Choose a paragraph from one of the readings. Take turns reading it for one minute. Count the total number of words you read. Practice saying the words you had trouble reading. Take turns reading the paragraph three more times. Did you read more words each time? Copy the chart below into your notebook and record your speeds.

	1st Speed	2nd Speed	3rd Speed	4th Speed
Words Per Minute				

Projects

Work in pairs or small groups. Choose one of these projects.

1 Create a brochure or poster that describes the Lower East Side Tenement Museum, its exhibits, and its tours. You may want to visit the library for additional information or use the Internet to find images to include in your brochure or on your poster. Remember to include the museum's location, operating hours, and telephone number. Share your brochure or poster with the class.

2 Find a wildlife expert in your community. Ask him or her about the endangered species that live in your area. Find out what volunteers can do to help protect these species. Share your findings with the class. Then brainstorm possible ways that your class could help in this effort.

3 The lotus plant is important in many cultures and religions. Research a legend or myth about a lotus flower and share it with a partner.

Further Reading

To find out more about the theme of this unit, choose from these reading suggestions.

Grey Owl, Vicky Shipton
This Penguin Reader® tells the amazing story of Grey Owl, a Native American who wanted to save his land and its forests and animals.

Homesick: My Own Story, Jean Fritz
In this blend of fact and fiction, the author describes the many things she loved about her childhood in China during the 1920s. But her parents' stories of home in America made her feel homesick for a place she had never seen.

Making It Home: Real Life Stories from Children Forced to Flee, Beverly Naidoo
Displaced from their homes by war, children, ages six to seventeen, from Kosovo, Bosnia, Afghanistan, Iraq, the Congo, Liberia, Sudan, and Burundi talk about their experiences as refugees. They describe the horror, the family separation, and the other struggles they face as asylum seekers adjusting to new places.

Put It All Together

TV News Show

You will present a TV news show about events in your community.

1 **THINK ABOUT IT** You have probably watched the news on TV—but do you know what reporters do before the cameras roll? They interview people, conduct research, and write a script. Their reports focus on the 5Ws of a story: *who, what, where, when,* and *why.*

Work in small groups. Make a list of recent or upcoming events in your community. For example:
- An election for mayor or city council
- The school board's decision to build a new school
- A concert by a local band
- The opening of a new skate park

Have each group member choose a different story idea from the list.

2 **GATHER AND ORGANIZE INFORMATION** Discuss and plan the overall structure of your show. If possible, watch a TV news show to get ideas. Choose one person to be your news anchor (the main person who presents the news on TV). The anchor will introduce each story and its reporter.

Research Check local newspapers or interview community members to find information for your story. Take notes and get answers to the 5Ws.

Order Your Notes Think about the best order in which to tell your story. Then make an outline showing your main points in this order.

Use Visuals Look for photos, maps, and other visuals to use during your news show. Think about how and when you will show each visual.

Prepare a Script As a group, write a short opening and closing for your news show. For example, the anchor might say: "Welcome to the Channel 6 Evening News. I'm Stanley Stevens. Tonight's top story will be of special interest to young people. Here's Julia Jenkins reporting live from Springfield's new skate park." Then use your outline and notes to write a script for your individual report. Start your story in a way that will catch people's interest. Remember to focus on the 5Ws.

3 PRACTICE AND PRESENT

Read your script over and over again until you know it well. As a group, practice presenting your TV news show until all members can deliver their stories confidently. Be sure to look "into the camera." Make smooth transitions between stories. Help each other with visuals as needed. Listen to each other, and make sure everyone is speaking loudly enough to be heard at the back of the room.

Deliver Your TV News Show Be sure your scripts and visuals are ready before you begin. Do not rush or mumble! Speak clearly, and pronounce names and numbers carefully. Emphasize key ideas by pausing, slowing down, speaking more loudly, or repeating them at the end of your story.

4 EVALUATE THE PRESENTATION

You will improve your skills as a speaker and a listener by evaluating each presentation you give and hear. Use this checklist to help you judge your group's TV news show and the news shows of your classmates.

- ☑ Was the news show presented in a professional and interesting way?
- ☑ Did the speakers look "into the camera" most of the time?
- ☑ Was each story about an event in your community?
- ☑ Could you hear and understand each speaker easily?
- ☑ What suggestions do you have for improving the show?

Speaking TIPS

Always face the audience (or imaginary TV camera) when you speak. Don't hide behind your script or visuals!

Use action verbs and descriptive adjectives to help the audience visualize the event.

Listening TIPS

Listen carefully to the other members of your group so you know when it is your turn to speak.

Listen for answers to the 5Ws. Does each story include these important details?

WRITING WORKSHOP

Expository Essay

In this workshop, you will use your skills to write an expository essay. As you have learned, an expository essay gives information about a topic. An expository essay may be written to report news about someone or something, to describe solutions to a problem, to respond to a work of literature, or for other reasons. A good expository essay begins with a paragraph that tells what the essay is about. Two or more body paragraphs develop the topic by adding ideas, details, and examples. This information is presented in a logical order. A concluding paragraph sums up the writer's main points in a lively and interesting way.

   Your writing assignment for this workshop is to expand one of the paragraphs you wrote for this unit into a five-paragraph expository essay.

1 **PREWRITE** Choose the paragraph you want to expand. Then think about your readers. What do they already know about your topic? What questions do you think they will have? List these questions in your notebook. Try to answer them in your essay. Also think about interesting details you want to add when you expand your paragraph into an essay.

List and Organize Ideas and Details Use a question-and-answer outline to organize information for your essay. A student named Blaise decided to expand her paragraph about a Boston museum. Here is the outline she prepared:

> I. What is the Museum of Science?
>   A. An exciting science museum
>   B. Located in Boston
> II. What is its mission?
>   A. Stimulate interest in science
>   B. Show importance of science
> III. What can a visitor do there?
>   A. Planetarium and movie theater
>   B. Courses and exhibits
> IV. What is my favorite exhibit?
>   A. Lecture on lightning
>   B. Demonstration of lightning
> V. What makes the museum special?
>   A. One of the foremost science museums
>   B. Educational, interactive, and fun

2 **DRAFT** Use the model on page 263 and your graphic organizer to help you write a first draft. Remember to include an introductory paragraph, three body paragraphs, and a concluding paragraph.

3 REVISE Read over your draft. As you do so, ask yourself the questions in the writing checklist. Use the questions to help you revise your essay.

SIX TRAITS OF WRITING CHECKLIST

- ☑ **IDEAS:** Do I provide good information in my essay?
- ☑ **ORGANIZATION:** Do I present ideas, details, and examples in an order that makes sense?
- ☑ **VOICE:** Does my writing show my interest in the topic?
- ☑ **WORD CHOICE:** Do I use words accurately?
- ☑ **SENTENCE FLUENCY:** Do my sentences begin in different ways?
- ☑ **CONVENTIONS:** Does my writing follow the rules of grammar, usage, and mechanics?

Here are the changes Blaise plans to make when she revises her first draft:

A Great Place to Visit

The Museum of Science in Boston, Massachusetts, is an exciting
                    which
museum. It can be visited many times without losing its appeal. The
                                                            site
museum was founded in the 1830s but opened at its present sight
                                                    which
along the Charles River in 1951. It offer exhibits and activities. They
are both educational and fun.

                                            e
The museum's mission is "to stimulat interest in and further

understanding of science and technology and their importance for
                                In fact,
individuals and for society." The Museum of Science was the first

all-inclusive science museum in the United States. It also has been
    a pioneer
important in introducing interactive exhibits.

The museum has a planetarium where laser light shows are set to

---

popular music. The museum also has a theater. It presents movies ^which about dinosaurs, sea life, the Grand Canyon, and other topics. One series of classes for high school kids are called "Mini Med-School." Each class focus on a different health issue and is taught by a doctor. ^who They specialize^s in that field. Courses for kids and adults are held at the museum throughout the year. Examples of the museum's many exhibits include *Beyond the X-ray*, *Butterfly Garden*, *Making Models*, *Natural Mysteries*, and *New England Habitats*.

My favorite exhibit at the museum is about lightning. After visitors are seated, one of the staff members talk about how lightning is made. The lecture is fascinating, but the demonstration that follows is even better! A machine actually produces bolts of lightning. Lightning right there in front of you! This exhibit is both dramatic and informative.

boston's Museum of Science is one of the foremost science museums in the nation. When individuals visit it they are encouraged to learn about science and technology, while at the same time having fun. It is a wonderful museum to explore, whether you are a resident of Boston or a tourist from far away.

4 EDIT AND PROOFREAD  Workbook Page 125

Copy your revised essay onto a clean sheet of paper. Read it again. Correct any errors in grammar, word usage, mechanics, and spelling. Here are the additional changes Blaise plans to make when she prepares her final draft.

Blaise Yafcak

A Great Place to Visit

The Museum of Science in Boston, Massachusetts, is an exciting museum which can be visited many times without losing its appeal. The museum was founded in the 1830s but opened at its present site along the Charles River in 1951. It offers exhibits and activities which are both educational and fun.

The museum's mission is "to stimulate interest in and further understanding of science and technology and their importance for individuals and for society." In fact, the Museum of Science was the first all-inclusive science museum in the United States. It also has been a pioneer in introducing interactive exhibits.

The museum has a planetarium where laser light shows are set to popular music. The museum also has a theater which presents movies about dinosaurs, sea life, the Grand Canyon, and other topics. Courses for kids and adults are held at the museum throughout the year. One series of classes for high school kids is called "Mini Med-School." Each class focuses on a different health issue and is taught by a doctor who specializes in that field. Examples of the museum's many exhibits include *Beyond the X-ray*, *Butterfly Garden*, *Making Models*, *Natural Mysteries*, and *New England Habitats*.

My favorite exhibit at the museum is about lightning. After visitors are seated, one of the staff members talks about how lightning is made. The lecture is fascinating, but the demonstration that follows is even better! A machine actually produces bolts of lightning. Lightning right there in front of you! This exhibit is both dramatic and informative.

Boston's Museum of Science is one of the foremost science museums in the nation. When individuals visit it they are encouraged to learn about science and technology, while at the same time having fun. It is a wonderful museum to explore, whether you are a resident of Boston or a tourist from far away.

5 **PUBLISH** Prepare your final draft. Share your essay with your teacher and classmates.

Acknowledging the Past, Reaching for the Future

*T*he United States is a country made up of millions of people who are far away from their homelands. American artists often explore the emotions that this situation can bring about. Sometimes they show hope and excitement, other times loneliness and grief.

Carmen Lomas Garza, *Camas para Sueños* (1985)

In *Camas para Sueños* (Spanish for "Beds for Dreams"), two girls sit on the roof of their home looking at the full moon. Inside the house their mother stretches out a bright pink blanket to make the bed. Mexican-American artist Carmen Lomas Garza painted this scene of herself and her sister as young girls. They wear almost matching outfits—spotted shirts, pants, and similar shoes—which highlight their closeness. Below, their mother works hard to make their home a clean, safe place to have pleasant dreams. This painting celebrates Garza's sense of place as a girl within her family. As a Mexican American she sometimes felt less than welcomed by the locals in her town in south Texas, but in her own home she felt safe.

▲ Carmen Lomas Garza, *Camas para Sueños*, 1985, gouache, 28⅛ x 20½ in., Smithsonian American Art Museum

264

Hung Liu,
The Ocean Is the Dragon's World,
1995, mixed media, 96 × 82½ in.,
Smithsonian American Art Museum ▶

Hung Liu, *The Ocean Is the Dragon's World* (1995)

Artist Hung Liu grew up in China in the 1950s when there was great political unrest. Liu did her artwork in the United States, but she uses her art to recreate a world that was lost in China. In *The Ocean Is the Dragon's World*, she painted a portrait of the great aunt of the last Emperor of China, who sits in the center of the canvas looking out at the viewer.

The decorated robes of the Empress fill the painting. You can also see peacock feathers (upper left) and flowers. Liu hung an actual empty metal birdcage onto the canvas! She also added a piece of bamboo painted with Chinese letters on the far right border. This added touch makes the painting look like the cover of a bound book (the Chinese read from right to left). Who knows what stories this grand courtly woman might have to tell?

Both of these artists either came from another country or were the first generation in their family to live in the United States. They use their art to explore the distance between the world their families left behind and the world they discovered in the United States.

Apply What You Learned

1 Why do you think Carmen Lomas Garza called her painting "Beds for Dreams"?

2 In what way is the subject matter of *The Ocean Is the Dragon's World* different from *Camas para Sueños*?

Big Question
If you were an artist creating an artwork that explored the idea of "home," would you concentrate on the past or would you look toward the future? Explain your answer.

Workbook
Pages 127–128

265

UNIT
5

THE BIG QUESTION

What is the human spirit?

DEUTSCHE BUNDESPOST

60

ANNE FRANK · 12.6.1929 · 31.3.19

1979

USA
37

CESAR E. CHAVEZ

2003

This unit is about the human spirit. You will read informational texts that describe people who conquer life's obstacles with determination. You will also read literature that describes individuals who stand up for what they believe in. Reading, writing, and talking about these topics will help you practice using academic language and help you become a better student.

READING 1: Social Studies Article

- From *César Chávez: We Can Do It!* by Sunita Apte

READING 2: Short Story

- "The Scholarship Jacket" by Marta Salinas

READING 3: Social Studies Article

- "Listen Up" by Phil Taylor

READING 4: Play

- From *The Diary of Anne Frank: The Play* by Frances Goodrich and Albert Hackett, adapted by Wendy Kesselman

Listening and Speaking

At the end of this unit, you will create and present a **radio commercial**.

Writing

In this unit you will practice **persuasive writing**, which tries to influence the reader to change his or her opinion about a topic. After each reading, you will learn a skill to help you write a persuasive paragraph. At the end of the unit, you will use these skills to help you write a persuasive speech.

QuickWrite

Write a few sentences about a time when you fought for what you believed in. Read them to a partner.

What You Will Learn

Reading
- Vocabulary building: *Context, dictionary skills, word study*
- Reading strategy: *Distinguish fact from opinion*
- Text type: *Informational text (social studies)*

Grammar, Usage, and Mechanics
Inseparable phrasal verbs

Writing
Write an advertisement

THE BIG QUESTION

What is the human spirit? The United States is proud of its Declaration of Independence, the document that proclaimed the United States to be free of British rule. In this document, there is a line that reads, *We hold these truths to be self-evident: that all men are created equal.* This means that all people should be treated fairly.

Do you think that all people are treated fairly in the United States? How does a person feel when he or she is treated unfairly? How can this affect the human spirit?

BUILD BACKGROUND

You will read an excerpt from a biography called **César Chávez: We Can Do It!** A biography is a form of nonfiction. The writer tells the life story of another person. Most biographies are about famous or admirable people.

Chávez was a Mexican-American farm worker. For decades, Mexican-American farm workers were poorly paid and discriminated against. Chávez decided to do something about it. He organized protests and fought for better pay and treatment. Chávez did not believe in using violence to advance the workers' cause. His life and work inspired many people to regard him as a hero.

▲ César Chávez

Learn Key Words

Read these sentences. Use the context to figure out the meaning of the **red** words. Use a dictionary to check your answers. Then write each word and its meaning in your notebook.

Key Words

chemicals
crops
discrimination
migrant workers
strike
union

1. Farmers should not spray their fields with **chemicals** that can harm farm workers.

2. The farmer grows two **crops**, grapes and oranges.

3. The farm workers did not receive fair pay. They were victims of **discrimination**.

4. The **migrant workers** traveled from Mexico to the United States to find work.

5. The auto workers went on **strike**. They refused to work until the factory owners made conditions safer.

6. The teachers joined together to form a **union**. Working together gave them more power to protect their rights.

Practice

Workbook
Page 129

Write the sentences in your notebook. Choose a **red** word from the box above to complete each sentence. Then take turns reading the sentences aloud with a partner.

▲ Union workers meet in a vineyard.

1. The _____ never had steady jobs. They moved from place to place looking for work.

2. There are laws to prevent _____ in American schools and businesses.

3. The farmer told us that his corn and wheat _____ are growing well.

4. The workers are going on _____ because they want to be paid more money.

5. Some _____ used on farms are so dangerous that farm workers must wear masks and rubber gloves to handle them.

6. The group of workers belong to the _____. They meet to discuss problems and find solutions in the workplace.

Learn Academic Words

Study the **red** words and their meanings. You will find these words useful when talking and writing about informational texts. Write each word and its meaning in your notebook. After you read the excerpt from *César Chávez: We Can Do It!*, try to use these words to respond to the text.

founded = established a business, organization, school, etc.	➡	Carlos **founded** the union. He started it last year.
impact = effect that an event or situation has on someone or something	➡	The union's efforts had a great **impact** on the factory's owners.
labor = work that requires a lot of physical effort	➡	The farm owners relied on the **labor** of the migrant workers.
persistence = determination to do something even though it is difficult or other people oppose it	➡	The workers showed great **persistence**. They continued to strike until their pay was increased.

Practice

Workbook
Page 130

Work with a partner to answer these questions. Try to include the **red** word in your answer. Write the sentences in your notebook.

1. Who **founded** the United States of America?

2. What one event has had the greatest **impact** on your life? Why?

3. Have you ever had to do hard **labor**? If so, what was it?

4. Has there ever been a time when you showed great **persistence**? Explain.

Migrant workers' lives are filled with hard labor. ▼

Word Study: Capitalization

There are rules for using capital letters. Some of these rules are listed below.

Use Capital Letters for . . .	Examples
The word *I*	Sometimes **I** work at night.
The first letter of the first word in every sentence	**T**he farm workers had come to see one man.
All proper nouns: • The names/titles of people • Geographical terms • Historical events, eras, calendar items • Streets, cities, states, countries, continents • Ethnic groups, national groups, languages	**F**red **R**oss, **S**eñor **C**hávez, **Dr. B**ouchard **L**ake **T**ahoe **C**ésar **C**hávez **D**ay **B**eacon **S**treet, **S**acramento, **C**alifornia **M**exican **A**merican, **S**panish

Practice  Workbook Page 131

Work with a partner. Copy the sentences below into your notebook. Capitalize each proper noun.

1. luis is from bogota, colombia.

2. We don't have to go to school on memorial day.

3. In the summer, we like to spend time near the pacific ocean.

4. My aunt, lisa velarde, speaks both spanish and italian.

READING STRATEGY   DISTINGUISH FACT FROM OPINION

Distinguishing a fact from an opinion will help you form ideas about what you read. A fact is something that can be proven. An opinion is what someone believes or thinks. To distinguish between facts and opinions, follow these steps:

- As you read, ask yourself whether you can check what you are reading in an encyclopedia, a history book, or with some other research. If you can, it's probably a fact.

- Look for phrases the author uses to give opinions, for example, *I think*, *I believe*, *I suppose*, *personally*.

- Look for adjectives that go with opinions, for example, *best*, *wonderful*, *luckiest*, *horrible*, *bad*.

As you read about César Chávez, look for facts and opinions within the text. How can you tell the difference between them?

 Workbook Page 132

Set a purpose for reading As you read, think about the difficulties César Chávez faced. How did they strengthen his spirit? How did this help him accomplish his goals?

César Chávez: We Can Do It!

Sunita Apte

▲ Chávez as a young boy, watching a family member pick crops

It was April 10, 1966. More than 10,000 people were gathered in Sacramento, the capital city of California. Most of them were Mexican-American farm workers. These workers toiled in fields all day, picking grapes, cotton, or other crops. The work was hard. Their lives were hard.

The farm workers had come to see one man. He was a Mexican American who gave them hope. His name was César Chávez. César had walked 547 kilometers (340 mi.) to Sacramento. It took him almost a month. He had walked to draw attention to the lives of farm workers. Now, the entire nation was paying attention.

A Hard Life

César Chávez knew about the farm worker's life. He had been a migrant farm worker for many years. He had moved from place to place to find work, picking crops. He had spent long hours in the hot sun. He had bent down all day, working in the fields.

---

toiled, worked hard

272

▲ Many migrant families drove to California to look for work during the Great Depression.

Farm workers weren't paid much for all their hard work. Often, the growers they worked for cheated them. Most farm workers made barely enough to live. To survive, the whole family had to work in the fields, including the children. César had been working in the fields since he was eleven years old.

Yuma

César's life hadn't always been so hard. He was born near Yuma, Arizona, in 1927. His family owned a small store and a farm. They were not rich, but life was good.

Then the Great Depression hit. People lost their jobs and had no money. No one could afford to shop at the store. César's parents had to sell it. During the Great Depression a terrible drought struck many states. It lasted for years. The river that watered the Chávez family farm eventually dried up.

The family struggled to survive. Soon, however, they lost the farm. At that point, they decided to leave Arizona and drive to California to look for work.

Great Depression, a period of economic troubles in the 1930s that left many people poor and without jobs

drought, period of time when there is no, or very little, rain

BEFORE YOU GO ON

1 Why were farm workers' families forced to work in the fields?

2 What caused the Chávez family to lose their farm?

💡 **On Your Own**
What do you think would be the most challenging aspect of the migrant-worker lifestyle?

273

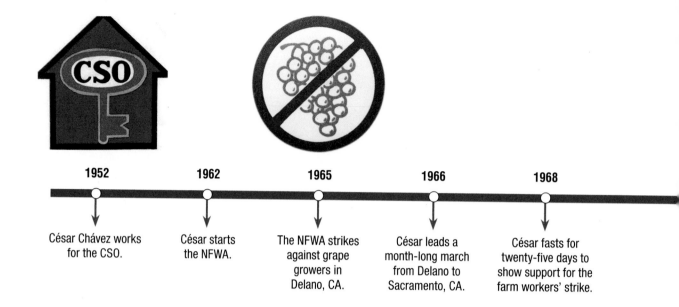

1952	1962	1965	1966	1968
César Chávez works for the CSO.	César starts the NFWA.	The NFWA strikes against grape growers in Delano, CA.	César leads a month-long march from Delano to Sacramento, CA.	César fasts for twenty-five days to show support for the farm workers' strike.

César's father often had trouble finding work in California. Sometimes, he would hear about a farm job. The family would drive long hours to get to the farm. When they arrived, there would be no job, or the job paid much less than the family had hoped.

The Chávez family also faced discrimination. Many white Californians looked down on Mexican Americans. Some restaurants had signs that read, "No Dogs or Mexicans Allowed." Mexican Americans were even supposed to sit in a special section at the movie theatre.

From School to the Fields

César's family finally settled in a poor neighborhood near San Jose, California. The neighborhood was called Sal Si Puedes, or "Get Out If You Can."

When César was fifteen years old, his father was hurt in a car accident. Instead of going to high school, César had to work in the fields. It was the only way his family could survive.

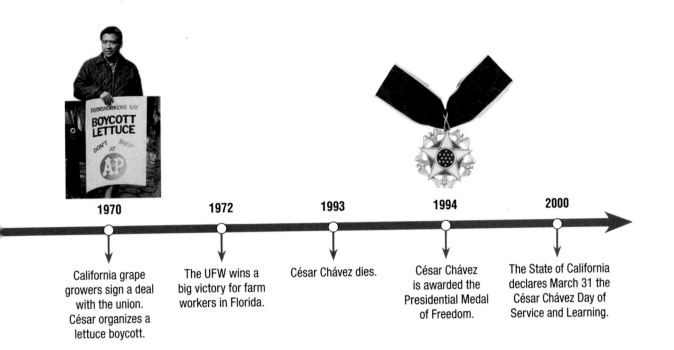

1970	1972	1993	1994	2000
California grape growers sign a deal with the union. César organizes a lettuce boycott.	The UFW wins a big victory for farm workers in Florida.	César Chávez dies.	César Chávez is awarded the Presidential Medal of Freedom.	The State of California declares March 31 the César Chávez Day of Service and Learning.

Farm work was grueling. César's back ached from bending down all day. His eyes stung from the chemicals sprayed in the fields to kill insects. His skin tore from yanking out beets. He had no rest breaks, no bathrooms, and no clean water to drink.

César wanted to go back to school. Instead, however, he joined the U.S. Navy. César hated the discrimination he experienced in the Navy. He felt that white people did not treat Mexican Americans fairly.

The Chance to Change Things

When César got out of the Navy, he married Helen Fabela. Together, they worked in the fields. César's time in the Navy had convinced him that Mexican-American farm workers needed to demand better treatment.

César talked to other farm workers about fighting for change. He listened to their problems. He became known around his neighborhood as someone worth talking to.

---

grueling, very difficult and painful

BEFORE YOU GO ON

1 What happened to the Chávez family when César was fifteen years old? What did this mean for César?

2 What made farm work grueling?

On Your Own
Have you ever felt discriminated against? Explain.

275

Fred Ross heard about César from a friend. Ross ran the Community Service Organization, or CSO. The CSO worked to help poor Mexican Americans. Ross hired César. At last, César would have a chance to change things.

César helped many people during his ten years at the CSO. Still, he thought that farm workers needed to form their own group to demand fair treatment. They needed a union.

In 1962, César quit the CSO to start the National Farm Workers Association, or NFWA. He wasn't sure it would be a success. To his surprise, many farm workers quickly joined the union. They were ready to fight for their rights.

The first big fight came three years later. In 1965, the union went on strike against some grape growers in Delano, California. Union members stopped work and demanded better pay.

"Don't Buy Grapes!"

Day after day, workers picketed grape farms. They marched up and down, shouting "¡Huelga!" or "Strike!"

The growers didn't give in. They thought the farm workers would run out of money. Then the workers would have to come back to their jobs.

César wanted to put pressure on the growers.

He needed the rest of America to support the strike. He sent union workers to cities across the United States. They went to supermarkets and told people, "Don't buy grapes."

The growers lost a lot of money because of the boycott. Still, they didn't give in.

▲ A National Farm Workers Association poster

---

rights, freedoms that are or should be
    allowed by law
give in, admit defeat
put pressure, attempt to make someone
    do something by using influence,
    arguments, or threats
boycott, act of refusing to buy the
    products or services of a company

César decided that something more was needed to grab the public's attention. So, he organized a march with sixty-seven other protestors. He began walking the 547 kilometers (340 mi.) from Delano to Sacramento on March 17, 1966. The marchers carried banners reading, "¡Viva la Causa!" Each day, more people joined the march.

Reporters and film crews followed the marchers. They learned how farm workers lived. They saw the migrant shacks. They shared the truth with people everywhere.

The growers didn't like the publicity. Finally, they agreed to the union's demands. On the steps of Sacramento's capitol building, César joyously announced the victory.

César continued the fight. It took four more years. Finally, in 1970, the rest of Delano's grape growers signed contracts with the union.

Then César turned his attention to California's lettuce growers. He organized strikes and boycotts against them. He was sent to jail for his work. In the end, however, his union won.

In 1975, California passed the Agricultural Labor Relations Act. This law promised basic rights for all farm workers.

▲ César and Helen Chávez march from Delano to Sacramento.

A True Friend of Farm Workers

César Chávez died in 1993, at the age of sixty-six. Fifty-thousand people came to his funeral.

For over thirty years, César had fought for a better life for farm workers. He had starved himself, marched hundreds of miles, spent time in jail, and even received death threats.

Through it all, César never lost hope. He never stopped believing that change was possible. "¡Sí, se puede!" he said. "Yes, it can be done." César proved that poor people could fight and win. He had done it.

---

shacks, buildings made of cheap materials
publicity, attention someone or something gets from newspapers, television, or other media sources
contracts, legal written agreements between two or more people or companies, which say what each side will do

BEFORE YOU GO ON

1 What was the CSO? What was its purpose?

2 What were the results of the grape strike?

On Your Own
Would you join a union? Why or why not?

277

COMPREHENSION  Workbook Page 133

Right There

1. How old was Chávez when he began working in the fields?
2. What did the Agricultural Labor Relations Act promise to do?

Think and Search

3. In what kinds of situations was Chávez discriminated against?
4. What kinds of growers did Chávez protest against?

Author and You

5. Why did Chávez focus his attention on farm workers?
6. Why do you think Chávez chose Sacramento as the final destination for his march against grape growers?

On Your Own

7. Do you think forming a union is an effective way for workers to communicate their wants and needs? Explain.
8. How important is the media's coverage of events such as union strikes? Explain.

▲ A union flag

IN YOUR OWN WORDS

Use the words below to summarize the reading for a partner.

A Hard Life	➡	migrant workers, growers, children
Yuma	➡	farm, drought, discrimination
From School to the Fields	➡	hard labor, Navy
The Chance to Change Things	➡	CSO, NFWA
"Don't Buy Grapes!"	➡	Delano, strike, march, contracts
A True Friend of Farm Workers	➡	funeral, fought for a better life, never lost hope

DISCUSSION

Discuss in pairs or small groups.

1. In what ways did the NFWA protest against growers?
2. Which way do you think was the most effective and why?

Q **What is the human spirit?** Do you think that obstacles, such as those faced by César Chávez, make a person stronger? Explain.

Listening TIP

When your classmates share their ideas, listen for details that support their opinions. Ask yourself, "Did the speaker explain why these ideas are important?"

READ FOR FLUENCY

It is often easier to read a text if you understand the difficult words and phrases. Work with a partner. Choose a paragraph from the reading. Identify the words and phrases you do not know or have trouble pronouncing. Look up the difficult words in a dictionary.

Take turns pronouncing the words and phrases with your partner. If necessary, ask your teacher to model the correct pronunciation. Then take turns reading the paragraph aloud. Give each other feedback on your reading.

EXTENSION

Workbook Page 133

In 2000, California declared March 31 the César Chávez Day of Service and Learning. Work with a partner to find out which other states recognize this day. Use the library or Internet to learn about the activities that occur and the opportunities for people to get involved. When your research is complete, share your information with the class. Explain where and how people honor this American hero.

▲ A woman holds a sign at an event honoring César Chávez.

Grammar and Writing

Inseparable Phrasal Verbs

A phrasal verb is created by combining a verb + one or more prepositions. A phrasal verb has its own special meaning, different from the meaning of the original verb. Many phrasal verbs are inseparable, which means that a noun or pronoun always follows, never comes before, the preposition(s). Read the following examples of phrasal verbs from *César Chávez: We Can Do It!*

Example: Often, the growers they **worked for** cheated them.
Definition: worked for = employed by

Example: César's family finally **settled in** a poor neighborhood near San Jose, California.
Definition: settled in = went to live in a new place

Example: Many white Californians **looked down on** Mexican Americans.
Definition: looked down on = acted as if someone wasn't good enough

---

Practice
Workbook
Page 134

Work with a partner. Find the following phrasal verbs in the excerpt from *César Chávez: We Can Do It!* Use the context of the sentence to create a definition for each phrasal verb. Then check the definitions in a dictionary.

1. hear about
2. look for
3. listen to
4. go back to
5. fight for
6. run out of
7. agree to
8. got out of

280

WRITING A PERSUASIVE PARAGRAPH

Write an Advertisement

At the end of this unit, you will write a speech. To do this, you will need to learn about persuasive writing, or writing in which the author tries to influence the reader's opinion. An advertisement is an example of persuasive writing. It is a message that encourages the reader to buy a product or service. When you write a print advertisement, it is important to identify your intended audience. Tailor your message to this audience. Begin with an attention-grabbing phrase or question. Then include facts and details that describe the product, its function, and how it will benefit the buyer.

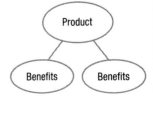

Here is a model advertisement. Before writing, the writer used a word web to organize his information. Notice how he includes facts and details that appeal to his audience.

Andrew Denkus

Grapes Are Great!

Grapes are known as nature's candy. But did you know that they have been celebrated for years because of their health benefits? Grapes are a great source of potassium and vitamins A and C, and they also contain powerful antioxidants. Researchers agree that by adding grapes to your diet, you can help prevent chronic illnesses, including heart disease, cancer, and age-associated diseases such as Alzheimer's. They also lower your cholesterol! Plus, they are a great high-energy, bite-size snack, perfect for busy people on the go. They are very refreshing and can even be frozen for a cool after-school treat. So whether you enjoy red, white, or seedless, show your strength in numbers, don't delay—buy your grapes today!

Practice

Workbook Page 135

Write a print advertisement for a product, such as a computer, or a service, such as babysitting. Use a graphic organizer to help you. Be sure to include phrasal verbs in your paragraph.

Writing Checklist

IDEAS:
- ✔ I began my ad with an interesting phrase or question.

WORD CHOICE:
- ✔ I included facts and details to try and persuade the audience.

281

Prepare to Read

What You Will Learn

Reading

- Vocabulary building: *Literary terms, word study*
- Reading strategy: *Predict 2*
- Text type: *Literature (short story)*

Grammar, Usage, and Mechanics
Punctuation in quotations

Writing
Write a review

THE BIG QUESTION

What is the human spirit? Teenagers in the United States are required to attend school. There they learn about academic subjects and develop skills that will help them in the future. Think about a time when you studied hard for a test and received a good grade on it. Did you feel that the result was worth the effort? What if you hadn't received a good grade? Would the experience have broken your spirit? Share your experiences with a partner.

BUILD BACKGROUND

In this section, you will read a short story called **"The Scholarship Jacket."** The word *scholarship* has several meanings; in this story, *scholarship* means *academic award*.

   "The Scholarship Jacket" is a story about a Mexican girl named Marta. She is the class valedictorian, or the student with the highest grades. Different schools have different ways of recognizing a valedictorian's academic achievement. Some schools invite the valedictorian to present a speech at their graduation ceremony. The valedictorian at Marta's school is rewarded with a special scholarship jacket. Marta expects to receive the jacket, but she is surprised when the school considers giving it to someone else.

A class valedictorian gives a speech at her graduation ceremony. ▶

Learn Literary Words

A **dialogue** is a conversation between characters. In poems, novels, and short stories, dialogue is usually shown by quotation marks (" ") to indicate a speaker's exact words. Punctuation marks (! . , ?) let the reader know how the conversation should be read. Read the dialogue from "The Scholarship Jacket" below.

Literary Words

dialogue
theme

> He turned to me and asked quietly, "What does a scholarship jacket mean?"
> I answered quickly; maybe there was a chance. "It means you've earned it by having the highest grades for eight years and that's why they're giving it to you."

The **theme** is a central message in a story. Sometimes a theme is directly stated in the text. More often, it is presented indirectly. The reader must decide what the theme is based on and what the text reveals about people and life. Some themes in literature include friendship, celebration, forgiveness, and bravery.

Practice  **Workbook Page 136**

Work with a partner. Read the excerpt from "The Scholarship Jacket" below. Then answer the questions.

> "I refuse to do it! I don't care who her father is, her grades don't even begin to compare to Marta's. I won't lie or falsify records. Marta has a straight A plus average and you know it." That was Mr. Schmidt and he sounded very angry. Mr. Boone's voice sounded calm and quiet.
> "Look, Joann's father is not only on the Board, he owns the only store in town; we could say it was a close tie and—"
> The pounding in my ears drowned out the rest of the words, only a word here and there filtered through. ". . . Marta is Mexican . . . resign . . . won't do it. . . ."

1. What are the spoken words, or the quotations, in the story excerpt?
2. Who is the speaker of each quotation?

Learn Academic Words

Study the **red** words and their meanings. You will find these words useful when talking and writing about literature. Write each word and its meaning in your notebook. After you read "The Scholarship Jacket," try to use these words to respond to the text.

academic = relating to work done in schools, colleges, or universities	→	Elena earned the highest grades in her class. She is proud of her **academic** achievement.
policy = a plan that is agreed to by a political party, government, or organization	→	It was the school's **policy** to give a special jacket to the class valedictorian.
principal = someone who is in charge of a school	→	The **principal** called me into her office to talk about my grades.
tradition = a belief or custom that has existed for a long time	→	Every year, the students at my school hold a bake sale to help raise money for charity. It is a **tradition**.

Practice  **Workbook Page 137**

Work with a partner to answer these questions. Try to include the **red** word in your answer. Write the sentences in your notebook.

1. What is your greatest **academic** achievement?

2. What is your school's **policy** regarding cell phones in the classroom?

3. Who is the **principal** of your school? Have you or someone you know ever been called to the principal's office? Why?

4. What is one **tradition** that your school celebrates every year?

Word Study: Words Ending with Consonant + *-le, -al, -el*

Words that end with a *consonant + -le, -al,* and *-el* can be difficult to spell because they share the sound, /əl/. Specific rules for when to use *-le, -al,* or *-el* do not exist. Therefore, it is best to memorize the spelling of each new word you learn. Read the examples below.

Word Ending	Example	Sentence
-le	lit**tle**	My grandfather tended to his **little** bean plants.
-al	princip**al**	The **principal** called me into his office.
-el	caram**el**	I took the **caramel** from my grandmother.

Practice
Workbook Page 138

Work with a partner. Copy the words from the box below into your notebook. Circle each word ending. Then say one of the words. Ask your partner to spell it aloud. Check your partner's spelling. Then have your partner say the next word. Continue until you can spell all of the words correctly.

bagel	crumple	dental	handle	jewel	unable

READING STRATEGY | MAKE INFERENCES

Making inferences helps you figure out the information that authors do not always give directly. When you make inferences (or infer), you are figuring out what the author means. To make inferences, follow these steps:

- As you read, think about the characters and setting. Pay attention to the events and situations described. What can you guess about the characters and setting?

- Think about your own experiences. Do they help you understand the events and situations that you are reading about?

- Now use the information in the story and your own experiences to make inferences.

As you read "The Scholarship Jacket," think about what the author means, but does not say directly. What inferences can you make from what the author wrote?

Workbook Page 139

285

Set a purpose for reading As you read, notice Marta's reactions to the discrimination she encounters. How is she able to retain her sense of spirit in the face of such negativity?

THE SCHOLARSHIP JACKET

Marta Salinas

The small Texas school that I attended carried out a tradition every year during the eighth grade graduation; a beautiful gold and green jacket, the school colors, was awarded to the class valedictorian, the student who had maintained the highest grades for eight years. The scholarship jacket had a big gold S on the left front side and the winner's name was written in gold letters on the pocket.

My oldest sister Rosie had won the jacket a few years back and I fully expected to win also. I was fourteen and in the eighth grade. I had been a straight A student since the first grade, and the last year I had looked forward to owning that jacket. My father was a farm laborer who couldn't earn enough money to feed eight children, so when I was six I was given to my grandparents to raise. We couldn't participate in sports at school because there were registration fees, uniform costs, and trips out of town; so even though we were quite agile and athletic, there would never be a sports school jacket for us. This one, the scholarship jacket, was our only chance.

In May, close to graduation, spring fever struck, and no one paid any attention in class; instead we stared out the windows and at each other, wanting to speed up the last few weeks of school. I despaired every time I looked in the mirror.

---

registration fees, monies paid when signing up for something
uniform, clothing that members of an organization, such as a sports team, wear
agile, able to move quickly and easily
despaired, felt very sad

Pencil thin, not a curve anywhere, I was called "Beanpole" and "String Bean" and I knew that's what I looked like. A flat chest, no hips, and a brain, that's what I had. That really isn't much fun for a fourteen-year-old to work with, I thought, as I absentmindedly wandered from my history class to the gym.

Another hour of sweating in basketball and displaying my toothpick legs was coming up. Then I remembered my P.E. shorts were still in a bag under my desk where I'd forgotten them. I had to walk all the way back and get them. Coach Thompson was a real bear if anyone wasn't dressed for P.E. She had said I was a good **forward** and once she even tried to talk Grandma into letting me join the team. Grandma, of course, said no.

I was almost back at my classroom's door when I heard angry voices and arguing. I stopped. I didn't mean to **eavesdrop**; I just hesitated, not knowing what to do. I needed those shorts and I was going to be late, but I didn't want to interrupt an argument between my teachers. I recognized the voices: Mr. Schmidt, my history teacher, and Mr. Boone, my math teacher. They seemed to be arguing about me. I couldn't believe it. I still remember the shock that **rooted** me flat against the wall as if I were trying to blend in with the **graffiti** written there.

P.E., Physical Education, or gym class
forward, basketball player whose main job is to shoot the ball at the basket
eavesdrop, listen secretly to other people's conversations
rooted, made it so someone or something cannot move
graffiti, rude or humorous writing and pictures on the walls of buildings

BEFORE YOU GO ON

1 Why couldn't Marta and her siblings participate in school sports?

2 What happened when Marta returned to her classroom?

On Your Own
Do you think students should be rewarded for their academic achievements? If so, in what ways?

287

"I refuse to do it! I don't care who her father is, her grades don't even begin to compare to Marta's. I won't lie or falsify records. Marta has a straight A plus average and you know it." That was Mr. Schmidt and he sounded very angry. Mr. Boone's voice sounded calm and quiet.

"Look, Joann's father is not only on the Board, he owns the only store in town; we could say it was a close tie and—"

The pounding in my ears drowned out the rest of the words, only a word here and there filtered through. " . . . Marta is Mexican . . . resign . . . won't do it. . . . " Mr. Schmidt came rushing out, and luckily for me went down the opposite way toward the auditorium, so he didn't see me. Shaking, I waited a few minutes and then went in and grabbed my bag and fled from the room. Mr. Boone looked up when I came in but didn't say anything. To this day I don't remember if I got in trouble in P.E. for being late or how I made it through the rest of the afternoon. I went home very sad and cried into my pillow that night so Grandmother wouldn't hear me. It seemed a cruel coincidence that I had overheard that conversation.

The next day when the principal called me into his office, I knew what it would be about. He looked uncomfortable and unhappy. I decided I wasn't going to make it any easier for him so I looked him straight in the eye. He looked away and fidgeted with the papers on his desk.

"Marta," he said, "there's been a change in policy this year regarding the scholarship jacket. As you know, it has always been free." He cleared his throat and continued. "This year the Board decided to charge fifteen dollars—which still won't cover the complete cost of the jacket."

I stared at him in shock and a small sound of dismay escaped my throat. I hadn't expected this. He still avoided looking in my eyes.

"So if you are unable to pay the fifteen dollars for the jacket, it will be given to the next one in line."

Standing with all the dignity I could muster, I said, "I'll speak to my grandfather about it, sir, and let you know tomorrow." I cried on the walk home from the bus stop. The first road was a quarter of a mile from the highway, so by the time I got home, my eyes were red and puffy.

"Where's Grandpa?" I asked Grandma, looking down at the floor so she wouldn't ask me why I'd been crying. She was sewing on a quilt and didn't look up.

Board, committee that controls how schools in an area are run
tie, situation in which two people in a competition have the same result or finish
resign, officially quit a job
dismay, disappointment and unhappiness
dignity, self-respect
muster, collect

✔ **LITERARY CHECK**
Which lines in this dialogue are Marta's? Which are the principal's?

BEFORE YOU GO ON

1 Who did Mr. Boone want to give the jacket to? Why?

2 How do you think the principal felt about having to give the jacket to Joann? Why?

On Your Own
What would you do if you were in Marta's situation?

289

"I think he's out back working in the bean field."

I went outside and looked out at the fields. There he was. I could see him walking between the rows, his body bent over the little plants, hoe in hand. I walked slowly out to him, trying to think how I could best ask him for the money.

There was a cool breeze blowing and a sweet smell of mesquite in the air, but I didn't appreciate it. I kicked at a dirt clod. I wanted that jacket so much. It was more than just being a valedictorian and giving a little thank you speech for the jacket on graduation night. It represented eight years of hard work and expectation. I knew I had to be honest with Grandpa; it was my only chance. He saw me and looked up.

He waited for me to speak. I cleared my throat nervously and clasped my hands behind my back so he wouldn't see them shaking. "Grandpa, I have a big favor to ask you," I said in Spanish, the only language he knew. He still waited silently. I tried again. "Grandpa, this year the principal said the scholarship jacket is not going to be free. It's going to cost fifteen dollars and I have to take the money in tomorrow, otherwise it'll be given to someone else." The last words came out in an eager rush. Grandpa

---

hoe, garden tool with a long handle, used to loosen soil
mesquite, tree bark used to cook food
expectation, the belief that one will get something
favor, thing one does for someone else out of kindness

straightened up tiredly and leaned his chin on the hoe handle.
He looked out over the field that was filled with the tiny green bean plants.
I waited desperately hoping he'd say I could have the money.

He turned to me and asked quietly, "What does a scholarship jacket mean?"

I answered quickly; maybe there was a chance. "It means you've earned it by having the highest grades for eight years and that's why they're giving it to you."

Too late I realized the significance of my words. Grandpa knew that I understood it was not a matter of money. It wasn't that. He went back to hoeing the weeds that sprang up between the delicate little bean plants. It was a time consuming job; sometimes the small shoots were right next to each other. Finally he spoke again.

"Then if you pay for it, Marta, it's not a scholarship jacket, is it? Tell your principal I will not pay the fifteen dollars."

I walked back to the house and locked myself in the bathroom for a long time. I was angry with Grandfather even though I knew he was right, and I was angry with the Board, whoever they were. Why did they have to change the rules just when it was my turn to win the jacket?

---

desperately, in an anxious manner
significance, importance or meaning

BEFORE YOU GO ON

1. What did Marta ask her grandfather?

2. Why was the scholarship jacket important to Marta?

On Your Own
Make a prediction: Do you think the principal will give the jacket to Joann if Marta does not have the money to buy it?

291

It was a very sad and withdrawn girl who dragged into the principal's office the next day. This time he did look me in the eyes.

"What did your grandfather say?"

I sat very straight in my chair.

"He said to tell you he won't pay the fifteen dollars."

The principal muttered something I couldn't understand under his breath, and walked over to the window. He stood looking out at something outside. He looked bigger than usual when he stood up; he was a tall gaunt man with gray hair, and I watched the back of his head while I waited for him to speak.

"Why?" he finally asked. "Your grandfather has the money. Doesn't he own a small bean farm?"

I looked at him, forcing my eyes to stay dry. "He said if I had to pay for it, then it wouldn't be a scholarship jacket," I said and stood up to leave. "I guess you'll just have to give it to Joann." I hadn't meant to say that; it just slipped out. I was almost to the door when he stopped me.

"Marta—wait."

I turned to him, waiting. What did he want now?

I could feel my heart pounding. Something bitter and vile tasting was coming up in my mouth; I was afraid I was going to be sick. I didn't need any sympathy speeches. He sighed loudly and went back to his big desk. He looked at me, biting his lip, as if thinking.

---

withdrawn, quiet and not wanting to be with people
muttered, spoke in a quiet voice
bitter, having a strong, bad taste
sympathy, concern for someone

292

"Okay, damn it. We'll make an exception in your case. I'll tell the Board, you'll get your jacket."

I could hardly believe it. I spoke in a trembling rush. "Oh, thank you, sir!" Suddenly I felt great. I didn't know about adrenaline in those days, but I knew something was pumping through me, making me feel as tall as the sky. I wanted to yell, jump, run the mile, do something. I ran out so I could cry in the hall where there was no one to see me. At the end of the day, Mr. Schmidt winked at me and said, "I hear you're getting a scholarship jacket this year."

His face looked as happy and innocent as a baby's, but I knew better. Without answering I gave him a quick hug and ran to the bus.

I cried on the walk home again, but this time because I was so happy. I couldn't wait to tell Grandpa and ran straight to the field.

I joined him in the row where he was working and without saying anything I crouched down and started pulling up the weeds with my hands. Grandpa worked alongside me for a few minutes, but he didn't ask what had happened. After I had a little pile of weeds between the rows, I stood up and faced him.

"The principal said he's making an exception for me, Grandpa, and I'm getting the jacket after all. That's after I told him what you said."

Grandpa didn't say anything, he just gave me a pat on the shoulder and a smile. He pulled out the crumpled red handkerchief that he always carried in his back pocket and wiped the sweat off his forehead.

"Better go see if your grandmother needs any help with supper."

I gave him a big grin. He didn't fool me. I skipped and ran back to the house whistling some silly tune.

---

adrenaline, a chemical produced by your body that makes your heart beat faster
winked, closed and opened one eye quickly
innocent, inexperienced
exception, exclusion from a rule

ABOUT THE **AUTHOR**

Marta Salinas was born in California. She attended college at the University of California, Irvine, where she studied writing. Today she is a writer and an environmental advocate.

✔ **LITERARY CHECK**
*What is the **theme** of this story?*

BEFORE YOU GO ON

1. How do you think Marta's grandfather felt after Marta won the jacket?

2. What do you think Marta learned from her experience with the principal?

On Your Own
Do you feel Mr. Boone and the principal should have been disciplined for their behavior? If so, how?

Review and Practice

READER'S THEATER

Speaking TIP

Use expressions and movements that match the lines you are reading.

Act out the following scene with a partner.

Marta: Grandpa, can you please give me fifteen dollars?

Grandpa: Why? What do you need it for?

Marta: My scholarship jacket.

Grandpa: You have to pay for the jacket? Your sister didn't have to pay for hers.

Marta: I know, but the school changed its policy.

Grandpa: Why do you want this jacket so badly?

Marta: Because I've earned it.

Grandpa: If you've earned it, Marta, you shouldn't have to pay for it. Tell your principal that I will not give you the money.

COMPREHENSION

Workbook Page 140

Right There

1. Why did Marta live with her grandparents?
2. What business does Marta's grandfather own?

Think and Search

3. Which two people in the story wanted Joann to receive the scholarship jacket?
4. How and why is Marta's behavior different each time she meets with the principal?

Author and You

5. How are the actions of Marta's grandfather an example of the human spirit?
6. What do you think the author's purpose was in writing this text?

7. Have you ever overheard a conversation you were not supposed to hear? What was it about?

8. How does your school reward students for their academic achievements?

DISCUSSION

Discuss in pairs or small groups.

1. Why do you think the principal gave Marta the scholarship jacket after all?

2. What other kinds of achievements can people earn besides academic achievements?

◉ **What is the human spirit?** How does performing a task well and being recognized for it affect a person's spirit?

◀ A champion swimmer holds a trophy.

RESPONSE TO LITERATURE

Workbook
Page 140

At the end of the story, the principal promises to give the scholarship jacket to Marta. How would the story be different if the principal had given Joann the jacket? Work with a partner. Write a new ending to the story. Include the reactions of Marta, Grandpa, and Mr. Schmidt.

Grammar and Writing

GRAMMAR, USAGE, AND MECHANICS

Punctuation in Quotations

Punctuation is important when you read quotations and include them in your writing. Use quotation marks (" ") and a comma (,) to separate quoted speech from the phrase that identifies the speaker. Also, be sure to capitalize the first word within a quotation. Read the examples below.

> "I think he's out back working in the bean field," Grandma said.
> He said, "I hear you're getting a scholarship jacket this year."

If the phrase that identifies the speaker comes between the quoted speech, use a comma after the first part of the quoted speech and after the phrase. Include both parts of the quoted speech in quotation marks.

> "Marta," he said, "there's been a change in policy regarding the scholarship jacket."

If the quoted speech is a question or an exclamation, use a question mark (?) or an exclamation point (!) instead of a comma at the end of the quoted speech.

> He said, "I refuse to do it!"
> "What does a scholarship jacket mean?" he asked.

Practice  Workbook Page 141

Work with a partner. Copy the sentences below into your notebook. Correctly punctuate each sentence.

1. I can't believe they changed the policy this year she said loudly
2. Why did they change their policy Grandpa asked
3. Grandpa said I will not give you the fifteen dollars
4. Dinner's ready Grandma yelled from the porch
5. No he firmly replied I will not give the jacket to someone who does not deserve it

296

WRITING A PERSUASIVE PARAGRAPH

Write a Review

You have learned that an advertisement is a form of persuasive writing. Another kind of persuasive writing is a review, or a writer's opinion about a book, movie, or other work. The purpose of a review is to persuade the reader to experience the work or to avoid it.

When you write a review, begin with a brief summary or description of the work. Then state your opinion of it—whether you liked it or did not like it and why. Provide reasons for your opinion, and support it with examples from the work, such as direct quotations or descriptions.

Here is a sample review. The writer used a chart to organize her information. Then she described the story, included her opinion, and used examples from the story to support it.

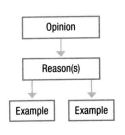

Opinion

↓

Reason(s)

↓

Example   Example

Blaise Yafcak

"The Scholarship Jacket"

"The Scholarship Jacket" is about a girl named Marta who earns her school's top prize, a scholarship jacket. Marta, whose family is poor, discovers that the school principal wants to give the jacket to the daughter of a school board member instead. The principal tries to prevent Marta from receiving the jacket by telling her she will have to pay for it. Marta asks her grandfather for the money, but he refuses to give it to her. I liked this story because I think both Marta and her grandfather are admirable. For example, I thought Marta showed a lot of strength when she looked the principal in the eye as he told her she would have to pay for the jacket. In addition, Marta's grandfather could simply have ignored the school's discriminatory ways and paid for the jacket. Instead he said, "Tell your principal I will not pay the fifteen dollars." These characters are strong and realistic. As a result, I recommend "The Scholarship Jacket" to anyone who has had to fight for what he or she believes in.

Writing Checklist

VOICE:
☑ I stated my opinion clearly.

WORD CHOICE:
☑ I used examples from the work to support my opinion.

Practice

Workbook
Page 142

Choose a book, CD, play, or film to review. Use a graphic organizer. State your opinion clearly and support it with examples from the work. Be sure to use reported speech correctly.

297

What You Will Learn

Reading

- Vocabulary building: *Context, dictionary skills, word study*
- Reading strategy: *Identify main idea and details*
- Text type: *Informational text (social studies)*

Grammar, Usage, and Mechanics
Present perfect with *for* and *since*

Writing
Write a letter to the editor

THE BIG QUESTION

What is the human spirit? Each of the five senses—sight, hearing, taste, smell, and touch—provides information about the world around us. Work with a partner. Copy the chart below into your notebook. Write three more items under each heading that you perceive with that sense. What is the importance of each sense? How would you react to the world differently if you lost one or more of these senses? What effect would this have on your spirit? Discuss with a partner.

Sight	Hearing	Taste	Smell	Touch
car	CD	lemon	flower	cotton ball

BUILD BACKGROUND

You will read a nonfiction magazine article called **"Listen Up"** about the football team from the California School for the Deaf-Riverside (CSDR).

CSDR gives hearing-impaired students a chance to succeed in academics and athletics. Over 500 students attend CSDR. They range in age from eighteen months to twenty-two years old.

One of the school's missions is to teach their students that being hearing-impaired does not have to limit what they can do. The school's football team is a perfect example of this. Although they are not able to hear each other, the players have learned how to work as a team and how to believe in themselves—even in the face of opposition.

Learn Key Words

Read these sentences. Use the context to figure out the meaning of the **red** words. Use a dictionary to check your answers. Then write each word and its meaning in your notebook.

1. We worked hard to **accomplish** our goal, and we were successful.

2. The players use a code to **communicate** with each other.

3. The team members are **hearing impaired**. They either cannot hear at all or are unable to hear well.

4. The other team plays well. It is our only **obstacle** to winning the state title.

5. If we defeat our **opponent**, we will be the new champions.

6. The coaches use **sign language** to converse with their players. Each hand movement they use has a special meaning.

Key Words

accomplish
communicate
hearing impaired
obstacle
opponent
sign language

Practice

Write the sentences in your notebook. Choose a **red** word from the box above to complete each sentence. Then take turns reading the sentences aloud with a partner.

1. Members of the debate team set goals and then work hard to _____ them.

2. Two team members were unable to participate. This was an _____ the team had not planned for.

3. The debate team lost to its _____ .

4. Not all people _____ by speaking aloud to each other.

5. Because he is _____, Andrew didn't hear the teacher call his name.

6. People who cannot hear often use _____ to communicate with each other.

▲ Two women converse using sign language.

299

Learn Academic Words

Study the **red** words and their meanings. You will find these words useful when talking and writing about informational texts. Write each word and its meaning in your notebook. After you read "Listen Up," try to use these words to respond to the text.

Academic Words

participate
perceive
prior
team

participate = take part in an activity or event	➡	Many students **participate** in after-school clubs and activities.
perceive = understand or think about something in a particular way	➡	We use our senses to **perceive** the world around us.
prior = before	➡	The team had a poor record **prior** to the coach's arrival. Then their performance improved.
team = a group of people who compete against another group in a sport, game, etc.	➡	There are many players on Andrea's basketball **team**.

Practice

Work with a partner to answer these questions. Try to include the **red** word in your answer. Write the sentences in your notebook.

1. In what kinds of school sports or clubs do you **participate**?

2. Which senses would you use to **perceive** a bouncing basketball?

3. Are there any special exercises you perform **prior** to playing a sport?

4. Have you ever been part of a **team**? If so, what kind?

Word Study: Antonyms

Antonyms are words that have the opposite or nearly opposite meanings from each other. For example, the antonym for the word *above* is *below*, and the antonym for *fast* is *slow*. Knowing antonyms can help build your vocabulary, and it also helps you to figure out the meanings of unfamiliar words.

> At first all they did was **lose** games, then they learned how to **win**.
> The crowd made a lot of **noise**, but all the players heard was **silence**.

Practice

Copy the chart below in your notebook and complete it by yourself. Then share your answers with a partner. Did you find the same antonyms? Check a thesaurus to see if there are other antonyms for each word.

Word	Antonym
forward	
doubt	
failure	
divide	
beginning	
strength	

READING STRATEGY   IDENTIFY MAIN IDEA AND DETAILS

Identifying the main idea and details in a reading helps you see key points the author is making. The main idea is the most important idea in the text. The details are small pieces of information that support the main idea. To identify the main idea and details, follow these steps:

- Read the first paragraph. What do you think is the most important idea?
- Read the whole text. Look for examples, facts, dates, and sentences that tell more about the main idea. These are the details.
- Remember that the main idea may be at the beginning, in the middle, or at the end of a paragraph.

As you read "Listen Up," identify the main idea of each paragraph and of the whole article. Then find details that support those main ideas.

READING 3

INFORMATIONAL TEXT

SOCIAL STUDIES

Set a purpose for reading In what ways can others help to strengthen our sense of self and lift our spirits? As you read, identify the people who made a difference to the CSDR team and how they did so.

LISTEN UP

Phil Taylor

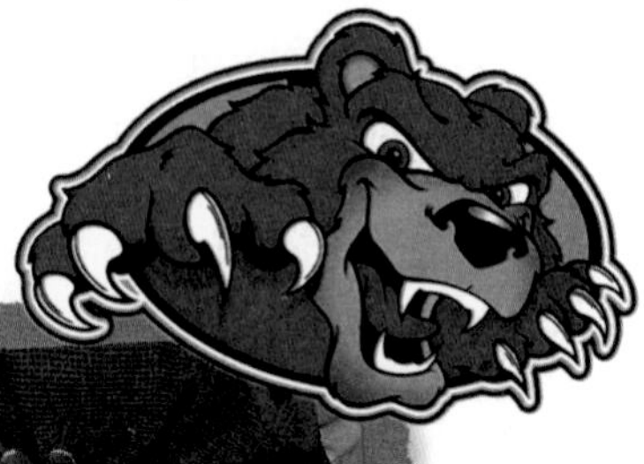

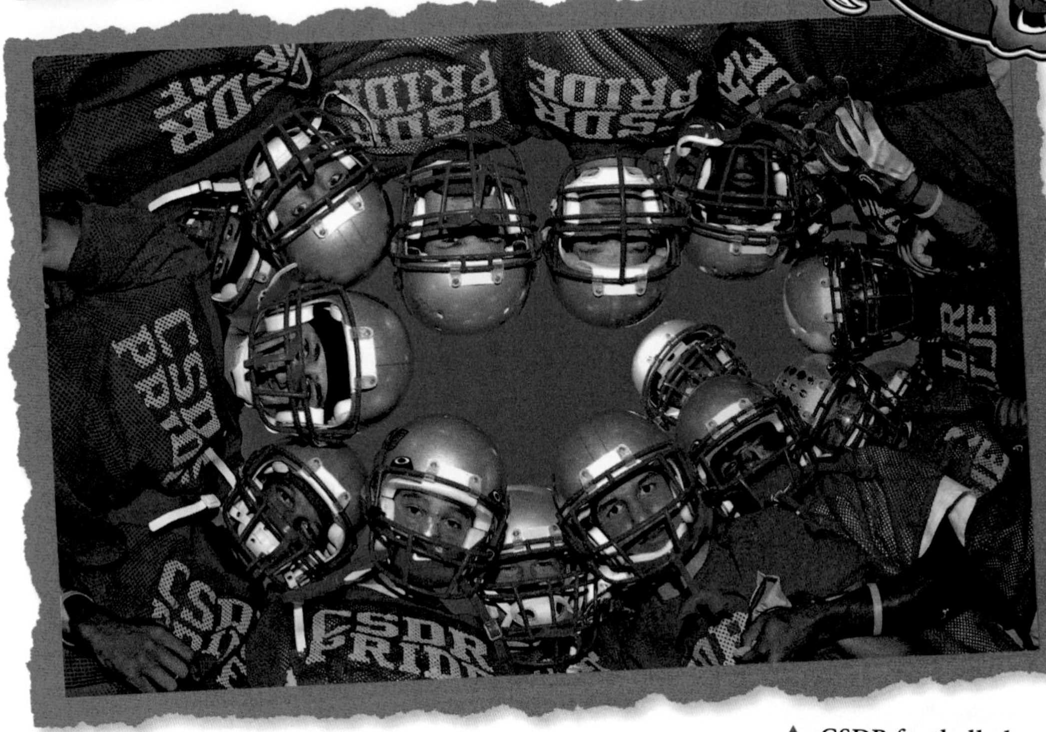

▲ CSDR football players

The sounds of high school football surrounded player Selwyn Abrahamson as he grabbed the football and ran upfield. There was the crash of pads as he tackled an opponent. There were the cheers of fans. There was the referee's whistle when he scored a touchdown. But Abrahamson heard only one thing:

Silence.

Abrahamson plays football for the California School for the Deaf-Riverside (CSDR). He and his teammates live in a quiet world. They cannot hear the words and noises that most of us take for granted.

pads, thick pieces of material players wear to protect their bodies
tackled, forced to the ground
fans, people who support a sports team

touchdown, play in football during which a team scores six points
take for granted, accept without question

But part of the school's mission is to teach students that being hearing impaired doesn't have to limit what they can accomplish in life. The varsity football team is proof of that.

The CSDR Cubs play against hearing and hearing-impaired schools. CSDR's entire team and all of its coaches are hearing impaired. Their comments for this story were made through a sign-language interpreter.

"We want to be known as a great team," says head coach Keith Adams. "Not a great deaf team; just a great team."

The Program

The Cubs are well on their way to becoming a great team. They finished with nine wins and one loss in 2004.

---

varsity, main team that represents a school in sports
coaches, people who give special lessons to a team
sign-language interpreter, person whose job is to put the words of sign language into spoken language

"I think we proved to other teams that they can't expect to beat us just because we're deaf," says senior player Gary Sidansky. "We proved some things to ourselves, too. If we can be this good at football, we can be just as good at anything else."

Losers to Winners

A lack of hearing isn't the only obstacle CSDR's football program has had to overcome. From 1998 through 2000, the Cubs won a total of two games. Players skipped practice whenever they felt like it. Those who did attend often went through drills at half-speed.

"The players didn't have any pride in themselves," said defensive coach Kaveh Angoorani. "I think their attitude was, 'We're not going to win anyway, so why should I show up on time? Why should I practice hard?'"

---

obstacle, thing that makes it difficult to succeed
drills, activities repeated often for practice
pride, feeling of satisfaction

◀ A player runs from his opponents.

BEFORE YOU GO ON

1 What makes the CSDR football team unique?

2 What is the mission of CSDR?

On Your Own
Do you like American football? Why or why not?

303

▲ A coach uses hand signals to communicate with a player.

That all changed when a new coach, Len Gonzales, took over in 2001. Gonzales played football at CSDR in the 1980s and 1990s. He went on to play at Gallaudet, a college for the hearing impaired in Washington, D.C.

Gonzales and his coaching staff brought more structure to the program. They insisted on off-season weight-lifting sessions. They also took the players to summer football camps. The extra work helped the players develop their skills and bond as a team.

The results weren't obvious overnight. CSDR didn't win any games during Gonzales's first season. But the Cubs began to show signs of improvement. They won five out of ten games in 2002.

In 2003, they won four games. Gonzales left before the winning 2004 season for family reasons. But Adams has continued to build on the foundation that Gonzales established.

Special Communication

Opponents used to count on an easy victory when they played CSDR. Not anymore. Now coaches from opposing teams try to learn the Cubs' signals.

Figuring out the team's system of communication isn't easy. CSDR uses a combination of American Sign Language and its own code, designed by the coaches, to call plays. The coaches signal the play to sophomore Mark Korn with

---

structure, organization or discipline
bond, understand and trust one another

foundation, basic idea
plays, actions of someone in a game or sport

hand gestures from the sidelines. Korn then relays the play to the team in the huddle. During the play, Korn taps the center when it's time to pass the ball. The other players go when they see the center make the pass.

The Cubs ask for no special treatment from their opponents. They request only that the referees wave their arms as well as blow their whistles to signal the end of a play. "There's really not that much difference between the way one of our games operates and the way a game between two hearing teams would operate," says Adams.

---

sidelines, parts of the football field where coaches and players who are not in the game stand
relays, shares information about
huddle, gathering of players to talk briefly about what they are going to do next
center, player who tosses the ball to his teammate at the beginning of every play

▼ Fans cheer for the team.

Loud and Clear

Even though the Cubs can't hear noise, they can make it. The players and coaches whoop and holler during the games—as do their cheerleaders, who are also students at CSDR. But even some of the cheering is done through sign language. It's not unusual to look in the stands at a game and see fans holding both arms straight up in the air and wiggling their fingers—the sign language gesture for applause.

"You don't have to be able to hear to know when you've done a good job," says senior player Bobby Neil.

You also don't have to hear to feel like a winner. At California School for the Deaf-Riverside, that message comes through loud and clear.

---

whoop, shout supportively
holler, yell or shout
stands, sections where fans sit to watch a game
applause, clapping to show support

BEFORE YOU GO ON

1 How do the team members communicate with each other and with their coaches?

2 What request does the CSDR team make before each game? Why?

On Your Own
Do you think you would be able to participate in a sport without your sense of hearing? Explain.

305

COMPREHENSION

Workbook
Page 147

Right There

1. What kinds of teams does CSDR play against?
2. What obstacles has the football program had to overcome?

Think and Search

3. What was the team's record from 1998 through 2000? What was it from 2000 through 2004?
4. How did the team change after Len Gonzales was hired?

Author and You

5. Why did the CSDR coaches design their own codes to call plays?
6. How do you think the author feels about the CSDR football team?

On Your Own

7. Name one goal you have had to work hard to achieve.
8. Did your attitude influence the outcome of that goal? Explain.

IN YOUR OWN WORDS

Work with a partner. Copy the chart below into your notebook. Complete the chart with main ideas and details from the article "Listen Up." Then use this information to summarize the article for your partner.

Head	Main Idea	Detail(s)
The Program		
Losers to Winners		
Special Communication		
Loud and Clear	Even though the Cubs can't hear noise, they can make it.	Players, coaches, and cheerleaders yell during the games.

 Listening TIP

Be patient. Give the speaker enough time to express his or her ideas clearly.

DISCUSSION

Discuss in pairs or small groups.

1. Why do you think opponents used to count on an easy victory when they played against CSDR?

2. Would you want to attend a CSDR football game? Why or why not?

Q **What is the human spirit?** What did Coach Adams mean when he said, "We want to be known as a great team. Not a great deaf team; just a great team." How is this an example of the human spirit?

READ FOR FLUENCY

Reading with feeling helps make what you read more interesting. Work with a partner. Choose a paragraph from the reading. Read the paragraph. Ask each other how you felt after reading the paragraph. Did you feel happy or sad?

Take turns reading the paragraph aloud to each other with a tone of voice that represents how you felt when you read it the first time. Give each other feedback.

EXTENSION

Workbook
Page 147

Work with a partner. Use the Internet or library to learn more about people, like the CSDR football players and those listed below, who have overcome disabilities to accomplish great things. Present your findings to the class.

- Ray Charles
- Itzhak Perlman
- Stephen Hawking
- Marlee Matlin
- Heather Whitestone

▲ Ray Charles

307

Grammar and Writing

GRAMMAR, USAGE, AND MECHANICS

Present Perfect with *for* and *since*

The present perfect is formed with *have/has* + past participle. Writers use the present perfect with *for* or *since* to talk about an action that started in the past and continues into the present.

Use *for* to tell about a period of time in the past. Use *since* to tell about a specific period of time in the past.

> The Cubs have been a winning team **for** three years.
> The Cubs have been a winning team **since** last year.

You can also use the present perfect with adverbs to talk about when or how often something has happened in the past. Look at the examples below.

> I have **always** been a fan of the Cubs.
> He has **often** gone to the games.
> Have you **ever** seen them play? No, I **never** have.
> They've **recently** played against that team.
> They've won 3 out of 6 games **so far**.

Practice

Workbook
Page 148

Copy the sentences below into your notebook. Choose the correct word to complete each sentence. Share your work with a partner. Take turns reading the sentences to each other.

1. We have been big fans (for / always) the last three years.
2. Tim Carson has kicked twelve field goals (for / since) the season began.
3. Mrs. Carson has seen every game (still / so far).
4. Has the team (ever / always) lost a game?
5. The team has (never / for) played well.
6. The players have (so far / never) missed a practice.

WRITING A PERSUASIVE PARAGRAPH

Write a Letter to the Editor

You have learned how to write an advertisement and a review. Now you will learn about another form of persuasive writing: letters to the editor. People write letters to editors of newspapers or magazines to express their opinions about a topic. Sometimes a letter to the editor includes an idea for solving a problem or improving something within the community. Now you will write a letter to the editor. Begin your letter by stating the issue that concerns you. Then give your opinion on the issue. Provide facts and/or examples to support your opinion. Conclude by restating your opinion in a strong and persuasive way.

Here is a sample letter to the editor. The writer used a word web to organize his thoughts. Notice how he clearly stated his opinion and supported it with facts and examples.

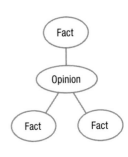

October 8, 2009

To the Editor,

I am writing about our school's football program. Currently, only boys are allowed to play the sport. However, I believe that girls, too, should be able to try out for positions on the team. Since the early 1970s, girls have earned spots on both junior high and high school football teams. These athletes proved that females are just as capable of running, kicking, catching, and passing as their male teammates. And although these girls faced many challenges— they were teased and treated unfairly by both coaches and other players—this hasn't prevented future generations of girls from wanting to play. I think the girls in our school should be given a similar chance to prove themselves. By not allowing girls to try out, our school is sending the wrong message about gender equality.

Sincerely,
Ari Janoff

Practice  **Workbook Page 149**

Write a letter to the editor of your school or local newspaper about an issue you feel strongly about in your school or community. List your ideas in a graphic organizer. Be sure to express your opinion clearly. Support your point of view with facts and/or examples. Be sure to use the present perfect correctly in your letter.

Writing Checklist

VOICE:
☑ I stated the issues clearly.

ORGANIZATION:
☑ I supported each statement with facts and/or examples.

What You Will Learn

Reading

■ Vocabulary building: *Literary terms, word study*

■ Reading strategy: *Read aloud*

■ Text type: *Literature (play excerpt)*

Grammar, Usage, and Mechanics

Simple past versus present perfect

Writing

Write a persuasive paragraph

THE BIG QUESTION

What is the human spirit? Imagine that you have to escape from an enemy. You move into a secret, cramped apartment, like the one shown below. You have to share it with seven other people. You cannot make any noise or go outside. How would you feel? What would you do all day? What would you miss most about the outside world? Would this experience break your spirit? Discuss with a partner.

BUILD BACKGROUND

You will read an excerpt from **The Diary of Anne Frank: The Play**. It is based on the book *Anne Frank: The Diary of a Young Girl*. Anne Frank wrote her diary in Amsterdam, Holland, between 1943 and 1945 while hiding from the Nazis during World War II.

Anne Frank and her family hid in a secret annex, a small hidden apartment, for over two years. They had to be very quiet during the day so no one would hear them. They could not leave the annex. They depended on Mr. Frank's work colleagues to bring them food and other necessities. These people heroically risked their lives to help the family.

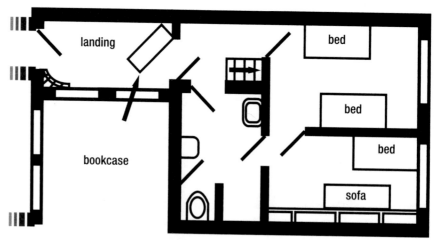

▲ A floor plan of the secret annex

Learn Literary Words

A **diary** is a book in which you write about your own life. Each day you write about your personal thoughts, opinions, and/or the events in which you participated.

Literary Words

diary
drama
stage directions

You will read a **drama** that is based on Anne Frank's diary. A drama is a play that is written and performed by actors. The written version of a drama is called a script. It is made up of dialogue and stage directions. Characters' names appear next to the dialogue they speak. **Stage directions** tell the actors how to speak and act; they can also describe the setting, sound effects, and lighting. Stage directions are often printed in italics and set within brackets [ ]. The actors do not read them aloud. For example, read the script excerpt below from *The Diary of Anne Frank: The Play.*

> **Mr. Frank:** [*quickly coming forward*] Peter. The first to arrive. [*Shaking his hand.*] Welcome, Peter. Peter van Daan, children.
> **Anne:** [*rushing toward him*] Welcome to the Annex!

Practice
Workbook Page 150

Read the script excerpt below with a partner. Then answer these questions: Who are the characters? What are the stage directions? Which lines are spoken?

Anne: [*looking down at the basket*] A cat! [*turning to Margot*] He has a cat!

Peter: [*self-conscious*] A black one.

Anne: We have a cat too. I wanted to bring her but. . . . [*glancing at her mother*] I know our neighbors will take care of her till we come back. I don't know what I'll do without her. But it'll be great having a cat here. . . .

Mrs. Frank: Anne dear, don't get so excited. Peter doesn't know you yet.

Anne: [*laughing*] He'll get to know me soon though. It's going to be so much fun having people around. A whole other family.

Learn Academic Words

Study the **red** words and their meanings. You will find these words useful when talking and writing about literature. Write each word and its meaning in your notebook. After you read the excerpt from *The Diary of Anne Frank: The Play,* try to use these words to respond to the text.

assisted = helped someone	➡	Angela's friends **assisted** her by carrying the heavy furniture into her apartment.
occupants = people who live in a building, room, etc.	➡	Eight **occupants** lived in the apartment.
published = printed and distributed	➡	Anne Frank's diary has been **published** in many different countries around the world.
regulations = official rules or orders	➡	The soldier arrested the woman because she did not obey the **regulations**.

Practice

Workbook Page 151

Write the sentences in your notebook. Choose a **red** word from the box above to complete each sentence. Then take turns reading the sentences aloud with a partner.

1. Over three hundred _____ lived in the building last year.

2. A theater employee _____ the elderly woman in finding a seat.

3. If you don't follow the theater's _____, you will be asked to leave.

4. After the success of their play, the writers _____ their script so that people around the world could read it.

▲ Anne Frank's diary has been published in multiple languages.

Word Study: Spelling the Sound /j/

In the excerpt from *The Diary of Anne Frank: The Play*, there are many words with the /j/ sound. There are different ways to spell this sound: *j* as in *jolly*, *g* as in *gem*, or *dge* as in *edge*. The letter *j* is usually used if the sound precedes an *a*, *o*, or *u*. The letter *g* is usually used when the sound is followed by an *e*, *i*, or *y*. The letters *dge* are often used when the sound comes at the end of a syllable or a word.

Sound of /j/		
j	**g**	**dge**
job	gentle	dodge
jury	original	ledge

Practice

Work with a partner. Copy the chart above into your notebook. Add the words in the box below to the chart under the correct headings. Then say a word from the chart. Ask your partner to spell it aloud. Have your partner say the next word. Continue until you can spell all of the words correctly.

badge	dangerous	enjoy	June	large	object

READING STRATEGY | READ ALOUD

Reading aloud brings a story and characters to life. It can make reading more fun, especially when you're reading a play, a poem, or a story. To read a play aloud, follow these steps:

- Read the list of characters and choose one person to be each character.
- Read your lines to yourself. Read the stage directions.
- Read the play aloud as a group. Listen carefully to the other actors so that you know when to say your lines.

As you read the excerpt from *The Diary of Anne Frank: The Play*, pay attention to your lines and stage directions. When you perform the play in a group, speak clearly and listen carefully to the other actors.

313

Set a purpose for reading As you read, think about the responsibilities Miep and Mr. Kraler shared in hiding the families. Would you have done the same?

from

The Diary of Anne Frank: The Play

Frances Goodrich and Albert Hackett, with Wendy Kesselman

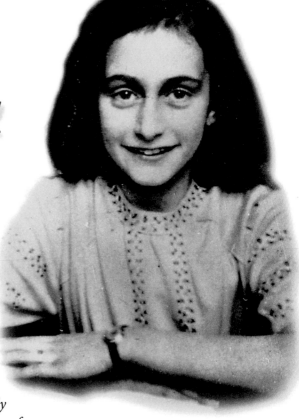

▲ Anne Frank

On June 12, 1942, Anne Frank received a diary for her thirteenth birthday. A few weeks later, on July 6, the family was forced to move into the "Secret Annex." They lived there for two years with the van Pels family (Anne calls them the van Daans in her diary) and another Jewish man. Mr. Frank's former work colleagues, Mr. Kraler and Miep Gies, helped the families survive.

ANNE: [*voiceover*] July sixth, 1942. A few days ago, Father began to talk about going into hiding. He said it would be very hard for us to live cut off from the rest of the world. He sounded so serious I felt scared. "Don't worry, Anneke. We'll take care of everything. Just enjoy your carefree life while you can." [*She pauses.*]

Carefree? I was born in Frankfurt on June twelfth, 1929. Because we're Jewish, my father emigrated to Holland in 1933. He started a business, manufacturing products used to make jam. But Hitler invaded Holland

---

cut off, separated
carefree, problem-free
emigrated, left one country to live in another
invaded, entered a place using military force

on May tenth, 1940, a month before my eleventh birthday. Five days later the Dutch surrendered, the Germans arrived—and the trouble started for the Jews. [*a pause*]

Father was forced to give up his business. We couldn't use streetcars, couldn't go to the theater or movies anymore, couldn't be out on the street after 9 P.M., couldn't even sit in our own gardens! We had to turn in our bicycles; no beaches, no swimming pools, no libraries—we couldn't even walk on the sunny side of the streets! My sister Margot and I had to go to a Jewish school. Our identity cards were stamped with a big black "J." And . . . we had to wear the yellow star. But somehow life went on. Until yesterday, when a call-up notice came from the SS. Margot was ordered to report for work in Germany, to the Westerbork transit camp. A call-up: Everyone knows what that means! [*She pauses.*]

At five-thirty this morning, we closed the door of our apartment behind us—ten days earlier than my parents had planned. My cat was the only living creature I said goodbye to. The unmade beds, the breakfast things on the table all created the impression we'd left in a hurry. [*a pause*]

And our destination? We walked two and a half miles in the pouring rain all the way to . . . Father's office building! Our hiding place, the "Secret Annex," is right behind it upstairs. Even though the Germans forced Father out, he still runs the office with Mr. Kraler and Miep, who've agreed to help us while we're in hiding. [*As Mr. Frank pulls a large tarpaulin off the kitchen table, he sees a rat move across the floor. Mrs. Frank shrieks.*]

MRS. FRANK: A rat!

MR. FRANK: Shhh! [*Quickly he motions her to be quiet, as Miep comes up the steps.*]

MR. FRANK: Ah, Miep!

MIEP: Mr. Frank. Thank God you arrived safely.

ANNE: Miep!

---

yellow star, badge that Jews were required to wear
SS, high-ranking members of the Nazi Party
Westerbork transit camp, place in Holland where people were put on trains that took them to the concentration camps
impression, idea
tarpaulin, piece of material used to cover and protect an object

▲ Anne Frank's diary

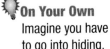

✔ **LITERARY CHECK**
What do the stage directions in this paragraph describe?

BEFORE YOU GO ON

1 Why do the Franks go into hiding?

2 Who helps them?

💡**On Your Own**
Imagine you have to go into hiding. What would you take with you?

315

▲ Anne's bedroom in the annex

▲ The secret annex was at the back of Mr. Frank's office building.

▲ The entrance to the annex was hidden by a swinging bookcase.

MIEP: Anne. Margot. [*as Margot and Mrs. Frank slowly sit up*] Mrs. Frank, you must be exhausted. If only we'd known we would have had it all ready for you.

MR. FRANK: You've done too much already, Miep. Besides, it's good for us to keep busy. As you see, Anne's my little helper.

MIEP: I can see that. [*She looks down the steps where Peter van Daan, a shy, awkward boy of sixteen, wearing a heavy coat with the conspicuous yellow star, waits nervously. He is carrying a cat in a basket.*] Peter— come in!

MR. FRANK: [*quickly coming forward*] Peter. The first to arrive. [*shaking his hand*] Welcome, Peter. Peter van Daan, children.

ANNE: [*Rushing toward him*] Welcome to the Annex!

MR. FRANK: Peter—Margot, Anne. You already know Mrs. Frank.

PETER: [*solemnly shaking hands with Mrs. Frank*] Mrs. Frank.

MRS. FRANK: Forgive me, Peter. I'm not quite myself. But I'm so glad you'll be with us.

MARGOT: I am too.

ANNE: [*looking down at the basket*] A cat! [*turning to Margot*] He has a cat!

PETER: [*self-conscious*] A black one.

ANNE: We have a cat too. I wanted to bring her but . . . [*glancing at her mother*] I know our neighbors will take care of her till we come back. I don't know what I'll do without her. But it'll be great having a cat here. Won't it, Pim? Won't it be fantastic?

MRS. FRANK: Anne dear, don't get so excited. Peter doesn't know you yet.

ANNE: [*laughing*] He'll get to know me soon though. It's going to be so much fun having people around. A whole other family. Won't it, Margot?

MARGOT: Yes.

ANNE: [*skipping around the room*] Like being on vacation in some strange pension or something. An adventure—romantic and dangerous at the same time!

---

conspicuous, very easy to notice
solemnly, seriously or sadly
self-conscious, shy; awkward
Pim, Anne's nickname for her father
pension, hotel or boarding house
romantic, emotional or dream-like

BEFORE YOU GO ON

1 How does Anne feel about hiding in the annex?

2 What do Anne and Peter have in common?

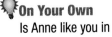**On Your Own**
Is Anne like you in any way? If so, how?

▲ Anne sitting at her school desk

▲ Peter van Daan

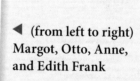

◄ (from left to right)
Margot, Otto, Anne,
and Edith Frank

MR. FRANK: [*watching Peter's anxious face*] What is it, Peter?

PETER: My parents. They were right behind me, one street away.

MR. FRANK: [*laying his hand on Peter's shoulder*] They'll be here.

PETER: You don't think they were. . . .

MRS. FRANK: Don't worry, Peter. [*smiling*] You're just like me.

ANNE: Mother's always jumping at every little thing. [*peeking into Peter's basket*] What's its name?

PETER: [*self-conscious*] Mouschi.

ANNE: [*to the cat*] Mouschi! Mouschi. I love cats. [*to Peter*] Where'd you go to school?

PETER: They set up a technical school in someone's house, once we were forbidden—

ANNE: [*breaking in*] I had to switch from my Montessori school to the Jewish Lyceum.

PETER: I know. I saw you there.

ANNE: You did? [*Mr. Kraler hurries up the stairs with Mr. and Mrs. van Daan. Mrs. van Daan is wearing a fur coat and carrying an umbrella and a large hat box. Mr. van Daan carries a satchel and his briefcase. All three are out of breath.*]

MR. FRANK: [*to Peter, smiling*] See—what did I tell you? Now we're all here.

MR. KRALER: [*obviously shaken*] Just in time. We had to take the long way around—there were too many Green Police on the streets. [*Mr. van Daan breaks open a package of cigarettes, nervously starts smoking*]

MR. FRANK: [*shaking hands with the van Daans*] Welcome, Mrs. van Daan. Mr. van Daan. You know my wife, of course, and the children. [*Mrs. Frank, Margot, and Anne shake hands with the van Daans.*]

MR. KRALER: We must hurry. The workmen will be here in half an hour.

MR. FRANK: Such trouble we're causing you, Mr. Kraler, after all you and Miep have done. And now we arrive early!

MR. KRALER: You couldn't let your daughter be taken away, Mr. Frank.

---

anxious, worried
technical school, school that teaches auto mechanics, machine repair, and other skills
satchel, small bag for carrying clothing, books, etc.
Green Police, Dutch police who supported the Nazis

BEFORE YOU GO ON

1 Why are Mr. and Mrs. van Daan the last to arrive?

2 Why is Mr. Kraler in a hurry to get the families settled in the annex?

On Your Own
What words would you use to describe Mr. Kraler and Miep?

319

◀ Miep and Mr. Frank

MIEP: Please don't worry. We will do everything we can to help you. Now I must run and get your ration books.

MRS. VAN DAAN: Wait—if they see our names on ration books, they'll know we're here, won't they?

MIEP: Trust me—your names won't be on them. I'll be up later. If you make a list every day, I'll try to get what you want. And every Saturday I can bring five library books. [*She hurries out.*]

MR. FRANK: Thank you, Miep.

ANNE: Five! I know what my five are going to be.

MRS. FRANK: Anne, remember, there are seven of us.

ANNE: I know, Mother.

MARGOT: [*troubled*] It's illegal, then, the ration books? We've never done anything illegal.

MR. VAN DAAN: I don't think we'll be living exactly according to regulations here. [*The carillon is heard playing the quarter hour before eight.*]

ANNE: Listen. The Westertoren!

MRS. FRANK: How will I ever get used to that clock?

ANNE: Oh, I love it!

MR. KRALER: Miep or I will be here every day to see you. I've hidden a buzzer to signal you when we come up, and tomorrow I'll have that bookcase placed in front of your door. Oh, and one last thing . . . the radio. . . . [*He points to a small radio hidden beneath a sheet.*]

---

ration books, booklets of coupons that allow people to buy food during wartime
illegal, not allowed by law
carillon, set of bells on a clock tower
buzzer, small device that makes a buzzing sound when you press it

ANNE: [*bounding over to the radio*] A radio! Fantastic!

MRS. VAN DAAN: A radio. Thank God.

MR. VAN DAAN: How did you get it? We had to turn ours in months ago.

MR. FRANK: Thank you, Mr. Kraler. For everything. (Mr. Kraler turns to go, as Anne drops a batch of silverware.)

MR. KRALER: [*to Mr. Frank*] Oh . . . you'll tell them about the noise?

MR. FRANK: I'll tell them.

MRS. FRANK: [*following Mr. Kraler to the top of the stairs*] How can we thank you really? How can we ever—

MR. KRALER: I never thought I'd live to see the day a man like Mr. Frank would have to go into hiding. [*He hurries out, as she stands still, watching him.*]

* * *

On August 4, 1944, the secret annex was raided by the Security Police. Anne and the seven others in hiding were arrested. They were transported to Auschwitz concentration camp. After a month there, Anne and Margot were sent to Bergen-Belsen concentration camp, where they both got typhus, a deadly disease. They died within a short time of each other in March 1945, only a few weeks before the camp was liberated by the British. Only Anne's father, Otto Frank, survived. In 1947, he published Anne's diary.

---

bounding, running with a lot of energy

✔ **LITERARY CHECK**

*What character in this **drama** would you like to play?*

ABOUT THE PLAYWRIGHTS

Frances Goodrich and Albert Hackett wrote the screenplays for some of Hollywood's most famous movies. *The Diary of Anne Frank: The Play*, written in 1955, was perhaps their greatest achievement. Wendy Kesselman's adaptation, based on an expanded and unedited version of the original diary, portrays a more realistic Anne.

BEFORE YOU GO ON

1 In what ways does Miep offer to help the families?

2 How will Miep and Mr. Kraler signal that they are coming up to the annex?

On Your Own
Do you like Anne? Why or why not?

321

Review and Practice

DRAMATIC READING

One of the best ways to understand and appreciate a play is to perform it. Work in small groups. Choose a section of *The Diary of Anne Frank: The Play* to act out for the class. Discuss each character in the play and how he or she should be portrayed. Then assign a character to each person in your group. Read your parts aloud. Pay attention to the stage directions. You may want to include the use of props or costumes to make your interpretation of the play more authentic. If so, be sure to use these items as you practice.

Keep practicing until you feel comfortable. Then act out your scene for the rest of the class.

COMPREHENSION  Workbook Page 154

Right There

1. Where is the annex located?
2. What did the Franks do to create the impression that they left their apartment in a hurry?

Think and Search

3. What kinds of items did the families bring with them to the annex?
4. In what ways do the families disregard Nazi regulations?

Author and You

5. Why do you think Anne calls the van Pells the "van Daans" in her diary?
6. Why do you think the playwrights created a play based on Anne's diary?

Speaking TIP

Face the audience when you speak to the other actors. If you turn away from the audience too much, people may not be able to hear or understand you.

On Your Own

7. Do you keep a diary? If so, what do you write about?

8. Have you or someone you know ever been discriminated against due to your race, culture, or religion? What happened? How did you feel?

DISCUSSION

Discuss in pairs or small groups.

1. When the Germans invaded Holland, how did life change for Anne and her family?

2. What dangers do Miep and Mr. Kraler have to face as they help the families?

Q **What is the human spirit?** Would you be willing to help others in need even if it was dangerous for you to do so? Why or why not? Do you think we have a responsibility to help others? Explain.

»)) *Listening* TIP

Pay attention to the speaker's tone of voice, gestures, and expressions. What do they tell you about how the speaker feels about the topic?

RESPONSE TO LITERATURE

Workbook
Page 154

You have learned about Anne Frank's diary. Now create a diary entry of your own. Write the date at the top of the page. Include your own personal thoughts and opinions, as well as things that happened to you. Use descriptive language. Then share your entry with a partner.

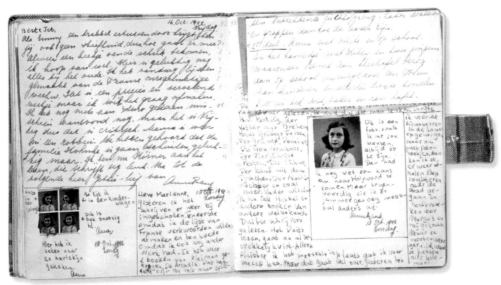

▲ Text and photos from Anne Frank's diary

Grammar and Writing

Simple Past versus Present Perfect

As you have learned, writers use the simple past to show that an action happened and ended at a specific time in the past. Form the simple past by adding *-d* or *-ed* to regular verbs. Remember that many verbs are irregular.

> Anne Frank's diary **inspired** me when I read it.

Writers use the present perfect to show that an action happened at an indefinite time in the past, or to show that an action began in the past and continues into the present. Form the present perfect with *has/have* and the past participle of the verb.

> Anne Frank's diary **has inspired** millions of students.

Practice
Workbook
Page 155

Copy the sentences below into your notebook. Choose the correct verb. Share your work with a partner. Take turns reading the sentences to each other.

1. The Franks originally (lived / have lived) in Germany.
2. I (read / have read) about Anne Frank many times.
3. We (talked / have talked) about the war in class today.
4. The author (wrote / has written) many books about the subject.
5. Seeing this play is one of the best things I (did / have done).
6. We (saw / have seen) the play last night.
7. They (visited / have visited) the Anne Frank house last year.
8. She (wanted / has wanted) to read *The Diary of Anne Frank* for a long time.

WRITING A PERSUASIVE PARAGRAPH

Write a Persuasive Paragraph

You have learned about different forms of persuasive writing. Now you will write a persuasive paragraph. Begin your paragraph by introducing a topic you feel strongly about. Clearly state your opinion on the issue. Support your opinion with facts and details. Anticipate opposing opinions and tell why they are incorrect. Conclude your paragraph by restating your opinion in a new way. Use strong words that will appeal to your readers' emotions.

Pros	Cons

Here is a sample paragraph. The writer used a pros-and-cons chart to organize his thoughts. Notice how he clearly states his opinion, supports it, and presents both sides of the argument.

George Delgrosso

The Diary of Anne Frank

I think Anne Frank's father, Otto Frank, was right to publish his daughter's diary. It is an important personal description of events as they happened during World War II. The diary reminds us about the awful effects of war. It is for these reasons that the diary is used as an educational tool in schools across the country. However, not all people share these views. Some people believe Mr. Frank was disrespectful in publishing Anne's private thoughts. But many people do not know that Mr. Frank edited Anne's diary before it was published. He did not include pages that he thought were too personal and private. He respected his daughter and, in publishing her story, has inspired millions of people around the world.

Practice

Workbook
Page 156

Write a persuasive paragraph about an issue you feel strongly about. Before writing, list your ideas in a graphic organizer. Be sure to use the simple past and the present perfect correctly.

Writing Checklist

ORGANIZATION:
☑ I presented both sides of the argument.

VOICE:
☑ I clearly stated my opinion.

Link the Readings

Critical Thinking

Look back at the readings in this unit. Think about what they have in common. They all tell about the human spirit. Yet they do not all have the same purpose. The purpose of one reading might be to inform, while the purpose of another might be to entertain or persuade. In addition, the content of each reading relates to the human spirit differently. Now copy the chart below into your notebook and complete it.

Title of Reading	Purpose	Big Question Link
From *César Chávez: We Can Do It!*		*One man works to make the lives of others better.*
"The Scholarship Jacket"	*to entertain*	
"Listen Up"		
From *The Diary of Anne Frank: The Play*		

Discussion

Discuss in pairs or small groups.

- How is Mr. Schmidt in "The Scholarship Jacket" similar to Miep and Mr. Kraler in the excerpt from *The Diary of Anne Frank: The Play*?

- **Q What is the human spirit?** What character traits did the people in the stories share? How do these character traits reflect the strength of the human spirit?

Fluency Check

Work with a partner. Choose a paragraph from one of the readings. Take turns reading it for one minute. Count the total number of words you read. Practice saying the words you had trouble reading. Take turns reading the paragraph three more times. Did you read more words each time? Copy the chart below into your notebook and record your speeds.

	1st Speed	2nd Speed	3rd Speed	4th Speed
Words Per Minute				

Projects

Work in pairs or small groups. Choose one of these projects.

1 Create a large "human spirit timeline" in your classroom. Draw pictures of people or groups whose lives and work have reflected the human spirit throughout history. Write a short paragraph that tells why each person or group belongs on the timeline.

2 Present a "Human Spirit Award" to someone in your school. Write a persuasive argument telling why the person you chose deserves the award. Read your argument to the class and take a vote. Invite the winner to your classroom and present that person with the award.

3 Interview someone in your community or in your school who has worked hard to help others. Before conducting your interview, prepare a list of questions to ask. If possible, invite the person to your school so that your class can ask questions. If this is not possible, use a tape recorder to be sure you do not miss anything. Share your interview with the class.

Further Reading

To find out more about the theme of this unit, choose from these reading suggestions.

The Last of the Mohicans, James Fenimore Cooper
This Penguin Reader® is an adaptation of the classic tale of adventure and struggle on the North American frontier.

The River, Gary Paulsen
Two years before this story begins, teenager Brian Robeson survived in the wilderness for fifty-four days with only a hatchet. Now he agrees to go back into the wilderness to teach a government worker how to survive.

Who Was Harriet Tubman? Yona Zeldis McDonough
Born a slave in Maryland, Harriet Tubman knew first-hand what it meant to be someone's property. After the Civil War brought an end to slavery, this amazing woman's long, rich life was proof of what just one person can do.

Put It All Together

LISTENING & SPEAKING WORKSHOP

Radio Commercial

You and a partner will create and present a radio commercial.

1 **THINK ABOUT IT** When you listen to the radio, you hear commercials. The purpose of a commercial is to persuade listeners to buy a product, attend an event, or support a cause. Radio commercials are very short: They typically last just thirty seconds or a minute.

Work in pairs to develop a list of products, events, or causes you could advertise in a radio commercial. These may be real or imaginary. For example:

- A new type of cell phone
- A community theater production
- A local fundraiser

2 **GATHER AND ORGANIZE INFORMATION** With a partner, choose a topic from your list. Then make notes about what to include in your radio commercial. What persuasive words could you use? What details should you use to describe the product, event, or cause? What sound effects or music would make your commercial interesting and memorable?

Research / Reflect If your topic is a real product, event, or cause, go to the library, talk to an adult, or conduct research on the Internet to get more information about it. Take notes on what you find. If your product is imaginary, create the details that you will need to describe it.

Order Your Notes Study your notes. Decide which arguments, examples, and supporting details you will use to persuade your listener. Then organize your ideas in an outline or another graphic organizer.

3 PRACTICE AND PRESENT Use your outline or graphic organizer as you practice your commercial. With your partner, choose which parts you will each present. Practice in front of a friend or family member, or tape-record yourself and listen to the tape. If you are using recorded sound effects, check that your equipment works and that you can use it easily.

Deliver Your Radio Commercial Give your presentation from the back of the room so your classmates can hear but not see you—as if you were radio announcers. Emphasize persuasive words by changing the volume or tone of your voice. Slow down when you come to the most important points.

4 EVALUATE THE PRESENTATION
You will improve your skills as a speaker and a listener by evaluating each presentation you give and hear. Use this checklist to help you judge your commercial and those of your classmates.

☑ Was the purpose of the commercial clear?

☑ Did the pair persuade you to buy the product, attend the event, or support the cause? Why or why not?

☑ Could you hear and understand the speakers easily?

☑ Did the speakers make effective use of tone of voice, music, and sound effects?

☑ What suggestions do you have for improving the radio commercial?

Speaking TIPS

Be sure to speak clearly and to repeat important details so that your listeners will understand and remember them.

Use sound effects, music, and your tone of voice to catch the listeners' attention.

Listening TIPS

What is the speaker trying to persuade you to do? If you don't understand, ask questions at the end of the presentation.

Listen for information that would make you want to buy the product, attend the event, or support the cause. Try to remember the important details.

WRITING WORKSHOP

Persuasive Speech

In persuasive writing, the writer expresses an opinion and tries to convince others to agree with it. A speech is one form of persuasive writing. Speechwriters aim to persuade listeners to think or act a certain way. A strong persuasive speech begins with a paragraph that clearly states the writer's opinion. The speech gives reasons, facts, and examples that support the writer's position. Speechwriters also present both sides of an issue. Then they explain why they think opposing arguments are incorrect. A persuasive speech concludes with a paragraph that restates the writer's opinion in a new and memorable way. Speechwriters often use strong, persuasive words to appeal to their listeners' feelings.

You will write a five-paragraph speech that tries to persuade your audience to agree with your opinion on an issue that matters to you.

1 PREWRITE Brainstorm a list of possible topics for your speech in your notebook. What do you think is an important issue in your school or community? How can you convince others to agree with your opinion on this issue? What action would you like your listeners to take after hearing your speech? Choose the issue that most interests you.

List and Organize Ideas and Details Use a pros-and-cons chart to organize your ideas. In the *Pros* column, give arguments that support your opinion. In the *Cons* column, give arguments that oppose your opinion, so that you can respond to them in your speech. A student named George decided to write a persuasive speech about the importance of volunteering. Here is the pros-and-cons chart he created:

Pros	Cons
Important to volunteer A way to help other individuals and the community Can meet new people and learn a lot	Not enough time to volunteer No local places to volunteer

2 DRAFT Use the model on page 333 and your pros-and-cons chart to help you write your first draft. Remember to state your opinion clearly in the first paragraph and to restate your opinion in the concluding paragraph.

3 **REVISE** Read over your draft. As you do so, ask yourself the questions in the writing checklist. Use the questions to help you revise your speech.

SIX TRAITS OF WRITING CHECKLIST

☑ **IDEAS:** Do I present both sides of the issue?

☑ **ORGANIZATION:** Do I support my opinion with reasons, facts, and examples in an order that makes sense?

☑ **VOICE:** Does my writing show my feelings about the issue?

☑ **WORD CHOICE:** Do I use persuasive words that will appeal to listeners?

☑ **SENTENCE FLUENCY:** Do my sentences flow well when read aloud?

☑ **CONVENTIONS:** Does my writing follow the rules of grammar, usage, and mechanics?

Here are the changes George plans to make when he revises his first draft:

The Importance of Volunteering

After disasters such as major hurricanes, people often join together
to assist the victims. ^who have suffered losses Whether through food drives, clothing drives, or

soup kitchens, the efforts of volunteers have helped individuals and

communities recover from times of darkness. By volunteering and

taking time out of <u>your</u> day to do something beneficial for others, <u>you</u>

can be that one person who changes someone's life. ^for the better

Many people I know volunteer out of "the goodness of their

hearts. Some also volunteer at more than one place. A few of the

organizations that welcome volunteers to work ^for them include the

Salvation Army, People to People, and meals on Wheels, as well as

some hospitals, libraries, soup kitchens, and thrift shops

For example ∧

You might choose to visit the elderly or to assist at a daycare center. As a volunteer you might find yourself aiding families who are coping with everyday problems. Volunteers can also be called upon to provide support to a community in a time of crisis. For example, emergency situations can require immediate action by a large number of volunteers to assist in running shelters or delivering food.

Many people don't volunteer because they "can't find the time," or because they "don't have any local organizations to contact." I believe that if they really wanted to help out, they could probably make the time in their schedules or travel a small distance out of their way. Volunteering is important! It not only helps others but also benefits the person who volunteers! As a volunteer, <u>you</u> can meet new people and learn new things. I been a volunteer *for* several years, and it is a very rewarding experience.

Why don't you explore volunteer opportunities in your community today?

¶ Volunteering is a way to show the good inside of you. When you harness this good, it can be used to change your life and the life of another.

4   EDIT AND PROOFREAD    Workbook Page 157

Copy your revised speech onto a clean sheet of paper. Read it again. Correct any errors in grammar, word usage, mechanics, and spelling. Here are the additional changes George plans to make when he prepares his final draft.

George Delgrosso

The Importance of Volunteering

After disasters such as major hurricanes, people often join together to assist the victims who have suffered losses. Whether through food drives, clothing drives, or soup kitchens, the efforts of volunteers have helped individuals and communities recover from times of darkness. By volunteering and taking time out of <u>your</u> day to do something beneficial for others, <u>you</u> can be that one person who changes someone's life for the better.

Many people I know volunteer out of "the goodness of their hearts." Some also volunteer at more than one place. A few of the organizations that welcome volunteers to work for them include the Salvation Army, People to People, and meals on Wheels, as well as some hospitals, libraries, soup kitchens, and thrift shops.

As a volunteer, you might find yourself aiding families who are coping with everyday problems. For example, you might choose to visit the elderly or to assist at a daycare center. Volunteers can also be called upon to provide support to a community in a time of crisis. For example, emergency situations can require immediate action by a large number of volunteers to assist in running shelters or delivering food.

Many people don't volunteer because they "can't find the time," or because they "don't have any local organizations to contact." I believe that if they really wanted to help out, they could probably make the time in their schedules or travel a small distance out of their way. Volunteering is important! It not only helps others but also benefits the person who volunteers! As a volunteer, <u>you</u> can meet new people and learn new things. I have been a volunteer for several years, and it is a very rewarding experience.

Why don't you explore volunteer opportunities in your community today? Volunteering is a way to show the good inside of you. When you harness this good, it can be used to change your life and the life of another.

---

5 **PUBLISH** Prepare your final draft. Share your speech with your teacher and classmates.

Workbook
Page 158

Everyday Obstacles, Everyday Courage

*T*he media often shows dramatic images that celebrate the human spirit, for example, a photograph of a space shuttle blasting off. But the power of the human spirit plays out in everyday actions as well. Many American artists have celebrated these less obvious examples of courage.

Residents of Bourbon County, Kentucky, *Fan Quilt, Mt. Carmel* (1893)

Splendid fans of many colors parade across this quilt. A group of women from Paris, Kentucky, made it more than 100 years ago. They pieced together different types of brightly colored fabric into forty-two separate squares. Then they sewed in the names of 110 men and women who lived in their county. The fan shapes are certainly fun, but not unusual for a quilt from this time period. The fact that so many people worked together to create this one quilt is wonderful proof of the community spirit they shared.

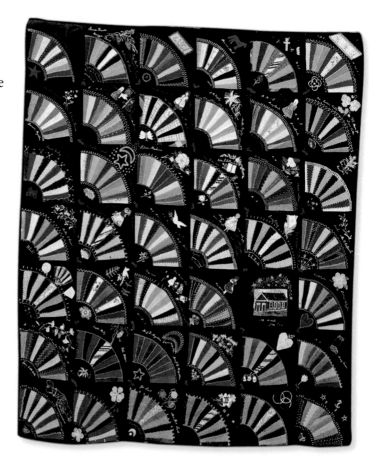

Residents of Bourbon County, Kentucky, *Fan Quilt, Mt. Carmel,* 1893, mixed media, 85 x 72¼ in., Smithsonian American Art Museum ▶

Daniel Chester French, *Spirit of Life* (1914)

In *Spirit of Life,* a young woman with wings raises a basin in her left hand and a pine branch in her right. Daniel Chester French, one of America's most famous sculptors, made this small sculpture in bronze as a model for a larger work. He planned to have water flow from the basin. French made the sculpture as a memorial for a businessman who had built health resorts in Saratoga Springs, New York. *Spirit of Life* marks a death by celebrating life.

Michael Olszewski, *Speaking to Hear* (1989)

In *Speaking to Hear,* artist Michael Olszewski places two small panels side by side. He wants to show how difficult it can be to tell two sides of a story from two different points of view. The panels are made from silk, a delicate fabric. Olszewski then used complicated stitching and embroidery to represent the words of a conversation.

In the left panel, Olszewski painted alternating orange and black stripes like a flag across the center of the silk. Then he added a solid red band down the middle. He reverses these images in the panel on the right. The two pieces seem to represent people coming from two different directions. But there's a feeling that the two "sides" are working toward some kind of understanding.

▲ Daniel Chester French, *Spirit of Life*, 1914, bronze, 30 x 34⅞ in., Smithsonian American Art Museum

▲ Michael Olszewski, *Speaking to Hear*, 1989, silk, parts A and B: both 22½ x 21¼ in., Smithsonian American Art Museum

These artworks offer wonderful examples of artists working in all sorts of ways to capture and honor the spirit and courage that people show in their everyday lives.

Apply What You Learned

1 How does each artwork relate to the idea of courage?

2 What kind of artwork would you create to illustrate how people face everyday obstacles with courage?

Big Question
Why do you think an artist might be interested in courage and the human spirit?

Workbook
Pages 159–160

335

How does the sky influence us?

This unit is about the sky. In it, you will read both literary and informational texts about space. Reading about this topic will give you practice using academic language and help you become a better student.

READING 1: Letter and Poems

- "Starry Nights"
- "Stars" by Sara Teasdale
- "Escape at Bedtime" by Robert Louis Stevenson

READING 2: Science Article

- "Earth and the Milky Way"

READING 3: Myth

- "The Girl Who Married the Moon," retold by Joseph Bruchac and Gayle Ross

READING 4: Science Articles

- "Return to the Moon" by Christy Brownlee
- "No Need to Establish a Moon Base" by Matt Kachur

Listening and Speaking

At the end of this unit, you will choose a topic and deliver an **oral report** about it.

Writing

In this unit you will learn about the elements of a **research report**, or a special kind of expository writing in which you present information that you have studied in depth.

QuickWrite

In your notebook, write a few sentences about the ways in which you think the sky influences us.

Prepare to Read

What You Will Learn

Reading
- Vocabulary building: *Literary terms, word study*
- Reading strategy: *Connect ideas*
- Text type: *Literature (letter and poetry)*

Grammar, Usage, and Mechanics
Punctuation in prose and poetry

Writing
Write an introductory paragraph

THE BIG QUESTION

How does the sky influence us? For centuries, the night sky has been a subject explored in both science and art. Why do you think people are so fascinated by the night sky? Work with a partner to answer these questions. Then make a list of objects that you can see in the night sky. Share your list with the class. Combine your answers to create a class list.

BUILD BACKGROUND

In this section, you will read an article called **"Starry Nights."** It is about Vincent van Gogh, a troubled painter who lived during the mid-1800s. Van Gogh was fond of writing letters. You will read an excerpt from one of the letters that he wrote to his sister, Wilhelmina. In it, van Gogh describes how his painting of a starry night differs from those of other painters.

You will also read two poems: **"Stars"** by Sarah Teasdale and **"Escape at Bedtime"** by Robert Louis Stevenson. Both poems describe the stars in the night sky, but do so in different ways.

▲ A self-portrait by Vincent van Gogh

Learn Literary Words

A **stanza** is a group of lines in a poem that are usually similar in length and pattern. Stanzas are separated by spaces. A stanza is like a paragraph of poetry. It states and develops a single main idea. For example, read the stanza below from the poem "Stars."

> And a heaven full of stars
> Over my head.
> White and topaz
> and misty red.

Sometimes the words in a stanza rhyme. **Rhyme** is the repetition of sounds at the ends of words. Poets use rhyme to create a song-like quality to their verses and to emphasize certain words and ideas. Many poems contain end rhymes, or rhyming words at the ends of lines. Reread the poem above. Notice how *head* and *red* is an example of an end rhyme.

Practice  **Workbook Page 161**

Read the poem "Canis Major" about the constellation of the same name. How many stanzas are there? What is the main idea of each stanza? Circle the rhyming words.

> The great Overdog
> That heavenly beast
> With a star in one eye
> Gives a leap in the east.
>
> He dances upright
> All the way to the west
> And never once drops
> On his forefeet to rest.
>
> I'm a poor underdog,
> But to-night I will bark
> With the great Overdog
> That romps through the dark.
> —*Robert Frost*

Learn Academic Words

Study the red words and their meanings. You will find these words useful when talking and writing about literature. Write each word and its meaning in your notebook. After you read "Starry Nights," "Stars," and "Escape at Bedtime," try to use these words to respond to the texts.

Academic Words

analyze
image
interpretation
visible

analyze = examine or think about something carefully in order to understand it	➡	Most artists **analyze** their subjects before painting them.
image = a picture that you can see through a camera, on a television, in a mirror, etc.	➡	The **image** of the child in the painting is very lifelike.
interpretation = an explanation of the meaning or significance of something	➡	My **interpretation** of the painting is different from yours. You think the painting looks realistic; I disagree.
visible = something that can be seen	➡	The stars in the painting are barely **visible**.

Practice

Workbook Page 162

Work with a partner to answer these questions. Try to include the red word in your answer. Write the sentences in your notebook.

1. **Analyze** the painting on the right.
2. What does the **image** represent?
3. What is your **interpretation** of the painting?
4. Are any objects **visible** in the painting? If so, what are they?

City in Shards of Light by Carolyn Hubbard-Ford ▶

340

Word Study: Lexical Sets

Lexical sets are sets of words that describe a central idea. For example, a lexical set for the word *light* includes the following words: *bright, brilliant, dazzling, illuminated, radiant, sparkling,* and *starry.* Read the lexical sets below.

dark	dim, gloomy, murky, shadowy
fast	fleeting, quick, rapid, speedy, swift
loud	deafening, ear-splitting, harsh, noisy, shrill, strident

Practice  Workbook Page 163

Work with a partner. Copy the chart below into your notebook. Take turns reading the words in the chart. Create a lexical set for each word. Include at least three words in each set.

beautiful	
slow	
strong	
sweet	

READING STRATEGY   CONNECT IDEAS

Connecting ideas in a poem helps you understand what the author wants you to know. When you connect ideas, look for the most important idea in each stanza and see how it fits with all of the other ideas. To connect ideas, follow these steps:

- Read the first stanza. What is the main idea?
- Now read the stanzas that follow. Make a note of the main ideas.
- Look at the list you made. How are the ideas similar?

As you read "Stars" and "Escape at Bedtime," look for ideas that are similar to each other. Think about what connects each idea to the next.

 Workbook Page 164

Starry Nights

Vincent van Gogh was born in 1853 in Holland. He became a painter when he was in his twenties and moved to France in 1886. Van Gogh spent the last years of his life in the south of France, painting landscapes and people. He suffered from mental illness and was confined at various times to mental hospitals, where he continued to paint until his death in 1890. Van Gogh sold only one painting during his lifetime. Today a van Gogh painting is worth millions of dollars. One of van Gogh's most famous paintings is called *Starry Night*.

Vincent van Gogh often wrote letters to his siblings. Some of these letters have been preserved in museums and are available for viewing. Following is an excerpt of a letter Vincent sent to his sister, Wilhelmina. In it, he describes painting the picture *Café Terrace on the Place du Forum, Arles, at Night*.

---

mental illness, a sickness relating to the mind

▼ *Starry Night* by Vincent van Gogh

Arles, 9 and 16 September 1888

My dear sister,

Your letter gave me a great deal of pleasure, and today I have the leisure to calmly reply. . . .

At present I absolutely want to paint a starry sky. It often seems to me that night is still more richly colored than the day; having hues of the most intense violets, blues, and greens. If only you pay attention to it you will see that certain stars are lemon-yellow, others pink or a green, blue and forget-me-not brilliance. And without my expatiating on this theme it is obvious that putting little white dots on the blue-black is not enough to paint a starry sky. . . .

In point of fact I was interrupted these days by my toiling on a new picture representing the outside of a café at night. On the terrace there are the tiny figures of drinkers. An immense yellow lantern illuminates the terrace, the façade and the sidewalk, and even casts its light on the pavement of the streets, which takes a pinkish violet tone. The gables of the houses in the street stretching away under a blue sky spangled with stars are dark blue or violet with a green tree. Here you have a night picture without black in it, done with nothing but beautiful blue and violet and green, and lemon-yellow. It amuses me enormously to paint the night right on the spot. They used to draw and paint the picture in the daytime after the sketch. But I find satisfaction in painting the thing immediately. . . .

▲ *Café Terrace on the Place du Forum, Arles, at Night* by Vincent van Gogh

---

hues, colors
expatiating, speaking or writing in detail about a particular subject
toiling, working hard
terrace, patio
façade, front or outside of a building
gables, top, triangular parts of walls
sketch, drawing

BEFORE YOU GO ON

1 How many paintings did van Gogh sell in his lifetime? How is this different from how they sell today?

2 How does van Gogh's work differ from the traditional representation of stars as white dots in a black sky?

On Your Own
Do you like van Gogh's paintings? Why or why not?

343

Stars

Sara Teasdale

Alone in the night
On a dark hill
With pines around me
Spicy and still,

And a heaven full of stars
Over my head,
White and topaz
And misty red;

Myriads with beating
Hearts of fire
That aeons
Cannot vex or tire;

Up the dome of heaven
Like a great hill,
I watch them marching
Stately and still,
And I know that I
Am honored to be
Witness
Of so much majesty.

✔ **LITERARY CHECK**
*How many stanzas
are in this poem?*

---

pines, tall trees common in
   North America
topaz, yellow-brown
myriads, uncountable
   numbers
aeons, very long periods
   of time
vex, bother
majesty, impressive or
   beautiful quality

ABOUT THE **POET**

Sara Teasdale (1884–1933)
most often composed poetry
about love, the beauty of
nature, and death. Her
poems became especially
popular during the early
twentieth century. In 1918, Teasdale's work
was recognized, and she was awarded the
Columbia University Poetry Society Prize, later
known as the Pulitzer Prize for Poetry.

Escape at Bedtime

Robert Louis Stevenson

The lights from the parlour and kitchen shone out
Through the blinds and the windows and bars;
And high overhead and all moving about,
There were thousands of millions of stars.
There ne'er were such thousands of leaves on a tree,
Nor of people in church or the Park,
As the crowds of the stars that looked down upon me,
And that glittered and winked in the dark.
The Dog, and the Plough, and the Hunter, and all,
And the star of the sailor, and Mars,
These shown in the sky, and the pail by the wall
Would be half full of water and stars.
They saw me at last, and they chased me with cries,
And they soon had me packed into bed;
But the glory kept shining and bright in my eyes,
And the stars going round in my head.

---

parlour, living room
blinds, objects that cover windows
ne'er, never
glittered, were very shiny
plough, farmer's tool
sailor, person who works on a ship

✔ **LITERARY CHECK**
*Read the last four lines of the poem. Which words **rhyme**? Do you notice a pattern?*

BEFORE YOU GO ON

1. How does the person in the poem "Stars" feel about stars?

2. In the poem "Escape at Bedtime," what are the Dog, the Plough, and the Hunter?

On Your Own
How do you feel when you look at stars?

DRAMATIC READING

One of the best ways to understand a poem is to memorize it. Work in groups of four. Reread, discuss, and interpret "Stars." Then work together to interpret any difficult words or phrases in the poem. Use a dictionary or ask your teacher for help if necessary.

After you have examined the poem carefully, assign one of the poem's stanzas to each member of the group. Memorize your assigned stanza. Then come back together as a group to recite the entire poem. Comment on one another's oral recitation and make helpful suggestions for improvements. You can even hold a contest in which each group within your classroom competes for the best oral recitation.

> 🔊 *Speaking* TIP
>
> Communicate your belief in what you are saying, so your classmates will believe it, too.

COMPREHENSION

 **Workbook Page 165**

Right There

1. Where and when was Vincent van Gogh born?
2. How old was van Gogh when he became a painter?

Think and Search

3. Name two different van Gogh paintings.
4. In van Gogh's letter to his sister, what colors does he claim to use in his most recent painting?

Author and You

5. Why do you think van Gogh was not able to sell more than one painting in his lifetime?
6. Why do you think his paintings sell for millions of dollars today?

On Your Own

7. Have you ever seen a van Gogh painting at a museum? If so, which one?
8. Van Gogh thought that the night is more richly colored than the day. Would you agree? Explain.

DISCUSSION

Discuss in pairs or small groups.

1. How are the two van Gogh paintings you read about similar?
2. Compare the two poems "Stars" and "Escape at Bedtime." How are they different?

 **How does the sky influence us?** Would you rather talk to a scientist who studies the stars or a poet who writes about them? Why?

RESPONSE TO LITERATURE

Workbook
Page 165

You read two poems that describe stars. Now, with a partner, write your own poem about the night sky. Your poem should contain three stanzas and words that rhyme. Read your completed poem aloud to your classmates.

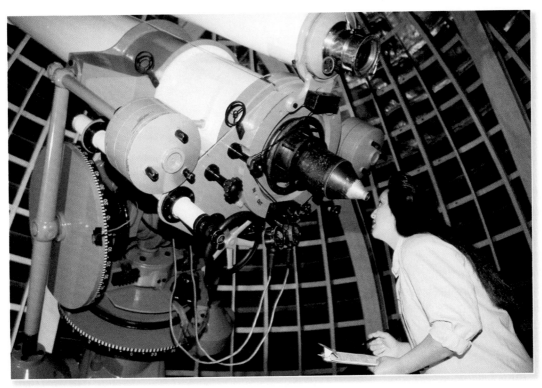

▲ An astronomer looking at the night sky through a telescope

Listening TIP

Listen for supporting details and reasons. Ask yourself, "Did the speaker explain why these ideas are important?"

Grammar and Writing

Punctuation in Prose and Poetry

Different rules of punctuation are used in prose and poetry. In prose, or ordinary written language, the first letter of the first word in every sentence is always capitalized. There is always a period, exclamation point, or question mark at the end of each sentence.

In poetry, these rules do not exist. The first letter of the first word in every line is often capitalized, but not always. There may or may not be a period, comma, semicolon, or colon at the end of each line. For example, the poet e.e. cummings used punctuation creatively within his poems and often ignored capitalization altogether. Read the excerpt below from his poem "i go to this window."

> i go to this window
>
> just as day dissolves
> when it is twilight (and
> looking up in fear
>
> i see the new moon
> thinner than a hair)
>
> — *e.e. cummings*

Practice

Copy the poem below into your notebook. Rewrite the poetic lines as prose. Remember to follow the rules of punctuation and capitalization. Then share your work with a partner.

> i walked along a darkened road
> the night sky shimmered with stars of gold
> the air smelled fresh the grass sweet
> as pebbles crunched beneath my feet
>
> i wandered
> without a destination
> content to observe
> the nights celebration

WRITING A RESEARCH REPORT

Write an Introductory Paragraph

At the end of this unit, you will write a research report. First, you will learn how to begin such a report. Then you will conduct research and write an introductory paragraph.

Sometimes it is helpful to make a list of research topics and then choose the one that is most interesting to you. Suppose you choose to write about space. Your first task would be to focus on a specific aspect of space, such as the stars. To narrow your topic even further, ask a question: *How do stars form?* After you identify the question you want to answer, begin your research.

After you have completed your research, you can write the introductory paragraph for your report. The paragraph should introduce the research topic with an interesting question or fact.

Here is a model of an introductory paragraph. The writer used an inverted pyramid to narrow his topic before writing. Notice how he begins his paragraph with an interesting question.

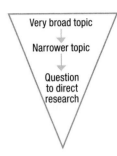

Very broad topic
↓
Narrower topic
↓
Question to direct research

Ari Janoff

The Life of a Star
What are the stages of a star's life cycle? Because the stars look the same night after night, you might not know that they change at all. In fact, a Greek philosopher named Aristotle believed that stars were made of a special, unchanging material that was only found in space. However, within the last hundred years, astronomers have learned that, like people, stars do experience a limited life cycle: All stars are born in the same way, they may shine for millions or billions of years, and then they die. The size of a star determines how long it will live and the life stages it will experience. These stages are described in detail within the paragraphs that follow.

Practice  **Workbook Page 167**

Select a topic related to space. Use a graphic organizer to narrow your topic and ask a question to guide your research. After conducting your research, write an introductory paragraph. Be sure to use correct punctuation.

Writing Checklist

ORGANIZATION:
☑ I introduced the question that directed my research.

CONVENTIONS:
☑ I used correct punctuation.

349

Prepare to Read

What You Will Learn

Reading
- Vocabulary building:
  Context, dictionary skills, word study
- Reading strategy:
  Use visuals
- Text type:
  Informational text (science)

Grammar, Usage, and Mechanics
Noun/pronoun agreement

Writing
Support the main idea

THE BIG QUESTION

How does the sky influence us? What do you know about space? Do you know what a galaxy is? A solar system? Do you know what makes up a solar system? Copy the K-W-L-H chart below into your notebook. Work with a partner. Complete the *K* column with information you know about space. Use the questions above as a guide. Write your reasons for wanting to learn about space in the *W* column. After reading the text, complete the *L* column with the new information you have learned, and the *H* column with a description about how you learned it.

K What do I **know**?	W What do I **want** to know?	L What did I **learn**?	H **How** did I learn it?

BUILD BACKGROUND

In this section, you will read an informational science article entitled **"Earth and the Milky Way."** It provides information about the Milky Way galaxy, our solar system, and objects that occupy the solar system, including planet Earth.

The Milky Way ▶

Learn Key Words

Read these sentences. Use the context to figure out the meaning of the **red** words. Use a dictionary to check your answers. Then write each word and its meaning in your notebook.

1. **Asteroids** circle the sun just as planets do.
2. The **comet** was bright enough to see without a telescope.
3. Astronauts wear heavy shoes on the moon because the moon's **gravity** is not as strong as Earth's gravity.
4. **Meteoroids** are pieces of rock or dust that travel through space.
5. Earth circles the sun. Earth takes one year to complete its **orbit**.
6. Earth is one of eight **planets** in our solar system.

Key Words

asteroids
comet
gravity
meteoroids
orbit
planets

Practice  **Workbook Page 168**

Write the sentences in your notebook. Choose a **red** word from the box above to complete each sentence. Then take turns reading the sentences aloud with a partner.

1. We could see the bright tail of the _____ in the night sky.
2. Mercury, Venus, Earth, and Mars are the four _____ closest to the sun.
3. The _____ traveled together in a belt around the sun.
4. Earth's _____ prevents us from floating into space.
5. Asteroids and Earth are similar in that they both _____ the sun.
6. The rocky _____ formed part of the comet's tail.

A view of Earth from space ▶

351

Learn Academic Words

Study the red words and their meanings. You will find these words useful when talking and writing about informational texts. Write each word and its meaning in your notebook. After you read "Earth and the Milky Way," try to use these words to respond to the text.

Academic Words

consists
criteria
features
located

consists = is made of or contains a number of different things		A galaxy **consists** of billions of stars.
criteria = facts or standards used in order to help you judge or decide something		Pluto is no longer considered to be a planet. It does not meet the necessary scientific **criteria**.
features = important, interesting, or typical parts of something		Some planets have **features** such as solid, rocky surfaces.
located = in a particular place or position		The sun is **located** at the center of our solar system.

Practice
Workbook Page 169

Write the sentences in your notebook. Choose a red word from the box above to complete each sentence. Then take turns reading the sentences aloud with a partner.

1. I want to learn more about space. Do you know where the planetarium is _____?

2. What _____ do scientists use to classify asteroids?

3. A comet _____ of large pieces of ice and dust.

4. Large water bodies are _____ that make Earth easily identifiable from space.

Rose Center, Hayden
Planetarium, in New York City ▶

Word Study: Greek and Latin Roots *astro, ology, geo*

Many words in English have Greek and Latin roots. Understanding
these roots can help you understand the English words that formed
from them.

Greek or Latin Root	Meaning	Words and definitions
astro	stars	**astronomy**: the scientific study of the stars and planets
ology	study of	**biology**: the scientific study of living things
geo	earth	**geology**: the scientific study of materials such as rocks and soil and how they have changed over time

Practice

Copy the chart below into your notebook. Find the definition of each
word in a dictionary. Write the definition in the chart. Then use each
word in a sentence. Read your sentences aloud to a partner.

Word	Definition	Sentence
astronaut		
psychology		
geography		

READING STRATEGY   USE VISUALS

Using visuals helps you understand the text better. Visuals are art,
photographs, diagrams, charts, maps, etc. Many informational texts
include visuals. To use visuals, follow these steps:

- Look at the visual. Ask yourself, "What does the visual show? How
  does it help me understand the reading?"
- Read the titles, headings, labels or captions carefully.
- Review the visuals as you read each section.

As you read "Earth and the Milky Way," look at the diagrams.
What do they tell you about the sky?

Set a purpose for reading As you read, look for examples of how the sky relates to planet Earth. How do the objects in the sky influence Earth?

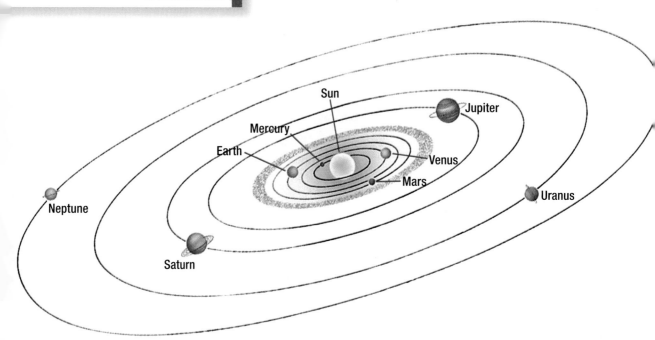

Earth and the Milky Way

From Earth, the stars appear as tiny dots in the sky. In fact, each star in the sky is an enormous glowing ball of gas, like our sun.

A huge, organized collection of stars is called a galaxy. Our solar system is located in the Milky Way galaxy. Our sun is one of more than 100 billion stars within this galaxy.

---

enormous, extremely large

Our Solar System

Our solar system consists of the sun, eight planets and their moons, an asteroid belt, and many comets and meteors. All of which orbit, or circle, the sun, which is the center of our solar system.

The Sun

Our sun is a medium-sized star. It is a huge, spinning ball of hot gas that lights Earth and provides us with heat. It is 149,680,000 kilometers (93,026,724 mi.) from Earth.

Scientists determine the temperature of the sun by measuring how much heat and light it emits. The sun's core can reach 5,500,000 to 15,000,000°C (10,000,000 to 27,000,000°F). The outer atmosphere of the sun is also extremely hot.

Since the sun is the closest star to Earth, astronomers study it to understand the nature of stars in general. They use special instruments to analyze the light from the sun, its effect on Earth's climate, the sun's magnetic field, solar wind, and many other solar phenomena.

---

emits, sends out; gives off
core, center

atmosphere, mix of gases that surround a star or planet
phenomena, facts or events that can be seen

A close-up view of the sun, showing a blast of hot gas ▶

BEFORE YOU GO ON

1 Which star in the Milky Way galaxy is closest to Earth?

2 What objects orbit the sun?

💡 **On Your Own**
What do you know about the planets in our solar system?

355

The Planets

There are eight planets that orbit our sun: Mercury, Venus, Earth, Mars, Jupiter, Saturn, Uranus, and Neptune.

In the past, a planet was defined as being a body (gaseous or solid) that orbits stars. Under this definition, Pluto was also considered to be a planet. However, astronomers found that Pluto has characteristics that make it different from the other planets: Pluto is much smaller, it has an odd orbit, and it tilts in a different direction.

As a result, in 2006, astronomers changed the definition of the word *planet*. Now, a planet is considered to be a body (gaseous or solid) that orbits the sun, is nearly round, and does not cross the path of another planet's orbit. Pluto's orbit crosses Neptune's path. For this reason, Pluto was reclassified as a smaller, dwarf planet.

The remaining eight planets are classified into one of two groups: the inner planets and the outer planets.

The four planets closest to the sun—Mercury, Venus, Earth, and Mars—are called the inner planets. They are small and have solid, rocky surfaces. Thousands of pieces of rock and metal, called asteroids, orbit the sun between Mars and Jupiter. They separate the inner planets from the outer planets.

The four outer planets are Jupiter, Saturn, Uranus, and Neptune. They are called gas giants because they are much larger than Earth and do not have solid surfaces. All four planets have rings.

These eight planets may not be the only planets in the Milky Way. Scientists are still finding new bodies that orbit our sun.

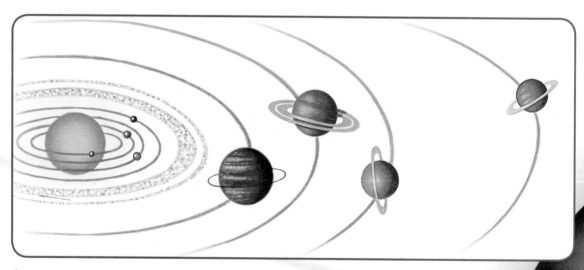

▲ The inner planets, asteroid belt, and outer planets of our solar system

356

▲ Saturn

Planet Facts

Jupiter

The biggest planet in the solar system is Jupiter. All the other planets could fit inside it. Two Earth-sized planets could fit inside the storm that has lasted on Jupiter for hundreds of years. This storm is called the Great Red Spot. It is about 28,000 kilometers (17,000 mi.) long and 14,000 kilometers (9,000 mi.) wide.

Jupiter has rings, but they are faint, dark, and narrow, so they are not easy to see. Jupiter's rings are made of tiny bits of rock and dust that orbit the planet. The dust is created as a result of tiny meteorites crashing into Jupiter's moons.

One of these moons, Ganymede, is bigger than the planet Mercury. Its diameter is about one third that of Earth.

Saturn

Saturn is the second biggest planet in the solar system. Like Jupiter, Saturn has a thick atmosphere, composed mostly of hydrogen and helium. Although Saturn has clouds and storms, they are much milder than those on Jupiter.

Unlike Jupiter's rings, Saturn's famous rings are made up of chunks of rock and ice. Saturn's rings are much larger and brighter than the rings of other planets.

---

diameter, length of a line that divides a circle in half

◀ Jupiter

BEFORE YOU GO ON

1 What are planets?

2 In what two groups are planets classified? Explain.

On Your Own
What planets would you like to learn more about and why?

357

▲ Venus

Venus

Venus is the closest planet in size to Earth. Venus's diameter is 95 percent of Earth's diameter, and its mass is 82 percent of Earth's mass. Venus is the planet that passes closest to Earth in its orbit. It is roughly 39,200,000 kilometers (24,588,879 mi.) from Earth at its closest approach. Venus is the hottest planet, with temperatures up to 480°C (896°F).

Mars

The biggest volcano in the solar system, Olympus Mons, is on Mars. It is 27 kilometers (17 mi.) tall and over 520 kilometers (320 mi.) across. It formed about 200 million years ago. Scientists now believe it to be extinct.

---

mass, amount of material in something
approach, movement toward or near

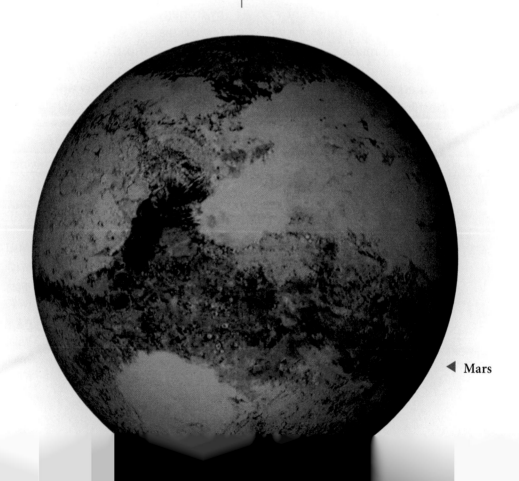

◀ Mars

▲ Comet Hale-Bopp

Asteroids, Comets, and Meteoroids

There are other objects smaller than planets and moons that also orbit the sun. They include asteroids, comets, and meteoroids.

Asteroids are rocky or metallic objects in many sizes and shapes. Most asteroids orbit the sun in a belt, or group, between the orbits of Mars and Jupiter. This area of the solar system is called the asteroid belt. Astronomers have discovered more than 10,000 asteroids.

Comets are large pieces of ice and dust that orbit the sun. When a comet travels near the sun, the energy in the sunlight changes the ice into gas. Gas and dust form a tail, which can be hundreds of millions of kilometers long.

Meteoroids are dust particles or bits of rock that travel through space. They usually come from comets or asteroids. When a meteoroid enters Earth's atmosphere, it burns up and produces a streak of light in the sky, called a meteor. Large meteoroids may not burn up completely. Meteoroids that hit a planet or moon are called meteorites.

A chunk of stony iron meteorite that landed on Earth ▶

BEFORE YOU GO ON

1. Which planet is the closest in size to Earth?

2. What is the area between Mars and Jupiter called? Why?

On Your Own
Would you like to be an astronomer? Why or why not?

359

The Stars

Most stars are in pairs or in clusters. The force of gravity holds these pairs or clusters together. Two stars that are locked together in orbit are called a binary star system. About half of all stars are in binary star systems. Larger groups of stars, or clusters, are also joined together by their gravitational pull.

Patterns of stars in the sky are called constellations. Constellations are different from star pairs or clusters because the connection among the stars is only visual. There is no gravitational or orbital connection, and distances between the stars in the constellation may be very great.

clusters, groups that are very close together
visual, relating to sight

▼ The Big Dipper

▲ The constellation Orion

◀ The constellations of the zodiac

There are eighty-eight recognized constellations. In ancient times, people called twelve of these constellations the zodiac. *Zodiac* is the Greek word for "animals," and most of the constellations in the zodiac are named after animals. Learning the constellations is a way to become familiar with the stars in the same way that people have been doing for thousands of years.

Star maps help astronomers locate stars in the same way that land maps help us find our way around Earth. Astronomers divide the sky into a grid similar to the latitude and longitude grid used on land maps. Astronomers use the star grid system to chart the positions of stars.

latitude, distance north or south of the equator
longitude, distance east or west of the meridian (imaginary line from the top of the world to the bottom that divides east and west)

in ancient times, times long ago
become familiar with, get to know; learn about

BEFORE YOU GO ON

1 What is a binary star system?

2 How is a star cluster different from a constellation?

On Your Own
Do you know the names of any other stars or constellations? If so, what are they?

361

COMPREHENSION

Workbook
Page 172

Right There

1. What does our solar system consist of?
2. What is a star?

Think and Search

3. How are asteroids and comets similar?
4. Put the following items in order by size, from smallest to largest: solar system, Milky Way, Ganymede, the sun, Mars.

Author and You

5. Why would scientists believe that the volcano on Mars is extinct?
6. Do you think the author believes that the study of space is important? Explain.

On Your Own

7. What do you find most interesting about space? Explain.
8. If you could travel to any planet, which one would you choose? Why?

IN YOUR OWN WORDS

Copy the chart below into your notebook. Then reread "Earth and the Milky Way." Write the most important fact about each topic in the chart. Use the facts to summarize the article for a partner.

Topics	Facts
Milky Way galaxy	Our solar system is located in the Milky Way galaxy.
Solar system	
Sun	
Planets	
Asteroids	
Comets	
Meteroids	
Stars	

DISCUSSION

Discuss in pairs or small groups.

1. Compare and contrast the inner and outer planets.
2. Why was Pluto reclassified as a dwarf planet?
 **How does the sky influence us?** How does the sun influence Earth? What would life on Earth be like without the sun?

Speaking TIP

Think about the topic in question. Offer ideas about only that topic and not something else.

READ FOR FLUENCY

It is often easier to read a text if you understand the difficult words and phrases. Work with a partner. Choose a paragraph from the reading. Identify the words and phrases you do not know or have trouble pronouncing. Look up the difficult words in a dictionary.

Take turns pronouncing the words and phrases with your partner. If necessary, ask your teacher to model the correct pronunciation. Then take turns reading the paragraph aloud. Give each other feedback on your reading.

EXTENSION

Workbook Page 172

Use the information you learned from "Earth and the Milky Way" to write riddles. For example: *I am made of the sun, eight planets, an asteroid belt, and comets and meteors. What am I?* (Answer: the solar system.) Ask each other your riddles.

◀ Computer-generated artwork of the planets as seen from Earth's moon

Grammar and Writing

GRAMMAR, USAGE, AND MECHANICS

Noun/Pronoun Agreement

A pronoun refers to a single noun or noun phrase. A pronoun can refer to the subject of a sentence, or a noun that performs an action and usually comes before the verb. A pronoun can also refer to an object, or a noun that receives the action and usually comes after the verb. To achieve noun/pronoun agreement, the noun and pronoun must agree in person and number. This agreement helps make it clear which noun the pronoun refers to.

Number	Subject Pronouns	Object Pronouns
singular	I, you, he, she, it	me, you, him, her, it
plural	we, you, they	us, you, them

Read the sentences from "Earth and the Milky Way" in the box below. In the second column, some nouns and noun phrases have been replaced with pronouns.

Sentences with Nouns	Sentences with Pronouns
Astronomers use **the star grid system** to chart the positions of stars.	**They** use **it** to chart the positions of stars.
This area of the solar system is called the asteroid belt.	**It** is called the asteroid belt.

Practice
Workbook Page 173

Copy the paragraph below into your notebook. Replace the underlined word(s) in each sentence with the correct pronoun. Use the pronoun chart above to help you.

My friends are going to be late for the light show at the planetarium. Most of <u>my friends</u> are held up in traffic. <u>My friend Jennifer and I</u> arrived half an hour ago. Jennifer has already seen several exhibits. <u>Jennifer</u> said the exhibits were very interesting! <u>Jennifer</u> liked <u>the exhibits</u> a lot. Jennifer said that a museum worker showed <u>Jennifer</u> how to use a telescope. <u>The telescope</u> had a very strong lens and Jennifer could see many details.

Support the Main Idea

You learned that a research report begins with an introductory paragraph. Following the introduction, each main idea is presented and expanded upon within its own paragraph.

The main idea is the most important point a writer tries to make in a paragraph. Details, including facts and examples, support the main idea. For example, imagine that the main idea of a paragraph is the following: *Neptune is a gas giant.* Your supporting details might include: *Neptune does not have a solid surface. Neptune has rings.*

Here is a model paragraph. The writer used a main-idea-and-details web to organize his information. Then he presented the main idea within its own paragraph and used details to support it.

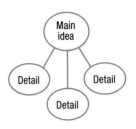

Pablo Espínola

Pluto Is No Longer a Planet

Although it lost its title as the ninth planet in our solar system, Pluto continues to interest astronomers. They are now studying the thousands of rocky, icy chunks, called dwarfs, which surround Pluto. These objects are located in an area called the Kuiper Belt. To learn more about this area, NASA launched a spacecraft in January 2006. The spacecraft, called New Horizons, will reach its destination in 2015. It will collect information about Pluto's surface and atmosphere. The spacecraft will also look for rings and moons. With the information they receive from Pluto and the Kuiper Belt, astronomers hope to learn about the conditions that existed when our solar system began.

Practice  **Workbook Page 174**

Write a paragraph that includes a main idea and supporting details. You might choose to expand upon the topic you wrote about in your introductory paragraph or you can choose to write about a new topic. Use a graphic organizer to determine which details best support your main idea. Be sure that all the nouns and pronouns in your paragraph agree.

Writing Checklist

ORGANIZATION:
☑ I used the main-idea-and-details web to organize my notes.

WORD CHOICE:
☑ I included specific examples that explain and support the main idea.

365

Prepare to Read

What You Will Learn

Reading

■ Vocabulary building: *Literary terms, word study*

■ Reading strategy: *Read for enjoyment*

■ Text type: *Literature (myth)*

Grammar, Usage, and Mechanics
Modal verb: *must*

Writing
Include paraphrases and citations

 THE BIG QUESTION

How does the sky influence us? In the last reading, you learned some information about the sun. What would life be like for humans without the sun? How do both the sun and the moon influence life on Earth? Discuss with a partner.

BUILD BACKGROUND

In this section, you will read a myth called **"The Girl Who Married the Moon."** Myths are very old, fictional stories that are passed down from one generation to the next. They were often created to explain things about the natural world.

"The Girl Who Married the Moon" is about a group of people called the Alutiiq, also known as Eskimo people. The early Alutiiq lived in large villages on Kodiak Island, near Alaska. The women of these villages were responsible for gathering food and sewing clothes. Women were therefore thought to be important to their group's survival.

The Alutiiq were also known for masking, or carving the likenesses of ancestors, animals, and mythological beings into wood or bark.

As you read "The Girl Who Married the Moon," pay attention to how these cultural features are reflected in the story.

◀ A man carves a traditional Native Alaskan mask.

VOCABULARY

Learn Literary Words

A **myth** is a short fictional tale. Myths explain the origins of elements of nature. Their purpose is to entertain and instruct. Every ancient culture has its own mythology that is passed from generation to generation as part of the oral tradition. Read the myth below. Try to determine which natural event it tries to explain.

> Once there was a Mexican people who loved the sun. The sun liked to be near them, and every day he slowly moved closer to Earth. Soon, Earth became too hot for the people on Earth to bear. They begged the sun to move higher into the sky, but he did not want to leave them.
>
> Then, one day, a boy offered to travel high into the sky with the sun, so that he would not be lonely. Soon, the pair were traveling higher and higher into the sky together, and that is where they have been ever since.

Sometimes, **personification** is used in myths. Personification gives human qualities to nonhuman animals or things. What nonhuman thing is personified in the myth above? What human qualities does it have?

Practice

Workbook
Page 175

Work with a partner. Take turns reading the examples of personification below. Identify the object being personified and the human qualities it has.

1. The sunflowers nodded their yellow heads in the summer breeze.
2. Throughout the night, thunder grumbled and growled.
3. The trees shivered in the winter cold.
4. I can hear raindrops dancing on the rooftop.
5. The moon peeked over the treetops.
6. I saw the lamp as it winked at me through the window.

Learn Academic Words

Study the **red** words and their meanings. You will find these words useful when talking and writing about literature. Write each word and its meaning in your notebook. After you read "The Girl Who Married the Moon," try to use these words to respond to the text.

ignored = did not pay attention to someone or something	➡	I **ignored** the noisy students as I read the story.
instructed = taught or showed someone how to do something	➡	Our teacher **instructed** us to visualize the events as they happened in the story.
job = a particular duty or responsibility that you have	➡	My **job** is to research the origins of the myth online. My partner will write the report.
restricted = not allowed to do something	➡	Students are **restricted** from using the computer for more than one hour at a time.

Practice

Workbook
Page 176

Write the sentences in your notebook. Choose a **red** word from the box above to complete each sentence. Then take turns reading the sentences aloud with a partner.

1. Her _____ was to collect the books after class and return them to the library.

2. The librarian _____ her to place the books on the counter.

3. She was _____ from using the books for more than one class period at a time.

4. She _____ the rules and kept the book for two days.

368

Word Study: Spelling Long *i*

In "The Girl Who Married the Moon," you will read many words that have the long *i* sound. There are several ways to spell this sound. Read the information in the chart below for some examples.

Spelling Long *i*			
i_e	-igh	-y	i
like	night	sky	island
wife	brightly	why	climb
admire	might	cycle	kind
mile	high	rely	final

Practice
Workbook
Page 177

Work with a partner. Copy the chart above into your notebook. Say a word from the chart, and ask your partner to spell it aloud. Then have your partner say the next word. Continue until you can spell all of the words correctly. Now practice spelling these words with your partner: *side, blind, fry, fright*. Add them to the chart under the correct headings.

READING STRATEGY **READ FOR ENJOYMENT**

Reading for enjoyment is important because it gives you a purpose for reading and improves your ability to read for specific information. When you read for fun, you may learn new words and ideas that you will see again in nonfictional texts. To read for enjoyment, follow these steps:

- Before you read, remember that your main purpose is reading for enjoyment. You will be learning, too, but this is mainly for fun.
- Pay attention to the characters, settings, and illustrations. Think about how they increase your enjoyment of the text.
- Stop from time to time and think about the reason you enjoyed a particular passage or chapter.

As you read "The Girl Who Married the Moon," focus on the characters and setting. Ask yourself, "How does the author make this fun, interesting, or exciting for me to read?"

Workbook
Page 178

Set a purpose for reading As you read, pay attention to the characters' jobs. How do these jobs influence us?

The Girl Who Married
THE MOON

Retold by Joseph Bruchac and Gayle Ross

Long ago, in the village of Chiniak, on the island of Kodiak, there were two cousins.

They had reached the age when they could choose a husband. Both of them had just been given the chin tattoos that showed they were now women. Both of them were strong and good-looking, and they were so well liked that almost any young man would have agreed to marry them. In fact, some elders said that these girls might easily choose—as did some of the women—to each have two husbands. Yet none of the young men in the village of Chiniak or any of the other villages on the island or even the nearby mainland interested those cousins.

---

cousins, relatives whose parents are siblings
tattoos, designs that are permanently put onto the skin
elders, rulers of a village or tribe

When the night had come and the work of the day was done, those two girls would always go down to the beach to play together in the sand and watch for the rising Moon above the water. As soon as he began to show his face, they would turn over their kayak and sit, leaning back against it, admiring the moon's beauty. They spent all their time at night staring at the sky. Whether it was winter or summer, they could always be found there on the beach.

One night, one of the girls said, "I have fallen in love with the Moon."

"I have fallen in love with the Moon, too," said the other girl. "If he ever comes down to earth, I will marry him."

Their parents worried about them when they heard that the two girls wished to marry the Moon. But no one told them to stop going to the beach at night.

---

kayak, canoe

BEFORE YOU GO ON

1 Describe the cousins. Why do they go to the beach every night?

2 How do the girls feel about the Moon?

On Your Own
The girls were given chin tattoos to symbolize their becoming young adults. Was there a particular way in which you celebrated this occasion? Explain.

371

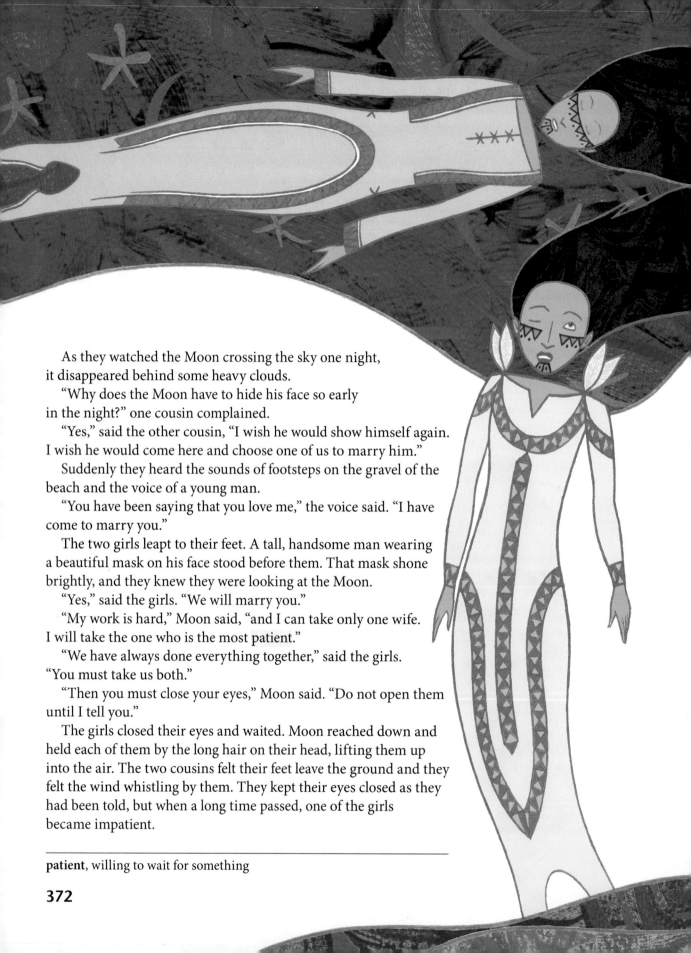

As they watched the Moon crossing the sky one night, it disappeared behind some heavy clouds.

"Why does the Moon have to hide his face so early in the night?" one cousin complained.

"Yes," said the other cousin, "I wish he would show himself again. I wish he would come here and choose one of us to marry him."

Suddenly they heard the sounds of footsteps on the gravel of the beach and the voice of a young man.

"You have been saying that you love me," the voice said. "I have come to marry you."

The two girls leapt to their feet. A tall, handsome man wearing a beautiful mask on his face stood before them. That mask shone brightly, and they knew they were looking at the Moon.

"Yes," said the girls. "We will marry you."

"My work is hard," Moon said, "and I can take only one wife. I will take the one who is the most patient."

"We have always done everything together," said the girls. "You must take us both."

"Then you must close your eyes," Moon said. "Do not open them until I tell you."

The girls closed their eyes and waited. Moon reached down and held each of them by the long hair on their head, lifting them up into the air. The two cousins felt their feet leave the ground and they felt the wind whistling by them. They kept their eyes closed as they had been told, but when a long time passed, one of the girls became impatient.

---

patient, willing to wait for something

372

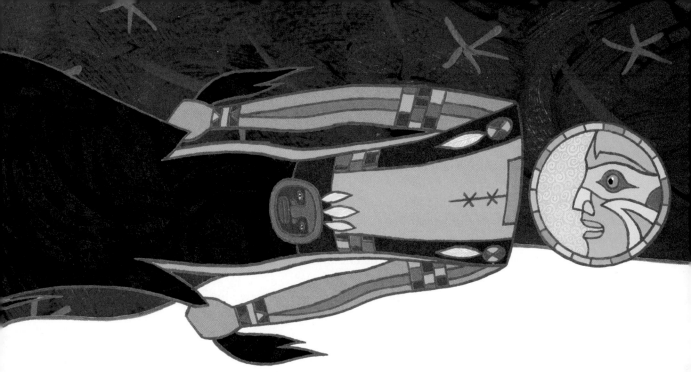

I must see where we are going, she thought. I will just open one eye a little.

But as soon as she opened her eye, she found herself falling down and landing back on the beach alone. Her long hair was gone from her head, and her cousin was gone from her forever.

The other girl, though, did not open her eyes. All through the night, she kept her eyes closed as Moon crossed the sky. When he told her to open her eyes at last, she found herself standing in Moon's house on the other side of the sky.

At first, she was happy to be the wife of Moon.

"Go wherever you wish," her husband told her. "Only do not look behind the blanket and go into my storehouse."

Moon's wife agreed. She would do as her husband said. She settled down to her new life in the land on the other side of the sky, but it was not always easy. Sometimes her husband would spend a long time with her. Sometimes he would be gone all night and then sleep all day after he came home. She never knew when he was going to go or how long he would be gone. Soon she became bored.

---

bored, tired and impatient

BEFORE YOU GO ON

1 What trait must Moon's wife have?

2 Whom did Moon drop? Why?

On Your Own
Are you a patient person? Explain.

373

"Why must you always leave me?" She said to her husband. "Why is it that you come and go in such a strange way?"

"It is the work I must do," said Moon. "That is why I cannot always be with you."

"Can I go with you when you do your work?"

"No," said Moon, "my work is too hard. You must stay home and be happy when I am with you."

Moon's wife listened, but she was not happy. That night when her husband left, she began to wander about the land on the other side of the sky. She walked farther and farther and came to a place where she saw many trails, and she began to follow one. At the end of that trail, she saw a person lying facedown.

"What are you doing?" she asked. But the person would not answer her or look her way.

She tried more trails and found the same thing at the end—a person lying facedown. And each time she asked what the person was doing, she received no answer. At last she could stand it no longer. At the end of the next trail she took, when she found a person lying down, she began to poke the person with her foot.

"Answer me," she said. "Answer me, answer me. What are you doing?"

Finally the person turned and looked at her. She saw he had only one bright eye, sparkling in the middle of his face. "I am working," the person said. "Do not bother me."

When Moon's wife returned home, her husband had not come back. She sat down to wait, but she was still bored. She looked around and saw his storeroom, with a dark woven blanket covering the door.

✔ **LITERARY CHECK**
What examples of personification exist in this story?

---

wander, walk slowly without having a clear direction or purpose
poke, quickly push someone or something
storeroom, room where goods are kept

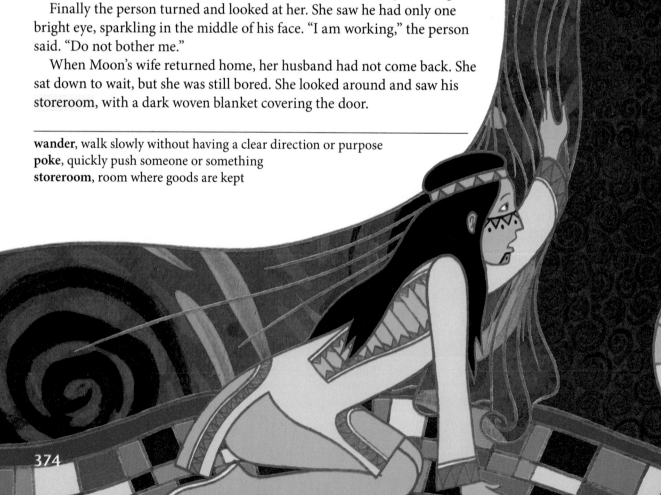

374

"It will not hurt to take one small look," she said. "Moon is my husband, and I should be able to go wherever I want in our house."

Then she went to the floor and pulled aside the blanket. There in the storeroom were the pieces of light her husband wore when he crossed the sky. There was a half-moon, a quarter moon, and all the other phases. The only one missing was the full moon, which her husband had worn when he left that evening. The pieces of light were so beautiful that Moon's wife could not resist.

---

quarter, one-fourth

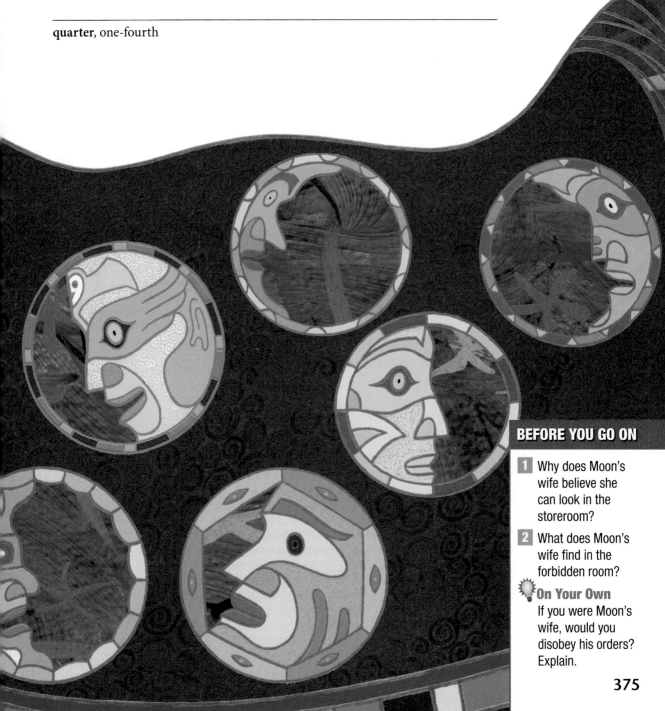

BEFORE YOU GO ON

1 Why does Moon's wife believe she can look in the storeroom?

2 What does Moon's wife find in the forbidden room?

On Your Own
If you were Moon's wife, would you disobey his orders? Explain.

375

"I must try on one of them," she said, "to see how my husband feels when he is carrying them across the sky."

She reached down and picked up the one that was almost full and placed it on her face. As soon as she did so, it stuck there. She tried to remove it, but it would not budge. Although she wept and cried, the piece of moon would not come off. Then she heard her husband's steps coming across the sky.

She climbed into their bed and covered her head with a blanket.

"What is wrong?" Moon asked.

"I have a pain on my face," said his wife. "I do not feel well. Leave me alone."

But Moon became suspicious. He went to his storeroom and saw that one of the pieces of light was gone. He went back to his wife and pulled the covers from her head.

"Husband," Moon's wife said, "I became bored while you were gone. I tried on this piece of moon and now it is stuck."

Then Moon laughed. He laughed and laughed. And with careful hands, he pulled that piece of moon from her face.

"What else have you done today?" Moon said, still laughing.

His wife told him about following the many trails that led to people lying with their faces down and with a single bright eye in each of their heads.

"Those people are the stars," Moon said. "They should not be bothered while they are doing their work. It is clear to me that you need work to do also, my wife. Since you have shown that you are able to carry the moon you can help me. From now on, I will carry the pieces of moon each cycle until it is full, and then you can carry the pieces of moon until it is dark. That way, we will both have time to rest and neither of us will grow bored."

So it is to this day. The man of the moon carries the pieces of light from the time of the moon's first quarter until it is full, and the woman of the moon carries them from the time it is full until the moon grows dark. So they share the duty of carrying light across the sky.

✔ **LITERARY CHECK**
What event in nature does this myth explain?

---

suspicious, doubtful
cycle, series of the moon's phases
duty, task

ABOUT THE **AUTHORS**

Joseph Bruchac grew up in Upstate New York with his Native American grandparents, from whom he learned traditional stories and the art of storytelling. Today, in addition to writing and storytelling, he works to preserve the culture of his people, the Abenaki.

Gayle Ross learned the art of storytelling from her grandmother. Today Ross writes about those myths and legends and shares them at schools and colleges across the country. Most often, she tells the stories of her father's people, the Cherokee. Ross is directly related to John Ross, who was chief of the Cherokee nation during the "Trail of Tears."

BEFORE YOU GO ON

1. How does Moon react when he learns his wife entered the storeroom?

2. Who were the people Moon's wife spoke to during her walk? What were they doing?

On Your Own
Did you like this myth? Why or why not?

377

Review and Practice

READER'S THEATER

Act out the following scene with a partner.

Moon: What's wrong?

Wife: My face hurts. I don't feel good.

Moon: Why? What happened while I was gone?

Wife: [*covering her face with her hands*] I was bored while you were away, so I tried on this piece of moon and now it won't come off.

Moon: [*laughing as he pulls the piece of moon off his wife's face*] What else did you do today?

Wife: I took a walk, and I saw the strangest thing—there were people with only one eye that sparkled in the middle of their faces.

Moon: Those people are the stars—you shouldn't bother them when they're working. It seems like you need some work to do. From now on, you'll help me carry the moon across the sky.

COMPREHENSION

Workbook
Page 179

Right There

1. Where did the two cousins live?

2. Why was Moon's wife unhappy?

Think and Search

3. What did Moon's wife do when she became bored?

4. Which two pieces of light were not in the storeroom when Moon returned home?

Author and You

5. Why do you think Moon told his wife to stay away from his storeroom?

6. What do you think the authors' purpose was in telling this story?

On Your Own

7. Can you name all of the moon's phases? If not, which ones do you know?

8. What other myths do you know? What are they about? How do they explain objects or events that exist in the natural world?

DISCUSSION

»))) Listening TIP

As you listen, think about how your classmates' ideas are similar to or different from your own.

Discuss in pairs or small groups.

1. What aspect of Moon's job was his wife not aware of when she first married him? How did this affect Moon's wife?

2. Do you think patience is a good quality for a person to have? Explain.

Q How does the sky influence us? Why do you think ancient peoples had myths about natural occurrences?

RESPONSE TO LITERATURE  Workbook Page 179

Like "The Girl Who Married the Moon," many myths explain natural events and occurences. Write your own myth. Illustrate your story. Then share it with the class.

◀ The phases of the moon

Grammar and Writing

Modal Verb: *must*

Modal verbs are helping verbs. Writers use them to give special meaning to other verbs. Modal verbs have no tenses, and they do not change according to person. *Must* is a modal verb.

Look at the chart. It shows five different ways in which *must* can be used.

Function	Example
To show **obligation**	It is the work I **must** do.
To show **strong advice**	Then you **must** close your eyes.
To show **certainty** about something	"I **must** try on one of them," she said, "to see how my husband feels when he is carrying them across the sky."
To express **necessity**	I **must** see where we are going.
Must not to express what is **prohibited** or **forbidden**	You **must not** open your eyes.

Practice

Copy the sentences below into your notebook. Rewrite each sentence using *must* or *must not*. Then read your sentences aloud to a partner. Decide which way the modal verb is used.

1. They have to get up early tomorrow.
2. He will hand in his homework today.
3. You are prohibited from using your cell phone in class.
4. You should not go swimming right after lunch.
5. We will go to soccer practice after school.
6. We will get tickets for the concert soon.
7. We cannot park our car here.
8. You have to arrive early to get good seats.

Include Paraphrases and Citations

You have learned how to write an introductory paragraph and how to support a main idea with details. A paraphrase, or a restatement of someone else's idea into your own words, can also be used to support a main idea. You should highlight paraphrased text by providing an "in-text citation," or the source of the information you are using (the author or title of the piece, and the page number, if known, in parentheses). The citation should also be included in an alphabetized "Works Consulted List." (See pages 461–462 for how to cite various sources.)

Paraphrase	Source

In the model below, the writer paraphrased information about a Choctaw myth. She used a source chart to manage her citations.

Madeline Shaw

A Choctaw Myth

To Native Americans, the natural world is very important and must be treated with respect. In the past, Native Americans also believed that most natural occurrences did not have simple explanations. Therefore, they used myths to explain how and why things occurred in nature. One myth, from the Choctaw tribe, tries to explain the reason for solar eclipses, or times when the moon passes between the earth and the sun, briefly blocking the sun's light. According to the myth, when a solar eclipse occurs, it's because a black squirrel is eating the sun. Therefore, whenever the Choctaw saw a black squirrel, they tried to frighten it away, hoping to protect the sun (Choctaw Legends and Stories).

Works Consulted List

"Eclipse of the Sun Blamed on Black Squirrel." Choctaw Legends and Stories. 13 September 2009 <http://www.tc.umn.edu/~mboucher/mikebouchweb/Choctaw/legends2.htm>.

Practice  **Workbook Page 181**

Write a paragraph about another myth. Be sure to paraphrase. List your citations in a graphic organizer. Include both an in-text citation and a Works Consulted List. Use the modal verb *must* correctly.

Writing Checklist

ORGANIZATION:
☑ I used paraphrased information to support the main idea.

CONVENTIONS:
☑ I correctly cited sources.

Prepare to Read

What You Will Learn

Reading

- Vocabulary building: *Context, dictionary skills, word study*

- Reading strategy: *Take notes*

- Text type: *Informational text (science)*

Grammar, Usage, and Mechanics
Cause-and-effect structures

Writing
Include quotations and citations

THE BIG QUESTION

How does the sky influence us? Look at the picture below. Does the thought of traveling to space interest you? If you were given the opportunity to accompany astronauts on a space mission, would you accept? Discuss with a partner.

BUILD BACKGROUND

In this section, you will read two persuasive articles. The first is called **"Return to the Moon."** It presents an argument in favor of American astronauts returning to the moon. The second article, **"No Need to Establish a Moon Base,"** argues against manned space flights and the construction of a permanent moon base. As you read, notice how both authors present clear opinions and support their views with facts.

An astronaut on a space walk near the International Space Station ▶

VOCABULARY

Learn Key Words

Read these sentences. Use the context to figure out the meaning of the **red** words. Use a dictionary to check your answers. Then write each word and its meaning in your notebook.

1. Some people want the United States to build a **base** on the moon. From there, astronauts could travel to Mars.

2. The meteorite left a **crater** on the moon's surface.

3. We used a telescope to see craters on the **lunar** surface.

4. One day, scientists hope to **mine** the moon's surface for water and oxygen.

5. Our moon is one of many in the vast **universe**.

6. The **voyage** resulted in the successful landing of a man on the moon.

Practice  **Workbook Page 182**

Key Words
base
crater
lunar
mine
universe
voyage

Write the sentences in your notebook. Choose a **red** word from the box above to complete each sentence. Then take turns reading the sentences aloud with a partner.

1. The spaceship's _____ from Earth to the moon took three days.

2. The spaceship landed on the _____ surface.

3. While on the moon, the astronauts stayed at the _____, where their food was stored.

4. The astronauts walked near a deep _____ .

5. They plan to _____ the lunar surface for additional materials.

6. Scientists want to know what is necessary to live on the moon. This information could help humans explore the rest of the _____.

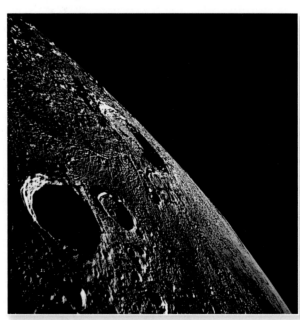

◀ Lunar craters

Learn Academic Words

Study the **red** words and their meanings. You will find these words useful when talking and writing about informational texts. Write each word and its meaning in your notebook. After you read "Return to the Moon" and "No Need to Establish a Moon Base," try to use these words to respond to the texts.

investigate = try to find out the truth about something	➡	Scientists **investigate** the moon and planets to learn more about the universe.
issues = subjects or problems that people discuss	➡	The government considers many **issues** when funding the space program.
promote = help something develop and be successful	➡	After considering the issues, the government decided to **promote** the construction of a permanent moon base.
research = serious study of a subject that is intended to discover new facts about it	➡	Astronauts conduct **research** both on Earth and in space.

Practice  **Workbook Page 183**

Work with a partner to answer these questions. Try to include the **red** word in your answer. Write the sentences in your notebook.

1. What aspects of space travel would you want to **investigate** if given the opportunity?

2. What **issues** would concern you if you were traveling to another planet?

3. What do you feel is the best way to **promote** a return to the moon?

4. What kind of **research** would you want to perform on a space mission?

◀ A NASA scientist analyzing research data at a campsite

Word Study: Acronyms

Acronyms and initials are used frequently in many forms of communication. An acronym is formed by adding the first letters or syllables of several words together. For example, the acronym NASA appears in the article "Return to the Moon." NASA is made from the first letters of the following words: *National Aeronautics and Space Administration*. Read additional examples of acronyms in the chart below.

Acronym	Words that Form Acronym
NATO	**N**orth **A**tlantic **T**reaty **O**rganization
SWAT	**S**pecial **W**eapons **A**nd **T**actics (team)
laser	**l**ight **a**mplification by **st**imulated **e**mission of **r**adiation
asap	**a**s **s**oon **a**s **p**ossible

Practice  Workbook Page 184

Work with a partner. Use a dictionary to find the definition of each acronym in the box below. Write the acronym and the words that form it in your notebook.

CD-ROM	radar	RAM	scuba	UFO	UNICEF

READING STRATEGY | TAKE NOTES

Taking notes keeps you focused on what you're reading. It also helps you understand and remember new information. To take notes, follow these steps:

- Think about your purpose for reading the text.
- Scan the text for the key information you need.
- Look for dates, names, places, and events.
- Write notes about the most important facts you need, not the details.
- Don't write in complete sentences. Use short notes, for example: *landed 6/21/69*

As you read "Return to the Moon" and "No Need to Establish a Moon Base," think about the information you want to remember. Take notes while you read. Review your notes and check that they're correct.

 Workbook Page 185

Set a purpose for reading As you read, think about whether or not we should return to the moon. Is there a need to establish a moon base? Compare the two sides of this issue.

Return to the Moon

Christy Brownlee

On July 21, 1969, millions of television viewers around the world tuned in to the news to watch an amazing event. For the first time ever, people were walking on the moon! The now-famous moon walkers were American astronauts Buzz Aldrin and Neil Armstrong.

Since that first moon walk, 10 more people have set foot on the gray globe's chalky surface. But no one has walked on the moon for more than thirty-four years. Now, the National Aeronautics and Space Administration (NASA) is gearing up to send astronauts back to the moon— eventually, to stay!

Why send astronauts back? Because our nearest neighbor in space is a great place to learn more about Earth and the rest of the universe. It could also serve as a launching pad for destinations farther than people have ever traveled.

Old Pals

Scientists believe that 4 billion years ago, a small planet the size of Mars smashed into Earth. The crash was so powerful that it chipped off a gigantic chunk of our planet and kicked it into space. That chunk is now the moon.

Since the moon is made of ancient Earth, some scientists think that studying it up close will tell us what our home planet was like long ago.

The moon could also give scientists a better look at what the rest of our universe is like. Earth's atmosphere and city lights can alter the images that scientists see in telescopes. By setting up telescopes on the moon's surface, researchers could get a clearer view of space.

---

atmosphere, air
alter, change
telescopes, instruments that allow people to see things that are very far away

▲ Astronaut Buzz Aldrin stands on the moon's surface during the first American lunar landing in 1969.

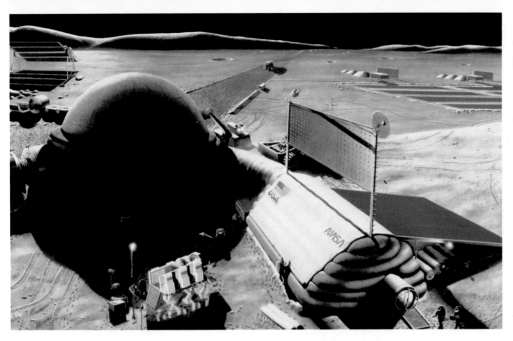

◀ A model lunar base

Home Base

Eventually, the moon could also act as a training camp for trips to planets. A trip to the moon takes a spacecraft only two and a half days. A trek to Mars could take almost nine months. "That lengthy time makes it much more difficult to go back if something goes wrong or there's something that we forgot," explains scientist Chris McKay, who works at NASA's Ames Research Center.

After it sends four astronauts to the moon for a brief period in 2018, NASA will have other astronauts visit it for longer stretches of time. Eventually, colonies of astronauts could live there for six months.

But the moon has no food or oxygen, a gas that humans must breathe to stay alive. So how can astronauts remain there for such long periods? On their first few trips, astronauts will take some supplies, such as oxygen packs and tasty meals, with them in separate cargo vehicles. But eventually, they plan to mine some supplies from the moon's surface itself. Some researchers believe that there's oxygen buried in the moon's dirt and water hidden in its deep craters.

Figuring out how to live on the moon could teach scientists the skills needed to keep exploring the rest of the universe. Says McKay: "A moon base is the first step to an essentially endless voyage into space."

---

trek, long, difficult journey

cargo vehicles, vehicles that are used to carry additional supplies

BEFORE YOU GO ON

1 In what ways do scientists think studying the moon could be beneficial to people on Earth?

2 How many years have passed since American astronauts last walked on the moon?

On Your Own
Do you think astronauts should return to the moon? Why or why not?

▲ An unmanned robot

No Need to Establish a Moon Base

Matt Kachur

When Americans landed on the moon in 1969, it was considered to be an American triumph. Today, there is talk of sending American astronauts back to the moon and constructing a permanent base there. However, both actions are unnecessary, dangerous, and expensive.

In truth, the need for manned space flights has decreased as the use of robots has increased. In fact, today's robots can perform most of the tasks previously assigned to humans and can do so in a more **precise** way. Recent achievements in space—such as discovering more than 100 planets outside our solar system and finding **evidence** of water on Mars—have come from unmanned space telescopes or robots.

Furthermore, unmanned space missions **pose** a smaller threat to human life than manned space missions. We often forget how dangerous manned space flights can be. Since 1967, they have been responsible for the deaths of seventeen people.

precise, exact

evidence, proof
pose, present

In addition to the cost in human life, manned space missions are expensive. One space shuttle launch alone can cost $360 million. Much of that money is used to create systems that keep humans alive in space. This, added to the cost of building a moon base, would require hundreds of billions of dollars. In order to meet this need, the U.S. government would have to cut important social programs or raise taxes.

It is for these reasons that it makes sense to abandon the idea of a return to the moon and the construction of a permanent base. Instead, we should invest our time, money, and energy into additional robotic projects.

---

abandon, leave behind
invest, spend

▲ The Hubble Space Telescope

The launch of the space
shuttle *Discovery* ▶

BEFORE YOU GO ON

1 Why has the need for manned space flights decreased?

2 What have robots achieved in space?

On Your Own
Do you think robots should replace humans in space? Explain.

389

COMPREHENSION

Workbook
Page 186

Right There

1. Who were the first astronauts to walk on the moon?
2. How many people have walked on the moon?

Think and Search

3. Why should NASA build a moon base?
4. Name three reasons why NASA should not build a moon base.

Author and You

5. Although he opposes a moon base, do you think the author of "No Need to Establish a Moon Base" thinks space exploration is important? Explain.
6. How could the moon's location be helpful to astronauts who are going to Mars?

On Your Own

7. Do you think it is important for humans to study space? Explain.
8. What benefits do you think further space exploration could bring?

IN YOUR OWN WORDS

Work with a partner. Copy the T-chart below into your notebook. Write the arguments presented in "Return to the Moon" and "No Need to Establish a Moon Base" beneath the corresponding heads. Then summarize one of the articles for your partner.

"Return to the Moon"	"No Need to Establish a Moon Base"

DISCUSSION

Discuss in pairs or small groups.

1. What do you think would happen if astronauts were able to find the supplies they needed to live on the moon?

2. Do you think there could be other forms of life in outer space? Why or why not?

Q How does the sky influence us? How much of a priority do you think space travel should be in the United States? Why?

Listening TIP

As you listen, evaluate the speaker's facts.

READ FOR FLUENCY

When we read aloud to communicate meaning, we group words into phrases, pause or slow down to make important points, and emphasize important words. Pause for a short time when you reach a comma and for a longer time when you reach a period. Pay attention to rising and falling intonation at the end of sentences.

Work with a partner. Choose a paragraph from the reading. Discuss which words seem important for communicating meaning. Practice pronouncing difficult words. Take turns reading the paragraph aloud and give each other feedback.

EXTENSION

Workbook Page 186

You read about robots in space. Work with a partner. Use the Internet or go to the library to research one particular space robot. Try to find the following information: the name of the robot, a picture of the robot, and a description of the robot's job(s) in space. Then present this information to your class.

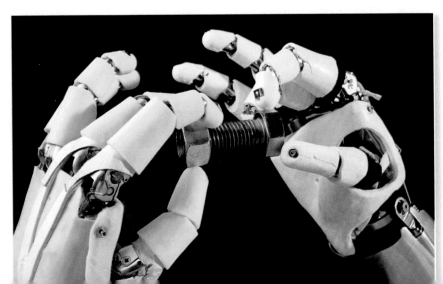

◀ Robotic hands completing a task at the Johnson Space Center in Houston, Texas

Grammar and Writing

Cause-and-Effect Structures

Cause-and-effect structures can help organize your writing. *Cause* explains why things happen. *Effect* explains what results from the cause. Words such as *because, so,* and *since* often signal causes and effects. Remember, an effect can sometimes come before a cause.

cause	effect

Space is a great place to learn, **so** we should send astronauts back into space.

cause	effect

Since the moon is made of ancient Earth, some scientists think that studying it up close will tell us what our home planet was like long ago.

effect	cause

We send astronauts to space **because** our nearest neighbor in space is a great place to learn more about Earth and the rest of the universe.

Practice
Workbook Page 187

Copy the following sentences into your notebook. Identify the cause and effect in each sentence. Then circle the word that signals the cause or effect.

1. We couldn't see the stars because the fog was very thick.
2. He is opposed to space travel because it costs a lot of money.
3. I will study astronomy since I am very good at math and science.
4. We didn't have time to go back to the planetarium because we had to study.
5. She needed to find more information about space travel, so she went to the library.
6. Because astronauts have gone to space, we know more about the solar system.
7. We need to learn more about Earth, so we should support space travel.
8. Since space travel is important, we should spend more money on it.

WRITING A RESEARCH REPORT

Include Quotations and Citations

You learned that a research report contains paragraphs with main ideas supported by facts, details, and paraphrases.

Quotation	Source

An effective research report will also include quotations from people who are experienced and knowledgeable about the research topic. Whenever you copy another person's writing or speech word for word, you must put the text in quotation marks. After the quotation, you must provide an in-text citation. (See pages 461–462 for how to cite various sources.)

Here is a sample paragraph. The writer used a source chart to organize his quotes and sources. Notice that he includes an in-text citation and a Works Consulted List.

> *Andrew Denkus*
>
> ### Space Tourism
>
> In 2001, the first space tourist, Dennis Tito, flew into space aboard a Russian spacecraft. Since that successful experience, several others have also paid enormous amounts of money, more than $20 million per trip, for the chance to spend time on the International Space Station. Experts predict that this new industry, space tourism, is sure to grow in the future. In fact, "private companies in Russia, Europe, and the United States are competing to become future leaders of space tourism" ("All about Space Tourism"). Company leaders believe that as space tourism becomes more affordable, it will also become more common. They envision the creation of new vehicles, similar to airplanes, that would be used to transport people into space. They even foresee luxury hotels orbiting Earth!
>
> #### Works Consulted List
>
> "All about Space Tourism." 2007. Space.com 25 October 2009 <http://www.space.com-space/tourism/>.

Practice

Write a paragraph that includes quotations and citations. Use a graphic organizer to list your quotations and citations. Be sure to use cause-and-effect structures correctly.

Writing Checklist

SENTENCE FLUENCY:
- ☑ I made sure quotations flowed smoothly within the paragraph.

CONVENTIONS:
- ☑ I correctly punctuated my quotations.

Link the Readings

Critical Thinking

Look back at the readings in this unit. Think about what they have in common. They all tell about the sky. Yet they do not all have the same purpose. The purpose of one reading might be to inform, while the purpose of another might be to entertain or persuade. In addition, the content of each reading relates to the sky differently. Now copy the chart below into your notebook and complete it.

Title of Reading	Purpose	Big Question Link
"Starry Nights" "Stars" "Escape at Bedtime"		
"Earth and the Milky Way"	*to inform*	
"The Girl Who Married the Moon"		*tells about the moon's phases*
"Return to the Moon" "No Need to Establish a Moon Base"		

Discussion

Discuss in pairs or small groups.

- Whose opinion would Sara Teasdale and Robert Lewis Stevenson agree with: the author's for "Return to the Moon" or the author's for "No Need to Establish a Moon Base"? Why?

- **How does the sky influence us?** What object in the sky do you think influences us the most? Why?

Fluency Check

Work with a partner. Choose a paragraph from one of the readings. Take turns reading it for one minute. Count the total number of words you read. Practice saying the words you had trouble reading. Take turns reading the paragraph three more times. Did you read more words each time? Copy the chart below into your notebook and record your speeds.

	1st Speed	2nd Speed	3rd Speed	4th Speed
Words Per Minute				

Projects

Work in pairs or small groups. Choose one of these projects.

1 Research plans for future space travel. Use the Internet, newspapers, and newsmagazines to learn about upcoming missions. Then write a newspaper article that reports your findings. Share the article with your classmates.

2 Use the Internet to create a profile of an astronaut or astronomer. Download or copy a picture of the person, or draw one. Display your picture and profile on a class bulletin board.

3 Create a star guide. Use the Internet and reference books to find out which constellations are visible from your town. On a clear night, go outside and see which constellations you can find. Then draw a map that shows where they are located in the night sky. Hang the map for your classmates to see.

4 Visit a planetarium. Report your experience to the class.

Further Reading

To find out more about the theme of this unit, choose from these reading suggestions.

The War of the Worlds, H. G. Wells
In this Penguin Reader® adaptation, a metal object falls from the sky over the south of England, and strange creatures come out of it. But they are not human—they are fighting machines from Mars. People start to wonder if Martians are trying to take over Earth.

Stars, Seymour Simon
In photo-essay format, *Stars* takes us on a tour of the galaxies. The book describes ordinary stars such as our sun, as well as stars called red giants and white dwarfs. It also explains how stars form, go through various stages of growth, and die.

They Dance in the Sky: Native American Star Myths, Ray A. Williamson and Jean Guard Monroe
This collection of stories includes star myths from Native American tribes. Wolves, bears, eagles, and other animals inhabit the stories and the night sky. The stars themselves tell tales of children who have danced away from home and of the great wounded sky bear, whose blood turns the autumn leaves red.

Put It All Together

LISTENING & SPEAKING WORKSHOP

Oral Report

You will give an oral report on a topic related to the sky.

1 **THINK ABOUT IT** Think about the poems, informational texts, and the myth you read about in this unit. The authors of these texts looked at the sky from many different perspectives. Which readings did you find most interesting? Why? Discuss your thoughts in small groups.

With your group, develop a list of topics related to the sky. For example:
- Space travel
- Constellations
- Weather
- The moon
- Clouds

2 **GATHER AND ORGANIZE INFORMATION** Choose a topic from your group's list. Decide how you want to approach your topic: for example, from a scientific, literary, artistic, or mythological perspective. Fill in the first two columns of a K-W-L chart as you brainstorm ideas for an oral report on this topic.

Research Go to the library or search the Internet to find information about your topic. Record what you find in the third column of your K-W-L chart. Choose the main points you want to include in your oral report, and make sure you have facts, details, and examples to support them.

Order Your Notes Copy your main points and supporting information onto note cards. Then arrange your cards in a logical order. Be prepared to share your sources with the audience.

Use Visuals Make or find photos, drawings, and/or other visuals that will help the audience understand your main points.

3 **PRACTICE AND PRESENT** Practice giving your oral report to friends or family members. Make sure your listeners can hear and understand you. Ask if your ideas are clear and easy to follow. Revise or rearrange your note cards if necessary. Keep practicing until you can speak confidently, looking at your audience and glancing occasionally at your note cards. Remember to show your visuals at the appropriate times.

Deliver Your Oral Report Before you begin, make sure your note cards and visuals are in order. Relax and focus on the ideas in your report, explaining them as if you were talking to a friend. Speak at a good pace, not too quickly or too slowly, and pronounce each word carefully. At the end of your report, ask your listeners if they have any questions.

4 **EVALUATE THE PRESENTATION**

You will improve your skills as a speaker and a listener by evaluating each presentation you give and hear. Use this checklist to help you judge your oral report and the reports of your classmates.

- ☑ Was the topic of the oral report clear?
- ☑ Did the speaker present the main points in a logical order?
- ☑ Were the main points supported by facts, examples, and details?
- ☑ Could you hear and understand the speaker easily?
- ☑ What suggestions do you have for improving the oral report?

 Speaking TIPS

Think of a way to grab the audience's attention and introduce your topic. You might use a quote, make a startling statement, or ask a question.

Connect with your audience by making eye contact with as many people as possible.

 Listening TIPS

Take notes on the most important points. If you have questions, write them down so you can ask them later.

Listen for the speaker's sources. Do you think his or her information is reliable?

WRITING WORKSHOP

Research Report

In this workshop, you will write a research report. In a research report, you present information about a topic you have studied in depth. Your purpose is to give readers a thorough understanding of the topic. You include research gathered from a variety of different sources and list all your sources at the end of the report. A good research report begins with a paragraph that introduces the writer's topic and states a controlling idea or focus. Each body paragraph presents a main idea supported by facts, details, and examples. A concluding paragraph sums up in a memorable way the information that the writer has explained.

Your assignment for this workshop is to write a five-paragraph research report about a topic related to the sky.

1 **PREWRITE** Select a topic that interests you. You might write about clouds and weather, stars and planets, astronauts and space travel, images of the sky in painting and poetry, or beliefs about the sky held by people in the past. After choosing a topic, ask yourself: "What do I want to know about my topic?" Use this question to narrow your focus and to guide your research.

Consult sources such as books, magazines, encyclopedias, and websites. Take notes on note cards.

List and Organize Ideas and Details
Create an outline to organize your ideas. A student named Haley decided to write about the history of the United States space program. Here is the outline she prepared.

I. Introduce the United States Space Program
    A. Headed by NASA
    B. Understanding of space shaped by endeavors
II. Projects Mercury and Gemini
    A. To see if humans could live in space
    B. To make longer distance space travel possible
III. Project Apollo
    A. To land humans on moon
    B. Alan Shepard first person to walk on moon
IV. Space Shuttles
    A. Useful in launch of Hubble Telescope
    B. Also put satellites in space for cell phones and TV
V. Conclude with U.S. Space Exploration
    A. Understanding of space has been expanded
    B. New information gained as technology advances

2 **DRAFT** Use the model on pages 402–403 and your outline to help you write a first draft. Be sure to use your own words when you write your report. If you use exact words from a source, punctuate the quotation(s) correctly. List all your sources accurately at the end of your report.

Citing Sources Look at the style, punctuation, and order of information in the following sources. Use these examples as models.

Book
Stanchak, John. <u>Civil War</u>. New York: Dorling Kindersley, 2000.

Magazine article
Kirn, Walter. "Lewis and Clark: The Journey That Changed America Forever." <u>Time</u> 8 July 2002: 36–41.

Internet website
Smith, Gene. "The Structure of the Milky Way." <u>Gene Smith's Astronomy Tutorial</u>. 28 April 1999. Center for Astrophysics & Space Sciences, University of California, San Diego. 20 July 2009 <http://casswww.ucsd.edu/public/tutorial/MW.html>.

Encyclopedia article
Siple, Paul A. "Antarctica." <u>World Book Encyclopedia</u>. 1991 ed.

---

3 **REVISE** Read over your draft. As you do so, ask yourself the questions in the writing checklist. Use the questions to help you revise your report.

SIX TRAITS OF WRITING CHECKLIST

☑ **IDEAS:** Does my first paragraph introduce my topic and focus?

☑ **ORGANIZATION:** Do I support main ideas with facts, details, and examples?

☑ **VOICE:** Is my tone serious and suited to the topic?

☑ **WORD CHOICE:** Do I use specific words that make the information clear?

☑ **SENTENCE FLUENCY:** Do my sentences vary in length and type?

☑ **CONVENTIONS:** Does my writing follow the rules of grammar, usage, and mechanics?

Here are the changes Haley plans to make when she revises her first draft:

The Space Program of the United States

The National Aeronautics and space Administration (NASA) is the

U.S. govermental branch responsible for space exploration. There have

been many important endeavors that have helped shape the U.S. space

program Knowledge about the moon, planets, and the rest of our

galaxy continues to add to our research about living in space.

Project Mercury was the first space program in the United States.

The goal of Project Mercury was to learn whether or not humans

could endure space flight. In May 1961, Alan Shepard became the

first American astronaut to travel into space. In February 1962,

John Glenn became the first American astronaut to orbit planet Earth.

The Gemini Project, which followed Project Mercury, was implemented

to discover ways of enabling longer distance space travel.

In 1961, President John F. Kennedy announced the goal of "landing

a man on the moon and returning him safely to the Earth" ("Man on

the Moon"). This was the aim of NASA's next mission, Project Apollo.

On June 20, 1969 Apollo 11 succeeded in its mission. Neil Armstrong,

the commander of the three-man crew, was the first person to walk

on the moon. As he stepped onto the moon, Armstrong famously said,

That's one small step for man, one giant leap for mankind ("The Apollo

11 Mission").

Reusable launch ships, also known as space shuttles, are now used for space exploration. Space shuttle missions have been very helpful in the launch and maintenance of the Hubble Telescope. it takes pictures that reach far out into space to increase our understanding about living in space. Space shuttles *are also important because they* put satellites in place that are used for cell phones and television. In addition, *since* space shuttles are able to orbit close to Earth. They have been able to aid in the repairing and replenishment of the International Space Station.

In all of these missions, communication has been strengthened, and our understanding of space has been expanded. great strides in exploring space have been made through the space program of the United States. Throughout the twenty first century, the United States will strive to learn more about space as technology advances.

Works Consulted List

Kerrod, Robin, and Giles Sparrow. The Way the Universe Works. New York: Dorling Kindersley, 2002.

"Man on the Moon: Kennedy Speech Ignited the Dream." CNN.com/space. 25 May 2001. Cable News Network. 08 October 2009 <http://archives.cnn.com./2001/TECH/space/Kennedy.moon>.

"The Apollo 11 Mission." Human Space Flight. 17 November 2005. National Aeronautics and Space Administration. 6 October 2009 <http://spaceflight1.nasa.gov/history/apollo/apollo11/>.

4 EDIT AND PROOFREAD

Workbook Page 189

Copy your revised draft onto a clean sheet of paper. Read it again. Correct any errors in grammar, word usage, mechanics, and spelling. Here are the additional changes Haley plans to make when she prepares her final draft.

Haley Coy

The Space Program of the United States

The National Aeronautics and space Administration (NASA) is the U.S. governmental branch responsible for space exploration. There have been many important endeavors that have helped shape the U.S. space program. Knowledge about the moon, planets such as Mars, and the rest of our galaxy continues to add to our research about living in space.

Project Mercury was the first space program in the United States. The goal of Project Mercury was to learn whether or not humans could endure space flight. In May 1961, Alan Shepard became the first American astronaut to travel into space. In February 1962, John Glenn became the first American astronaut to orbit planet Earth.

The Gemini Project, which followed Project Mercury, was implemented to discover ways of enabling longer distance space travel. Then, in 1961, President John F. Kennedy announced the goal of "landing a man on the moon and returning him safely to the Earth" ("Man on the Moon"). This became the aim of NASA's next mission, Project Apollo. On June 20, 1969, Apollo 11 succeeded in its mission. Neil Armstrong, the commander of the three-man crew, was the first person to walk on the moon. As he stepped onto the moon, Armstrong famously said, "That's one small step for man, one giant leap for mankind" ("The Apollo 11 Mission").

Reusable launch ships, also known as space shuttles, are now used for space exploration. Space shuttle missions have been very helpful in the launch and maintenance of the Hubble Telescope. it takes pictures that reach far out into space to increase our understanding about living

---

in space. Space shuttles are also important because they put satellites in place that are used for cell phones and television. In addition, since space shuttles are able to orbit close to Earth, they have been able to aid in the repairing and replenishment of the International Space Station.

   In all of these missions, communication has been strengthened, and our understanding of space has been expanded. Great strides in exploring space have been made through the space program of the United States. Throughout the twenty-first century, the United States will strive to learn more about space as technology advances.

Works Consulted List

Kerrod, Robin, and Giles Sparrow. The Way the Universe Works. New York:

   Dorling Kindersley, 2002.

"Man on the Moon: Kennedy Speech Ignited the Dream." CNN.com/space.

   25 May 2001. Cable News Network. 08 October 2009

   <http://archives.cnn.com./2001/TECH/space/Kennedy.moon>.

"The Apollo 11 Mission." Human Space Flight. 17 November 2005.

   National Aeronautics and Space Administration. 6 October 2009

   <http://spaceflight1.nasa.gov/history/apollo/apollo11/>.

5 **PUBLISH** Prepare your final draft. Share your research report with your teacher and classmates.

Workbook
Page 190

Capturing Cosmic Beauty

*M*any of us live in urban areas where there are a lot of lights on at night, so we do not get a good look at the stars. But if you sit in a dark field where there are no city lights, you can see the sky the way our ancestors saw it: a great area filled with countless stars. Artists often try to capture the beauty and mystery of the sky in their artwork.

Alma Thomas, *The Eclipse* (1970)

The moon moved in front of the sun during an eclipse that Alma Thomas once saw. She captures this eclipse with a dark, solid blue circle that sits off-center in her painting. Small painted blocks of cooler colors, such as green and light blue, spread out from the center. By the time she got to the edge of the canvas, Thomas was working in warmer oranges and yellows, which run right off the borders. Despite its cool center, the entire painting gives off a joyful celebration of color and light.

"A world without color would seem dead," Thomas once said. "Color is life. Light is the mother of color. Light reveals to us the spirit and living soul of the world."

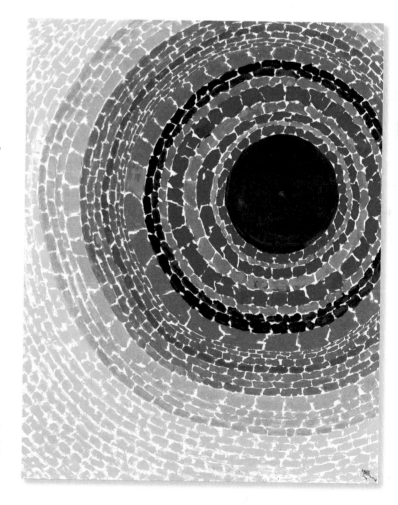

Alma Thomas, *The Eclipse*,
1970, acrylic, 62 × 49¾ in.,
Smithsonian American Art Museum ▶

◀ Charles Burchfield,
Orion in December, 1959,
watercolor and pencil, 39⅞ × 32⅞ in.,
Smithsonian American Art Museum

Charles Burchfield, *Orion in December* (1959)

One December night, artist Charles Burchfield could not sleep. He looked out of his bedroom window and watched the clouds sweep across the sky. Then suddenly he saw three stars in a row. He knew at once that it was Orion, a famous constellation. Orion was named after a Greek mythical figure who was a hunter. The three brightest stars represent his belt, and the three smaller stars that drop down from the belt represent his sword.

In *Orion in December*, Burchfield uses few colors to capture not only the coldness of that evening but also the beauty and sense of calm he felt. The stars in Orion rest in the center of the painting and form an upside-down V of dots above the point of a treetop. Burchfield outlined the trees with strong black lines, which gives them a ghostly appearance. He also outlined each star with a strong black circle, but added a white glow around those circles to give them a soft light.

Artists usually appreciate light and shadow that we never really notice. They are drawn to the dramatic play of light in the sky as the sun and moon rise and set each day.

Apply What You Learned

1 Both artists capture light in different ways. What is similar about the two paintings, and what is different?

2 Do you agree with Alma Thomas that "color is life [and] light is the mother of color"? Explain your answer.

 Big Question
Why do you think the sky is such a popular topic for so many artists?

Workbook
Pages 191–192

405

Contents
Handbooks and Resources

Study Skills and Language Learning

HOW TO LEARN LANGUAGE

Learning a language takes time, but, just like learning to swim, it can be fun. Whether you're learning English for the first time or adding to your knowledge of English by learning academic or content-area words, you're giving yourself a better chance of success in your studies and in your everyday life.

Learning any language is a skill that requires you to be active. You listen, speak, read, and write when you learn a language. Here are some tips that will help you learn English more actively and efficiently.

Listening

1. Set a purpose for listening. Think about what you hope to learn from today's class. Listen for these things as your teacher and classmates speak.

2. Listen actively. You can think faster than others can speak. This is useful because it allows you to anticipate what will be said next. Take notes as you listen. Write down only what is most important, and keep your notes short.

3. If you find something difficult to understand, listen more carefully. Do not give up and stop listening. Write down questions to ask afterward.

4. The more you listen, the faster you will learn. Use the radio, television, and Internet to practice your listening skills.

Speaking

1. Pay attention to sentence structure as you speak. Are you saying the words in the correct order?

2. Think about what you are saying. Don't worry about speaking fast. It's more important to communicate what you mean.

3. Practice speaking as much as you can, both in class and in your free time. Consider reading aloud to improve your pronunciation. If possible, record yourself speaking.

4. Do not be afraid of making mistakes. Everyone makes mistakes!

Reading

1. Read every day. Read as many different things as possible: Books, magazines, newspapers, and websites will all help you improve your comprehension and increase your vocabulary.

2. Try to understand what you are reading as a whole, rather than focusing on individual words. If you find a word you do not know, see if you can figure out its meaning from the context of the sentence before you look it up in a dictionary. Make a list of new vocabulary words and review it regularly.

3. Read texts more than once. Often your comprehension of a passage will improve if you read it twice or three times.

4. Try reading literature, poems, and plays aloud. This will help you understand them. It will also give you practice pronouncing new words.

Writing

1. Write something every day to improve your writing fluency. You can write about anything that interests you. Consider keeping a diary or a journal so that you can monitor your progress as time passes.

2. Plan your writing before you begin. Use graphic organizers to help you organize your ideas.

3. Be aware of sentence structure and grammar. Always write a first draft. Then go back and check for errors before you write your final version.

HOW TO BUILD VOCABULARY

1. Improving Your Vocabulary
Listening and Speaking
The most common ways to increase your vocabulary are listening, reading, and taking part in conversations. One of the most important skills in language learning is listening. Listen for new words when talking with others, joining in discussions, listening to the radio or audio books, or watching television.

You can find out the meanings of the words by asking, listening for clues, and looking up the words in a dictionary. Don't be embarrassed about asking what a word means. It shows that you are listening and that you want to learn. Whenever you can, use the new words you learn in conversation.

Reading Aloud
Listening to texts read aloud is another good way to build your vocabulary. There are many audio books available, and most libraries have a collection of them. When you listen to an audio book, you hear how new words are pronounced and how they are used. If you have a printed copy of the book, read along as you listen so that you can both see and hear new words.

Reading Often
Usually, people use a larger variety of words when they write than when they speak. The more you read, the more new words you'll find. When you see new words over and over again, they will become familiar to you and you'll begin to use them. Read from different sources—books, newspapers, magazines, Internet websites—in order to find a wide variety of words.

2. Figuring Out What a Word Means
Using Context Clues
When you come across a new word, you may not always need to use a dictionary. You might be able to figure out its meaning using the context, or the words in the sentence or paragraph in which you found it. Sometimes the surrounding words contain clues to tell you what the new word means.

Here are some tips for using context clues:
- Read the sentence, leaving out the word you don't know.
- Find clues in the sentence to figure out the new word's meaning.
- Read the sentence again, but replace the word you don't know with another possible meaning.
- Check your possible meaning by looking up the word in the dictionary. Write the word and its definition in your vocabulary notebook.

3. Practicing Your New Words

To make a word part of your vocabulary, study its definition, use it in your writing and speaking, and review it to make sure that you really understand its meaning.

Use one or more of these ways to remember the meanings of new words.

Keep a Vocabulary Notebook

Keep a notebook for vocabulary words. Divide your pages into three columns: the new words; hint words that help you remember their meanings; and their definitions. Test yourself by covering either the second or third column.

Word	Hint	Definition
zoology	zoo	study of animals
fortunate	fortune	lucky
quizzical	quiz	questioning

Make Flashcards

On the front of an index card, write a word you want to remember. On the back, write the meaning. You can also write a sentence that uses the word in context. Test yourself by flipping through the cards. Enter any hard words in your vocabulary notebook. As you learn the meanings, remove these cards and add new ones.

Say the Word Aloud

A useful strategy for building vocabulary is to say the new word aloud. Do not worry that there is no one to say the word to. Just say the word loud and clear several times. This will make you feel more confident and help you to use the word in conversation.

Record Yourself

Record your vocabulary words. Leave a ten-second space after each word, and then say the meaning and a sentence using the word. Play the recording. Fill in the blank space with the meaning and a sentence. Replay the recording until you memorize the word.

The Dictionary

When you look up a word in the dictionary, you find the word and information about it. The word and the information about it are called a dictionary entry. Each entry tells you the word's spelling, pronunciation, part of speech, and meaning. Many English words have more than one meaning. Some words, such as *handle*, can be both a noun and a verb. For such words, the meanings, or definitions, are numbered. Sometimes example sentences are given in italics to help you understand how the word is used.

Here is part of a dictionary page with its important features labeled.

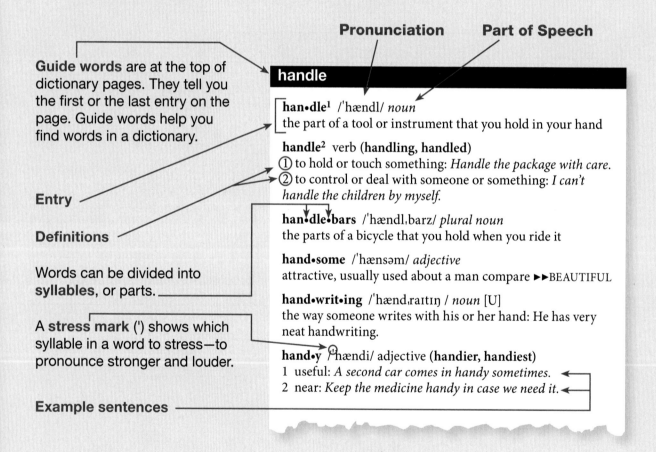

Pronunciation **Part of Speech**

Guide words are at the top of dictionary pages. They tell you the first or the last entry on the page. Guide words help you find words in a dictionary.

Entry

Definitions

Words can be divided into **syllables**, or parts.

A **stress mark** (') shows which syllable in a word to stress—to pronounce stronger and louder.

Example sentences

handle

han•dle[1] /ˈhændl/ *noun*
the part of a tool or instrument that you hold in your hand

handle[2] *verb* (**handling, handled**)
① to hold or touch something: *Handle the package with care.*
② to control or deal with someone or something: *I can't handle the children by myself.*

han•dle•bars /ˈhændlˌbarz/ *plural noun*
the parts of a bicycle that you hold when you ride it

hand•some /ˈhænsəm/ *adjective*
attractive, usually used about a man compare ▶▶BEAUTIFUL

hand•writ•ing /ˈhændˌraɪtɪŋ / *noun* [U]
the way someone writes with his or her hand: He has very neat handwriting.

hand•y /ˈhændi/ *adjective* (**handier, handiest**)
1 useful: *A second car comes in handy sometimes.*
2 near: *Keep the medicine handy in case we need it.*

The Thesaurus

A thesaurus is a kind of dictionary. It is a specialized dictionary that lists synonyms, or words with similar meanings, for words. You can use a print thesaurus (a book) or an online thesaurus on the Internet.

A thesaurus is a useful writing tool because it can help you avoid repeating the same word. It can also help you choose more precise words. Using a thesaurus regularly can help build your vocabulary by increasing the number of words you know that are related by an idea or concept.

In a thesaurus, words may either be arranged alphabetically or be grouped by theme. When the arrangement is by theme, you first have to look up the word in the index to find out in which grouping its synonyms will appear. When the thesaurus is arranged alphabetically, you simply look up the word as you would in a dictionary.

The entry below is from a thesaurus that is arranged alphabetically.

sad *adjective* Tending to cause sadness or low spirits : blue, cheerless, depressed, depressing, dismal, dispiriting, downcast, gloomy, heartbreaking, joyless, melancholy, miserable, poignant, sorrowful, unhappy. See **happy** (antonym) in index.
—See also **depressed, sorrowful**.

Choose synonyms carefully. You can see from the thesaurus entry above that there are many synonyms for the word *sad*. However, not all of these words may be the ones you want to use. For example, *depressed* can mean that you have an illness called depression, but it can also mean that you feel sad. If you are not sure what a word means, look it up in a dictionary to check that it is, in fact, the word you want to use.

HOW TO TAKE TESTS

In this section, you will learn some ways to improve your test-taking skills.

1. Taking Tests

Objective tests are tests in which each question has only one correct answer. To prepare for these tests, you should study the material that the test covers.

Preview the Test

1. Write your name on each sheet of paper you will hand in.
2. Look over the test to get an idea of the kinds of questions being asked.
3. Find out whether you lose points for incorrect answers. If you do, do not guess at answers.
4. Decide how much time you need to spend on each section of the test.
5. Use the time well. Give the most time to questions that are hardest or worth the most points.

Answer the Questions

1. Answer the easy questions first. Put a check next to harder questions and come back to them later.
2. If permitted, use scratch paper to write down your ideas.
3. Read each question at least twice before answering.
4. Answer all questions on the test (unless guessing can cost you points).
5. Do not change your first answer without a good reason.

Proofread Your Answers

1. Check that you followed the directions completely.
2. Reread questions and answers. Make sure you answered all the questions.

2. Answering Different Kinds of Questions

This section tells you about different kinds of test questions and gives you specific strategies for answering them.

True-or-False Questions

True-or-false questions ask you to decide whether or not a statement is true.

1. If a statement seems true, make sure that it is *all* true.
2. Pay special attention to the word *not*. It often changes the meaning of a statement entirely.
3. Pay attention to words that have a general meaning, such as *all*, *always*, *never*, *no*, *none*, and *only*. They often make a statement false.
4. Pay attention to words that qualify, such as *generally*, *much*, *many*, *most*, *often*, *sometimes*, and *usually*. They often make a statement true.

414

Multiple-Choice Questions

This kind of question asks you to choose from four or five possible answers.

1. Try to answer the question before reading the choices. If your answer is one of the choices, choose that answer.
2. Eliminate answers you know are wrong. Cross them out if you are allowed to write on the test paper.

Matching Questions

Matching questions ask you to match items in one group with items in another group.

1. Count each group to see whether any items will be left over.
2. Read all the items before you start matching.
3. Match the items you know first, and then match the others. If you can write on the paper, cross out items as you use them.

Fill-In Questions

A fill-in question asks you to give an answer in your own words.

1. Read the question or exercise carefully.
2. If you are completing a sentence, look for clues in the sentence that might help you figure out the answer. If the word *an* is right before the missing word, this means that the missing word begins with a vowel sound.

Short-Answer Questions

Short-answer questions ask you to write one or more sentences in which you give certain information.

1. Scan the question for key words, such as *explain*, *compare*, and *identify*.
2. When you answer the question, give only the information asked for.
3. Answer the question as clearly as possible.

Essay Questions

On many tests, you will have to write one or more essays. Sometimes you are given a choice of questions that you can answer.

1. Look for key words in the question or questions to find out exactly what information you should give.
2. Take a few minutes to think about facts, examples, and other types of information you can put in your essay.
3. Spend most of your time writing your essay so that it is well planned.
4. Leave time at the end of the test to proofread and correct your work.

STUDY SKILLS AND LEARNING STRATEGIES

1. Understanding the Parts of a Book
The Title Page
Every book has a **title page** that states the title, author, and publisher.

The Table of Contents and Headings
Many books have a **table of contents**. The table of contents can be found in the front of the book. It lists the chapters or units in the book. Beside each chapter or unit is the number of the page on which it begins. A **heading** at the top of the first page of each section tells you what that section is about.

The Glossary
While you read, you can look up unfamiliar words in the **glossary** at the back of the book. It lists words alphabetically and gives definitions.

The Index
To find out whether a book includes particular information, use the **index** at the back of the book. It is an alphabetical listing of names, places, and subjects in the book. Page numbers are listed beside each item.

The Bibliography
The **bibliography** is at the end of a nonfiction book or article. It tells you the other books or sources where an author got information to write the book. The sources are listed alphabetically by author. The bibliography is also a good way to find more articles or information about the same subject.

2. Using the Library
The Card Catalog
To find a book in a library, use the **card catalog**—an alphabetical list of authors, subjects, and titles. Each book has a **call number**, which tells you where to find a book on the shelf. Author cards, title cards, and subject cards all give information about a book. Use the **author card** when you want to find a book by an author but do not know the title. The **title card** is useful if you know the title of a book but not the author. When you want to find a book about a particular subject, use the **subject card**.

The Online Library Catalog
The **online library catalog** is a fast way to find a book using a computer. Books can be looked up by author, subject, or title. The online catalog will give you information on the book, as well as its call number.

416

3. Learning Strategies

Strategy	Description and Examples
Organizational Planning	Setting a learning goal; planning how to carry out a project, write a story, or solve a problem
Predicting	Using parts of a text (such as illustrations or titles) or a real-life situation and your own knowledge to anticipate what will occur next
Self-Management	Seeking or arranging the conditions that help you learn
Using Your Knowledge and Experience	Using knowledge and experience to learn something new, brainstorm, make associations, or write or tell what you know
Monitoring Comprehension	Being aware of how well a task is going, how well you understand what you are hearing or reading, or how well you are conveying ideas
Using/Making Rules	Applying a rule (phonics, decoding, grammar, linguistic, mathematical, scientific, and so on) to understand a text or complete a task; figuring out rules or patterns from examples
Taking Notes	Writing down key information in verbal, graphic, or numerical form, often as concept maps, word webs, timelines, or other graphic organizers
Visualizing	Creating mental pictures and using them to understand and appreciate descriptive writing
Cooperation	Working with classmates to complete a task or project, demonstrate a process or product, share knowledge, solve problems, give and receive feedback, and develop social skills
Making Inferences	Using the context of a text and your own knowledge to guess meanings of unfamiliar words or ideas
Substitution	Using a synonym or paraphrasing when you want to express an idea and do not know the word(s)
Using Resources	Using reference materials (books, dictionaries, encyclopedias, videos, computer programs, the Internet) to find information or complete a task
Classification	Grouping words, ideas, objects, or numbers according to their attributes; constructing graphic organizers to show classifications
Asking Questions	Negotiating meaning by asking for clarification, confirmation, rephrasing, or examples
Summarizing	Making a summary of something you listened to or read; retelling a text in your own words
Self-evaluation	After completing a task, judging how well you did, whether you reached your goal, and how effective your problem-solving procedures were

Grammar Handbook

In English there are eight **parts of speech**: nouns, pronouns, adjectives, verbs, adverbs, prepositions, conjunctions, and interjections.

Nouns

Nouns name people, places, or things. There are two kinds of nouns: **common nouns** and **proper nouns**.

A **common noun** is a general person, place, or thing.

person	thing	place
The **student** brings a **notebook** to **class**.		

A **proper noun** is a specific person, place, or thing. Proper nouns start with a capital letter.

person	place	thing
Joseph went to **Paris** and saw the **Eiffel Tower**.		

A noun that is made up of two words is called a **compound noun**. A compound noun can be one word or two words. Some compound nouns have hyphens.

One word: **newspaper, bathroom**
Two words: **vice president, pet shop**
Hyphens: **sister-in-law, grown-up**

Articles identify nouns. *A, an,* and *the* are articles.

A and *an* are called **indefinite articles**. Use the article *a* or *an* to talk about one general person, place, or thing.

Use *an* before a word that begins with a vowel sound.

I have **an** idea.

Use *a* before a word that begins with a consonant sound.

> May I borrow **a** pen?

The is called a **definite article**. Use *the* to talk about one or more specific people, places, or things.

> Please bring me **the** box from your room.
> **The** books are in my backpack.

Pronouns

Pronouns are words that take the place of nouns or proper nouns. In this example, the pronoun *she* replaces, or refers to, the proper noun *Angela*.

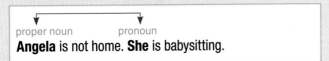

Pronouns can be subjects or objects. They can be singular or plural.

	Subject Pronouns	Object Pronouns
Singular	I, you, he, she, it	me, you, him, her, it
Plural	we, you, they	us, you, them

A **subject pronoun** replaces a noun or proper noun that is the subject of a sentence. A **subject** is who or what a sentence is about. In these sentences, *He* replaces *Daniel*.

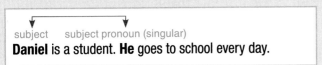

In these sentences, *We* replaces *Heather* and *I*.

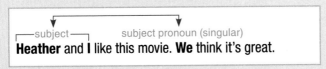

An **object pronoun** replaces a noun or proper noun that is the object of a verb. A verb tells the action in a sentence. An **object** receives the action of a verb.

In these sentences the verb is *gave*. *Him* replaces *Ed*, which is the object of the verb.

An object pronoun can also replace a noun or proper noun that is the **object of a preposition**. Prepositions are words like *for*, *to*, or *with*. In these sentences, the preposition is *with*. *Them* replaces *José* and *Yolanda*, which is the object of the preposition.

Pronouns can also be possessive. A **possessive pronoun** replaces a noun or proper noun. It shows who owns something.

	Possessive Pronouns
Singular	mine, yours, hers, his
Plural	ours, yours, theirs

In these sentences, *hers* replaces the words *Kyoko's coat*. It shows that Kyoko owns the coat.

Adjectives

Adjectives describe nouns. An adjective usually comes before the noun it describes.

tall grass	**big** truck	**two** kittens

An adjective can also come *after* the noun it describes.

The bag is **heavy**. The books are **new**.

Do not add *-s* to adjectives that describe plural nouns.

the **red** houses	the **funny** jokes	the **smart** teachers

Verbs

Verbs express an action or a state of being.

subject   verb   subject   verb
Jackie **walks** to school. The school **is** near her house.

An **action verb** tells what someone or something does or did. You cannot always see the action of an action verb.

Verbs That Tell Actions You Can See		Verbs That Tell Actions You Cannot See	
dance	swim	know	sense
play	talk	remember	name
sit	write	think	understand

A **linking verb** shows no action. It links the subject with another word that describes the subject.

Linking Verbs		
look	is	appear
smell	are	seem
sound	am	become
taste	were	
feel		

In this sentence, the adjective *tired* tells something about the subject, *dog*. *Seems* is the linking verb.

> Our dog **seems** tired.

In this sentence, the noun *friend* tells something about the subject, *brother*. *Is* is the linking verb.

> Your brother **is** my friend.

A **helping verb** comes before the main verb. It adds to the main verb's meaning. Helping verbs can be forms of the verbs *be, do,* or *have*.

	Helping Verbs
Forms of *be*	am, was, is, were, are
Forms of *do*	do, did, does
Forms of *have*	have, had, has
Other helping verbs	can, must, could, have (to), should, may, will, would

In this sentence, *am* is the helping verb; *walking* is the action verb.

> helping action
> verb   verb
> I **am walking** to my science class.

In this sentence, *has* is the helping verb; *completed* is the action verb.

> helping   action
> verb   verb
> He **has completed** his essay.

In questions, the subject comes between a helping verb and a main verb.

> person
> **Did** Liang **give** you the CD?

Adverbs

Adverbs describe the action of verbs. They tell *how* an action happens. Adverbs answer the question *Where*? *When*? *How*? *How much*? or *How often*?

Many adverbs end in *-ly*.

easily	slowly	carefully

Some adverbs do not end in *-ly*.

seldom	fast	very

In this sentence, the adverb *everywhere* modifies the verb *looked*. It answers the question *Where*?

> verb   adverb
> Nicole looked **everywhere** for her cell phone.

In this sentence, the adverb *quickly* modifies the verb *walked*. It answers the question *How*?

> verb   adverb
> They walked home **quickly**.

Adverbs also modify adjectives. They answer the question *How much*? or *How little*?

In this sentence, the adjective *dangerous* modifies the noun *road*. The adverb *very* modifies the adjective *dangerous*.

> adverb adjective noun
> This is a **very** dangerous road.

Adverbs can also modify other adverbs. In this sentence, the adverb *fast* modifies the verb *runs*. The adverb *quite* modifies the adverb *fast*.

> verb adverb adverb
> John runs **quite** fast.

Prepositions

Prepositions can show time, place, and direction.

Time	Place	Direction
after	above	across
before	below	down
during	in	into
since	near	to
until	under	up

In this sentence, the preposition *above* shows where the bird flew. It shows place.

> preposition
> A bird flew **above** my head.

In this sentence, the preposition *across* shows direction.

> preposition
> The children walked **across** the street.

A **prepositional phrase** starts with a preposition and ends with a noun or pronoun.

In this sentence, the preposition is *near* and the noun is *school*.

> prepositional phrase
> The library is **near the new school**.

Conjunctions

A **conjunction** joins words, groups of words, and whole sentences.

Conjunctions			
and	for	or	yet
but	nor	so	

In this sentence, the conjunction *and* joins two proper nouns: *Jonah* and *Teresa*.

noun	noun
Jonah **and** Teresa are in school.	

In this sentence, the conjunction *or* joins two prepositional phrases: *to the movies* and *to the mall*.

prepositional phrase	prepositional phrase
They want to go to the movies **or** to the mall.	

In this sentence, the conjunction *and* joins two independent clauses: *Amanda baked the cookies,* and *Eric made the lemonade.*

independent clause	independent clause
Amanda baked the cookies, **and** Eric made the lemonade.	

Interjections

Interjections are words or phrases that express emotion.

Interjections that express strong emotion are followed by an exclamation point.

Wow! Did you see that catch?
Hey! Watch out for that ball.

Interjections that express mild emotion are followed by a comma.

Gee, I'm sorry that your team lost.
Oh, it's okay. We'll do better next time.

CLAUSES

Clauses are groups of words with a subject and a verb. Some clauses form complete sentences; they tell a complete thought. Others do not.

This clause is a complete sentence. Clauses that form complete sentences are called **independent clauses**.

> subject   verb
> The dog's **tail wagged**.

This clause is not a complete sentence. Clauses that don't form complete sentences are called **dependent clauses**.

> subject   verb
> when the **boy patted** him.

Independent clauses can be combined with dependent clauses to form a sentence.

In this sentence, *The dog's tail wagged* is an independent clause. *When the boy patted him* is a dependent clause.

> ┌independent clause─┐┌─independent clause─┐
> The dog's tail wagged when the boy patted him.

SENTENCES

Sentences have a subject and a verb, and tell a complete thought. A sentence always begins with a capital letter. It always ends with a period, question mark, or exclamation point.

> subject action verb
>   ↓   ↓
> The **cheetah runs** very fast.
>
> helping
> verb   subject action verb
> ↓   ↓   ↓
> **Do you play** soccer?
>
> subject   linking verb
> ↓   ↓
> **I am** so late!

426

Simple Sentences and Compound Sentences

Some sentences are called simple sentences. Others are called compound sentences. A **simple sentence** has one independent clause. Here is an example.

┌──────── independent clause ────────┐
The dog barked at the mail carrier.

Compound sentences are made up of two or more simple sentences, or independent clauses. They are joined together by a **conjunction** such as *and* or *but*.

┌──── independent clause ────┐   ┌──── independent clause ────┐
The band has a lead singer, **but** they need a drummer.

Sentence Types

Sentences have different purposes. There are four types of sentences: declarative, interrogative, imperative, and exclamatory.

Declarative sentences are statements. They end with a period.

We are going to the beach on Saturday.

Interrogative sentences are questions. They end with a question mark.

Will you come with us?

Imperative sentences are commands. They usually end with a period. If the command is strong, the sentence may end with an exclamation point.

Put on your life jacket. Now jump into the water!

Exclamatory sentences express strong feeling. They end with an exclamation point.

I swam all the way from the boat to the shore!

End Marks

End marks come at the end of sentences. There are three kinds of end marks: periods, question marks, and exclamation points.

Use a **period** to end a statement (declarative sentence).

The spacecraft *Magellan* took pictures of Jupiter.

Use a **period** to end a command or request (imperative sentence) that isn't strong enough to need an exclamation point.

Please change the channel.

Use a **question mark** to end a sentence that asks a question. (interrogative sentence).

Where does Mrs. Suarez live?

Use an **exclamation point** to end a sentence that expresses strong feeling (exclamatory sentence).

That was a great party! Look at that huge house!

Use an **exclamation point** to end an imperative sentence that gives an urgent command.

Get away from the edge of the pool!

Periods are also used after initials and many abbreviations.

Use a **period** after a person's initial or abbreviated title.

Ms. Susan Vargas	Mrs. Fiske	J. D. Salinger
Gov. Lise Crawford	Mr. Vargas	Dr. Sapirstein

Use a **period** after the abbreviation of streets, roads, and so on.

Avenue	Ave.	Road	Rd.
Highway	Hwy.	Street	St.

Use a **period** after the abbreviation of many units of measurement. Abbreviations for metric measurements do *not* use periods.

inch	in.	centimeter	cm
foot	ft.	meter	m
pound	lb.	kilogram	kg
gallon	gal.	liter	l

Commas

Commas separate, or set off, parts of a sentence, or phrase.

Use a comma to separate two independent clauses linked by a conjunction. In this sentence, the comma goes before the conjunction *but*.

> ┌— independent clause ┐   ┌—independent clause ┐
> We went to the museum, **but** it is not open on Mondays.

Use commas to separate the parts in a series. A series is a group of three or more words, phrases, or very brief clauses.

	Commas in Series
To separate words	Lucio's bike is red, white, and silver.
To separate phrases	Today, he rode all over the lawn, down the sidewalk, and up the hill.
To separate clauses	Lucio washed the bike, his dad washed the car, and his mom washed the dog.

Use a comma to set off an introductory word, phrase, or clause.

	Commas with Introductory Words
To separate words	Yes, Stacy likes to go swimming.
To set off a phrase	In a month, she may join the swim team again.
To set off a clause	If she joins the swim team, I'll miss her at softball practice.

Use commas to set off an interrupting word, phrase, or clause.

	Commas with Interrupting Words
To set off a word	We left, finally, to get some fresh air.
To set off a phrase	Carol's dog, a brown pug, shakes when he gets scared.
To set off a clause	The assignment, I'm sorry to say, was too hard for me.

Use a comma to set off a speaker's quoted words in a sentence.

Jeanne asked, "Where is that book I just had?"
"I just saw it," said Billy, "on the kitchen counter."

In a direct address, one speaker talks directly to another. Use commas to set off the name of the person being addressed.

Thank you, Dee, for helping to put away the dishes.
Phil, why are you late again?

Use a comma between the day and the year.

My cousin was born on September 9, 2003.

If the date appears in the middle of a sentence, use a comma before and after the year.

Daria's mother was born on June 8, 1969, in New Jersey.

Use a comma between a city and a state and between a city and a nation.

My father grew up in Bakersfield, California.
We are traveling to Acapulco, Mexico.

If the names appear in the middle of a sentence, use a comma before *and* after the state or nation.

> My friend Carl went to Mumbai, India, last year.

Use a comma after the greeting in a friendly letter. Use a comma after the closing in both a friendly letter and formal letter. Do this in e-mail letters, too.

> Dear Margaret,   Sincerely,   Yours truly,

Semicolons and Colons

Semicolons can connect two independent clauses. Use them when the clauses are closely related in meaning or structure.

> The team won again; it was their ninth victory.
> Ana usually studies right after school; Rita prefers to study in the evening.

Colons introduce a list of items or important information.

Use a colon after an independent clause to introduce a list of items. (The clause often includes the words *the following, these, those,* or *this*.)

> The following animals live in Costa Rica: monkeys, lemurs, toucans, and jaguars.

Use a colon to introduce important information. If the information is in an independent clause, use a capital letter to begin the first word after the colon.

> There is one main rule: Do not talk to anyone during the test.
> You must remember this: Stay away from the train tracks!

Use a colon to separate hours and minutes when writing the time.

> 1:30   7:45   11:08

Quotation Marks

Quotation Marks set off direct quotations, dialogue, and some titles. A **direct quotation** is the exact words that somebody said, wrote, or thought.

Commas and periods *always* go inside quotation marks. If a question mark or exclamation point is part of the quotation, it is also placed *inside* the quotation marks.

> "Can you please get ready?" Mom asked.
> My sister shouted, "Look out for that bee!"

If a question mark or exclamation point is *not* part of the quotation, it goes *outside* the quotation marks. In these cases there is no punctuation before the end quotation marks.

> Did you say, "I can't do this"?

Conversation between two or more people is called **dialogue**. Use quotation marks to set off spoken words in dialogue.

> "What a great ride!" Pam said. "Let's go on it again."
> Julio shook his head and said, "No way. I'm feeling sick."

Use quotation marks around the titles of short works of writing or other art forms. The following kinds of titles take quotation marks:

Chapters	"The Railroad in the West"
Short Stories	"The Perfect Cat"
Articles	"California in the 1920s"
Songs	"This Land Is Your Land"
Single TV episodes	"Charlie's New Idea"
Short poems	"The Bat"

Titles of all other written work and artwork are underlined or set in italic type. These include books, magazines, newspapers, plays, movies, TV series, and paintings.

Apostrophes

Apostrophes can be used with singular and plural nouns to show ownership or possession. To form the possessive, follow these rules:

For singular nouns, add an apostrophe and an *s*.

| Maria's eyes | hamster's cage | the sun's warmth |

For singular nouns that end in *s*, add an apostrophe and an *s*.

| her boss's office | Carlos's piano | the grass's length |

For plural nouns that do not end in *s*, add an apostrophe and an *s*.

| women's clothes | men's shoes | children's books |

For plural nouns that end in *s*, add an apostrophe.

| teachers' lounge | dogs' leashes | kids' playground |

Apostrophes are also used in **contractions**. A contraction is a shortened form of two words that have been combined. The apostrophe shows where a letter or letters have been taken away.

I will
I'll be home in one hour.
do not
We **don't** have any milk.

Capitalization

There are five main reasons to use capital letters:

1. To begin a sentence and in a direct quotation
2. To write the word *I*
3. To write a proper noun (the name of a specific person, place, or thing)
4. To write a person's title
5. To write the title of a work (artwork, written work, magazine, newspaper, musical composition, organization)

Use a capital letter to begin the first word in a sentence.

Cows eat grass. They also eat hay.

Use a capital letter for the first word of a direct quotation. Use the capital letter even if the quotation is in the middle of a sentence.

Carlos said, "We need more lettuce for the sandwiches."

Use a capital letter for the word *I*.

How will I ever learn all these things? I guess I will learn them little by little.

Use a capital letter for a proper noun: the name of a specific person, place, or thing. Capitalize the important words in names.

Robert E. Lee   Morocco   Tuesday   Tropic of Cancer

Capital Letters in Place Names	
Streets	Interstate 95, Center Street, Atwood Avenue
City Sections	Greenwich Village, Shaker Heights, East Side
Cities and Towns	Rome, Chicago, Fresno
States	California, North Dakota, Maryland
Regions	Pacific Northwest, Great Plains, Eastern Europe
Nations	China, Dominican Republic, Italy
Continents	North America, Africa, Asia
Mountains	Mount Shasta, Andes Mountains, Rocky Mountains
Deserts	Mojave Desert, Sahara Desert, Gobi Desert
Islands	Fiji Islands, Capri, Virgin Islands
Rivers	Amazon River, Nile River, Mississippi River
Lakes	Lake Superior, Great Bear Lake, Lake Tahoe
Bays	San Francisco Bay, Hudson Bay, Galveston Bay
Seas	Mediterranean Sea, Sea of Japan
Oceans	Pacific Ocean, Atlantic Ocean, Indian Ocean

Capital Letters for Specific Things	
Historical Periods, Events	Renaissance, Battle of Bull Run
Historical Texts	Constitution, Bill of Rights
Days and Months	Monday, October
Holidays	Thanksgiving, Labor Day
Organizations, Schools	Greenpeace, Central High School
Government Bodies	Congress, State Department
Political Parties	Republican Party, Democratic Party
Ethnic Groups	Chinese, Latinos
Languages, Nationalities	Spanish, Canadian
Buildings	Empire State Building, City Hall
Monuments	Lincoln Memorial, Washington Monument
Religions	Hinduism, Christianity, Judaism, Islam
Special Events	Boston Marathon, Ohio State Fair

Use a capital letter for a person's title if the title comes before the name. In the second sentence below, a capital letter is not needed because the title does not come before a name.

I heard Senator Clinton's speech about jobs. The senator may come to our school.

Use a capital letter for the first and last word and all other important words in titles of books, newspapers, magazines, short stories, plays, movies, songs, paintings, and sculptures.

Lucy wants to read The Lord of the Rings.
The newspaper my father reads is The New York Times.
Did you like the painting called Work in the Fields?
This poem is called "The Birch Tree."

Reading Handbook

People often think of reading as a passive activity—that you don't have to do much, you just have to take in words—but that is not true. Good readers are active readers.

Reading comprehension involves these skills:

1. Understanding what you are reading.
2. Being part of what you are reading, or engaging with the text.
3. Evaluating what you are reading.
4. Making connections between what you are reading and what you already know.
5. Thinking about your response to what you have read.

Understanding What You Are Reading

One of the first steps is to recognize letters and words. Remember that it does not matter if you do not recognize all the words. You can figure out their meanings later. Try to figure out the meaning of unfamiliar words from the context of the sentence or paragraph. If you cannot figure out the meaning of a word, look it up in a dictionary. Next, you activate the meaning of words as you read them. That is what you are doing now. If you find parts of a text difficult, stop and read them a second time.

Engaging with the Text

Good readers use many different skills and strategies to help them understand and enjoy the text they are reading. When you read, think of it as a conversation between you and the writer. The writer wants to tell you something, and you want to understand his or her message.

Practice using these tips every time you read:

- Predict what will happen next in a story. Use clues you find in the text.
- Ask yourself questions about the main idea or message of the text.
- Monitor your understanding. Stop reading from time to time and think about what you have learned so far.

Evaluating What You Are Reading

The next step is to think about what you are reading. First, think about the author's purpose for writing. What type of text are you reading? If it is an informational text, the author wants to give you information about a subject, for example, about science, social science, or math. If you are reading literature, the author's purpose is probably to entertain you.

When you have decided what the author's purpose is for writing the text, think about what you have learned. Use these questions to help you:

- Is the information useful?
- Have you changed your mind about the subject?
- Did you enjoy the story, poem, or play?

Making Connections

Now connect the events or ideas in a text to your own knowledge or experience. Think about how your knowledge of a subject or your experience of the world can help you understand a text better.

- If the text has sections with headings, notice what these are. Do they give you clues about the main ideas in the text?
- Read the first paragraph. What is the main idea?
- Now read the paragraphs that follow. Make a note of the main ideas.
- Review your notes. How are the ideas connected?

Thinking about Your Response to What You Have Read

You read for a reason, so it is a good idea to think about how the text has helped you. Ask yourself these questions after you read:

- What information have I learned? Can I use it in my other classes?
- How can I connect my own experience or knowledge to the text?
- Did I enjoy reading the text? Why or why not?
- Did I learn any new vocabulary? What was it? How can I use it in conversation or in writing?

WHAT ARE READING STRATEGIES?

Reading strategies are specific things readers do to help them understand texts. Reading is like a conversation between an author and a reader. Authors make decisions about how to effectively communicate through a piece of writing. Readers use specific strategies to help them understand what authors are trying to communicate. Ten of the most common reading strategies are Previewing, Predicting, Skimming, Scanning, Comparing and Contrasting, Identifying Problems and Solutions, Recognizing Cause and Effect, Distinguishing Fact from Opinion, Identifying Main Idea and Details, and Identifying an Author's Purpose.

HOW TO IMPROVE READING FLUENCY

1. What Is Reading Fluency?

Reading fluency is the ability to read smoothly and expressively with clear understanding. Fluent readers are better able to understand and enjoy what they read. Use the strategies that follow to build your fluency in these four key areas: accuracy and rate, phrasing, intonation, expression.

2. How to Improve Accuracy and Rate

Accuracy is the correctness of your reading. Rate is the speed of your reading.

- Use correct pronunciation.
- Emphasize correct syllables.
- Recognize most words.

3. How to Read with Proper Rate

- Match your reading speed to what you are reading. For example, if you are reading a mystery story, read slightly faster. If you are reading a science textbook, read slightly slower.
- Recognize and use punctuation.

4. Test Your Accuracy and Rate

- Choose a text you are familiar with, and practice reading it multiple times.
- Keep a dictionary with you while you read, and look up words you do not recognize.
- Use a watch or clock to time yourself while you read a passage.
- Ask a friend or family member to read a passage for you so you know what it should sound like.

5. How to Improve Intonation

Intonation is the rise and fall in the pitch of your voice as you read aloud. Pitch means the highness or lowness of the sound. Follow these steps:

- Change the sound of your voice to match what you are reading.
- Make your voice flow, or sound smooth, while you read.
- Make sure you are pronouncing words correctly.
- Raise the pitch of your voice for words that should be stressed, or emphasized.
- Use proper rhythm and meter.
- Use visual clues.

Visual Clue and Meaning	Example	How to Read It
Italics: draw attention to a word to show special importance	He is *serious*.	Emphasize "serious."
Dash: shows a quick break in a sentence	He is—serious.	Pause before saying "serious."
Exclamation point: can represent energy, excitement, or anger	He is serious!	Make your voice louder at the end of the sentence.
All capital letters: can represent strong emphasis or yelling	HE IS SERIOUS.	Emphasize the whole sentence.
Boldfacing: draws attention to a word to show importance	He is **serious**.	Emphasize "serious."
Question mark: shows curiosity or confusion	Is he serious?	Raise the pitch of your voice slightly at the end of the sentence.

6. How to Improve Phrasing

Phrasing is how you group words together. Follow these steps:

- Use correct rhythm and meter by not reading too fast or too slow.
- Pause for key words within the text.
- Make sure your sentences have proper flow and meter, so they sound smooth instead of choppy.
- Make sure you sound like you are reading a sentence instead of a list.
- Use punctuation to tell you when to stop, pause, or emphasize.

7. How to Improve Expression

Expression in reading is how you express feeling. Follow these steps:

- Match the sound of your voice to what you are reading. For example, read louder and faster to show strong feeling. Read slowly and more quietly to show sadness or seriousness.
- Match the sound of your voice to the genre. For example, read a fun, fictional story using a fun, friendly voice. Read an informative, nonfiction article using an even tone and a more serious voice.
- Avoid speaking in monotone, or using only one tone in your voice.
- Pause for emphasis and exaggerate letter sounds to match the mood or theme of what you are reading.

Viewing and Representing

WHAT ARE VIEWING AND REPRESENTING?

Viewing

Viewing is something you do every day. Much of what you read and watch includes visuals that help you understand information. These visuals can be maps, charts, diagrams, graphs, photographs, illustrations, and so on. They can inform you, explain a topic or an idea, entertain you, or persuade you.

Websites use visuals, too. It is important for you to be able to view visuals critically in order to evaluate what you are seeing or reading.

Representing

Representing is creating a visual to convey an idea. It is important for you to be able to create and use visuals in your own written work and presentations. You can use graphic organizers, diagrams, charts, posters, and artwork to illustrate and explain your ideas. Following are some examples of visuals.

HOW TO READ MAPS AND DIAGRAMS

Maps

Maps help us learn more about our world. They show the location of places such as countries, states, and cities. Some maps show where mountains, rivers, and lakes are located.

Many maps have helpful features. For example, a **compass rose** shows which way is north. A **scale** shows how miles or kilometers are represented on the map. A **key** shows what different colors or symbols represent.

◀ Three trails on which cowboys drove cattle north from Texas

Diagrams

Diagrams are drawings or plans used to explain things or show how things work. They are often used in social studies and science books. Some diagrams show pictures of how objects look on the outside or on the inside. Others show the different steps in a process.

This diagram shows what a kernel of corn looks like on the inside.

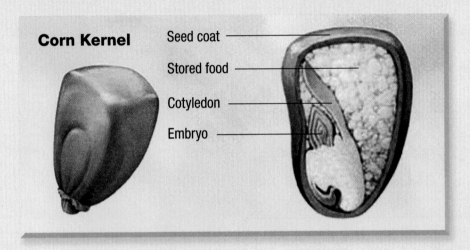

Corn Kernel

Seed coat

Stored food

Cotyledon

Embryo

A **flowchart** is a diagram that uses shapes and arrows to show a step-by-step process. The flowchart below shows the steps involved in baking chicken fingers. Each arrow points to the next step.

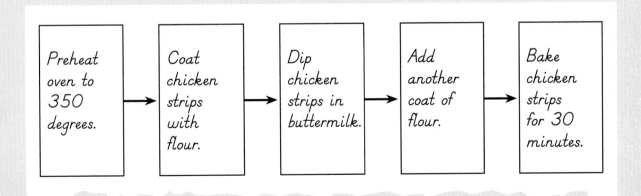

Preheat oven to 350 degrees. → Coat chicken strips with flour. → Dip chicken strips in buttermilk. → Add another coat of flour. → Bake chicken strips for 30 minutes.

Graphs organize and explain information. They show how two or more kinds of information are related, or how they are alike. Graphs are often used in math, science, and social studies books. Three common kinds of graphs are **line graphs**, **bar graphs**, and **circle graphs**.

Line Graphs

A line graph shows how information changes over a period of time. This line graph explains how, over a period of about 100 years, the Native-American population of Central Mexico decreased by more than 20 million people. Can you find the population in the year 1540? What was it in 1580?

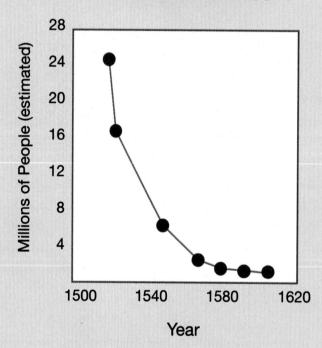

**Native-American Population
of Central Mexico**

Bar Graphs

We use bar graphs to compare information. For example, this bar graph compares the populations of the thirteen United States in 1790. It shows that, in 1790, Virginia had over ten times as many people as Delaware.

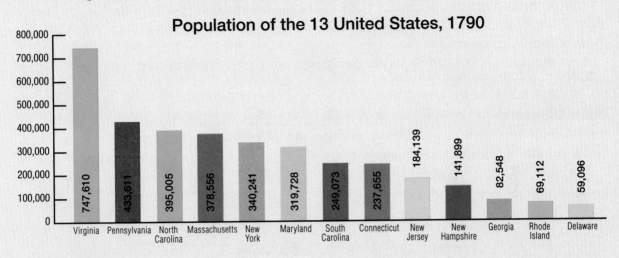

Population of the 13 United States, 1790

State	Population
Virginia	747,610
Pennsylvania	433,611
North Carolina	395,005
Massachusetts	378,556
New York	340,241
Maryland	319,728
South Carolina	249,073
Connecticut	237,655
New Jersey	184,139
New Hampshire	141,899
Georgia	82,548
Rhode Island	69,112
Delaware	59,096

Circle Graphs

A circle graph is sometimes called a pie chart because it looks like a pie cut into slices. Circle graphs are used to show how different parts of a whole thing compare to one another. In a circle graph, all the "slices" add up to 100 percent. This circle graph shows that only 29 percent of the earth's surface is covered by land. It also shows that the continent of Asia takes up 30 percent of the earth's land.

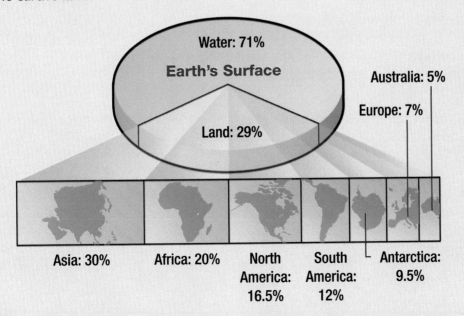

Water: 71%

Earth's Surface

Land: 29%

Australia: 5%

Europe: 7%

Asia: 30% Africa: 20% North America: 16.5% South America: 12% Antarctica: 9.5%

443

HOW TO USE GRAPHIC ORGANIZERS

A graphic organizer is a diagram that helps you organize information and show relationships among ideas. Because the information is organized visually, a graphic organizer tells you—in a quick snapshot—how ideas are related. Before you make a graphic organizer, think about the information you want to organize. How are the ideas or details related? Choose a format that will show those relationships clearly.

Venn diagrams and **word webs** are commonly used graphic organizers. Here is an example of each.

Venn Diagrams

A Venn diagram shows how two thing are alike and different. The diagram below compares oranges and bananas.

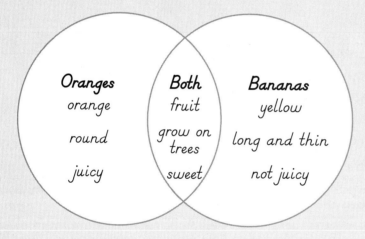

Word Webs

A word web is often used to help a writer describe something. The word web below lists five sensory details that describe popcorn.

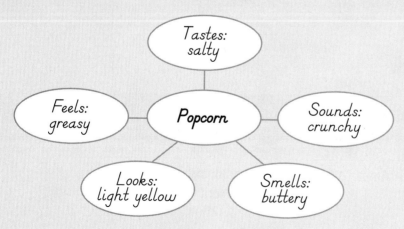

Writing Handbook

Narration

When writers tell a story, they use narration. There are many kinds of narration. Most include characters, a setting, and a sequence of events. Here are some types of narration.

A **short story** is a short, creative narrative. Most short stories have one or more characters, a setting, and a plot. A few types of short stories are realistic stories, fantasy stories, science-fiction stories, and adventure stories.

Autobiographical writing is a factual story of a writer's own life, told by the writer, usually in the first-person point of view. An autobiography may tell about the person's whole life or only a part of it.

Biographical writing is a factual story of a person's life told by another person. Most biographies are written about famous or admirable people.

Description

Description, or descriptive writing, is writing that gives the reader a mental picture of whatever is being described. To do this, writers choose their words carefully. They use figurative language and include vivid sensory details.

Persuasion

Writers use persuasion to try to persuade people to think or act in a certain way. Forms of persuasive writing include advertisements, essays, letters, editorials, speeches, and public-service announcements.

Exposition

Exposition, or expository writing, is writing that gives information or explains something. The information that writers include in expository writing is factual. Here are some types of expository writing.

A **compare-and-contrast essay** analyzes the similarities and differences between or among things.

A **cause-and-effect essay** explains causes or effects of an event. For example, a writer might examine several causes of a single effect or several effects of a single cause.

Writers use a **problem-and-solution essay** to describe a problem and offer one or more solutions to it.

A **how-to essay** explains how to do or make something. The process is broken down into steps, which are explained in order.

A **summary** is a brief statement that gives the main ideas of an event or a piece of writing. One way to write a summary is to read a text and then reread each paragraph or section. Next put the text aside and write the main ideas in your own words in a sentence or two.

Research Writing

Writers often use research to gather information about topics, including people, places, and things. Good research writing does not simply repeat information. It guides the readers through a topic, showing them why each fact matters and creating a complete picture of the topic. Here are some types of research writing.

Research report A research report presents information gathered from reference books, interviews, or other sources.

Biographical report A biographical report includes dates, details, and main events in a person's life. It can also include information about the time in which the person lived.

Multimedia report A multimedia report presents information through a variety of media, including text, slides, photographs, prerecorded music and sound effects, and digital imaging.

Responses to Literature

A **literary essay** is one type of response to literature. In a literary essay, a writer discusses and interprets what is important in a book, short story, essay, article, or poem.

Literary criticism is another type of response to literature. Literary criticism is the result of a careful examination of one or more literary works. The writer makes a judgment by looking carefully and critically at various important elements in the work.

A book **critique** gives readers a summary of a book, encouraging the reader either to read it or to avoid reading it. A movie critique gives readers a summary of a movie, tells if the writer enjoyed the movie, and then explains the reasons why or why not.

A **comparison of works** compares the features of two or more works.

Creative Writing

Creative writing blends imagination, ideas, and emotions, and allows the writer to present a unique view of the world. Poems, plays, short stories, dramas, and even some cartoons are examples of creative writing.

Practical and Technical Documents

Practical writing is fact-based writing that people do in the workplace or in their day-to-day lives. A business letter, memo, school form, job application, and a letter of inquiry are a few examples of practical writing.

Technical documents are fact-based documents that identify a sequence of activities needed to design a system, operate machinery, follow a procedure, or explain the rules of an organization. You read technical writing every time you read a manual or a set of instructions.

In the following descriptions, you'll find tips for tackling several types of practical and technical writing.

Business letters are formal letters that follow one of several specific formats.

News releases, also called press releases, announce factual information about upcoming events. A writer might send a news release to a local newspaper, local radio station, TV station, or other media that will publicize the information.

Guidelines give information about how people should act or how to do something.

Process explanations are step-by-step explanations of how to do something. The explanation should be clear and specific and can include diagrams or other illustrations. Below is an example.

KEYSTONE
CD-ROM

Usage Instructions
1. Insert the *Keystone* CD-ROM into your CD drive.
2. Open "My Computer."
3. Double-click on your CD-ROM disk drive.
4. Click on the *Keystone* icon. This will launch the program.

THE WRITING PROCESS

The **writing process** is a series of steps that can help you write effectively.

Step 1: Prewrite

During **prewriting**, you collect topic ideas, choose a topic, plan your writing, and gather information.

A good way to get ideas for a topic is to **brainstorm**. Brainstorming means writing a list of all the topic ideas you can think of.

Look at your list of topic ideas. Choose the one that is the most interesting to you. This is your **topic**, the subject you will write about.

Plan your writing by following these steps:

- First, decide on the **type** of writing that works best with your topic. For example, you may want to write a description, a story, or an essay.
- The type of writing is called the **form** of writing.
- Then think about your **audience**. Identifying your audience will help you decide whether to write formally or informally.
- Finally, decide what your reason for writing is. This is your **purpose**. Is your purpose to inform your audience? To entertain them?

How you gather information depends on what you are writing. For example, for a report, you need to do research. For a description, you might list your ideas in a graphic organizer. A student named Becca listed her ideas for a description of her week at art camp in the graphic organizer below.

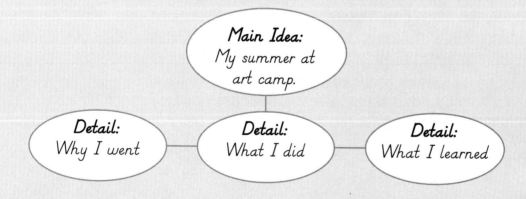

Step 2: Draft

In this step, you start writing. Don't worry too much about spelling and punctuation. Just put your ideas into sentences.

Here is the first paragraph that Becca wrote for her first draft.

> I saw an art contest advertised in the newspaper last spring. I entered my best drawing. I have always loved art. The prize was a week at an art camp in June with 9 other kids. I was very happy when I won.

Step 3: Revise

Now it's time to revise, or make changes. Ask yourself these questions:

- Are my ideas presented in the order that makes the most sense?
- Does my draft have a beginning, a middle, and an end?
- Does each paragraph have a main idea and supporting details?

If you answered *no* to any of these questions, you need to revise. Revising can mean changing the order of paragraphs or sentences. It can mean changing general words for specific words. It can mean correcting errors.

Once you decide what to change, you can mark the corrections on your draft using editing marks. Here's how Becca marked up her first paragraph.

> When ^ ^ I saw an art contest advertised in the newspaper last spring, I entered my best drawing. (I have always loved art.) The prize was a week at an art camp in June with ~~9~~ nine ^ other kids. I was very ~~happy~~ excited ^ when I won.

Step 4: Edit and Proofread

In this step, you make a second draft that includes the changes you marked on your first draft. You can also add details you may have thought of since writing your first draft. Now you're ready to **proofread**, or check your work for errors and make final corrections.

Here's Becca's first draft after she finished proofreading.

My Week at Art Camp

I have always loved art. When I saw an art contest advertised in the newspaper last spring, I entered my best drawing. The prize was a week at an art camp in June with nine other students. I was very excited when I won.

The camp was located at the Everson museum of art. On the first day, we looked at paintings by different artists. My favorite was by a painter named Monet. He painted colorful land scapes of boats and gardens. On the second day, we began our own paintings. I choose to paint a picture of the duck pond on the campus. I worked hard on my painting because we were going to have an art show of all our work at the end of the week.

I learned alot about painting at camp. I especially liked learning to use watercolors. For example I found out that you can make interesting designs by sprinkling salt on a wet watercolor painting.

I had a great time at art camp. The show at the end of the week was a big success, and I made some new friends. I hope to go again next year.

Step 5: Publish

Prepare a final copy of your writing to **publish**, or share with your audience. Here are some publishing tips.

- Photocopy and hand out your work to your classmates.
- Attach it to an e-mail and send it to friends.
- Send it to a school newspaper or magazine for possible publication.

Here is the final version of Becca's paper.

My Week at Art Camp

I have always loved art. When I saw an art contest advertised in the newspaper last spring, I entered my best drawing. The prize was a week at an art camp in June with nine other students. I was very excited when I won.

The camp was located at the Everson Museum of Art. On the first day, we looked at paintings by different artists. My favorite was by a painter named Monet. He painted colorful landscapes of boats and gardens. On the second day, we began our own paintings. I chose to paint a picture of the duck pond on the campus. I worked hard on my painting because we were going to have an art show of all our work at the end of the week.

I learned a lot about painting at camp. I especially liked learning to use watercolors. For example, I found out that you can make interesting designs by sprinkling salt on a wet watercolor painting.

I had a great time at art camp. The show at the end of the week was a big success, and I made some new friends. I hope to go again next year.

Once you have shared your work with others, you may want to keep it in a **portfolio**, a folder or envelope with your other writing. Each time you write something, add it to your portfolio. Compare recent work with earlier work. See how your writing is improving.

RUBRICS FOR WRITING

What Is a Rubric?

A **rubric** is a tool, often in the form of a chart or a grid, that helps you assess your work. Rubrics are helpful for writing and speaking assignments.

To help you or others assess your work, a rubric offers several specific criteria to be applied to your work. Then the rubric helps you indicate your range of success or failure according to those specific criteria. Rubrics are often used to evaluate writing for standardized tests.

Using a rubric will save you time, focus your learning, and improve your work. When you know the rubric beforehand, you can keep the specific criteria for the writing in your mind as you write. As you evaluate the essay before giving it to your teacher, you can focus on the specific criteria that your teacher wants you to master—or on areas that you know present challenges for you. Instead of searching through your work randomly for any way to improve or correct it, you will have a clear and helpful focus.

How Are Rubrics Structured?

Rubrics can be structured in several different ways:

1. Your teacher may assign a rubric for a specific assignment.
2. Your teacher may direct you to a rubric in your textbook.
3. Your teacher and your class may structure a rubric for a particular assignment together.
4. You and your classmates may structure a rubric together.
5. You can create your own rubric with your own specific criteria.

How Will a Rubric Help Me?

A rubric will help you assess your work on a scale. Scales vary from rubric to rubric but usually range from 6 to 1, 5 to 1, or 4 to 1, with 6, 5, or 4 being the highest score and 1 being the lowest. If someone else is using the rubric to assess your work, the rubric will give your evaluator a clear range within which to place your work. If you are using the rubric yourself, it will help you improve your work.

What Are the Types of Rubrics?

A **holistic rubric** has general criteria that can apply to a variety of assignments. An **analytic rubric** is specific to a particular assignment. The criteria for evaluation address the specific issues important in that assignment. The following pages show examples of both types of rubrics.

Holistic Rubrics

Holistic rubrics such as this one are sometimes used to assess writing assignments on standardized tests. Notice that the criteria for evaluation are focus, organization, support, and use of conventions.

Points	Criteria
6 Points	• The writing is focused and shows fresh insight into the writing task. • The writing is marked by a sense of completeness and coherence and is organized with a logical progression of ideas. • A main idea is fully developed, and support is specific and substantial. • A mature command of the language is evident. • Sentence structure is varied, and writing is free of fragments. • Virtually no errors in writing conventions appear.
5 Points	• The writing is focused on the task. • The writing is organized and has a logical progression of ideas, though there may be occasional lapses. • A main idea is well developed and supported with relevant detail. • Sentence structure is varied, and the writing is free of fragments. • Writing conventions are followed correctly.
4 Points	• The writing is focused on the task, but unrelated material may intrude. • Clear organizational pattern is present, though lapses occur. • A main idea is adequately supported, but development may be uneven. • Sentence structure is generally fragment free but shows little variation. • Writing conventions are generally followed correctly.
3 Points	• Writing is focused on the task, but unrelated material intrudes. • Organization is evident, but writing may lack a logical progression of ideas. • Support for the main idea is present but is sometimes illogical. • Sentence structure is free of fragments, but there is almost no variation. • The work demonstrates a knowledge of conventions, with misspellings.
2 Points	• The writing is related to the task but generally lacks focus. • There is little evidence of an organizational pattern. • Support for the main idea is generally inadequate, illogical, or absent. • Sentence structure is unvaried, and serious errors may occur. • Errors in writing conventions and spellings are frequent.
1 Point	• The writing may have little connection to the task. • There has been little attempt at organization or development. • The paper seems fragmented, with no clear main idea. • Sentence structure is unvaried, and serious errors appear. • Poor diction and poor command of the language obscure meaning. • Errors in writing conventions and spelling are frequent.
Unscorable	• The response is unrelated to the task or is simply a rewording of the prompt. • The response has been copied from a published work. • The student did not write a response. • The response is illegible. • The words in the response are arranged with no meaning. • There is an insufficient amount of writing to score.

Analytic Rubrics

This analytic rubric is an example of a rubric to assess a persuasive essay. It will help you assess presentation, position, evidence, and arguments.

Presentation	Position	Evidence	Arguments
6 Points Essay clearly and effectively addresses an issue with more than one side.	Essay clearly states a supportable position on the issue.	All evidence is logically organized, well presented, and supports the position.	All reader concerns and counterarguments are effectively addressed.
5 Points Most of essay addresses an issue that has more than one side.	Essay clearly states a position on the issue.	Most evidence is logically organized, well presented, and supports the position.	Most reader concerns and counterarguments are effectively addressed.
4 Points Essay adequately addresses issue that has more than one side.	Essay adequately states a position on the issue.	Many parts of evidence support the position; some evidence is out of order.	Many reader concerns and counterarguments are adequately addressed.
3 Points Essay addresses issue with two sides but does not present second side clearly.	Essay states a position on the issue, but the position is difficult to support.	Some evidence supports the position, but some evidence is out of order.	Some reader concerns and counterarguments are addressed.
2 Points Essay addresses issue with two sides but does not present second side.	Essay states a position on the issue, but the position is not supportable.	Not much evidence supports the position, and what is included is out of order.	A few reader concerns and counterarguments are addressed.
1 Point Essay does not address issue with more than one side.	Essay does not state a position on the issue.	No evidence supports the position.	No reader concerns or counterarguments are addressed.

Friendly Letters

A friendly letter is less formal than a business letter. It is a letter to a friend, a family member, or anyone with whom the writer wants to communicate in a personal, friendly way. Most friendly letters are made up of five parts: the **date**, the **greeting** (or salutation), the **body**, the **closing**, and the **signature**. The greeting is followed by a comma, and the paragraphs in the body are indented.

The purpose of a friendly letter is usually to share personal news and feelings, to send or to answer an invitation, or to express thanks.

In this letter, Maité tells her friend Julio about her new home.

Greeting   **Date**

March 2, 2009

Dear Julio,

    I was so happy to receive your letter today. I am feeling much better. My mom and I finally finished decorating my room. We painted the walls green and the ceiling pink. At first, my mom was nervous to paint the ceiling something other than white, but I knew it would look good. Now that my bedroom is finished, Manhattan is starting to feel more like home.

    Over the weekend I went to the Museum of Natural History. The whale exhibit made me think of back home and how you and I would spend hours at the beach. I am starting to adjust to city life, but I miss the smell of salt in the air and collecting sea glass on the shore.

Body

    My parents said I can spend the summer with my grandparents at their beach house. They said I could invite you for a couple of weeks. We'll go swimming every day. I can't wait!

Your friend,   ⟵ **Closing**

Maité   ⟵ **Signature**

455

Business Letters

Business letters follow one of several formats. In **block format**, each part of the letter begins at the left margin. A double space is used between paragraphs. In **modified block format**, some parts of the letter are indented to the center of the page. No matter which format is used, all letters in business format have a date, an inside address, a greeting (or salutation), a body, a closing, and a signature. These parts are shown on the model business letter below, formatted in block style.

June 11, 2009 ⟵——————— **Date**

Edward Sykes, Vice President
Animal Rights Group ⟵——————— **Inside Address**
154 Denver Street
Syosset, NY 11791

Dear Mr. Sykes: ⟵——————— **Greeting**

Many students at Bellevue High School would like to learn about animal rights for a project we're starting next fall. We've read about your program on your website and would like to know more about your activities.

Would you send us some information about your organization? We're specifically interested in learning what we as students can do to help protect animals. About 75 students have expressed interest so far—I think we'll have the people power to make the project a success and have an impact. ⟵——— **Body**

Please help us get started. Thank you for your time and consideration.

Sincerely, ⟵——— **Closing**

Pedro Rodriguez ⟵——— **Signature**
Pedro Rodriguez

The **inside address** shows where the letter will be sent. The **greeting** is punctuated with a colon. The **body** of the letter states the writer's purpose. The **closing** "Sincerely" is common, but "Yours truly" or "Respectfully yours" are also acceptable. The writer types his or her name and writes a **signature**.

Forms are preprinted documents with spaces for the user to enter specific information. Some include directions; others assume that users will follow the labels and common conventions. Two common forms in the workplace are fax cover sheets and applications. When you fill out forms, it is important to do the following:

- Fill them out accurately and completely.
- Write neatly in blue or black ink.
- Include only information that is asked for on the form.

Forms usually have limited space in which to write. Because space is limited, you can use standard symbols and abbreviations, such as *$10/hr.* to mean "10 dollars per hour."

FAX COVER SHEET

To: *Mr. Robert Thompson*   **From:** *Laura Rivas*

Fax: *(001) 921-9833*   **Pages:** *2 (including cover sheet)*

Date: *12/04/09*

Re: *Job Application*

Message:

Dear Mr. Thompson:

Thank you for meeting with me today about the sales associate position at Story Land Bookshop. The following page is my completed application form.

Sincerely,

Laura Rivas

Filling in an Application for Employment

Story Land Bookshop

PRE-EMPLOYMENT QUESTIONNAIRE
EQUAL OPPORTUNITY EMPLOYER
Date: 12/04/2009

PERSONAL INFORMATION

Name (last name first)
Rivas, Laura

Social Security No.
145-53-6211

Present Address
351 Middleton Road

City
Osborne

State
TX

Zip Code
78357

Permanent Address
Same

City

State

Zip Code

Phone No.
(001) 661-1567

Referred by
Josh Logan

EMPLOYMENT DESIRED

Position
Sales associate

Start Date
Immediately

Salary Desired
$10/hr.

	Yes	No
Are you presently employed?	☐ Yes	☑ No
May we contact your former employer?	☑ Yes	☐ No
Were you ever employed by this company?	☐ Yes	☑ No

EDUCATION

Name and Location of School
Osborne High School, Osborne, TX

Yrs Attended
3

Did you graduate?
Expect to graduate 2010

FORMER EMPLOYERS

Name and Address of Employer
Blue River Summer Camp
127 Horse Lane
Millwood, TX 78721

Salary
$195 per week

Position
Junior camp counselor

Date Month and Year
6/20/09 to 9/20/09

Reason for Leaving
Summer ended

Reference Skills

There is a wide range of print and electronic references you can use to find many different kinds of information.

Encyclopedias

Encyclopedias contain facts on a great many subjects. They provide basic information to help you start researching a topic. Use encyclopedias for basic facts, background information, and suggestions for additional research.

Periodicals

Periodicals are magazines and journals. Once you've used a periodical index to identify the articles you want to read, ask a librarian to help you locate the periodicals. Often, past issues of magazines are stored electronically on microfilm, a database, or CD-ROMs. The librarian can help you use these resources. Use the table of contents, the titles, and other magazine features to help you find information.

Biographical References

These books provide brief life histories of famous people in many different fields. Biographical references may offer short entries similar to those in dictionaries or longer articles more like those in encyclopedias. Most contain an index to help you locate entries.

Nonfiction Books

Nonfiction books about your topic can also be useful reference tools. Use titles, tables of contents, prefaces, chapter headings, glossaries, indexes, and appendixes to locate the information you need.

Almanacs

Almanacs are published annually. They contain facts and statistics about many subjects, including government, world history, geography, entertainment, business, and sports. To find a subject in a printed almanac, refer to the index in the front or back. In an electronic almanac, you can usually find information by typing a subject or key word.

Electronic Databases

Available on CD-ROMs or online, electronic databases provide quick access to a wealth of information on a topic. Using a search feature, you can easily access any type of data, piece together related information, or look at the information in a different way.

PROOFREADING

All forms of writing—from a letter to a friend to a research paper—are more effective when they are error-free. Once you are satisfied with the content of your writing, polish the grammar, usage, and mechanics.

Challenge yourself to learn and apply the skills of proofreading to everything you write. Review your writing carefully to find and correct all errors. Here are the broad categories that should direct your proofreading:

☑ **CHECK YOUR SPELLING:** Use a dictionary or an electronic spelling checker to check any spelling of which you are unsure.

☑ **CHECK YOUR GRAMMAR AND USAGE:** Use a writing handbook to correct problems in grammar or usage.

☑ **REVIEW CAPITALIZATION AND PUNCTUATION:** Review your draft to be sure you've begun each sentence with a capital letter and used proper end punctuation.

☑ **CHECK THE FACTS:** When your writing includes facts gathered from outside sources, confirm the accuracy of your work. Consult reference materials. Check names, dates, and statistics.

Editing Marks		
To:	**Use This Mark:**	**Example:**
add something	∧	We ate rice, bean, and corn.
delete something	ℒ	We ate rice, beans, and corns.
start a new paragraph	¶	¶We ate rice, beans, and corn.
add a comma	⌄	We ate rice, beans and corn.
add a period	⊙	We ate rice, beans, and corn⊙
switch letters or words	∼	We ate rice, baens, and corn.
change to a capital letter	≡	we ate rice, beans, and corn.
change to a lowercase letter	✗	WE ate rice, beans, and corn.

Proofreading and Preparing Manuscript

Before preparing a final copy, proofread your manuscript.

- Choose a standard, easy-to-read font.
- Type or print on one side of unlined 8 1/2" x 11" paper.
- Set the margins for the side, top, and bottom of your paper at approximately one inch. Most word-processing programs have a default setting that is appropriate.
- Double-space the document.
- Indent the first line of each paragraph.
- Number the pages in the upper right corner.

Follow your teacher's directions for formatting formal research papers. Most papers will have the following features: Title page, Table of Contents or Outline, Works Consulted List.

Crediting Sources

When you credit a source, you acknowledge where you found your information and you give your readers the details necessary for locating the source themselves. Within the body of the paper, you provide a short citation, a footnote number linked to a footnote, or an endnote number linked to an endnote reference. These brief references show the page numbers on which you found the information. Prepare a reference list at the end of the paper to provide full bibliographic information on your sources. These are two common types of reference lists:

A **bibliography** provides a listing of all the resources you consulted during your research. A **works consulted list** lists the works you have referenced in your paper.

The chart on the next page shows the Modern Language Association format for crediting sources. This is the most common format for papers written in the content areas in middle school and high school. Unless instructed otherwise by your teacher, use this format for crediting sources.

MLA Style for Listing Sources

Book with one author	Pyles, Thomas. *The Origins and Development of the English Language.* 2nd ed. New York: Harcourt Brace Jovanovich, Inc., 1971.
Book with two or three authors	McCrum, Robert, William Cran, and Robert MacNeil. *The Story of English.* New York: Penguin Books, 1987.
Book with an editor	Truth, Sojourner. *Narrative of Sojourner Truth.* Ed. Margaret Washington. New York: Vintage Books, 1993.
Book with more than three authors or editors	Donald, Robert B., et al. *Writing Clear Essays.* Upper Saddle River, NJ: Prentice Hall, Inc., 1996.
Single work from an anthology	Hawthorne, Nathaniel. "Young Goodman Brown." *Literature: An Introduction to Reading and Writing.* Ed. Edgar V. Roberts and Henry E. Jacobs. Upper Saddle River, NJ: Prentice-Hall, Inc., 1998. 376–385. [Indicate pages for the entire selection.]
Introduction in a published edition	Washington, Margaret. Introduction. *Narrative of Sojourner Truth.* By Sojourner Truth. New York: Vintage Books, 1993, pp. v–xi.
Signed article in a weekly magazine	Wallace, Charles. "A Vodacious Deal." *Time* 14 Feb. 2000: 63.
Signed article in a monthly magazine	Gustaitis, Joseph. "The Sticky History of Chewing Gum." *American History* Oct. 1998: 30–38.
Unsigned editorial or story	"Selective Silence." Editorial. *Wall Street Journal* 11 Feb. 2000: A14. [If the editorial or story is signed, begin with the author's name.]
Signed pamphlet or brochure	[Treat the pamphlet as though it were a book.]
Pamphlet with no author, publisher, or date	*Are You at Risk of Heart Attack?* n.p. n.d. ["n.p. n.d." indicates that there is no known publisher or date.]
Filmstrips, slide programs, videocassettes, DVDs, and other audiovisual media	*The Diary of Anne Frank.* Dir. George Stevens. Perf. Millie Perkins, Shelly Winters, Joseph Schildkraut, Lou Jacobi, and Richard Beymer. Twentieth Century Fox, 1959.
Radio or television program transcript	"Nobel for Literature." Narr. Rick Karr. *All Things Considered.* National Public Radio. WNYC, New York. 10 Oct. 2002. Transcript.
Internet	*National Association of Chewing Gum Manufacturers.* 19 Dec. 1999 <http://www.nacgm.org/consumer/funfacts.html> [Indicate the date you accessed the information. Content and addresses at websites change frequently.]
Newspaper	Thurow, Roger. "South Africans Who Fought for Sanctions Now Scrap for Investors." *Wall Street Journal* 11 Feb. 2000: A1+ [For a multipage article, write only the first page number on which it appears, followed by a plus sign.]
Personal interview	Smith, Jane. Personal interview. 10 Feb. 2000.
CD (with multiple publishers)	Simms, James, ed. *Romeo and Juliet.* By William Shakespeare. CD-ROM. Oxford: Attica Cybernetics Ltd.; London: BBC Education; London: HarperCollins Publishers, 1995.
Signed article from an encyclopedia	Askeland, Donald R. "Welding." *World Book Encyclopedia.* 1991 ed.

Technology Handbook

WHAT IS TECHNOLOGY?

Technology is a combination of resources that can help you do research, find information, and write. Good sources for research include the Internet and your local library. The library contains databases where you can find many forms of print and nonprint resources, including audio and video recordings.

The Internet

The Internet is an international network, or connection, of computers that share information with each other. It is a popular source for research and finding information for academic, professional, and personal reasons. The World Wide Web is a part of the Internet that allows you to find, read, and organize information. Using the Web is a fast way to get the most current information about many topics.

Words or phrases can be typed into the "search" section of a search engine, and websites that contain those words will be listed for you to explore. You can then search a website for the information you need.

Information Media

Media is all the organizations, such as television, radio, and newspapers that provide news and information for the public. Knowing the characteristics of various kinds of media will help you to spot them during your research. The following chart describes several forms of information media.

Types of Information Media	
Television News Program	• Covers current news events • Gives information objectively
Documentary	• Focuses on one topic of social interest • Sometimes expresses controversial opinions
Television Newsmagazine	• Covers a variety of topics • Entertains and informs
Commercial	• Presents products, people, or ideas • Persuades people to buy or take action

Other Sources of Information

There are many other reliable print and nonprint sources of information to use in your research. For example: magazines, newspapers, professional or academic journal articles, experts, political speeches, press conferences.

Most of the information from these sources is also available on the Internet. Try to evaluate the information you find from various media sources. Be careful to choose the most reliable sources for this information.

463

HOW TO USE THE INTERNET FOR RESEARCH

Keyword Search

Before you begin a search, narrow your subject to a keyword or a group of **keywords**. These are your search terms, and they should be as specific as possible. For example, if you are looking for information about your favorite musical group, you might use the band's name as a keyword. You might locate such information as band member biographies, the group's history, fan reviews of concerts, and hundreds of sites with related names containing information that is irrelevant to your search. Depending on your research needs, you might need to narrow your search.

How to Narrow Your Search

If you have a large group of keywords and still don't know which ones to use, write out a list of all the words you are considering. Then, delete the words that are least important to your search, and highlight those that are most important.

Use search connectors to fine-tune your search:

AND: narrows a search by retrieving documents that include both terms.
For example: *trumpets AND jazz*

OR: broadens a search by retrieving documents including any of the terms.
For example: *jazz OR music*

NOT: narrows a search by excluding documents containing certain words.
For example: *trumpets NOT drums*

Good Search Tips

1. Search engines can be case-sensitive. If your first try at searching fails, check your search terms for misspellings and search again.
2. Use the most important keyword first, followed by the less important ones.
3. Do not open the link to every single page in your results list. Search engines show pages in order of how close it is to your keyword. The most useful pages will be located at the top of the list.
4. Some search engines provide helpful tips for narrowing your search.

Respecting Copyrighted Material

The Internet is growing every day. Sometimes you are not allowed to access or reprint material you find on the Internet. For some text, photographs, music, and fine art, you must first get permission from the author or copyright owner. Also, be careful not to plagiarize while writing and researching. Plagiarism is presenting someone else's words, ideas, or work as your own. If the idea or words are not yours, be sure to give credit by citing the source in your work.

HOW TO EVALUATE THE QUALITY OF INFORMATION

Since the media presents large amounts of information, it is important to learn how to analyze this information critically. Analyzing critically means you can evaluate the information for content, quality, and importance.

How to Evaluate Information from Various Media

Sometimes the media tries to make you think a certain way instead of giving all the facts. These techniques will help you figure out if you can rely on information from the media.

- ✔ Ask yourself if you can trust the source, or if the information you find shows any bias. Is the information being given in a one-sided way?

- ✔ Discuss the information you find from different media with your classmates or teachers to figure out its reliability.

- ✔ Sort out facts from opinions. Make sure that any opinions given are backed up with facts. A fact is a statement that can be proved true. An opinion is a viewpoint that cannot be proved true.

- ✔ Be aware of any loaded language or images. Loaded language and images are emotional words and visuals used to persuade you.

- ✔ Check surprising or questionable information in other sources. Are there instances of faulty reasoning? Is the information adequately supported?

- ✔ Be aware of the kind of media you are watching. If it's a program, is it a documentary? A commercial? What is its purpose? Is it correct?

- ✔ Read the entire article or watch the whole program before reaching a conclusion. Then develop your own views on the issues, people, and information presented.

How to Evaluate Information from the Internet

There is so much information available on the Internet that it can be hard to understand. It is important to be sure that the information you use as support or evidence is reliable and can be trusted. Use the following checklist to decide if a Web page you are reading is reliable and a credible source.

- ☑ The information is from a well-known and trusted website. For example, websites that end in **.edu** are part of an educational institution and usually can be trusted. Other cues for reliable websites are sites that end in **.org** for "organization" or **.gov** for "government." Sites with a **.com** ending are either owned by businesses or individuals.

- ☑ The people who write or are quoted on the website are experts, not just everyday people telling their ideas or opinions.

- ☑ The website gives facts, not just opinions.

- ☑ The website is free of grammatical and spelling errors. This is often a hint that the site was carefully made and will not have factual mistakes.

- ☑ The website is not trying to sell a product or persuade people. It is simply trying to give correct information.

- ☑ If you are not sure about using a website as a source, ask your teacher for advice. Once you become more aware of the different sites, you will become better at knowing which sources to trust.

HOW TO USE TECHNOLOGY IN WRITING

Personal Computers

A personal computer can be an excellent writing tool. It enables a writer to create, change, and save documents. The cut, copy, and paste features are especially useful when writing and revising.

Organizing Information

Create a system to organize the research information you find from various forms of media, such as newspapers, books, and the Internet.

Using a computer and printer can help you in the writing process. You can change your drafts, see your changes clearly, and keep copies of all your work. Also, consider keeping an electronic portfolio. This way you can store and organize copies of your writing in several subject areas. You can review the works you have completed and see your improvement as a writer.

It is easy to organize electronic files on a computer. The desktop is the main screen, and holds folders that the user names. For example, a folder labeled "Writing Projects September" might contain all of the writing you do during that month. This will help you find your work quickly.

As you use your portfolio, you might think of better ways to organize it. You might find you have several drafts of a paper you wrote, and want to create a separate folder for these. Every month, take time to clean up your files.

Computer Tips

1. Rename each of your revised drafts using the SAVE AS function. For example, if your first file is "essay," name the first revision "essay2" and the next one "essay3."
2. If you share your computer with others, label a folder with your name and keep your files separate by putting them there.
3. Always back up your portfolio on a server or a CD.

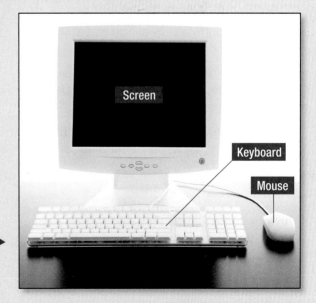

Personal computer ▶

467

Glossary

academic relating to work done in schools, colleges, or universities

accompanied went somewhere with someone

accomplish do something successfully

achieved succeeded in doing something, especially by working hard

affects produces a change in someone or something

aid help or support given to someone

analyze examine or think about something carefully in order to understand it

approach a way of doing something or dealing with a problem

assisted helped someone

assumed thought that something was true without having proof

asteroids large objects made of rock that move around in space

attached emotionally connected to

attitudes thoughts or feelings about something or someone

authoritative respected and trusted as being true, or making people respect or obey you

author's influences different factors that affect what an author writes about

available able to be used or seen

barriers things, such as rules or problems, that prevent you from doing something

base the main place where the work of a company or expedition is done

beneficial good or useful

benefit something that helps you or gives you an advantage

challenge something difficult that you need skill or ability to do

character motive a reason that explains a character's thoughts, feelings, actions, or speech

characters the people or animals that take part in the action of a story

chemicals substances, especially those made by or used in chemistry

climate the typical weather of a particular area

climax the high point in the action of a story's plot

code a way to use words, letters, or numbers to send secret messages

comet an object in the sky—like a bright ball with a tail—that moves through space

commensal a type of relationship between two organisms in which one partner benefits from the relationship, while the other partner is neither helped nor harmed

communicate express your thoughts or feelings so other people understand them

community all the people living in one place

conflict a struggle between opposing forces

confrontation an argument or fight

consent permission to do something

consists is made of or contains a number of different things

correspond write to someone and receive letters from him or her

crater a round hole in the ground made by something that has fallen on it or exploded on it

created made or invented

criteria facts or standards used in order to help you judge or decide something

crops plants such as wheat, corn, fruit, etc., that a farmer grows

cultivate try to develop a friendship with someone

cultural relating to a particular society and its way of life

customs special ways of doing something by a person or group

designer a person whose job is to make plans or patterns for clothes, furniture, equipment, etc.

device a thing that you use for a particular purpose

dialogue a conversation between characters

diary a book in which you write about the things that happen to you each day

discrimination unfair treatment of some people because of their race, ethnic group, religion, or gender

disease an illness or unhealthy condition

distributes gives something to different people or places

drama a story written to be performed by actors

elements simple chemical substances

encounter an occasion when you meet someone without planning to

endangered species a type of animal or plant that soon might not exist

enemies people or countries that are not friendly to you or want to harm or fight you

environment the land, water, and air in which people, animals, and plants live

exhibit a public show of objects such as paintings, photographs, etc.

experiment a careful test you do to see if something is true

external conflict conflict between a character and an outside force

features the important, interesting, or typical parts of something

fever an illness which causes an increase in your body's temperature

focus pay special attention to a particular person or thing instead of others

foreshadowing the author's use of clues to hint at what might happen later in a story

founded established a business, organization, school, etc.

fugitive someone who is trying to avoid being caught

function the purpose of something

goal something you want to do in the future

gravity the force that makes things fall to the ground when they are dropped

hearing impaired unable to hear well, or unable to hear at all

heritage the traditional beliefs, values, customs, etc., of a family, group of people, or country

hypothesis an idea that is suggested as an explanation of something, but that has not yet been proven to be true

ignored did not pay attention to someone or something

illegal not allowed by law

image a picture that you can see through a camera, on a television, in a mirror, etc.

imagery the use of words or phrases to describe ideas or actions in literary works

immigrants people who enter another country in order to live there

impact the effect that an event or situation has on someone or something

indicate say or do something that shows what you want or intend to do

individuals people; not a whole group

injured hurt

inspectors officials whose jobs it is to visit places and see if there is anything wrong with them

instructed taught or showed someone how to do something

interact talk to other people and work together with them

interaction the activity of talking with other people and working together with them

interpretation an explanation of the meaning or significance of something

invention something completely new that is made for the first time

investigate try to find out the truth about something

involved included in a project or situation

irony a situation that is unusual or amusing because something strange happens, or the opposite of what is expected happens

irrigate make water flow to dry land or crops

issues subjects or problems that people discuss

items things in a set, group, or list

job a particular duty or responsibility that you have

labor work that requires a lot of physical effort

legend a widely told story about the past that may or may not be true

located in a particular place or position

lunar relating to the moon

meteoroids pieces of rock or dust that travel through space

migrant workers people who go to another area or country in order to find work

migration the act of moving from one place to another

mine dig into the ground for coal, iron, gold, etc.

mission the purpose or the most important aim of an organization

monitor carefully watch, listen to, or examine something over a period of time, to check for any changes or developments

mosquitoes flying insects that drink blood from people or animals and that can spread disease from one person to another

mutualistic a relationship between two organisms from which both organisms benefit

myth a fictional story that explains natural events such as wind or rain

natural resources all the land, minerals, energy, etc., that exist in a country

nature the world and everything in it that people have not made, such as animals, weather, plants, etc.

neighborhood a small area of a town and the people who live there

network a group of people, organizations, etc., that are connected or that work together

nomads people who travel from place to place, especially as members of a tribe

objective something that you are working hard to achieve

obstacle something that makes it difficult for you to succeed

occupants people who live in a building, room, etc.

occurs happens

opponent someone who tries to defeat someone else in a game or competition

oral tradition stories passed along by word of mouth from one generation to the next

orbit the path that one thing follows when it moves around another in space

outcome the final result of a meeting, process, etc.

parasites plants or animals that live on or in another plant or animal and get food from it

participate take part in an activity or event

partnership a relationship in which two or more people, organizations, etc., work together to achieve something

patent a special document that says you have the right to make or sell a new invention or product and that no one else is allowed to do so

perceive understand or think about something in a particular way

periodic table a specially arranged list of the elements

persistence the determination to do something even though it is difficult or other people oppose it

personification the representation of a thing or a quality as a person

planets large objects in space, such as Earth, that move around a star such as the sun

plot a sequence of connected events in a fictional story

point of view the perspective from which a story is written

policy a plan that is agreed to by a political party, government, or organization

political relating to the government or politics of a country

population the number of people or animals living in a place

positive good or useful

preserved kept something from being harmed or damaged

principal someone who is in charge of a school

prior before

promote help something develop and be successful

protection the act of keeping a person or thing safe from harm or damage

published printed and distributed

rare not happening or seen very often

reacted behaved in a particular way because of what someone has said or done

reaction the way you behave in response to someone or something

refuge a safe place

region a large area

regulations official rules or orders

rejected decided not to do something

removed took something away from where it was

research serious study of a subject that is intended to discover new facts about it

residents the people who live in a place

resources a supply of materials used to complete a task

response something that is said, written, or done as a reaction or reply to something else

restricted controlled something or kept it within limits

rhyme when a word ends in the same sound as another

role the position or job that something or someone has in a particular situation or activity

route the way from one place to another

runaway someone who has left the place where he or she is supposed to be

setting the time and place of a story's action

shelter a place that protects you from bad weather or danger, or the protection that is given to you

significant noticeable or important

sign language a language that consists of hand movements instead of spoken words

similarities the qualities of being similar or the same

source where something comes from

speaker the imaginary voice a poet uses when writing a poem

stage directions notes in a drama that tell the actors what they should do and how they should do it

stanza a group of lines in poetry that are usually similar in length and pattern and are separated by spaces

strike a time when people stop working, usually because they want more money or better conditions

structure a building or something that has been built

substitute someone who does someone else's job

survive continue to live after an accident or illness

suspense the feeling of uncertainty about what will happen next in a literary work

symbiosis a relationship between two living things that exist together and depend on each other

472

symbol a picture, letter, or sign that means or stands for something else

symbolize represent a quality or a feeling

team a group of people who compete against another group in a sport, game, etc.

technology all the knowledge and equipment used in science

tenement a large building divided into apartments, especially one that is located in a poor area

theme the central message, concern, or purpose in a literary work

theory an idea that explains how something works or why something happens

tradition a belief or custom that has existed for a long time

transmit send or pass something from one person to another

transportation the process or business of moving people or goods from one place to another

tribe a group of people of the same race, language, customs, etc., that live in one place

Underground Railroad network of secret routes that escaping slaves followed to freedom

union a group of workers who have joined together to protect their pay and working conditions

universe all of space, including all the stars and planets

violence behavior that hurts someone in a physical way

virus a very small living thing that causes illness, or the illness caused by this

visible able to be seen

volunteers people who offer to do something without expecting to be paid

voyage a long trip, especially by ship or in a space vehicle

Index of Skills

Index of Authors, Titles, Art, and Artists

Acknowledgments

UNIT 1

"The First Americans." Copyright © Pearson Longman, 10 Bank Street, White Plains, NY 10606.

Excerpt from *Riding Freedom* by Pam Muñoz Ryan, Scholastic Inc./Scholastic Press. Copyright © 1998 by Pam Muñoz Ryan. Used by permission.

Excerpt from *1000 Inventions and Discoveries* edited by Roger Bridgeman. Copyright © Dorling Kindersley, 2006. Reprinted by permission of Penguin Books, Ltd.

Excerpt from *Seedfolks* by Paul Fleischman. Copyright © 1997 by Paul Fleischman. Used by permission of HarperCollins Publishers.

UNIT 2

"The Train to Freedom." Copyright © Pearson Longman, 10 Bank Street, White Plains, NY 10606.

"The Drinking Gourd." Public domain.

"Five New Words at a Time" by Yu-Lan (Mary) Ying, *The New York Times* Op-ed, March 6, 1993. Copyright © 1993 The New York Times Company. Reprinted by permission.

"Quilt" from *A Suitcase of Seaweed and Other Poems* by Janet S. Wong. Copyright © 1996 Janet S. Wong. Reprinted with the permission of Margaret K. McElderry Books, an Imprint of Simon & Schuster Children's Publishing Division.

"The Great Fever" Copyright © Pearson Longman, 10 Bank Street, White Plains, NY 10606.

Excerpt from the interview with Gary Paulsen in *Author Talk*, compiled and edited by Leonard S. Marcus. Copyright © 2000 by Leonard S. Marcus. Used by permission of the author.

Excerpt from *Hatchet* by Gary Paulsen. Reprinted with permission of Atheneum Books for Young Readers, an Imprint of Simon & Schuster Children's Publishing and by permission of Flannery Literary Agency. Copyright © 1987 Gary Paulsen.

UNIT 3

"Aguinaldo" (adapted) from *Salsa Stories* by Lulu Delacre. Scholastic Inc./Scholastic Press. Copyright © 2000 by Lulu Delacre. Used by permission.

"Marilia's Besitos de Coco Recipe" from *Salsa Stories* by Lulu Delacre. Scholastic Inc./ Scholastic Press. Copyright © 2000 by Lulu Delacre. Used by permission.

"Sowing the Seeds of Peace" by Mandy Terc. In memory of the founder of Seeds of Peace, John Wallach, for his vision, and the campers of Seeds of Peace, for their courage. Reprinted by permission of the author.

"Seeds of Peace: Cultivating Friendships." Copyright © Pearson Longman, 10 Bank Street, White Plains, NY 10606.

Excerpt from *Blue Willow* by Pam Conrad. Copyright © 1991 by Pam Conrad. Reprinted by permission of Maria Carvainis Agency.

"Partnerships in Nature." Copyright © Pearson Longman, 10 Bank Street, White Plains, NY 10606.

UNIT 4

"97 Orchard Street" and "The Pros and Cons of Tenement Life." Adapted from *Cobblestone*, "Tenement Life," February 2004, Copyright © 2004 Carus Publishing Company, published by Cobblestone Publishing, 30 Grove Street, Suite C, Peterborough, NH 03458. All rights reserved. Used by permission of the publisher.

"Somebody's Son" by Richard Pindell. Reprinted by permission of the author.

"Operation Migration" by Joyce Styron Madsen, *Boys' Quest*, June 1, 2002. Adapted by permission of the publisher.

Excerpt from "I years had been from home" from *The Poems of Emily Dickinson*, edited by Thomas H. Johnson. Copyright © 1951, 1955, 1979, 1983 by the President and Fellows of Harvard College. Reprinted by permission of the publishers and the Trustees of Amherst College, Cambridge, MA and The Belknap Press of Harvard University Press.

Credits

Smithsonian American Art Museum
List of Artworks

UNIT 1 Invention and Change
Page 66
Hans Hofmann
Fermented Soil
1965
oil on canvas
48 x 60 in.
Smithsonian American Art Museum, Gift of S. C. Johnson & Son, Inc.

Page 67
Samuel Colman
Storm King on the Hudson
1866
oil on canvas
32⅛ x 59⅞ in.
Smithsonian American Art Museum, Gift of John Gellatly

UNIT 2 The Challenge of Illness
Page 132
Alice Eugenia Ligon
Embroidered Garment
about 1949
embroidered muslin and cotton crochet
43¾ x 38½ in.
Smithsonian American Art Museum, Gift of Herbert Waide Hemphill Jr.

Page 133
J. Bond Francisco
The Sick Child
1893
oil on canvas
32 x 48 in.
Smithsonian American Art Museum, Museum purchase

UNIT 3 Embracing Family, Friends, and Neighbors
Page 202
Franz Kline
Merce C
1961
oil on canvas
93 x 74⅝ in.
Smithsonian American Art Museum, Gift of S. C. Johnson & Son, Inc.

Page 203
Charles "Chaz" Bojórquez
Placa/Rollcall
1980
acrylic on canvas
68¼ x 83⅛ in.
Smithsonian American Art Museum, Gift of the artist
© Smithsonian American Art Museum

UNIT 4 Acknowledging the Past, Reaching for the Future
Page 264
Carmen Lomas Garza
Camas para Sueños
1985
gouache on paper
28⅛ x 20½ in.
Smithsonian American Art Museum, Museum purchase through the Smithsonian Latino
Initiatives Pool and the Smithsonian Institution Collections Acquisition Program
© 1985 Carmen Lomas Garza

Page 265
Hung Liu
The Ocean Is the Dragon's World
1995
oil on canvas, painted wood panel, and metal bird cage
96 x 82½ in.
Smithsonian American Art Museum, Museum purchase in part through the Lichtenberg Family Foundation
© Smithsonian American Art Museum

UNIT 5 Everyday Obstacles, Everyday Courage
Page 334
Residents of Bourbon County, Kentucky
Fan Quilt, Mt. Carmel
1893
cotton, wool, silk, velvet, lace, paint, chromolithographic paper, and canvas
85 x 72¼ in.
Smithsonian American Art Museum, Gift of Herbert Waide Hemphill Jr.

Page 335
Daniel Chester French
Spirit of Life
1914
bronze
51 x 28 x 30 in.
Smithsonian American Art Museum, Museum purchase through
the Luisita L. and Franz H. Denghausen Endowment

Michael Olszewski
Speaking to Hear
1989
silk with acid dyes
parts A and B: both 22½ x 21¼ in.
Smithsonian American Art Museum, Gift of KPMG Peat Marwick
© 2007 Smithsonian American Art Museum

UNIT 6 Capturing Cosmic Beauty
Page 404
Alma Thomas
The Eclipse
1970
acrylic on canvas
62 x 49¾ in.
Smithsonian American Art Museum, Gift of the artist

Page 405
Charles Burchfield
Orion in December
1959
watercolor and pencil on paper
39⅞ x 32⅞ in.
Smithsonian American Art Museum, Gift of S. C. Johnson & Son, Inc.